EMPIRE BURLESQUE

● ● ● ● ● ● ● ● ● ● ● ●

NEW AMERICANISTS

A Series Edited by Donald E. Pease

EMPIRE BURLESQUE

The Fate of Critical Culture in Global America • *Daniel T. O'Hara*

DUKE UNIVERSITY PRESS • DURHAM & LONDON 2003

© 2003 Duke University Press   All rights reserved

Printed in the United States of America on acid-free paper ⊗

Designed by Rebecca M. Giménez   Typeset in Adobe Minion

by Keystone Typesetting, Inc.   Library of Congress Cataloging-

in-Publication Data appear on the last printed page of this book.

CONTENTS

●●●●●●●●●●●●●●●●●●●●●●●●●●●●

● ●

III. Analyzing Global America

IV. Reading Worlds

PREFACE

Five of the eleven chapters of this book were written during a study leave in 2000. Four of the remaining chapters were substantially revised since their original journal publication in the 1990s. And the other two previously published book chapters have been significantly revised so that they may better articulate this book's critical argument. This process was a painfully protracted gestation. Two developments contributed to this fact. The first, more personal one was becoming chair of my department for four years (1995–1999). Some of those experiences find their way into this book as object lessons. The other, more impersonal development was the final collapse of the Cold War national-security welfare state and its so-called liberal ideology and the sudden emergence, still in process, of a global horizon for the United States and its institutions. One consequence of such events for this book was that its extended writing became virtually a process of divination, that is, a quest to read "the signs of the times" in order to discover a possible future for liberal American culture and the profession of literary studies. In other words, I read "events" as they interacted in the last decade as if they were what Harold Bloom first called, with reference to the experience of poetry, "scenes of instruction," from which we may learn the history of the imagination to come. Will it survive, and how?

Such is the question still informing all the chapters of this book. If this sounds as though I still hope to believe in the prophetic function of literature and criticism, this is a correct judgment.

Such a focus explains the occasional origins of several chapters. Writing about Frank Lentricchia's decision in the mid-1990s to give up criticism and become a writer of memoir and fiction, or about Freud after a controversial Library of Congress exhibition in 1997, or about Henry James for the 150th anniversary celebration in 1993 of his birth at New York University—such occasions and their aftermaths afforded me vantage points on the emergence of the processes we now term "globalizing literary studies," in the context of this prophetic hope.

This book works analytically on several different levels at once. It is a *description* of the debilitating effects of globalization on the university in general and the field of literary studies in particular. It is a *critique* of literary studies' embrace of globalization theory in the name of a blind and vacant modernization. It is a *meditation* on the ways in which critical reading (and writing) can facilitate an ethical alternative to such institutionalized practices of modernization. More specifically, it is a psychoanalytic *diagnosis* of the globalization of American studies in terms of the New Americanists' abjection and transference, their habitual modernizing "bandwagon" mentality, regardless of consequences. Consequently, this book is as much a critical *parody* of globalization as an analysis of it. In this respect, *Empire Burlesque* resembles my last book, *Radical Parody: American Culture and Critical Agency after Foucault* (1992). The term "radical parody" describes the position or style that the parodist shares with others by virtue of a network of professional and cultural identifications, conscious and otherwise. *Empire Burlesque* thus targets aspects of the critic's own mode of scholarly production. This book, in short, is "ungrounded," as it supplements comically the culture and profession it takes as its immediate conditions of possibility. Such a radical contingency of reading, for better or worse, is this book's critical practice.

The critical history and cultural theory informing *Empire Burlesque*, as the introduction elaborates, argue that in the field of American studies, it was the transference from the Cold War national focus to an international global framework that resulted in the Americanists' self-abjection. This double movement of de-identification and displacement from one's cultural locale completed the process of abjection of academic Americanists begun by the challenges from within of multiculturalism. Globalization entails a transition from a heavily invested national narrative to quasi-anonymous tales of displacement and departure without returns, the literary critical simulacra of the geopolitically and economically driven migrations around the world. Every element of the Cold War national security state and its liberal welfare culture underwent negative transformation. This book terms the ironic imperial outcome of these complex differential processes "global America." Global America names the totalizing fetish whose claims to unity are predicated on denying the differences that it cannot subsume under its logics of representation, cultural and professional. As the global marketplace outsourced the military-industrial complex to more profitable locales, the manufacturing and professional meritocratic bases of upward mobility for the ethnic hierarchies of former immigrant populations suffered downgrading and displacements by new technologies and the new workforces being groomed for them here and, especially, abroad. The globalization of the academy—its new canon of texts, its hot topics for discussion at conferences and for publication, its targeted audiences, its slicker international means of production and distribution—has positioned the literary scholar within a space for which the American empire serves as the horizon of future possibilities. In cultivating a renewed taste for critical reading within such a new cultural space, this book represents a comprehensive attempt to check the flights from the professional and cultural situation characteristic of the contemporary scene. The turn to ethics this book envisions arises precisely in this context when the critic, in the contingency of reading, has to recognize his or her education by the text being read as the text's aporias are themselves recognized. The critic's work of reading thereby creates an ethical figure that has not been accommodated to empire but is the shadowy alterity at the heart of its globalizing order, its bad conscience, so to speak.

In its reading of canonical and uncanonical writers and cultural figures, whether Henry James, Freud, Said, Mankind (aka Mick Foley, a former professional wrestler with a literary bent), or Cordwainer Smith (a classic sci-fi writer of the 1950s and early 1960s whose real name was Paul Linebarger and whose real job, besides being a professor of Asian studies at Johns Hopkins, was working in the Far East for Army Intelligence), *Empire Burlesque* provides examples of the kind of aesthetico-ethical criticism that globalization would appear to have superseded. This book thereby enacts a desire to construct an ethos that would resist this mode of critical performance. That an ironic Cold War sci-fi writer so perfectly anticipates the mind-set of globalization is a scene of instruction to reckon with, as this book attempts to turn the profession toward the spectacle of its own self-burlesque, so as to shock it back into its sense of ethical responsibility.

The deconstructive theories of Jacques Derrida and Paul de Man find their analytic place here at this point in the book's argument. The catachrestic figure of "global America" is at once the American empire and its spectral double. Beyond the global processes of displacement and abjection, radical parody and self-burlesque, this book uses de Man's late work on a material sublime (on how "to see as the poets see") to critique the representational aesthetics of modernity. Derrida's recent Levinasian-inflected work on justice and human rights, in combination with his Benjaminian speculations on Marxism's "messianic promise," clears the ground for an imagination of a different future for American studies, one other than the return in reality of what has been symbolically foreclosed. This different future, more generally for U.S. literary and cultural studies, is in particular to be hospitable to all the others, with their futures, who would still have been arriving right now, including the others in ourselves.

The chapters in part 1, "Reading as a Vanishing Act," look at the fate of reading as a critical practice in recent criticism. They argue that under the reigning New Historicist dogmas of multiculturalist identity politics, its greatest proponent (Edward W. Said) fails to understand its academic successes (chapter 1, "Edward W. Said and the Fate of Critical Culture"); its theoretical model gets seriously mistaken (chapter 2, "Why Foucault No Longer Matters"); and its bad-faith, self-congratulatory academic politics have driven Frank Lentricchia, arguably the leading literary critic of his generation, out of the business of criticism and into writing not only caustic memoir but also savage fiction (chapter 3, "Lentricchia's Frankness and the Place of Literature").

Part 2, "Globalizing Literary Studies," examines the theoretical, ethical, and institutional effects of the transformation of American critical identity under the impact of recent geopolitical, ideological, and economic developments. Unless and until U.S. criticism learns to read itself as potentially innovative, it will become, more than it ever was before, subject to marginalization, to a kind of social death (chapter 4, "Redesigning the Lessons of Literature"). Even when critics have attempted to argue for an ethical basis underlying the aesthetics of critical reading (as chapter 5, "The Return to Ethics and the Specter of Reading," shows), they have too often substituted slogans and sound bites for close analysis of texts. As chapter 6, "Class in a Global Light: The Two Professions," spells out in some detail, the profession can ill afford the luxury of its moral and political posturings. It is already a self-divided profession, radically split along class lines, and unless it changes its ways, it will suffer reduction entirely to the service function of instructing the offspring of global elites in the niceties of communication.

To further this goal of self-critique, the chapters in part 3, "Analyzing Global America," propose, first, to experiment with the language of Derrida's recent Levinasian-inflected work on a deconstructive ethics (chapter 7, "Transference and Abjection: An Analytic Parable"). Chapter 8, "Ghostwork: An Uncanny Prospect for New Americanists," then proposes to envision a thought experiment, to stage an uncanny encounter between Freud's late theories of the cultural superego and a deconstructive reading of the New Americanist project. The ultimate "bad conscience" par excellence of New Historicist orthodoxy is, of course, Paul de Man, and in chapter 9, "Specter of Theory," it is to his critical theory, especially in its late manifestations, that I urge us now to turn, a spectral turning already begun in the previous two chapters.

The last part of this book, "Reading Worlds," consists of two long chapters. The first of these, "Empire Baroque: Becoming Other in Henry James," was originally written in the winter of 1992–1993 for two events scheduled for June 1993, the two-week-long 150th birthday celebration for Henry James at New York University, and the twentieth anniversary "New Americanist" conference for the international journal of literature and culture *boundary 2* at Dartmouth College. Portions of this text were read at both events. It has been much revised, updated, and expanded since then, especially with respect to the New Historicist turn in James studies and a recently proposed New Americanist pedagogy for teaching "the other Henry James," that is, the multicultural Henry James. In many respects, chapter 10 most fully puts into practice my theoretical analysis of reading as an ethics of and for criticism.

The final chapter, "Planet Buyer and the Catmaster: A Critical Future for Transference" explores two short tales and one short novel. The first tale, "Minor Heroism: Something about My Father," is by Allan Gurganus. As read, it represents the ambiguous—and ambivalent—triumph (or what I call "abject felicity") of multiculturalism *avant le lettre*, indeed, virtually its apotheosis, as foreseen, ironically, by Gurganus in 1973. Similarly, the second tale, "The Burning of the Brain," and the novel, *Nostrilia*, science fictions by Cordwainer Smith, published in 1958 and 1966, respectively, envision a critical future for transference phenomena that is apocalyptic in its excruciating intensities and cosmic in its prophetic scope. That Gurganus is a Left-oriented gay writer and Smith a Cold War critical humanist and Army Intelligence operative only makes their unexpected agreement on multicultural identity politics in their then emergent institutional forms all the more important, I think, as scenes of instruction for us today.

Finally, I need here to take note formally of the conceptual and discursive intermixing in this book. Just as Foucault and Derrida, Jon Elster and Lacan, Marx and Levinas, and so on interpenetrate the theoretical space of the book in improvised, hybrid associations, so too, at the level of style and genre, *Empire Burlesque*, in deploying essay, analysis, memoir, parody, parable, allegory, and, of course, burlesque, more than lives up to its name. Whether this is a weakness or a strength of mine, or of the cultural moment, is a critical judgment I must leave for others to make as they read the book.

ACKNOWLEDGMENTS

● ●

All or substantial portions of chapters 2, 3, 4, 5, 6, and 10 have appeared in earlier versions in *Reconstructing Foucault: Essays in the Wake of the 80s*, ed. Ricardo Miguel-Alonso and Silvia Caporale-Bizzini (Amsterdam: Rodopi, 1994); *boundary 2, Annals of Scholarship, Critical Terms for Literary Study,* 2d ed., ed. Frank Lentricchia and Thomas McLaughlin (Chicago: University of Chicago Press, 1995); and *Narrative Turns and Minor Genres in Postmodernism*, ed. Theo D'haen and Haris Bertens (Amsterdam: Rodopi, 1995). I am grateful to the publishers and editors of these publications for permission to reprint these now revised essays in their new context.

I want to thank the two readers of the manuscript from Duke University Press. Their constructive criticisms and helpful suggestions, I trust, have made this a much better book. I must also thank Donald E. Pease Jr., the editor of Duke's "New Americanists" series, and the press's executive editor, J. Reynolds Smith. Their invaluable work has made this book possible in its present form in every way. The critical history and cultural theory that I discuss here in my own way is largely indebted to Pease's published and unpublished work. I really cannot express my gratitude well enough. For an example of his most important recently published work, see Donald E. Pease, "C. L. R. James's *Mariners, Renegades, and*

Castaways and the World We Live In," which serves as the introduction to C. L. R. James's *Mariners, Renegades, and Castaways: The Story of Herman Melville and the World We Live In* (Hanover: University Press of New England, 2001).

Finally, I offer this book as my memorial to the spirit of my father, Daniel J. O'Hara, who died in July 1996.

INTRODUCTION

We Welcoming Others, or What's

Wrong with the Global Point of View?

● ●

Suppose someone said to you, "empire burlesque"; what would you think? Perhaps the first thing to come into your mind would not be "the fate of critical culture in global America." In the following pages, I will try to justify why you should make the connection between this book's title and its subtitle.

I admit that "empire burlesque" in itself is a curious phrase. On its face, it consists of two nouns. Given the usual expectations of standard English syntax, the first noun in any such phrase functions automatically as an adjectival modifier. "Empire burlesque" would then mean a kind of burlesque, as if there could be a "republic" or "democracy" burlesque, too, or if it could be an analogue of a furniture style.

"Burlesque" is a term, however, that could refer to a place, as well as to a type of show. "Empire burlesque" could then be construed as the name of a theater where, presumably, a "higher," grander, more sophisticated, more international style of show would occur. This potential meaning would be inherently ironic, not to say paradoxical, since "burlesque," as one recent edition of a literary handbook puts it, is traditionally considered a "low" form of comedy "characterized by ridiculous exaggeration and distortion," in which "the sublime may be made absurd, honest emotions may be turned to sentimentality, and a serious subject may be treated frivolously or a frivolous subject seriously."[1] As the handbook goes on to say, "the essential quality that makes for burlesque is the often raucous discrepancy between subject matter and style" (72). The nonsensical and the dignified in content and form are repeatedly mismatched with each other to the point of total confusion. One may think of the classic radio comedy bit, for example, Abbott and Costello's "Who's On First?", which has its origins in burlesque in which a passionate earnestness and a routine self-evidence get all mixed up with increasingly hilarious consequences.

Whether "burlesque" is taken in a broad fashion as a potential variation of meaning haunting literature and the other arts at every turn depending on the dubious adequacy of form and content to each other, or in a more restricted sense as a popular form of entertainment in which comedians tell risqué jokes and perform outrageous, often topical skits while big-bosomed women strip off their fetishistic outfits slowly to a honky-tonk bump-and-grind beat, burlesque is clearly related to parody and travesty. Parody is usually restricted to making fun of a particular work or style. Travesty is often what burlesque does to the pompous but secretly abject subject, such as the supposed sacredness of womanhood or the idealized purity of differences—class, gender, racial, or whatever. But burlesque actually takes in entire worlds or epochs for its objects of fun, with great comic effect when lampooning the social and moral and rhetorical contradictions and hypocrisies of some upper-class model or form of life. The English music hall tradition of comedy as it morphs into Monty Python in the team's send-up of the life of Christ in their great film *Life of Brian* is the best recent example of what I have in mind.

However, there are "high" or elite literary examples, as well. "Book Ninth" of Henry James's novel *The Wings of the Dove* (1902) opens with its male protagonist, Merton Densher, sitting in his Venice rooms as if in "his own theatre, in his single person," repeatedly rehearsing the fresh details of his sexual conquest of his manipulative lover, Kate Croy.[2] The terms of this rehearsal, a renewed "hallucination of intimacy" between lovers, with a "perpetual orchestra . . . playing low and slow," "the fiddlers" underscored in his fantasy, all suggest the gross vulgarity of a solitary act that undercuts Densher's sense of relational potency and so calls into question the fragile presumptions of his social world (400). Similarly, the class doubleness in which "high" and "low" cultures shadow each other is the specter of burlesque haunting the global order now emerging.

This is why, in "empire burlesque," we can also hear, if we listen hard enough, with sufficiently ironic a spirit, the parodic echo of a Miltonic inversion, as if what the title travestied were an imperial world to be submitted to the burlesque treatment in more detail, or perhaps even an empire in the process of burlesquing itself, wittingly or not. (That Bob Dylan titles his 1985 album *Empire Burlesque* might underscore such a possibility.) In any event, what I mean by it is that newly emerged global scene of instruction in which American critical identity, informed (and misinformed) by ideas, theories, literatures, cultures, and other realities "elsewhere" (as well as "here"), is now being (re)formed and performed with a growing frequency and influence as if it were the ultimate horizon of experience. Since the fall of the Berlin Wall and the massacre in Tiananmen Square, both events of 1989, the profession of American criticism in the widest sense—including academia, journalism, and the other media and policy-shaping institutions—has shifted its focus from a largely internal (internal to these professions) multicultural ethos in a New Historicist mode to the economic, political, and cultural processes of globalization. In the global perspective of these national and international institutions (of the university, the media, and intellectual and humanitarian foundations), American critical identity is enacting itself, as in a place or theater, as part of a traveling show (of conferences, theories, readings, memoirs, and publishing ventures), in which all the would-be emperors have, progressively, no clothes.

"Empire," of course, is a term that refers to a political reality, a set of political institutions and organizations of life, an imperial world system. Does empire in this sense exist literally now? Even according to its most systematic theorists, Michael Hardt and Antonio Negri, in their book *Empire,* its political manifestations or materializations are at best nascent and intermittent at the moment, largely limited to administrative, police, and humanitarian operations. While not nothing, these realizations of empire are not yet empire in the traditional sense. Given the power of the telecommunications industry, the rise of the Internet, and the emergence of the new tech-based economy, the postmodern form of empire may perhaps remain mostly virtual, except for projects and operations, scenes of instruction and events of entertainment. However that may be, empire, whether virtual or not, whether "straight" or "burlesque," appears to be the economic and cultural horizon of our lives to come on the planet.[3]

My theoretical take on the formation and operation of this global perspective on American critical identity as "empire burlesque" derives largely from Jacques Derrida's later work, especially *Specters of Marx* and related texts. In *Aporias*, for one example, Derrida demonstrates in a careful reading of Heidegger's "being-toward-death," the keystone of his existential analysis in *Being and Time*, that any attempt to found empirical and historical disciplines of knowledge on a priori foundations by means of establishing secure and inviolate borders, is doomed to failure. This is so even as all empirical and historical disciplines or knowledges presuppose one or another ontological pre-understanding that necessarily informs the nature and scope of their investigations, no matter how much they feign ignorance (or the self-evidence), for disciplinary purposes, of all such transcendental speculations: "While the richest or most necessary [anthropological knowledge] cannot found itself in any other way than on presuppositions that do not belong to [such knowledge or its competence] . . . conversely, this fundamental [system of presuppositions or ontology] cannot protect itself from a hidden [anthropological] contamination."[4] This deconstructive version of the hermeneutic circle is more radical than any existential one, since the intermixing between the realms of transcendental presupposition and that of empirical field "data" founds both realms on uncertain, not to say undecidable, bases. In this ironic way, theory does direct practice, even as practice always already—that is, in an a priori manner—infiltrates any theory's core. Such structural indetermination, which promotes a radical overdetermination, is the ultimate aporia or impasse of intellectual work, which can only be suffered or survived, lived on from repeatedly.

Although the wordplay in the last paragraph may sound like the philosophical equivalent of a burlesque comic's routine, it does have a serious point. Derrida is conceptualizing the limits of any structure in terms of its finitude, when facing the always imminent prospect of death. Structural finitude is an analogy for and an instance of human finitude. Any structure of thinking, including that inherent in material and cultural institutions and discourses, possesses a "ground-and-supplement" organization in which, at certain points or moments, the differences between this division or partition or borderline blur into one another, intermixing. These places of structural "mortality" (or entropy) are sites where a potentially infinite reflection on itself haunts the structure. This is the so-called *mise en abîme* effect. "Empire burlesque" is my name for this effect as it haunts, comically, the emerging structure of global American literature and culture. The low-life vulgarity that shadows Morton Densher's fantasy space is class and sexually specific, but those contingent dimensions depend on this structural peculiarity that transforms even James's empire baroque into our empire burlesque.

One of the explicit consequences of such a condition is that every concept, trope, or figure, every argument or system, gives off the traces of what it would exclude, what it must attempt to exclude, in order to order itself. Spectral lineaments of all these "others" haunt our most "positive" constructions. Our conceptual and rhetorical entities are thus never able to be "identical to themselves, hence no longer simply identifiable, and to that extent no longer determinable. Such totalities [can] therefore no longer authorize simple inclusions of a part in the whole" (7). Nation-states, even would-be global empires, share with intellectual entities this indeterminable and radically intermixed quality or conditionality, necessarily transgressing their own self-declared borders. Deconstruction, in this sense, is the rhetoric of such phantom excess, of such excessive spectral expenditure; it is, in this way, the ironic rhetoric of empire, empire's self-divided shadow, since empire would expend itself excessively, totally, if it could do so, in every moment, since exceeding all borders defines the principle of its paradoxical order, what Derrida calls its principle of self-ruin.[5]

In other words, that is, in my own words once again, empire is a priori its own burlesque; it is itself and its self-travestying double or alter ego or spectral other. We can see this phenomenon in the way American professions, with their celebrity mystique, and service industries, with their proletarian professionalism, are joining hands as if they are their own mirror images. We can also see it in the abjection of everyday American life simultaneously appearing with the transference of wealth and value to the diverse processes of globalization. This critical transference gets played out in the brutal low-life antics of popular culture, particularly in the latest form of "bread and circuses," professional wrestling, or in the passions of the memoir genre and other kinds of self-writing and the tacky self-revelations of the Jerry Springer–type talk show.

Shadowed by its spectral other (and double), by its alter ego, as it were, an intellectual entity, whether concept, trope, or law, both defines a field, a figure, or a domain and transgresses its own limits, trespassing on the spectral thresholds of other such entities, locales, or "places." The now notorious global flows of high finance and cultural representations are just two of the latest (and best) examples of this strangely ubiquitous "immaterializing" work, this "ghost" work.[6]

So when I speak of intellectual entities such as "American critical identity" or "a global perspective," I am aware of the inherent paradoxical limitations of such generalizing phrases. They are at once too determinate and also overdetermined, contradictorily open to a plurality of differences. Nonetheless, conceptual, rhetorical, and institutional realities make it necessary for a critic to form one identity, one perspective, even if it is not intended to be taken as the only one possible. Such moments of identity formation (and reformation) define critical generations in a profession.

Of course, literary studies, or more broadly English studies, whether amalgamated officially or not with comparative literature or cultural studies, and whether associated closely with contemporary media or not, in short, "our profession" (broadly speaking), appears not to be doing too well in reproducing itself from one generation to another without suffering traumatic deprofessionalizing changes affecting the processes of institutional renewal.[7] I do not wish to recite here the vicissitudes of our profession; you will hear enough of that in the pages to follow, although far less than in previous books of mine.[8] Owing, in large part, to Derrida's later work, I have learned to begin (with) welcoming others.

If Derrida is right and every intellectual entity, including geopolitical representations, hosts its double/other, playing host to, and being the guest of, this guest, even its hostage, then what? Then, a spectral trace disseminates and haunts with its invisible but palpable mark every text, archive, or topology. Such haunting is virtually what Derrida names, after a usage of Hélène Cixous, the *arrivant*. This *arrivant* is the absolute other ever to come. Death, "my death," as the impossible possibility totally mine, paradoxically embodies this specter of the *arrivant*.[9] The "death" or "passing" of every entity of representation is then inscribed at the core of each word as the spectral trace of radical alterity. The figure of the absolute *arrivant*, the ever first and last comer, is what Derrida sees in the immigrant, the émigré, the political exile, the migrant worker (we may also say, with justice, "the gypsy scholar"). This is why Odysseus, the Wandering Jew, and various other errant figures of nomadic hybridity haunt the following passage (from *Aporias*) as avatars of this "messianicity without messianism":[10]

> No, I am talking about the absolute *arrivant*, who is not even a guest. He who surprises the host—who is not yet a host or an inviting power —enough to call into question, to the point of annihilating or rendering indeterminate, all the distinctive signs of a prior identity, beginning with the very border that delineated home and assured lineage, names and language, nations, families and genealogies. The absolute *arrivant* does not yet have a name or an identity. It is not an invader or an occupier, nor is it a colonizer, even if it can also become one. It is not even a foreigner identified as a member of a foreign, determined community. Since the *arrivant* does not have any identity yet, its place of arrival is also de-identified: one does not yet know or one no longer knows which is the country, the place, the nation, the family, the language, and the home in general that welcomes the absolute *arrivant*. This absolute *arrivant* as such is, however, not an intruder, an invader, or a colonizer, because invasion presupposes some self-identity for the aggressor and for the victim. Nor is the *arrivant* a legislator or the discoverer of a promised land. (33–34)

An amazing, if somewhat mystifying, passage. So many echoes and traces shimmer and pass here that one does not know quite what to comment on. What appears next in the passage, however, is clearly the ghost of the infant messiah:

> As disarmed as a newly born child, [the absolute *arrivant*] no more commands than is commanded by the memory of some originary event when the archaic is bound with the final extremity, with the finality par excellence of the *telos* or of the *escathaton*. It even exceeds the Border of any determinable promise. . . . this border [where one cannot discriminate] among the figures of the *arrivant*, the deal, and the *revenant* (the ghost, he, she, or that which returns). (34–35)

A monstrous birth for this spectral messiah, one probably occurring in a dressing room of the empire burlesque? Thinking of the future, in(to) futurity, appears to take such a rough form.

Derrida's far-from-mystical but openly visionary point is that an order constitutes itself by excluding what appear to be radically hetero-geneous elements, which nonetheless also continue to exist both within and without the order, on both sides of its borders, in vestigial forms of emergent traces of what is really not present there now or at any other moment yet promising ever to come still. Such a structural order of spectral traces surviving, living on, is a decentered and decentering order. It is significantly marginal, even as it is self-exceeding, multiple and yet empirelike, a kind of ersatz counterimperial simulacrum haunting every material project of empire with its burlesque mirror image. This shadowy alterity at the heart of any positive order is what Derrida calls the absolute *arrivant* and what I am calling, with respect to American critical identity in a global perspective, "empire burlesque."

Let me give two examples, one scientific and the other geopolitical. It is now a commonplace of modern physics to discuss quantum mechanics as a supplement of classical Newtonian and Einsteinian physics that has special applications to the realm of subatomic particles. This develop-ment would suggest that classical mechanics and quantum mechanics are the ground and supplement, respectively, in the organization of the theo-retical structure of modern physics. But we also now know that the laws operating at the subatomic level and those at the cosmic scale intermix at high energies, so that the neat division between realms breaks down, as in our experiments we must take into account both the subatomic effects of our own instruments on transformation and detection and the classical features, such as gravity, in our increasingly radical experiments. This "deconstructive moment" in modern physics is signaled by the special mathematical formalization used to manage the infinities that would otherwise ensue as we calculate the results of these experiments. Both Heisenberg's famous uncertainty principle and Niels Bohr's equally fa-mous complementary principle are just two further signs of the opera-tion of this deconstructive moment. Ordinary logic no longer works.

My other example comes from the new realities of life on the border between Mexico and the United States. What has emerged, especially since NAFTA passed in 1993, is a zone existing on both sides of the border that exhibits the permeability of structures, the intermixing of elements within and between structures, and the disjunctive temporality of the resulting cultural space between and within structures. What "time" is it there, on the border? What historical conjuncture, what mode of existence, is it of the past or the future? Who can tell? When asked whether they feel themselves to be Mexicans living in the United States or Americans working in Mexico, the respective populations of service and high-tech workers respond that they feel their first loyalty is to this border zone itself, whether identified with the place of work or of home or even of shopping! Often they speak of their hectic "commute" between home and work as the self-identifying sign of their time. Without specifically reading too much into this, we could fairly say, I think, that on the border, the specter of America's global future is arriving virtually at every moment.

This spectral moment, which is also a spatial structure interrupting all centered structure, is anachronistic, anarchic, radically anterior and futural alike, which is why Derrida figures it as the absolute *arrivant* (the absolutely "arriving" one, "the newcomer," or "the arrival"). It is the messiah moment ever coming. Does this coming-messiah moment of apocalyptic differentiation and de-identification form the principal "apocalyptic" interest of global capital? Or given my empire burlesque frame, does it mean that the global scene of instruction for American critics should await the arrival of Nathan Lane from *The Bird Cage* dressed as Jesus in drag? The messiah moment is more discrete and secretive than that, even "here and now."

We can also approach this moment via a more domestic scene, involving my admittedly precocious nineteen-month-old granddaughter, Maria. This scene, I confess, struck me as being so like the famous one of Freud's grandson, in *Beyond the Pleasure Principle*, playing with the spool of ribbon that it felt truly uncanny when I experienced it.

My daughter, Maria's mother, Jessica, leaves for school each evening at five o'clock and returns after ten o'clock, long after Maria has gone to bed. As I was watching her, one day, soon after her mother left for school, Maria picked up one of her baby books, said to me, "Bye-bye" and "I miss you," ran to a corner of the room next to the door, paused for a long moment, then turned around quickly, a sharp volte-face, rushed toward me, calling out, "I'm back, I'm back," and fell into my opening arms. This play was then performed repeatedly, ritualistically, for the next twenty or so minutes. The game of return, it appears, would be repeated again and yet again, at other times.

The open secret of Maria's performance of this unconscious fantasy, her acting it out, in which she spontaneously impersonated the mother she wished to see return—Maria going to the wall herself and then returning as other—lay not in the driven desire completing its imaginary circuit, or in her adoption of the active part in the symbolic scenario, both of which processes are, of course, significant in other contexts. No, what I found most fascinating here was the moment when Maria paused in the corner by the door, with her face to the place where the walls at the front of the house converged. In that "borderline" space of the real, she paused only for an apparently blank moment, a pregnant pause; it was always the same moment, the same virgin interval again, and took as long each time no matter how excited and raucous the game of return got. This "pure" moment between the going out and the coming back was not only where her unconscious wish received its formal "appearance" and yet remained in hiding, inapparent. It was also that wish openly, if spectrally, incarnated. William Blake called this imaginatively receptive moment welcoming the creative response of the future "the fugitive moment," which Satan's Watch-Fiends—all the dark emanations of Church, Nation, Mill, and School—could not capture or pervert to their rationalized, instrumental, profit-making ends. What I am calling Derrida's messiah moment embodies this uncanny structure of visionary fantasy in its most welcoming creative response to otherness, in oneself most of all, as an innovative repetition, just as Maria's game of return introduced for her the new role of student performance artist of desire. Derrida's messiah moment may thus be the mother of all moments. Besides, if there is an empire, can a messiah be far behind, whether burlesque in mode or not?

We might think of such a messiah moment not in terms of the mother's actual or remembered return but in light of the expectation, the hope, of a new coming increasingly disjoined from the habitual traces of the return. This openness of systems to the future, disconnected from any master narrative prefiguring the course of events, this radical contingency, is what I read from my granddaughter's drama. It is what can be read from the living-on-the-border I have alluded to; it is what experimental physicists read from their instruments every day. When enough of these moments arise, who knows but that the new world order's apocalypse may be at hand? At the very least, a substantive transformation in U.S. institutions, especially those of education, could be forthcoming.

Going Global!

As an editor of *boundary 2: an international journal of literature and culture*, I have been exposed in a variety of ways to the global point of view for some time now. My editorial colleagues and I have discussed it repeatedly, in person, over the phone, in conference calls, via e-mail, by means of the formal reports done on essays and reviews submitted, and so on. We have seen it both as the latest threat to critical thinking and as a unique opportunity for provoking its radical renewal. These discussions have occurred not only in the United States but around the world, in Tunisia, Bermuda, Berlin, and elsewhere; and privy to these discussions have been the local and specific intellectuals of the host locations.

In 1998 I coedited with Alan Singer, a Temple University colleague, a special issue of *boundary 2* entitled "Thinking through Art: Aesthetic Agency and Global Modernity."[11] Neither this professional exposure nor my intellectual participation in the global phenomenon overtaking literary and cultural studies has lessened my skepticism about it as a critical point of view, however much I may intend to make use of it. The reason for my continued skepticism and growing fascination for it was clarified recently for me by some research I conducted outside the field of literary and cultural criticism.[12]

But before discussing some of the results of that research, I need to say something about the subject within my field. The January 2001 issue of *PMLA* was devoted almost entirely to the special topic "Globalizing Literary Studies."[13] Coordinated by Giles Gunn, this issue contains nine articles by Paul Jay, Stephen Greenblatt, Arhiro Anas, Basem L. Ra'ad, David Chioni Moore, William Slaymaker, Robert Eric Livingston, Ian Baucom, and Wai Chee Dimoc. It also includes two talks on the topic given at the Modern Language Association Convention in 1999 by Edward W. Said, then president of the MLA, and by Rey Chow. Two things are noteworthy about the issue. The first is the absence of any "expert" governmental participants or consultants. Because there was considerable scholarship on display, this can only mean that such "expert" knowledge of the foreign policy institutions was deliberately being excluded as ideologically questionable, even tainted by its entanglements with the American empire. The second thing of note, besides this ideological purity on the part of the American empire's literary and cultural critics, was their basic acceptance of the current and foreseeable status quo in their—and my—field, as signaled in one of Said's final comments: "The politics of identity and nationally grounded system of education remain at the core of what most of us do, despite changed boundaries and objects of research" in the profession of literary studies (68). I note these two features of this institutionally sanctioned special issue of *PMLA*—its ideological purity and its professional self-satisfaction—because they are the two this book most contests. Writing about globalization and not making use of all of what social sciences, government agencies, and the new media may have to offer on the topic is as silly as writing an essay on Shakespeare without checking out all of the relevant scholarship. More significantly, discussing globalization without recognizing its potentially revolutionary effects on any and all politics of identity, its possibly utopian subversion of the culture of representation itself, not to mention the structure of literary studies, is not a position that this book hopes to occupy.

Like my *boundary 2* colleagues, I have assumed that whether one was critical of it or not, with respect to the global point of view, its adoption meant that one presumed, in some sense, what Bruce Robbins, one of our associated editors and an editor of *Social Text*, refers to as the unprecedented global "hegemony" of the United States of America.[14] That is, the global point of view assumes the existence and power of the American empire, whether conceived in terms of military might, economic and political influence, or cultural domination; and whether condemned or used against itself in alliance with its critical others here and abroad, America, global America, in any or all of these dimensions, is the great imperial shadow haunting the global point of view.[15]

The global point of view looks at a rapidly modernizing, so-called developing rest of the world outside of Europe and North America and can read into this process of modernization a necessary Westernization, and into this Westernization, it can read in turn an inescapable Americanization. Modernization, Westernization, and Americanization are the trinity of global capitalism driving the forces of globalization. And these forces are leveling and homogenizing all the differences in the world, disciplining them by destroying everywhere local customs, national cultures and traditions, and entire ways of life of ancient civilizations. At the same time, however, the global point of view also assumes that the globalization of technological change, especially in telecommunications, of political, financial, and social institutions, and of cultural representations has made possible new chances for, and new instruments of, substantial collaboration among America's critics, within and without. Of course, the network of spy satellites known as Echelon, which can easily trace all e-mail messages and tap any phone conversation in the world, may put a damper on these critics as they organize their various forms of resistance. . . . But that is another more problematic story.[16]

At the very least, critics of the presumed overwhelming American hegemony may do their work on the thousands or so "businessmen, bankers, government officials, intellectuals, and journalists from scores of countries" who meet each year at the World Economic Forum in Davos, Switzerland, by lobbying these representatives of the "Davos cult," as it has been called, to use their influence and power in support of institutions and policies fostering international recognition and enforcement of human rights and other worthy causes of a new, socially democratic vision of the world.[17] Some of the critics of these critics, I must say, are even more skeptical than I am. Judith Butler, for one significant example, is cited by Bruce Robbins in his book *Feeling Global: Internationalism in Distress*, as claiming that the "Davos cult" and its critical proponents are following, wittingly or not, a barely disguised American agenda to make well-placed representatives of global cultural capital feel better about their elite roles in administering empire.[18] A therapeutic smart bomb, as it were.

However that may be, what's wrong with the global point of view, no matter who adopts it or for what purposes, is that it overestimates power. Despite all the hoopla and lamentation, American power after the Cold War has lessened, not grown. By all measures—military, economic, political, cultural—America has lost ground vis-à-vis the rest of the world. It is true that the spectacle of American power, especially in its military aspect, has become greater, but like a Hollywood action blockbuster, the special effects of American presence in the world may be sublime, even though our cinematic hero is just another robotic, muscle-bound goon who suffers from a bad heart from steroid abuse. In short, America may not "be back," after all. The events of September 11, 2001, tragically confirm this point.

Samuel P. Huntington, no apologist for America's critics, to say the least, founder and coeditor of *Foreign Policy*, among other considerable distinctions, persuasively argues the pessimistic view of American and Western power in *The Clash of Civilizations and the Remaking of World Order*.[19] With startling blurbs of praise from Francis Fukuyama, writing in the *Wall Street Journal* ("The book is dazzling in its scope and grasp of the intricacies of contemporary global politics"), and from Richard Bernstein, writing in the *New York Times* ("A benchmark for informed speculation . . . [and] a searching reflection on our global state"), and from Wang Gungwa, writing in *The National Interest* ("This is what is so stunning [about this book]: It is not just *about* the future but may actually help to shape it"), and from both Henry Kissinger and Zbigniew Brzezinski (but I'll spare you their unsponsored, if even more extravagant, praise), Huntington's book, often critical of these very figures, is an immediate disciplinary classic and an international best-seller. Here is its thesis:

> Culture and cultural identities . . . civilization identities, are shaping the patterns of cohesion, disintegration, and conflict in the post–Cold War world.
>
> For the first time in history global politics is both multipolar and multicivilizational; modernization is distinct from Westernization and is producing neither a universal civilization in any meaningful sense nor the Westernization of non-Western societies.
>
> The balance of power among civilizations is shifting: the West is declining in relative influence; Asian civilizations are expanding their economic, military, and political strength; Islam is exploding demographically with destabilizing consequences for Muslim countries and their neighbors; and non-Western civilizations generally are reaffirming the value of their own cultures.
>
> The West's universalist pretensions increasingly bring it into conflict with other civilization, most seriously with Islam and China; at the local level fault line wars largely between Muslims and non-Muslims, generate "kin-country rallying," the threat of broader escalation, and hence efforts by core states to halt these wars.

The survival of the West depends on Americans reaffirming their Western identity and Westerners accepting their civilization as unique not universal and uniting to renew and preserve it against challenges from non-Western societies. Avoidance of a global war of civilization depends on . . . accepting . . . global politics. (20–21)

One can see in this last point Huntington's domestic political agenda, of course: a kind of realistic, hardheaded, pragmatic exposure to multiculturalism, so as to better reaffirm and defend Western civilization. Nonetheless the facts and figures, graphs and tables, and authoritative national and international archival materials, not to mention the praise of his critical opponents as well as his friends, make Huntington, the Albert J. Weatherhead III University Professor at Harvard, where he is also the director of the John M. Olin Institute for Strategic Studies and the chairman of the Harvard Academy for International and Area Studies, an authority to be reckoned with, however lamentable or comforting that may be. And of course, in my field of literary and cultural studies, no one writing about or from the global point of view bothers even to mention Huntington's considerable achievement.[20] No one, that is, except Edward W. Said, in a previously unpublished essay collected in his *Reflections on Exile and Other Essays*. Said attacks the original 1992 *Foreign Policy* essay by Huntington that became his 1996 book, but one of the things disabling Said's polemical critique is that in twenty-five pages, he quotes Huntington's essay only once, and that a single sentence. (For more on this, see chapter 1 in this volume.)

Let me make it clear that, first of all, Huntington does not argue for the lessening of American and Western power as a desirable goal. Nor, secondly, does he argue that the emerging world order of civilization—identity politics at large, as it were—including Sinic, Japanese, Hindu, Islamic, Orthodox, Western, Latin American, and African constituents and all of their panoply of core states, member states, lone countries, torn states, and cleft states, resembles some United States of the World, an *actual* global America, with liberal pluralistic values and institutions. In fact, for Huntington (and this is my third point), the driving force for this "new world order" is not so much globalization as such as the resurgence of indigenization, that is, the resurgence of so-called reactionary cultural identities based largely on the global religious revival, and not global capital, a "fundamentalist" religious revival operative within the United States, too, all of which is a virtually universal response to the discontents, dislocations, and alienations that inevitably accompany modernization everywhere it occurs, whether in explicitly Western guise or not. Huntington, in other words, argues for a realpolitik position that recognizes the role of so-called unreason or feeling in compensating imaginatively for, and so ameliorating to some degree, the worst effects of the modern rationalization of the world. Once again, the tragedy of September 11, 2001, in New York City confirms this thesis strikingly.

I agree with this much of Huntington's thesis, and I want to suggest that given such a revised global point of view, one can read the multicultural identity politics within the United States and Western countries generally as the new civic religion of social democracy pervading the new internationalism.

Another way of putting all this is to say that the two comparatively monolithic ideologies of the Cold War—Americanism and Communism—have been displaced by several competing civilizational visions of identity in difference based less purely on geopolitical strategies than on long-standing albeit very "messy" cultural affinities and identifications, mostly religious in nature. And this transference or displacement within "the new world order," and to this vision of that order, often feels like the (admittedly necessary) abjection of the previous forms of life. Rather than two grand narratives structuring the horizon of the entire world there is now a postmodern plurality of possible story germs, most of them avowedly religious in nature, and all clearly mythopoeic in their lineaments.

If one wanted to play devil's advocate at this point, one could suggest that Huntington's "realistic" position in fact repeats, ironically enough, the metanarrative theory of romanticism as the emancipated resurgence of apparently outmoded cultural traditions in compensatory reaction to the Enlightenment's instrumental reason. In Europe and America, according to this grand narrative, one position of the bourgeois avant-garde stands in opposition to another. Or one moment in the making of a broad middle-class society opposes another moment. Could it be that Huntington's realistically displaced romantic vision is actually a mechanism through which global capital ensures itself a more (rather than less) heterogeneous and differential world?

One of the myths of critical theory, of course, perhaps derived from Marcuse or the Frankfurt school more generally, is the idea that capitalism requires a leveling and homogeneous "one-dimensional" playing field to operate in. In fact, as we see from the way the conditions of production and consumption in different locales are played off against each other, capitalism thrives best when cost and price margins between and among various regions, states, or hemispheres keep the cycle of investment, production, consumption, relocation, renewed investment, and so on, flowing freely. A multicivilizational world order, as opposed to a one-world or even a simplistically split or halved world order, makes for better opportunities to maximize the potential chances for greater differential profits.

It is important to see that this vision of a complex, heterogeneous, differentially interrelated world should not be identified with any one actual state or civilization or cultural institution (such as "literature"), not to mention any one political or financial institution such as the United Nations or the World Bank. Nonetheless, I believe that it is important to keep this vision as such in circulation as both the valued representation of alterity and *différance,* opposed to all utopian and dystopian single visions, and the preferred model of existence of capital in this epoch of its global manifestation. I will christen it, as a figure of the ultimate power in our moment of existence, after Emerson's "new ideal America in the West" and call it "global America." I will use this term here to designate the complex imaginative phenomenon of globalization. But I want to underscore the point that the name "global America" refers to no mode or style of existence of any other entity than itself. No person(s), no class, no people, no organization, no institution is singularly intended, nothing other than the otherwise anonymous, impersonal, and unnameable thing and agency, global capital.

What's wrong with the global point of view? In my sense, nothing— so long as one recognizes in its critical or exculpatory versions that "global America" (or any of its avatars) is another uncanny phantom or specter, just like any other would-be unifying and totalizing representation of cultural (or other) identity, a fantasmatic fetish of identity. What really exists, of course, as we all know, is the realm of virtual life (or death), the undead dimension of capital, which is the sole kingdom at hand.[21]

Between Marx and "Mankind"

In a special issue of *boundary 2* entitled "The University," its editor, Paul A. Bové, in his opening note, sounds the theme of the issue (and indeed of much recent criticism) when he makes it clear that "the issues of education within globalization affect regions of the world unevenly but with repeated demands that the systemic effects and intents of globalization be analyzed everywhere they appear—and as such, that is, not merely as local instances of traditional problems or as instances of 'imperialism' on an old nationalist model."[22] Bové has put his finger on what is at once the opportunity and the problem that the term "globalization" poses for understanding the changes transforming the university, disciplines and professions generally, the nation-state as a political institution, and "globally" the future of life on the planet. What does this "globalization, as such," attitude imply? As "an object of analysis," what is it that one is to analyze? Bové cites Henry Adams from his *Education* as his authority when he remarks that it was "Karl Marx, who alone, after 1848, foresaw radical change" in such global terms (1). What is it that we, following Marx (or Adams), can now see?

What these questions point to and underscore is the power of "globalization" as a new master term for criticism. Like "culture," "power," "gender," "structure," "presence," or "form," "globalization" implies specific realities that everyone at the moment already knows (or is presumed to know) and yet sounds suggestively vague enough to hold for a while a mysterious resonance. This is the opportunity and the problem of the term.

The specific realities everyone is presumed to already know when "globalization" is deployed are these: With the end of the Cold War, capitalism is no longer tied necessarily to the political and cultural forms of the nation-state, to the social institutions of any one civilization, or to the current or traditional lifestyles and customs of particular peoples. Large multi- and transnational corporations can now rationalize in their best interests without much restraint the production, distribution, advertising, and sale of the commodities they offer, wherever and whenever they can get the best deal. If it makes more sense to the bottom line to manufacture clothes in China, centralize distribution in Memphis, Tennessee, advertise out of New York City, and stimulate and feed the markets of the

Pacific Rim or of Russia, then so be it, no matter what consequences for others—economic, political and social, ethical and so on—may follow. Consequently we can see how "globalization" refers specifically to this free-floating quality, this differential sense of the freedom to move anywhere, at any time, from one locale to another around the world, to take advantage of the latest and immediately foreseeable opportunities while leaving the problems behind. Capitalism thrives best, it is presumed, when all of its options remain open, even if this results in the destruction of the environment, the dislocation and migration of millions of people, the transformation of traditional ways of life beyond recognition, the alienation and abjection, not to mention the violent resistances, of the dispossessed and the displaced, the resurgence of ethnic and religious identities and conflicts across borders and within regions—and the list goes on. Capitalism's power to penetrate at will into, and to withdraw from, any place (or time) in the world is what "globalization" (like "empire," or any other "god term") can ultimately mean.

Of course, put like this, "globalization" takes on mythical proportions. A Zeus or a Satan comes to mind. But what lies behind such unavoidable mythopoeia is indeed real enough, all too real, in fact: the ubiquitous substitution of provisional associations for permanent communities, associations based on comparatively immediate material interests or gains, the "cash-nexus," as Marx would have said, versus the connections based on immemorial ways of life.

With fewer and fewer internal or external checks on capitalism and with its obvious appeal to immediate material self-interest, nothing appears able to withstand its corrosive power to dissolve all bonds, personal, professional, whatever. Within the modern American university system to which Bové alludes, this has meant (1) the division of the faculty into a small and ever shrinking class of professionals with tenure (or at least with its possibility) and a growing class of part-timers, gypsy scholars, higher education's migrant workers, without any possibility of tenure, who are willing and able to teach anywhere, at a moment's notice, as administrators decree; (2) the dismantling of the tenure system, sometimes as outright abolition by a certain date, other times via the gradual proletarianization, the deprofessionalization, of working conditions—via modern corporate efficiency measures, including the perfunctory and lame displays of administrators inviting faculty "input" or "feedback";

(3) the shift from public support for research and publication to private foundational support or market-based, for-profit-only sources; (4) the adoption of a multicultural ethical imperative and its "politically correct" manifestations, which facilitates the assimilation of university personnel —administrators, faculty, staff, and students—to the diverse demands of global capital's various markets. And on and on it could go.

To put in a nutshell what globalization as such can mean for the university or any other institution, here or abroad, I will use a hypothetical scene and its bluntly allegorical interpretation that has become a popular touchstone in the circles of international journalists, policy makers, and global critics, who have given "globalization" its original cachet:

> Think of a stretch limo in the pot-holed streets of New York City, where homeless beggars live. Inside the limo are the air-conditioned post-industrial regions of North America, Europe, the emerging Pacific Rim, and a few other isolated places with their trade summitry and computer-information highways. Outside is the rest of mankind, going in a completely different direction.[23]

Of course, any institution, people, or individual who reads this scene, an admittedly fabulous and obviously impossible fantasy scene of instruction, would want to be, it is also presumed, within global capital's stretch limo (if only to escape various sorts of "heat") no matter what one's critical, even revolutionary, motives and radical contentions might be. Marx, after all, did some of his best work of analysis and theory in the British Museum, in London's Bloomsbury neighborhood.

Some people, I am sure, when reading this global scene of instruction or when thinking about the different aspects of globalization, will want to offer alternative takes on the term or its aspects. Especially troublesome may be the diminishment of individual and collective agency my story of "globalization, as such" appears to imply. As Marx himself remarks, however, men—and women, too, of course—make their histories, but not as they think. Let me lay my cards all out on the table, then. Whatever the reality may be with respect to this question of agency, the rhetoric of "globalization, as such," in the texts of policy makers or their critics, regardless of anyone's intentions in the matter, assumes a tactical or at most a strategic choice among options predefined as possible by present circumstances. No person or group, however ingenious in resistance or passionate (or "anarchic" or "multitudinous") in revolutionary aspiration, can abolish these present circumstances and choose the impossible fantasy, whatever it could be, that is, choose as certain the messianic future that is always coming, the utopian future of the work of universal liberation. I don't think it is a capitulation to a pandemic cynicism or "weak" neopragmatism to share such an assumption, at least for now.

One consequence of this global perspective is that all calls for resistance and revolution—especially the calls coming from other riders in the air-conditioned stretch limo, even from the newest riders, those best and brightest from "outside," from "the rest of mankind," here and abroad, who have hitched a ride, as it were—ring not so much false or hollow as something more troubling because something less classifiable and more ambiguous, unstable, mixed in its motive, something decidedly undecidable, what I will call "the authentic gimmick."

Now, by "the authentic gimmick," I mean not just to invoke the specious simulacrum, the postmodern decoy of the supposed "real thing," the copy of a copy of a copy of some explicitly fabricated norm, some designed makeshift model or improvised property. I also, and even more so, mean to suggest the specific move or technique, constitutive of a rhetorical practice, of a professional or political agenda or program, and of a subject position, identity, persona, or "personality" that permits the cultural work in question—whatever it may be—to be envisioned at all, in however abject a form or mode. As a practice, program, and subject position, "the authentic gimmick" can best be demonstrated by (and in) the "field" or the "arena," "the discipline" or the "culture," the "lifestyle," associated with the sort of labor performed in the American "catch-as-catch-can" profession of pro wrestling, especially in its latest "hard-core" style.

In pro wrestling, "the gimmick" is the term used openly by everyone concerned—promoters, wrestlers, commentators, fans—to refer to what the wrestler says, does, and represents at the moment in his or her career. It is the "commodity-theme." Pro wrestling today is a knowing parody, a witting travesty, of global capital—the best, most developed example of empire burlesque. Wrestlers come from every part of the world and assume identities that span various time periods (past, present, and future)—"the Road Warriors" have been a famous tag team for over fifteen years now—and various cultures, nations, peoples, all the living and even the undead! ("The Undertaker" from "Death Valley" is a case in point of the latter.) The only thing that matters is the survival and enhancement of the now multinational "federation" or transnational communications and entertainment conglomerate that sells the matches and wrestlers, the T-shirts, the videos, the computer games, the children's toys ("Bone-Crunchin' Buddies"), the collectable cards, and so on to international audiences of proles *and* elites around the world. In disclosing and, most recently, reflecting rather analytically on its representative status as a self-conscious parody of global capital, as in the text of the pro wrestler Mick Foley's best-selling memoir *Mankind: Have a Nice Day! A Tale of Blood and Sweatsocks,* American pro wrestling is becoming a radical parody of "globalization, as such."[24] To put it in terms of our stretch limo global scene of instruction, in pro wrestling, the "inside" and the "outside" of the business are coming out and slipping in virtually all the time.

Consider Foley's original "authentic gimmick." As "Cactus Jack Manson," from "Truth or Consequences, New Mexico," Foley was a sadomasochistic outlaw messiah type, a kind of Clint Eastwood pale rider on angel dust. He talked crazy, fought in barbed-wire matches, and Japanese death matches, with C-4 explosives, the object of which was to survive slamming your opponent onto a board, the back of which was rigged with the plastique, and getting the pin fall. Foley as Cactus Jack did amazing stunts, took extraordinary risks, and endured a great amount of punishment. Unexpectedly, as this bizarro "heel," he won fan approval vis-à-vis the "pretty-faced heroes." Cast as the pure embodiment of diabolical madness, Cactus Jack, to the fan, felt more "authentic" in his gimmick. Could this neopragmatist genuine fictionality be what Harold Bloom meant by entitling his book about "the American difference" *Agon: Towards a Theory of Revisionism*? However that may be, Foley's authentic gimmick was solid and stable enough that he had a recognizable commodity-identity and a habitus flexible enough to adapt to changing circumstances. As a practice, as a performance, and as (self-) promotion, it worked. Such is professional wrestling's not so strange identity politics, with a vengeance. Under late capitalism, within the American university, method, position, polemic, and critical personality make up criticism's authentic gimmickry.

Let's look a bit more closely at this notion of the authentic gimmick.

Mick Foley, reflecting on "the best gimmicks in wrestling," claims that they are "actually extensions of a real-life personality." By this, Foley means a professional dramatization of one's familiar "habits of mind" (488). Foley notes that the proof or test of such a gimmick is whether it catches on with the audience, and if it does so, it is because the gimmick has been authenticated in and by "blood." As everyone knows, and as even the wrestlers now readily admit, the outcomes of the matches are predetermined. But how these preset conclusions are reached, that is, how the scripts are improvised on, with little or no special rehearsal for specific matches—all of that is left to the wrestlers themselves to work out, in "the act," as it were.

This is one reason that Foley, in his personae of Cactus Jack, Mankind, and Dude Love (the latter two being, respectively, the heavy metal dog-muzzled menace and the sixties nerdy would-be Dead Head), has suffered eight concussions, broken his nose twice and his jaw once, had four front teeth knocked out, and his right ear ripped off, received over 325 stitches, and at the age of thirty-four, after fifteen years in the business, been forced by his condition to retire for his own good. I could have listed more of his injuries, and have not bothered to mention all the indignities and (self-) humiliations he endured, but I think I have made my point, which is that it is the amount of pain incurred and sacrifice made, in deploying and executing the authentic gimmick, that marks it as such. The spectral riders in that global stretch limo should bleed a little, bear (and bare) scars, wring a bit of pathos out of their professional situations, sing somewhat of their sufferings—hence the glut of memoirs coming from American professionals nowadays, perhaps.

In any event, it is clearly the case that pro wrestling and pro lit crit, American style, are not the same thing in every particular, to say the least, even in a global perspective. At least, not yet. The former is more honest about its authentic gimmickry, for one thing.

But I can easily imagine a tag team death match between . . . Oh, well, perhaps, I'd better not say, after all.

Of course, we teachers and scholars of the English language and its literatures and cultures really have no direct way of authenticating our gimmicks. We have our "agons" and festive contests and preset rituals, but no blood gets spilled, no bones are broken, no lives are cut short. Thank God, I guess. But I think it is for this reason that our profession hates itself, even as its state of abjection is generally more disdained than even pro wrestling by other American professionals, and our profession's leading members seek gratuitous connections with groups and causes, here and globally, in which the threat or promise of violence and bloodshed, of real revolution—for the highest moral purposes, naturally— looms over the horizon.

Empire and Identity

The chapters of this book thus trace the emergence over the last decade or so of a new global scene of instruction for the formation of critical identity in America. Each generation of critics, no matter how technically or professionally focused, bears the date mark of its moment of formation. It rehearses the traumatic experience of its ritual inscription by that moment in the cultural history of the institution via the performance and conceptualization of an identity theme. And it expresses this theme repeatedly in its most representative allegorical interpretations of texts, figures, careers, theories, and contexts. The god that failed of Marxism, the Cold War, the counterculture, the rise of professionalization—these moments have been subsumed by globalization. It represents the horizon of possibility within which critical work now is practiced.

Central to this development of a new global scene of instruction for American critical identity is a different experience of work and time, of borders and subjectivity. The new technologies of communications make every corner of the globe available for presentation at any moment of the day or night. They also open up every moment to the demands and imperatives of work, so much so that it appears increasingly to be the case that people are virtually dreaming, submerged in a semiautomatic preconscious state, almost all the time, under the threat of producing more and more production, of whatever sort it may be. The lives we are living now are progressively less and less our own. And this phenomenon of possessed dispossession is systematically becoming the common global experience: for individuals and entire peoples alike. Another way of "plotting" it, following all the signs, such as robotics, genetic engineering, the Internet revolution, virtuality unbound, the pervasiveness of sci-fi culture, is that a new form of life is emerging, simultaneously, all over the world. Global capital, that spectral phantom, is materializing itself. In a fundamental sense, the subject of this book is this process of materialization in the critical field.

John le Carré, famous for his stylish and erudite spy fiction, has written his own portrait of global capital in his 1999 novel *Single and Single*.[25] No one person or group or people can incarnate this new form of life, global capital, for very long, but where any one does, the impersonation makes one resemble some "Prince of Shimmer," both "clumsy buffoon" and "nimble god" (33). Tiger Single and his son, Oliver, lawyers and international bankers, are each invested in turn with this quality of global capital, as are the Russian mobsters, the Orlov brothers, and ultimately their diabolic henchman, Alix Hoban. This ceaseless circulation of sites of manifestation, of scenes of instruction, from character to character, country to country, moment to moment, is like vapor-trails tracing the instantaneous passages of subatomic particles stringing the universe together.

The postmodern sense of identity, of being split into multiple selves, with no one identity theme being able to incorporate all the parts into a single synoptic story, now coincides with a new pervasive experience of agency—a nonhuman yet rational agency that occupies and drives human beings both selectively and repeatedly; opportunistically, pragmatically, and provisionally; and expectantly and anxiously. Le Carré's protagonist, Oliver Single, puts it nicely to himself, about himself, in the third person: "He was nobody, doing everybody's bidding. He was an understudy who hadn't learned his lines" (287). This sense of being in many parts, both seriatim and at times all at once, without really knowing what they are, and having nonetheless to improvise, even as the pressures of living up to the imperative expectations of these unknown roles keep mounting, in short, of being lived by an alien force—this experience of becoming momentarily but repeatedly the global subject haunts le Carré's novel, which deserves the kind of complete analysis that is beyond my limited scope here. I simply wanted to use it to express, as succinctly as I can in this brief introduction, the general nature of the experience of this new form of life that, for want of any better term, we can indeed call, for now, the global subject.

In the terror of the discipline that such scenes of instruction can exact, under the continuous sentence of possible death, what can one do but get busy "transposing [oneself] to other places" (9)? . . . This "Prince of Shimmer" is out of here!

> Stepping forward . . . he felt his feet being kicked from under him. His head flew over his feet, and the next thing he knew he was lying on his back on the floor and a steel-hand heel was being driven so viciously into his stomach that the lights went out and he thought he was dead. But he wasn't, because when the lights came on again, the man who had kicked him was lying on the ground clutching his groin and groaning, and he had been put there, as Oliver quickly deduced, by Aggie, brandishing a submachine gun and wearing a panther suit and Apache war paint. (385)

Le Carré's "hero," rescued by his "heroine," might not have recognized her "had it not been for her rich Glaswegian accent" as she delivered, with "schoolmarmish emphasis," the novel's final words: "Oliver, on your feet, please, stand up, Oliver, *now!*" (385).

PART ONE

● ● ● ● ● ● ● ● ● ● ● ●

Reading as a Vanishing Act

1

Edward W. Said and the Fate of Critical Culture

● ●

I have read Edward W. Said's *Reflections on Exile and Other Essays* with mixed emotions.[1] The essays collected in the volume cover thirty-five years and are, to a large extent, the summation of a career, and not just any career. Said's career, from the mid-1960s until the present moment, has been enormously influential. In fact, it has been formative of the intellectual and imaginative lives of many critics, particularly of my generation, in literary and cultural studies. Moreover, before his recent severe illness, during the Reagan and first Bush presidencies, Said had become a media figure, speaking eloquently, with reasonableness and passion, on behalf of political positions at the time representative of millions of people around the world. With the collection of these essays, it seems not only has a book been assembled but also one has been closed. No doubt Said's chronic leukemia makes this sense of closure more poignantly urgent than does his simply being a sixty-six-year-old public critic. In short, my sense of grateful indebtedness to Said's work and example is tainted with the sense of imminent loss, a loss both of the man and, even more selfishly, of the figure as it has performed its role in the critical culture of my generation. American criticism, to put it starkly, does not currently possess any comparable figure of intelligence, achievement, passion, or genius. Admittedly, this mixture of feelings on my part betrays a human, all-too-human, perspective, a selfish sorrow. I just cannot envision any literary or cultural critic in the future achieving a similar professional and public stature.

Beyond these self-involved considerations, another cause of my mixed feelings is the historical sense associated with these essays. By this I mean not their critical approach but their strangely dated quality, especially and paradoxically the two newest, previously unpublished ones: the book's introduction, "Criticism and Exile," and its final chapter, "The Clash of Definitions: On Samuel Huntington." This last essay serves as the book's de facto conclusion. Together, these two new pieces aspire to cover professional and geopolitical history from the Cold War to the new millennium, even as they frame a volume composed entirely of old work, none of which has been significantly updated. To be fair, several of these critical essays have become classics in literary and cultural studies and have received prestigious awards. Nonetheless, added to my personal ambivalence, is an intellectual conflict of a more impersonal sort.

I find "Criticism and Exile," the new introduction to the volume, anachronistic. As it outlines the current scene in criticism, it presents that scene as still being haunted by what things were like in 1978 when Said's third book, *Orientalism,* appeared. (His first two books, of course, were *Joseph Conrad and the Fiction of Autobiography* [1966] and *Beginnings: Intention and Method* [1975].) That is, Said sees criticism today as still a contest between an emerging discourse of historical critique and political liberation performed by feminists, African Americanists, ethnic studies critics, postcolonialists, and so on, all of whom, at the margins of the profession, stand in opposition to the orthodoxy and hegemony of what he terms "the formalist consensus" (xx), which consists in New Criticism aligned to, and revised or refined by, deconstruction. Naturally, Said takes note of some of the progress of the multicultural critics in their challenge to the formalist consensus, but nowhere does he reflect on the obvious fact that he and his allies have won the contest, have in fact been ensconced for some time at the center of the profession. Said himself is a recent past president of the Modern Language Association. Instead, he suggests that the grip of the formalist consensus on the levers of institutional power is still tight: "Signs [of a strikingly different approach to formalism] emerging in the study of literature are strongly evident" in the various critical movements previously mentioned (xx), all of which,

Said contends, base their approach, unlike their opponents, on the primacy and priority of experience over form. The historical irony of Said's remark, the featured contributor to the special issue of *PMLA* entitled "Globalizing Literary Studies" (January 2001) discussed in the introduction, strikes one like a truck.[2] What it testifies to is the need, the drive, on Said's part to continue the rebellions of his critical youth long past the time when that response is decently appropriate.

Beginning in 1970 with Geoffrey Hartman's famous collection *Beyond Formalism,* American literary study has repeatedly been staging a radical break with formalism under the aegis of one newer criticism or other. And long ago this break was effected. Between traditional thematic approaches and the New Historicist approaches of identity politics, formalism has been swept away. To his immense credit, Said is often at his best when decoding the formal structures of literary and other texts, but he has nevertheless always argued for a contrapuntal reading of texts that submits formal analysis to the standard of historical experience as the final arbiter of critical judgment. As he discusses at length in "The Politics of Knowledge" (372–85) and demonstrates brilliantly in his essay on *Moby Dick* (356–71), however, contrapuntal criticism of a subtle and effective kind is a hard act for critical disciples to follow. The wavering balance in the interval between critical modes is an impossible place to occupy for very long.

The contemporary critical scene is dominated by an antiformalist, antitheoretical, and antiaesthetic orthodoxy, an institutional hegemony, every bit as repressive and exclusionary as any political regime or ideological state apparatus. By saying this, I don't mean to suggest that I think hegemony in any situation is ever completely uncontested. What I do mean to suggest is that within the profession of literary and cultural studies, the levers of power are in the hands of people who at most pay only lip service to the lessons of theory and the realities of form on their hasty ways to the simulacra of political critique or utopian vision that they believe they ought to embrace and promote. And Said's less-than-adequate performance here in facing this development helps to allow such hegemony to continue unchallenged by a voice that could have made an important difference. Admittedly, no one in literary and cultural studies today in America is executed for a devotion to, say, Paul de Man's work. But the ironic title of a recent publication, *Material Events: Paul de Man and the Afterlife of Theory,* tells the whole sad tale. To make de Man acceptable now, he must appear to be at least vaguely "materialistic," even as he is recognized as a rather pathetic ghost persisting in the fading twilight of theory's heyday.

Nearly a third of the essays collected in *Reflections on Exile and Other Essays,* which contains forty-seven chapters, rehearse this story of theory's demise. Essays such as "Opponents, Audiences, Constituencies, and Community" (1982), "Michel Foucault, 1927–1984" (1984), "Michel Foucault and the Imagination of Power" (1986), "The Politics of Knowledge" (1991), "Identity, Authority, and Freedom: The Potentate and the Traveler" (1991), "On Lost Causes" (1997), and the celebrated title essay, "Reflections on Exile" (1984), among others, track at once the supreme achievement of a critical career and the unmaking of any critical culture based intellectually on the principles of formalism and theory. What Said proposes as the highest principle of criticism is the existential foundation of experience—an admittedly problematic foundation indeed. The earliest essay in the collection, "Labyrinths of Incarnations: The Essays of Maurice Merleau-Ponty," originally published in a 1967 issue of *The Kenyon Review,* uncannily foretells Said's selection of critical foundations. I choose a passage as a case in point, virtually at random, from his introduction "Criticism and Exile":

> The study of literature is not abstract but is set irrecusably and unarguably within a culture whose history influences, if it does not determine, a great deal of what we say and do. I have been using the phrase "historical experience" throughout because the words are neither technical nor esoteric but suggest an opening away from the formal and technical toward the lived, the contested, and the immediate, which in these essays I keep returning to again and again. . . . The point here, however, is that at present the study of literature has gone in two opposed and in my opinion ridiculously tendentious directions: one, into a professionalized and technical jargon that bristles with strategies, techniques, privileges, and valorizations, many of them simply verbal or "postmodern" and hence lacking in engagement with the world, or two, into a lackluster, ostrich-like, and unreflective pseudohealthiness that calls itself "traditional scholarship." Historical experience, and in particular the experience of dislocation, exile, migration,

and empire, therefore opens both of these approaches to the invigorating presence of a banished or forgotten reality which in the past two hundred years has dominated human existence in an enormous variety of ways. It is this general and particular experience that my own kind of criticism and scholarship in this book are trying to reclaim, understand, and situate. (xxxi–xxxii)

This is not the occasion to elaborate on the problematic nature of experience as a basis for criticism, especially as Said puts it here. Suffice it to say, experience in an individual or a collective sense is as much the playing field of fantasy as it is the theater of historical reality. But this portrait of the current scene in American criticism—the simple opposition between tepid traditionalism and terroristic theory—caricatures the situation in 1978 much better than it describes that of today. Could it be that Said is out of touch with the fact that his side in the struggle for hegemony in the profession has won? Can he not know that his legions— the partisans of experience, particularly when the experience is of dislocation, alienation, and the exile occasioned by differences in identity and the politics derived therefrom—are in power? The critical establishment is Said's, certainly not Paul de Man's, not really ever R. P. Blackmur's, even if here Said treats de Man in passing with respect and Blackmur at some length with reverence and critical discrimination (246–67). How could this situation not in large part be the result of Said's own work? But any contest between theory and experience, formalism and history, is never a real contest at all, when these are the terms of the contest. Who would willingly embrace the skeleton of theory with pleasure when the body of experience so seductively beckons, as does the partially veiled face and bulging figure of "Dante in Exile" on the cover of Said's volume? (Said's name obscures Dante's eyes and thus the gaze they would form.) And yet, do we ever teach experience? In literary and cultural studies, don't we teach the linguistic, rhetorical, and cultural codes that constitute the historical schemata of our experience in the discourses that we use to speak to ourselves and to each other? And these schemata are never immediately given to our perception or to our critical reflection; rather, they must always be formally deduced, conceptualized by theory, so as then to be critically analyzed in speculative acts of reading that break up and mediate, for better or worse, the so-called natural flow of experience.

A critical culture that espouses Said and company's viewpoint on the foundational nature of experience is bound to lose its object of analysis, the symbolic order, as it dissolves into the endless mirages of the ersatz archives of imaginary experiences. This loss of its object of study may explain why criticism today, especially of Said's avowedly "secular" sort, cannot deal with the global resurgence of religion, fundamentalist or otherwise, which for the peoples and classes largely concerned could justifiably be seen as "the greatest single fact" of the last quarter of a century (xiv), and not as Said one-dimensionally puts it, "the migration and displacement" of millions of people as a consequence of global capital's policies. In fact, the resurgence of religion has been the most effective political reaction to the "development" projects of global capital during this period. Perhaps, for reasons of class identification and professional advancement, matters of religion and class are just too difficult for the partisans of experience to experience and so critically reflect on. One of the purposes of my argument in this book is precisely to produce a critical language and approach better able to register the realities of class and religion for the critic than that of New Historicist identity politics.

My mixed emotions, then, include not only admiration, respect, gratitude, and identification but also an anticipation of grief and an immediate sense of disappointment. Edward W. Said knows better than he writes here and has performed criticism better than what this book's introduction mounts for initial display. Many of the other essays here set a standard for criticism that indicts the introduction for its obvious blind spots and distortions. One wonders what he was thinking when he wrote it, or what he is thinking as he announces "a forthcoming book on humanism in America," in which he plans "to affirm the continued relevance of humanism for our time" (xxxi). Such humanism, as we have seen, would have to be nontechnical, jargon free, even antiprofessional, worldly or secular, and politically engaged, based on the overwhelming historical experience of the last century and a half, "the vast migration" of peoples into exile because of the emergence of a global economy and culture, with all the accompanying imperialistic realities and revolutionary prospects for resistance, liberation, and reconciliation, except those, of course, which are founded on popular revivals of religious visions. The ultimate goal of such critical humanism, as Said anticipates it here, would be the appropriate inclusion of all the world's peoples "within the same universe of discourse inhabited by Western culture" (xxvii). And so, what do I find wrong with this humanistic vision?

It has already come about. Through the telecommunications industry, virtually the entire world has been included "within the same universe of discourse inhabited by Western culture." And more and more, as the world's economy becomes a global consumer economy in ways increasingly appropriate to the avowed representations, the identity politics, of the world's peoples, such inclusion is becoming progressively more humanistic and secular, worldly. This is precisely why peoples not of the global class, nor of its faith in Enlightenment rationality, have turned in massive numbers to the religions of their ancestors for a vision of life outside "the same universe of discourse inhabited by Western culture." One of the reasons that many within the profession of literary and cultural studies have been turning to spokespeople for "the third culture," all those scientist-intellectuals such as Stephen Hawking, Roger Penrose, and Stephen Jay Gould who discuss the intellectual and spiritual questions of life, is because they at least do not shy away from confronting such ultimate metaphysical questions, however they choose to answer them. My point is that writing an essay entitled "Jungle Calling" in homage to the veritable pagan mystique of Johnny Weismuller's Tarzan, as Said does here (327–36), is clearly not going to do the trick of satisfying the demand that a critic look candidly at his own present class status or religious bias. This piece, by the way, appears as creditable an enthusiastic performance as Adrian Leverkuhn singing with Harry Carrey "Take Me Out to the Old Ball Game." As Seamus Deane puts it in his review of Said's 1999 memoir *Out of Place,* "one of the strange effects of colonialism is often to defer an individual's recognition of natal culture and set in its place a simulacrum of both the natal and the imperial cultures that thereafter remains foundational, no matter how much it is exposed to a later critique."[3] Coming to terms, in some depth, with the rich spiritual (as opposed to purely intellectual) legacies of Islam is not something that Said, originally a Christian Arab, has ever thought to do in public: too much of the people, too much risk of otherworldly thinking, perhaps? Or just too intimate?

The other realities that Said not so much ignores as he is outright hostile to are indeed religious and popular in nature. Throughout these essays, whenever he speaks of religion and its dogmatic institutions and ideological role, no matter what the society or period in question, he speaks with open contempt or thinly veiled dismissal in his tone. He even reserves his harshest judgments of other critics and positions or movements for those of their statements that sound even remotely like priestly declarations of putative doctrine: "Cultures are always made up of mixed, heterogenous, and even contradictory discourses, never more themselves in a sense than when they are not just being themselves, in other words, not being in that state of unattractive and aggressive affirmativeness into which they are twisted by authoritarian figures who, like so many pharisees or mullahs, pretend to speak for the whole culture. In fact, no such situation is really possible, despite the many efforts and reams of paper expended fruitlessly for that purpose" (xv). I will leave the evidently shortsighted ironies of Said's statement stand unglossed.

Once again, I think, this hostility to religion and its formative influence on cultures, modern or otherwise, arises from Said's intellectual class position. His embrace of a program of progressive Enlightenment reason, no doubt revised and corrected, an expanded rationality like that of the romantics and Victorian poets and prophets, permeates his identification with Adorno and the Frankfurt school's neo-Marxist critique of the authoritarian personality and totalitarianism, so as to cast religious culture off the great global stage and out way beyond the pale. Nowhere is this clearer in the collection than in its concluding essay, "The Clash of Definitions: On Samuel Huntington." Before looking at Said's performance there, I need to say something more about religion and its relation or potential relation to criticism.

Of course, religious cultures, like any other forms of culture, are generally diverse, internally divided, complexly manifold, and contestatory, not simplemindedly unitary, covering a wide range of possibilities of belief and practice. Nonetheless, whether one appeals to the classic analyses of religious culture in Marx, Nietzsche, or Freud or to more recent analyses and popular histories, such as those of Kenneth Burke or Karen Armstrong, the portrait that emerges shows established religious cultures as tending, in moments of political and social crisis, to fix identities, close canons, and create or reassert dogma. Religious cultures are the most extreme forms of identity politics and cannot be so easily dismissed as purely imaginary or epiphenomenal. Yeats rightly characterized the object of all religions, the belief in the supernatural, as "the most violent force in history." He took it for the topic of all his major work, especially after 1914, because religious experience informs the creation and renewal of the symbolic order determinate of any group (orthodox or revolutionary), any people, nation, empire, or world system, and Yeats was trying to lead the emerging Irish nation to the reformation of its spiritual culture, in opposition to materialistic British colonialism and its blatantly hypocritical "Christian" advocates. No matter what the critical standards prescribed by progressive post-Enlightenment intellectuals may be, for the masses around the world, for better or worse, religion is the one reality.

Among the 617-plus pages of this latest volume in the acclaimed Harvard University Press series edited by Said entitled "Convergence: Inventions of the Present," only "Reflections on Exile," this book's title essay, makes any significant mention of religious discourse in a positive vein, when Said cites Erich Auerbach's citation of Hugo of St. Victor's twelfth-century meditation on exile for its "hauntingly beautiful lines" on the subject. Here is the entire complex nexus of citations:

> Hugo of St. Victor, a twelfth-century monk from Saxony, wrote these hauntingly beautiful lines:
>
> "It is, therefore, a source of great virtue for the practised mind to learn, bit by bit, first to change about [six] invisible and transitory things, so that afterwards it may be able to leave them behind altogether. The man who finds his homeland sweet is still a tender beginner; he to whom every soil is as his native one is already strong: but he is perfect to whom the entire world is as a foreign land. The tender soul has fixed his love on one spot in the world; the strong man has extended his love to all places; the perfect man has extinguished his."
>
> Erich Auerbach, the great twentieth-century literary scholar who spent the war years as an exile in Turkey, has cited this passage as a model for anyone wishing to transcend national provincial limits. Only by embracing this attitude can a historian begin to grasp human experience and its written records in their diversity and particularly; otherwise he or she will remain committed more to the exclusions and reactions of prejudice than to the freedom that accompanies knowledge. But note that Hugo twice makes it clear that the "strong" or "perfect" man achieves independence and detachment by *working through* attachments, not by rejecting them. Exile is predicated on the

existence of, love for, and bond with, one native place; what is true of all exile is not that home and love of home are loss, but that loss is inherent in the very existence of both. (185)

Thus Said says one should "regard experiences as if they were about to disappear" (185). "What is it that anchors them in reality? What would you save of them? What would you give up? Only someone who has achieved independence and detachment, someone whose homeland is 'sweet' but whose circumstances make it impossible to recapture that sweetness, can answer those questions. (Such a person would also find it impossible to derive satisfaction from substitutes furnished by illusion or dogma" [185–86].) It seems that Said has benefited, in an important way, from the ascetic lesson of this cloistral vision of the world.

Said concludes his own meditation on exile by claiming that exile's duality of vision, its attachment in detachment, its death-in-life and life-in-death, does not make up a prescription for "an unrelieved grimness of outlook," but it does make possible "originality of vision" as it enforces on the exile "an awareness" of cultural diversity that takes a "contrapuntal" form (186). Old and new cultural environments for one with the mind of exile, for the critic of culture, in other words, exist in "contrapuntal juxtapositions" (186). Such habitual irony of vision diminishes orthodox judgment and elevates appreciative sympathy, so long as one remembers to act as if "one were at home wherever one happens to be" (186). As a true citizen of the world, in sum, whose nostalgia and cosmopolitanism are recognized, by the exile at least, as part of "the habit of dissimulation" that the realities of the experience of exile must repeatedly break up (186), one is steeled for the next traumatic displacement to come:

> This remains risky, however: the habit of dissimulation is both wearying and nerve-wracking. Exile is never the state of being satisfied, placid, or secure. Exile, in the words of Wallace Stevens, is "a mind of winter" [sic] in which the pathos of summer and autumn as much as the potential of spring are nearby but unobtainable. Perhaps this is another way of saying that a life of exile moves according to a different calendar, and is less seasonal and settled than life at home. Exile is life led outside habitual order. It is nomadic, decentered, contrapuntal; but no sooner does one get accustomed to it than its unsettling force erupts anew. (186)

Hugo of St. Victor's "hauntingly beautiful" words thus shape in a purely secularized aesthetic or primal manner the worldly viewpoint of critical consciousness as it positions itself contrapuntally vis-à-vis the culture it inhabits at the moment. Exile is the condition of possibility for this critical consciousness, which is nothing other than "the habit of dissimulation," the play of critical masks called forth by one's current circumstances. As Said in "Between Two Worlds" cites Adorno as noting, the critic's text, the exile's writing, becomes "a place to live" while there remains no "slackening of intellectual tension" (568). In the end, however, the critic of cultures is not even allowed to live in his or her own writing (568). Exile is like a condition of absolute, haunting sleeplessness; no slackening of intellectual tension is permitted, no security or placidity allowed. Where, then, does critical consciousness and its culture dwell? Where can it dwell? Only globally, in endless physical and mental traveling. In short, "in" the postmodern academy? However we answer this question, it is necessary to recall that such critical consciousness and its nomadic and eccentric critical culture of permanent exile can only exist materially via institutional circumstances like those of a rich American foundation, think tank, or elite university. The resolutely disillusioned exile's self-conscious irony is a luxury item for a certain class of left wing affluent academics, a situation unavailable to most peoples of the earth, for whom the passions of their religious, ethnic, and class identities can know no purifying ascesis of the secular spirit.

But surely, of all people, Said must know this. His critical intelligence is just too demonstrable and strong. How, then, to explain this apparent lapse in critical judgment? A clue to the Said enigma comes once again from Seamus Deane's review of the recent memoir. Deane remarks perceptively on the way, near the end of *Out of Place,* that the world of Said's parents gets increasingly labeled as "ersatz" or "fractured," "eerily out of touch," "semi-fantastic" (15). This is the world that his parents had built in emulation of British models, a life of an upper-class Palestinian family living in Cairo, deliberately summering in Lebanon in a desolate valley and not near the ocean, visiting poorer relatives on special occasions back in Palestine. This is one of the now familiar imaginary worlds of modernity as briefly materialized by global capital everywhere today. Ironically enough, its most pseudo-idyllic scene is brilliantly captured by Said in his memoir not of Palestine or his family's British models of life but in

American prep school when he recalls a strange experience he had in 1948 as a precociously fashionable thirteen-year-old camper spending part of the summer deep in the Maine woods:[4]

> The rest of the time [at the camp] was quite routine as I had stopped deriving any pleasure from the place, and none at all from my fellow-campers. . . . One later experience emblematized the peculiarity of a camp summer. . . . There was an overnight canoe trip . . . that involved portage from one lake to another in the bland Maine forests, as well as long trajectories when we rowed across vast blazing hot tracts of brown-water lakes. My canoe was manned by me in the stern and another camper in the bow. Comfortably stretched out in the space between us was a counselor, Andy, with a long Czech name, who in his shiny red bathing suit, moccasins, and smoking pipe sat for hours reading a book whose title and contents I could not decipher. The odd thing was that after quickly going down a page with his left index finger he would methodically detach the page from the book, roll it up into a ball, and toss it casually into the lake. (137)

Perhaps, in our global epoch of spectral capital unbound, this uncanny allegory of reading has come back to haunt Said, making his lapses in critical judgment and equally our potential responses to them perfectly anticipated by the ritually dismissive actions of "plain" old American camp counselor Andy. Bland Andy, in sum, is Said's secret Epicurean god image? For some reason, Said notes Andy's hyphenated identity but does nothing with it. Are we to presume he may be Jewish and another refugee from war's terror?

However that may be, it is the case that *Reflections on Exile and Other Essays* is handicapped by its essential nonrecognition of religion's influence in the contemporary world and how such an understanding informs Samuel Huntington's book *The Clash of Civilizations,* the subject of Said's last chapter and a slashing, unfair critique. Here is Said at his reductively polemical, dismissive worst:

> The core of Huntington's visions (not really original with him) is the idea of an unceasing clash, a concept of conflict which slides somewhat effortlessly into the political space vacated by the unremitting bipolar war of ideas and values embodied in the unregretted Cold

War. I do not, therefore, think it is inaccurate to suggest that what Huntington is providing in this [book] of his—especially since it is primarily addressed to Washington-based opinion and policy-makers who subscribe to *Foreign Affairs,* the leading U.S. journal of foreign policy discussion—is a recycled version of the Cold War thesis, that conflicts in today's and tomorrow's world will remain not economic or social in essence but ideological; and if that is so then one ideology, the West's, is the still point or locus around which for Huntington all others turn. In effect, the Cold War continues, but this time on many fronts, with many more serious and basic systems of values and ideas (like Islam and Confucianism) struggling for ascendancy and even dominance over the West. . . . So strong and insistent is Huntington's notion that other civilizations necessarily clash with the West, and so relentlessly aggressive and chauvinistic is his prescription for what the West must do to continue winning, that we are forced to conclude that he is really most interested in continuing and expanding the Cold War by means other than advancing ideas about understanding the current world scene or trying to reconcile different cultures. Little in what he says expresses the slightest doubt or skepticism. Not only will conflict continue, he says on the first page, but "conflict between civilizations will be the latest phase in the evolution of conflict in the modern world." It is as a very brief and rather crudely articulated manual in the art of maintaining a wartime status in the minds of Americans and others that Huntington's [book] has to be understood. I would go so far as to say that it argues from the standpoint of Pentagon planners and defense industry executives who may have temporarily lost their occupations after the end of the Cold War, but have now discovered a new vocation for themselves. Huntington at least has the merit of underlining the cultural component in relationships among different countries, traditions, and peoples. (570–71)

For Said, it is clearly a crime to write for the opinion makers and policy makers in Washington, a crime to take seriously Islam and Confucianism as systems of belief (Said reduced them to ideas and values, to ideology), a crime to recognize not two major conflicting powers in the world but several, a crime to belong to a guild, a profession, a "priesthood" that has a particular interest rather than a universal one, a crime to win the endorsement of opposing rivals in the making of global policy, a crime even to subscribe to *Foreign Affairs* (I confess, I can't afford it). What Said cannot see is that Huntington actually respects the core ideological (to use Said's world) self-definitions of each of his clashing civilizations, which have essentially constituted, repeatedly, in moments of crisis, cultural identities based on religious or ethical dogmas that substantially downplay, if not bitterly oppose, modern, democratic, secular worldviews. I am no expert in geopolitics, but then, who is, these days? But I do recognize when a critic is not playing fair, and such is the case of Said on Huntington. By saying this, I do not mean to suggest any general defense of Huntington's proposals and positions, especially those on American culture. My point in raising the question of Said's slam of Huntington is to account for my strong sense of disappointment at this celebrated critic's poor judgment. In twenty-two pages of rather crude polemic, Said cites Huntington directly in only one sentence. Such scholarly bad faith and critical injustice ironically accompany a self-serving utopian vision of secular liberation every bit as lame and blind as anything the mouthpieces of global capital have ever proclaimed, and I quote from it regretfully as I conclude this first chapter.

> [Critical humanism] prepares the way for a dissolution of cultural barriers as well as of the civilizational pride that prevents the kind of benign globalism already to be found, for instance, in the environmental movement, in scientific cooperation, in the universal concern for human rights, in concepts of global thought that stress community and sharing over racial, gender, or class dominance. It would seem to me, therefore, that efforts to return the community of civilizations to a primitive stage of narcissistic struggle must be understood not as descriptions about how in fact they behave but rather as incitements of wasteful conflict and unedifying chauvinism. And that seems to be exactly what we do not need. (590)

One does not have to be a disciple of Nietzsche or Hobbes—or an American superpatriot—to feel now sad at this dismissive conclusion. One need only think of Said's Andy.

2

Why Foucault No Longer Matters

● ●

Foucault, really from the beginning of his career, concerns himself with what he comes to call the subject of knowledge, the subject of power, and the subject of self-stylization. *Madness and Civilization* (1961), *The Birth of the Clinic* (1963), and *Death and the Labyrinth: The World of Raymond Roussel* (1963) respectively focus on the different generic formations of these different subjects, with their different rules of discursive configuration and practice.[1] By the late interviews of the early 1980s, these different subjects are fully conceived.[2] The subject of knowledge, for example, is the would-be "neutral I" formed in and by the analytic operations performed on the "deranged," objectified "characters" of the insane, the patient, the delinquent, within the institutional and discursive confines of the asylum, the clinic, the prison. This subject of knowledge presumes a virtual omniscience vis-à-vis these defective characters, thanks to its occupation of the post-Enlightenment position of scientific rationality or instrumental reason, the "technological," positivistic norm of the bourgeois mind-set.

The subject of power, then, is this subject of knowledge's dark double or "evil" twin. It is the internally split, "sick" inmate formed in and by the practices of the ultimately self-supervising and self-punishing modern disciplinary society of always potentially "dangerous" or "infamous"—

because predictably unpredictable, deviations from the norm—"individuals." The subject of power is a cautionary object lesson.

Finally, the subject of self-stylization is the agonistically structured, conflicted, mobile, and radically unstable identity formed in and by a Baudelairean "aesthetics of existence." The subject of knowledge, the would-be master, and the subject of power, this master's specular shadow and slave, as internalized styles of enunciation in a reflective mediation without end, together constitute this subject of self-stylization as a composite figure called "oneself," as in Foucault's phrase for this problematics, *rapport à soi* (I will simply use the more familiar "self"). Foucault sees this rapport à soi as the problemization of sexuality definitive for any ethics, ancient or modern. The genres of treatise and case study produce and perform these different subjects of knowledge and power, which in turn relate as "oneself" in the modern genres of ethical meditation and reflection. These genres include much of what we call "literature," such as journals, diaries, essays, fiction, even lyric poetry of some kinds, any and all of which can and do incorporate the discursive modes and subject positions of other genres in the constitution of their own stylistic practice of "ironic heroization," of pastiche and parody.[3] Such an "aesthetic of existence" is, for Foucault, a latter-day analogue to that of the Greeks and Romans. It is practiced in the interstices of the power/knowledge networks by an elite educated few, from whatever class origins, whose ability to read and write imaginatively and critically allows them to live life as if it were a work of art, the beautiful memory of which they can pass on, as an exemplary gift, to edify posterity. In failing to understand the literary connections among these subjects, Foucault's American New Historicist followers and critics mistake his project and so their own, as we have just seen in the last chapter.

For Foucault, then, Kant's "pure reason," "practical reason," and "aesthetic judgment" become, ironically, the subject of knowledge, the subject of power, and the subject of self-stylization. The discourses of the scientific or philosophical treatise (such as Descartes's *Meditations*), of the practical or professional training manual and case study (such as Clausewitz's *On War*), and of the spiritual exercise or literary meditation working through one's ideals, wishes, and dreams (such as Montaigne's *Essays*) compose these three different subjects of knowledge, of power, and of desire. That is, the knowing subject, the willing subject, and the desiring subject arise in forms of writing devoted to the "objective" knowledge of things, to the "subjective" constitution of internally self-disciplining and self-supervising subjects and societies, and to the aesthetic achievement of a distinctive imaginative expression for oneself to be given to a few others. Psychoanalytic analogues for these different subjects could be the ego, superego, and id, although more precise analogues would be the subject positions in the natural sciences, in the social sciences, and in the humanities and arts, the tripartite division that composes the conflict of the faculties in the modern university. The modes of theoretical treatise, professional critique, and reflective meditation, as they repeatedly appear and overlap in Foucault's work, all operate under the sign of "radical parody"—a self-conscious mimicry and ironic pastiche of such modes knowing no bounds.[4] Identity politics are the last thing, then, on Foucault's mind. Losing identities, like Beckett's fictional narrators, would be more like it.

What can one know? What should one will? What can one hope for? These Kantian questions Foucault proposes to respond to by saying, with mock simplicity: "oneself." As I have suggested, "oneself" is a loose trilateral coalition or unstable amalgam of discursive subject positions, the last of which, that of the desiring subject, attempts to incorporate the subject positions of knowledge and power in a stylized contest of reflective meditation on the ethical dimensions of self-formation based on the pedagogic model of mentor and student. This situation is ever open to potential shifts, reversals, dissolutions, and renewed formations. In other words, one can really know only oneself as the past subject of a belated knowledge. One can really will only oneself as the present subject of a pervasive power. One can really hope for only oneself as the future creation of an aesthetics of existence. But this temporally structured, "ecstatic" (or "out-standing") "oneself" is no mere isolated "individual"; rather, it is a recurring singularity as an irruptive site of cultural enunciation. "Oneself" is plural, mobile, unstable. It operates at a level neither solely specific nor purely universal, but which is that of regularity, generality, cutting across historical periods and societies thanks to the similarity (amid significant differences) in the forms of critical problemization of the subject. The self is neither so particular and dense with detail as to be unnameable, nor is it universal and so purely formal and empty of material contents. Rather, it is contingently representative. And it is made so by the ways in which the work of thought repeatedly constructs and construes certain issues and themes as conflicts and problems to be produced and reflected on as ethical predicaments within the diverse histories making up Western culture.

The self, as in Foucault's late formulation "rapport à soi," would be usefully characterized as a contingently representative site of cultural enunciation, a recurring influential figure, persona, or mask in the Western cultural imaginary as it (re)enacts its symbolic economy of destructively empowering abjection and repression with its scapegoat rituals of mimetic rivalry. Foucault himself, of course, has partially occupied this site and has partially impersonated this cultural mask for our "postmodern" moment. Why Foucault no longer matters thus has something, but not everything, to do with the ritual passing of this recent moment. As we saw in the last chapter, the success of his heirs contributes to such critical misunderstanding. As we will see in later chapters, even thinkers as different from Foucault and each other as Derrida and Ricoeur, however, understand this version of the self.

The most important reason for Foucault's increasing irrelevance has to do with more than the fading of postmodern "theory" culture. It has to do with a failure of reading. This failure emerges most clearly in the position taken by the major critics of Foucault's late work.[5] Edward W. Said, Charles Taylor, and Richard Rorty, among others, all find the late work to be a solecism in relation to the earlier work, whatever their problems or satisfactions with any phase of Foucault's career.[6] How the history of the ethical self-stylization fits with the archaeology of the subject of knowledge and the genealogy of the subject of power defines the problem Foucault's critics have with him, even though I think he has already addressed this problem.[7] Perhaps, however, he hasn't made himself understood, or perhaps, given their expectations, he could not have done so anyway. Or given one of their apparently leading assumptions, namely, that the aesthetic is a fully known and predetermined category of irresponsible or purely private fantasy, what else but misapprehension could result?[8]

Foucault's critics simply cannot see what statements such as the following have to do with his earlier projects, despite their clear relation to the book on Raymond Roussel and a host of articles on literary and artistic works published in the 1960s.[9] For argument's sake, however, what *can* the following statements have to do with Foucault's archaeological or genealogical critiques of the discourse of knowledge and power for instituting the modern subject as an exclusionary, normalizing model of human being? Here are the statements. First, from "What Is Enlightenment?" (1984), comes Foucault apropos Baudelaire's poetics of dandyism and its monumentalizing of the moment: "This ironic heroization of the present [that finds the glamour of the eternal, of poetry, in it], this transfiguring play of freedom with reality, this ascetic elaboration of the self—Baudelaire does not imagine that these have any place in society itself, or in the body politic. They can only be produced in another, a different place, which Baudelaire calls art."[10] This statement seems to describe and endorse the modern view of art as a would-be separate world of its own that, via its allusive intertextual forms, transcends and compensates imaginatively for an otherwise meaningless life of alternating sharp sensation and savage torpor. The second statement, from a later review, appears to apply this modern view of art to life itself, in the rhetorical mode of a rare belated discovery and complaint:[11] "Our society has hardly any remnant of the idea . . . that the principal work of art which one has to take care of, the main area one must apply aesthetic values, is oneself, one's life, one's existence. We find this in the Renaissance but in a slightly academic form, and yet again in nineteenth-century dandyism, but those were only episodes" (*FR*, 362). In this regard, the four or five centuries of experimentation found in ancient Greco-Roman culture constitute a full-blown epic of living the aesthetic view of life. The Greeks and Romans, in Foucault's eyes, make the aesthetics of existence the sustained focus of elaborate philosophical and practical care, an authentic cultivation of self perfected by the Stoics. Following in Baudelaire's wake, we can find in the Greeks and Romans, in the Renaissance courtiers, in the "decadent" aesthetes and dandies, not only examples to contemplate and discriminate but, in all their writings, a rich resource, a collective archive, of techniques of self-fashioning, some of which may prove imaginatively useful and practically effective for us now even in our different conditions.

Foucault, with these two statements and others like them, consigns himself to what appears to be an individualist and escapist celebration of decadent aestheticism, postmodern style.[12] In the world elsewhere of art, it appears one can envision one's life as a text composing a work of art.

Such a vision either finds some favor or, more generally, suffers a lot of condemnation, but in both cases it is judged as not following from his prior positions.[13] If the earlier work demonstrates, to everyone's satisfaction or not, that the human subject is the formal production of a historically contingent, hazardous play of conflicting discourses, with no hard core of individual identity, only its simulacrum and the fraying margins of barely repressed differences, how can Foucault also maintain in his later work that the human subject has a will, can express a unique agency, know and reflect on itself and elaborate, self-consciously, an aesthetics of existence? This is the question that all Foucault's critics put to him.[14]

If we accept its assumptions about, and view of, the earlier work as adequate characterizations, then this is a difficult, perhaps impossible, question to answer. In fact, this view of the earlier work in his critics is a falsifying and reductive received idea. Again and again, Foucault argues, nowhere more compellingly than in the whole of *Discipline and Punish*, that the broadly normalizing discourses of Western society—the discourses of reason, will, truth—manufacture the modern soul as a uniquely different and so individualized variation on, and deviation from, the normative model of bourgeois or instrumental rationality. It is the duty of the modern soul to strive to become as normal as possible, and it is the function of the asylum, the prison, and the clinic to produce a wealth of cautionary examples and object lessons demonstrating what can happen when the empowered norm is strayed too far from, and it must correct or at least confine the deviations via the state apparatus. The madman, the patient, the delinquent, and so on are extreme warnings of how individual variations can go too far from the centralized enforced mode of rationality, a norm by which each subject measures itself, judges itself, and conducts its self-revisions. If Western society once taught the imitation of Christ, it now teaches via selective counterpoint the mimicry of instrumental reason.[15]

In other words, the open secret of liberal Western culture is that it already practices an aesthetics of existence for everyone under the guise of a normalizing rationality and its empowering repression of some designated extreme cases but not of all individualizing differences. In fact, knowledge—precise, comprehensive, analytic—of such differences grants effective power over subjects, and no more effectively than in the service of global capital. The normative center and the periphery of predetermined differences define the modern regime of truth and its apparatus of power. Authors, as strange geniuses, are, after all, permitted as objects of awe and demystification alike. Nowhere is this curious power/knowledge mechanism of making normal and deviant subjects clearer than in the history of human sexuality, which Foucault discovers encompasses in its grand scope some 2,500 years of "desiring man." Throughout this history, the sexual "deviant," "the homosexual" in particular, has been the most cautionary of individual cases, the most dangerous, because the problem of such love, especially the love of a man for a boy under the former's pedagogical care, constitutes a recurrent "problem" that, in the different responses developed, discloses the important differences between ancient, Christian, and modern societies, something Foucault's critics tend to forget or ignore. It is the nature of such differences that I want to underscore in what follows, and not the "problem" of man-and-boy love.

Classical culture, supported by slavery and imperial conquest, composes a completely "virile" or male-dominated world. Yet, significantly, there is not, for most of its history until the triumph of Christianity under Constantine, a single state-enforced normalizing code of behavior and belief for the noble elite. Instead, there are variously proposed, self-elected rules of living in relation to oneself and others: Platonic, Aristotelian, Epicurean, Stoic, and so on. Especially with the rise of Imperial Rome, religion becomes purely formal and ritualistic even as superstition flourishes, and morality, in the sense of the public mores of civil society, becomes a matter for the army. Ethics, however, comes into its own now. Ethics concerns the relation to oneself—rapport à soi—and from the consciously constructed and elaborated nature of this relation flows one's relations with others. Although there are models of this relation to oneself, there is no single model imposed and enforced by the state. And though there are prohibited or recommended behaviors, these are various and constructed differently, leaving, unlike Christian or modern codes, much to individual judgment. In fact, ancient culture individualizes subjects not via a single coercive norm but via a contest of would-be good judgments ever open to further reflection, discussion, and decision. The classical self is in principle "freer" than the modern subject, but, one must recall, this self is solely a noble option that a slave class makes materially possible. One must also recall that the culture making the modern subject possible has been under relentless critique and in the process of change for some time.

Of course, Foucault does not believe that we can or should, even if we could, return to the culture of the Greeks or Romans, precisely because of its basis in enforced slavery. He does believe, however, that since we live in a time when religion has been in official decline, especially for the large intellectual and professional class, when the state has lost its legitimacy for most people and much of its social function, and when various global elite groups are forming their differentiating identities in opposition to both the centralizing norm and its prescribed deviations, we could perhaps learn from the examples of ancient culture. That is, we could learn from classical culture's collective archive some of the techniques for practicing the relation to oneself, and so invent our own diverse "aesthetics of existence." This would be especially useful since, as Marxism has failed, the Enlightenment assumption of a necessary, rather than contingent, link between socioeconomic forces and cultural positions has become less and less tenable. Foucault therefore concludes, "we have to get rid of this idea of an analytical or necessary link between ethics and other social or economic or political structures" (FR, 350). Instead, the only link between these different economic, civil, and cultural spheres is the contingent link of an aesthetic vision formed in the ascetic relation to oneself as an ethical self-stylization potentially having a pervasively exemplary or influential import among those capable of educating themselves in the discipline of self making. Given such a post-Kantian, Nietzschean position, which is coherent with his earlier work, is it any wonder that "oppositional" critics of all sorts would now dismiss or forget Foucault?[16]

What such critics want, and what Foucault has always refused to supply, is a fixed, predetermined, necessary connection of cause and effect, a clear and distinct idea of the grand design holding together, for good or ill, all aspects of human existence.[17] This is not to say that his vision of power in the mid-1970s lacks features of such a totalizing scheme or grand design, only that we must remember that Foucault refuses to formulate his vision of power in these terms, preferring instead to speak of a microphysics of power, a microanalytics of its mechanisms, carried out by specific intellectuals at their sites within the apparatus of the modern disciplinary society. Synoptic cause-and-effect analyses of the entirety of our existence, presented by would-be universal intellectuals who are certain of their truth and somehow outside what they criticize— such a prophetic prospect is something Foucault has always resisted, offering instead a series of partial and contingent critiques (what he calls historical ontologies of ourselves) covering but not exhausting the array of critical disciplines in the natural, social, and human sciences as well as the array of those discursive practices that do not easily fit, such as military discipline or penal reform, within the academy's disciplinary boundaries.[18] Among the socioeconomic, civil, and cultural spheres there is for Foucault no necessary link of cause to effect in a strict regime of truth, only a possible aesthetic connection of detailed similitudes and homologies in an open-ended strategic game of differential critique. "The aesthetics of existence," in short, defines with a later name what Foucault has practiced all along.

Primarily what we can learn from the Greco-Roman technologies of the self, in this context, is that the self is not simply found, not authentically discovered deep within us, but rather made, artificially invented and projected before us, as it were, out of all the discourses available to us. This self is plural, mobile, unstable, open to revision, and dependent on reading and writing for its "creation." This is also something we can learn from ancient culture—especially its use of the *hypomnemata,* or copybooks, records, and journals, the materials for Foucault's analysis in *The Use of Pleasure* and *The Care of the Self.* Because this is so important for understanding Foucault's late work, and for understanding why, because of it, he no longer can matter for us, I cite the crucial passages at some length:

> In the technical sense, the *hypomnemata* could be account books, public registers, individual notebooks serving as memoranda. Their use as books of life, guides for conduct, seems to have become a current thing among a whole cultivated public. Into them one entered quotations, fragments of works, examples, and actions to which one had been witness or of which one had read the account, reflections or reasonings which one had heard or which had come to mind. They constituted a material memory of things read, heard, or thought, thus offering these as an accumulated treasure for rereading and later meditation. They also formed a raw material for the writing of more

systematic treatises in which were given arguments and means by which to struggle against some defect (such as anger, envy, gossip, flattery) or to overcome some difficult circumstance (a mourning, an exile, downfall, disgrace). . . . They [the *hypomnemata*] do not constitute an "account of oneself"; their objective is not to bring the *arcana conscientiae* to light, the confession of which—be it oral or written—has a purifying value. The movement that they seek to effect is the inverse of this last one. The point is not to pursue the indescribable, not to reveal the hidden, not to say the non-said, but, on the contrary, to collect the already-said, to reassemble that which one could hear or read, and this to an end which is nothing less than the constitution of oneself. The *hypomnemata* are to be resituated in the context of a very sensitive tension of that period. Within a culture very affected by traditionality, by the recognized value of the already-said, by the recurrence of discourse, by the "citational" practice under the seal of age and authority, an ethic was developing which was very explicitly oriented to the care of oneself, toward definite objectives such as retiring into oneself, teaching oneself, living with oneself, being sufficient to oneself, profiting by and enjoying oneself. Such is the objective of the *hypomnemata*: to make of the fragmentary *logos* transmitted by teaching, listening, or reading a means to establish as adequate and as perfect a relationship of oneself to oneself as possible. (*FR*, 364–65)

The classical culture of memory changes, owing to the introduction of the hypomnemata in Plato's time, from an oral-based to a written-based culture. These copybooks are aids to memory originally used for administrative or accounting purposes. Gradually, they take on the features of commonplace books and finally become the many meditative "books of life" for a later Imperial age of Roman Stoics. Out of the raw materials of the diverse discourses gathered therein, these hypomnemata become the collective archive of self-invention that Foucault particularly highlights. I think that the ultimate reason why Foucault no longer matters for us now is that his most influential critics, perhaps because of Foucault's own lack of clarity on this matter, have failed to realize that he comes to see all of his works, but especially volumes 2 and 3 in *The History of Sexuality*, as latter-day hypomnemata of precisely the sort he characterizes at the end of the foregoing quotation. These volumes are his commonplace books of unfinished self-fashioning, which sensitive, like-minded readers can choose to complete in their own ways via their similar reading/writing/ listening/responding activities. This is why the style of these spiritual exercises is so lucid, succinct, and transparent in its sparing use of rhetorical flourishes. They lack, conspicuously so, the often obscuring, elaborate periods and Dionysian rhapsodies of the earlier work. In this way, they can better act as records of a spiritual exercise creating a self different from any Foucault knows or, perhaps any we know.[19] These volumes are sites for the enunciation of Foucault's invented rapport à soi as an open game of friendship for the reader able and willing to use these "books of life" as tools in the production and performance of his or her own rapport à soi, which is simultaneously, given the composite structure of the subject, a complex socializing form of human agency practiced via reading/writing/listening/responding and the principal precondition for the work of thought. Here, for my argument's sake, I must cite at some length once again:

> For a long time I have been trying to see if it would be possible to describe the history of thought as distinct both from the history of ideas—by which I mean the analysis of systems of representation—and from the history of mentalities—by which I mean the analysis of attitudes and types of action (*schémes de comportment*). It seemed to me there was one element that was capable of describing the history of thought: this was what one could call the element of problems or more exactly, problemizations. What distinguishes thought is that it is something quite different from the set of representations that underlies a certain behavior; it is also something quite different from the domain of attitudes that can determine this behavior. Thought is not what inhabits a certain conduct and gives it its meaning; rather, it is what allows one to step back from this way of acting or reacting, to present it to oneself as an object of thought and question it as to its meaning, its conditions, and its goals. Thought is freedom in relation to what one does, the motion by which one detaches oneself from it, establishes it as an object, and reflects on it as a problem. (*FR*, 388)

The kinds of reading/writing/listening/responding that Foucault's "books of life" require make possible the aesthetic distance productive of, and entailed by, the work of thought as he envisions it. To put it in its most provocatively polemical form: why Foucault no longer matters is precisely because we no longer know how to read what he means by the aesthetics of existence and its relationship to the work of thought, a relationship he sees in terms of the ancient care of the self, or *epimeleia heauton*. Generally, for today's global elites, the aesthetic is a category to be dismissed as not serious enough for thought, and this American view is New Historicist, often put forward in a smugly critical or delighted fashion.[20] The following is my approach to understanding in a different manner what Foucault means by "the aesthetics of existence" and its relation to the work of thought, which I suspect will also be open to misunderstanding.[21]

In *The Use of Pleasure* and *The Care of the Self,* Foucault analyzes the classical rapport à soi into a fourfold grid of ethical contingencies: the problematic material to be worked on (*substance éthique*), the subject-positioning or constraining rationale for ethical work (*mode d'assujet-tissement*), the self-forming ascetic activity (*pratique de soi*), and the kind of being into which one aspires to transform oneself (*téléologie*). For the ancients, the ethical substance is the aphrodisia (the body's desirable and pleasurable behaviors, sexual and otherwise); the discursive mode of subjection (and "subjectification") is anything from an appeal to self-interest to one of universal reason or human nature; the practice of self is a variety of elective disciplines including those of carefully reading/writing/listening/responding; and the ethical goal is self-mastery, however conceived and recognized. Although never mentioned in this connection, Aristotle clearly informs Foucault's fourfold grid of ethical contingencies. Material, necessary, sufficient, and formal (or "final") modes of causality in Aristotle have been revised by Foucault into contingent conditions of ethical capacity. Similarly, a complex revisionary theory of interpretation informs Foucault's ethical grid. The ethical substance can be seen as the material from the collective archives; the mode of subjection can be seen as the intellectual rationale for its transformation into another text; the practice of self can be seen as the professional disciplines of the scholar-critic-theorist-teacher—reading/writing/listening/responding—that one performs on oneself and for others. And the ethical goal can be seen as the self-mastery of the aesthetics of existence as a work of thought repeatedly open to the possibilities of becoming another as oneself. About this strange aim, more later.

The primary objection to this ethics of interpretation is that it is a species of formalist perfectionism, or that contentless mode of self-overcoming that reifies one part of the human being and deifies another part in an endless cycle of aesthetic alienation. Both Kant and Nietzsche, among others, have been accused of such formalist perfectionism.[22] The Foucauldian aesthetics of existence do have a content, however, principally self-mastery and the quest for it, because of his selection of the ancients from the collective archive. The ethics of interpretation informing this selection also have a content, I believe, and it is the belief that the highest human good is to shape a distinctive self out of the moral exemplars in the collective archive, and to give oneself as this distinctively shaped invention or aesthetic experiment to others through one's critical acts of magnanimous judgment. Such critical agency makes up the culture of care. Why care? Who cares? Today, in global America, I'm not sure any response will be given, and so I suspect that virtually no one cares, in this context. Hence Foucault's not mattering now.

In any event, for Foucault, the self-mastering person becomes an individuated but still composite self, according to a self-elected rule. This self is thereby worthy of being remembered as an exemplary figure for representative articulation in the history of ethical culture. Such a hero of the ascetic ideal, by transcending both blind desire and reflexive resentment, would be a central focus in a society of like-minded ascetic intellectuals, or friends in self-mastering self-fashioning. Such an ascetic aesthetics of existence does not imply the discovery of an authentic self deeply hidden in the recesses of the psyche. Nor does it presume to divide the aesthetics of existence into the private pleasure taken in, and created by, the imaginative shaping of a life into a work of art from public ethics. Rather, Foucault's aesthetic ethics would project for others the exemplary image of a life lived according to the difficult and chosen dictates of self-mastery, which for Foucault consists primarily in repeatedly emptying the mind of its habitual thoughts so as to be repeatedly open as possible to the latest twist and turn in the work of thought. The ethical agent in Foucault is an enacted role for thought, an embodied act of thought, an unfolding story in thought's history, thought's living work or figure, the play of its mask as the mask speaks, which is freely embraced and espoused as a singular persona contingently adopted and adapted, revised and elaborated, according to the ideal of self-mastery as the discipline of repeatedly trying, of experimentally essaying, to think otherwise. Self-mastery for Foucault, unlike for the Stoics, is not the extirpation of the passions, however destructive for oneself and others they may be, but this revisionary projection of a life transforming itself again and again into the work of thought both within the collective archive of culture and at the site of the text. To alter a bit Yeats's late formulation, it is character isolated by a past heroic deed to engross the present and dominate the future's memory.[23] The culture of care is, in this light, the collective archive of the ethical imagination, which encompasses a wide variety of figures such as Martin Luther King Jr., Emerson, and Margaret Fuller as soul makers.

So long as the goal is the general agonistic one of self-mastery, of surmounting blind desire and reflexive resentment alike, and the rationale remains the imaginative achievement of ascetic glory, whether or not any particular person is fully successful at transforming the substance for ethical work, and what that problematic substance may be—sexual acts, dietary regimes, thinking—will matter less than the passionate devotion to the chosen process of soul making. Like Keats's "ardour of pursuit," such a process is ideally revisionary, repeatedly creative of the object in passionate pursuit and so productive of differences without end: "The object [is] to learn to what extent the effort to think one's own history can free thought from what it silently thinks, and so enable it to think differently."[24] This aesthetics of existence, of difference, could not be ethically further from the identity politics dominating our time, which is another reason why Foucault no longer matters.[25] Feminists, African Americanists, neoconservatives—all sorts of critics appear now, to retrieve their own histories, again and again to secure their common identities, in opposition to other groups, and not to learn to break old habits of thought by improving, by experimenting with losing themselves in the thinking of others, and so remake their souls by overcoming, if they can, imaginative inertia and suspicious resentment: "Those images that yet / Fresh images beget."[26] As we saw in the preceding chapter, even a Said succumbs to the seductive mirages of this contemporary critical situation.

The passion of soul making is contingently representative, I think, of human cultures, whether in its strictly religious or more secularized forms.[27] The major division between cultures, for Foucault, is that between a culture that imposes a single, schematic, normalizing model, a centralizing pattern for rigorous imitation, and a culture that permits, indeed encourages, the revisionary production and performance of a differential plurality of concrete examples. Whether the model is Christ or Horatio Alger, so long as it constitutes one law for the ox and the lion, it is an imaginative mode of tyranny. Such a culture may possess a morality, an imposed standard of public and customary mores, but it is not ethical, since there is no freely selected rapport à soi possible, except as now in the modes of pure negation, such as absolute irony, radical parody, and empire burlesque.[28]

As I have suggested, Foucault appears to think that postmodern culture could begin to provide the conditions giving rise to a freely chosen rapport à soi, that sympathetic attunement to oneself as another and another as oneself that has its own array of selective ethical figures.[29] I do not think that this possibility exists any longer because to select from the collective archive of the ethical imagination one's own portfolio of heroically ascetic profiles requires the critical ability to reflect in a compassionate manner largely unavailable in the current climate of identity politics, group thinking, and political correctness of whatever sort.[30] What is required for a rapport à soi in its fourfold vision is an appreciative work of critical reflection, a new way of working for us, open to the contingent play of culture, its discourses, objects, and texts. Such a working would appreciate for its self-critical frisson my use of the foregoing trope (of the portfolio) from fashion modeling in this ethical context and not automatically use it to hoist me on my own petard, as it were. Nor would the recent sensation caused by revelations of Foucault's personal sexual preferences and behavior finally matter, since what should matter for intellectuals is the capacity for envisioning and striving toward self-mastery of desire and resentment via an elected mode of self-discipline, in the name of a socially recognized and critically representative rationale of some concrete kind that is not simply modeled after a centrally produced, imposed, and circulated norm supposedly universal and certainly abstract and one-dimensional. In sum, what should count for the critical intellectual is the practice of self and what can be learned from its appreciative form of analysis.

To think differently—nowadays? It may mean thinking that certain kinds of intellectual accomplishment are to be valued for their disciplined beauty as much as are the achievements of artists and athletes. Precisely because experience is contingent, fragmented, overdetermined discursively, incomplete, curtailed, precisely because the full development of things into their perfected forms rarely if ever really happens, "culture" is the dimension of life where such perfection can be envisioned and imaginatively rendered as an ethics of style given to oneself and for the edification of others. The relation of oneself to oneself, rapport à soi, when practiced well according to a chosen rule of ethical self-creation, is a form of the beautiful life to be recollected in pleasure and for inspiration. Each of us can produce such a game of life, with its own rule, standard, goal, and truth. Each of us does so, in fact, wittingly or not; but only some games are open to others because they are known to ourselves and generally recognized as such, and other such games are closed systems because they are secret to all, perhaps including, as psychoanalysis suggests, especially ourselves. However else conceived—according to a political or judicial model of agency and judgment—the relation to self in its ultimate literary or narrative form among the Stoics, Foucault reminds us, "is also defined as a concrete relationship enabling one to delight in oneself, as in a thing one both possesses and has before one's eyes," no matter what may befall oneself or the others with whom one shares such serene pleasure.[31] "The individual who has finally succeeded in gaining access to himself" in this manner, Foucault notes, "is, for himself [and others], an object of pleasure" in this special sense of the aesthetics of existence and its ethical stylization of a living being self-possessed of and by its distinctive virtue (66). Such is the thinking differently informing Foucault's late work, his commonplace "books of life," open to all but really understandable to few, for now. To think in this way, in our time, explains why I think that Foucault can no longer matter for the critical hegemony of the moment, since we can increasingly understand less and less of the kind of thing he may be meaning to say.[32]

Giving Spirit: An Ironic Postscript

As we have seen, then, Foucault is made to matter no longer as a professional matter of course. He is incorporated as an ersatz caricature of himself via reductive paraphrase and, even worse, citation without reading closely what is cited. He thus assumes the spectral life of the latest professional shibboleth, and then presumably must disappear, or if he does reappear, he will do so in a new light as determined by the practical circumstances of that moment and then dismissed once again.

For example, for one more example, in an otherwise helpful introduction to Foucault's "care of the self" as possibly also a "care of the other" in a poststructuralist ethics of pedagogy, Margaret Toye usefully summarizes the major features of his ethics of self-stylization in more detail. However, she is nonetheless unable to specify the basis for self-transcendence in Foucault's care of the self, and so she suggestively supplements his ethics with a Derridean revision of Levinas's ethics of the other.[33] Because I do something like this in this book, I admire her suggestion, even as I find her practice of nonreading problematic. But Toye can do so—that is, she can read Foucault's ethics without their social or communal dimension, as needing her supplement—because she abstracts from the details of the Greek male-to-male lifestyle of mentor and student, master and protégé, which provides the substance of any careful reading of *The Use of Pleasure* and *The Care of the Self*. How to remake the power dynamics of penetration, of youth and age, of pleasure and good example, and finally of love and honor versus mistrust and gain: this is the specific problemization that the Greeks wrestle with in ways Foucault thinks useful for our own erotic agons and their "politics of friendship"[34] (I deal with this topic at length in my *Radical Parody*). The issue is not to agree with Foucault in this view but to elucidate carefully what he has said, rather than simply practicing citation without analysis. What Toye has done here is, of course, nothing unusual. In fact, it is precisely because it is so routine that it makes plain the usual procedures of modern professionalization in global America—the outmoding of the latest model, paradigm, or example to make possible the production of the next latest one.

Such outmoding operations are the procedures and techniques, the technological capital, of a profession. "Modernization" is the big name for this sort of highly valued resource. It is the current driving force in the globalization of Western economies, as well as many other competing economies around the world. "Global America" is the impossible name for these revisionary technological processes of outmoding modernization. Why Foucault no longer matters? Ask global America!

As the figure of the impossible par excellence, however, global America also and at the same time, a time never present, promises, on the basis of all the archives of the past, the patterns of potential renewal ever to come in and as the future. Global America is both Specter and Creator, Satan and Messiah, tradition's blessing and curse. Toye's Foucault and Foucault's Toy(e).

Another way of thinking about this is in terms of different kinds of reading. Reading can be a procedure by which an already known conventional understanding returns to itself, gets itself reconfirmed, yet again once more. Or reading may act as a technique of discovery, a probing of the unknown, a leap in the dark whose aftershocks reverberate and scatter who knows where, with who knows what, if any, effects. Reading as return to oneself or as self-scattering: recollection or dissemination.

To understand reading as dissemination better, one would have to think of the relation to heritage, tradition, archives, canons, and non-canons as participating both in the economy of exchange, circulation, and return with interest and in the impossible economy of the gift without guilt, indebtedness, or reciprocal restitution.

The film *The Hurricane* represents both economies, exchange and gift, in terms of reading, almost just right. Rubin "Hurricane" Carter, a famous African American boxer, is railroaded into prison for life by corrupt cops for murders he did not commit. The book he writes about his ordeal falls into the hands of a young black man being instructed in literacy by Canadian volunteers who happen to be white lawyers, too. After many trials (in several senses of the word), the good turn that Carter's story of heroic suffering does for the self-esteem and aspirations of his self-chosen greatest reader and heir comes back to the book's author: the radical Canadian lawyers get Carter released from prison on the basis of technical but important violations of police procedure. This is the economy of exchange in terms of reading cultural traditions. What goes around, after a while, comes around with interest or with a vengeance.

Gifting is another matter. In *Given Time* and *The Gift of Death*, Derrida elucidates the aporia of the gift via sustained critical meditations on Mauss's anthropological analyses, Heidegger's ontological understanding of Being, Baudelaire's tale "Counterfeit Money," and Kierkegaard's *Fear and Trembling*. To put Derrida's point in a nutshell: "The truth of the gift suffices to . . . annul the gift."[35]

Let's put this in light of *The Hurricane*. If Carter either intends or later depends on the economy of exchange, of return with interest, and if his self-elected protégé in heroic suffering does likewise, then this presence of the gift in the economy of exchange destroys the gift as such. But if this truth of the gift that escapes and so propels by producing the economy of exchange is recognized, then the gift can never appear; it remains like one's own conscious death, an infinite or asymptotic limit, and as such, it becomes an aporia that annuls itself in the light of its own paradoxical truth as the ultimate given of existence. A giving without any possibility of exchange, not even the thought of possible exchange, an absolute expenditure without return, a radical and apocalyptic dissemination— what could this impossible be, how could one think of this, in what figure(s), under what mask(s), through whose persona(e)?

Let's return to the film one more time. From director Norman Jewison's point of view, *The Hurricane* participates fully, completely, totally (if successful), in the economy of exchange. Beyond this obvious and self-evident reality, however, there may be glimpses of the gift to be, well, glimpsed. To disseminate *The Hurricane* in worldwide release promises an iteration of its gift potential sublimely apocalyptic in scale, scope, and speed, beyond the will, intentions, limited identificatory mechanisms, and anticipated returns of director, author, studio, or multinational distributor. It is just putting into play, and so, perhaps, playing, giving out, among millions of others whose hopes for literacy, freedom, and impersonal justice cannot in advance be understood, predicted, imagined, or mastered, the spirit of the gift.

On a more limited scale, perhaps, it is in the spirit of the gift that Foucault offers us his pedagogic couple offering their heirs the beautiful example of their ethical self-stylizations of male-to-male love. That is, it is in our reading of his careful reading of their reading that the gift may be disclosed.[36] To a similar end I offer here what can be comically called the copy-books of global America.

3

Lentricchia's Frankness

and the Place of Literature

● ●

I begin with two quotations from Frank Lentricchia's surreal memoir, *The Edge of Night: A Confession,* which define its complex imaginative motivation. The first quotation satirizes the current status of literary study as a profession of "pre-Reading": "I live in the literary academy, the Imperial Place of Explanation, among those-who-always-already-know, among the Princes and Princesses of Pre-Reading, the executioners of mystery."[1] The second quotation satirizes the critic's desire to become an author, by giving himself a new name, entirely of his own invention, which would stand as the mark of his distinctive signature in, and on, the world: "I change the subject fast and ask them, since they're all studying Irish (which they dislike having to do), if someone can tell me my name in Irish. The inventive Simon comes forward quickly with 'Frunc,' a perfect description of my inner life at the moment" (159). The moment in question is a hair-raising drive through the Irish countryside in a car driven by a jet-lagged American critic and passengered by a bunch of Irish children.

I summon up these two quotations to bring out an important point about the literary motive informing *The Edge of Night,* about which Lentricchia is, typically, entirely frank. For him, the profession has become a factory for manufacturing well-established commodities produced according to already-known designs. Whether "multicultural" or "liberal humanist" or "neoconservative," for Lentricchia, literary study holds no surprises. This is especially so as it transforms itself into cultural studies out of embarrassment over the politically incorrect social positions of most canonical authors, particularly all those modern makers of surprising formal inventions of the creative imagination such as Pound, Yeats, Stevens, Frost, and Eliot. To put it a bit schematically: whereas, as Foucault would predict, these modern authors, because of their irresistible formal innovations, often discover themselves, in their works, becoming beautifully other than what they or we would expect, we postmodern critics, official celebrants of the sublime, practice our theories and methods by rote, performing in our works predictable roles according to purely predetermined scripts, with no space or time for the smallest improvisation. Get the product out, whatever market it serves, as quickly and professionally as possible, and forget about surprise, innovation, discovery, or learning. Yet, as the second quotation makes clear, there is no easy escape from this situation by christening oneself an author, that embodied representative of the literary imagination, for our identities are not ours to create autonomously, by singular fiat, but negotiated composite formations constituted in the give-and-take of social experience, however destitute, surprising, absurd, or painful that may turn out to be.

We are at a crossroads in the profession. When a leading American critic—arguably the most imaginative reader of his critical generation—turns away from literary study to create a work of literature, in disgust with his profession and with a desire to discover a freer range of vision, this phenomenon must serve as a cautionary tale, a genuine scene of instruction. The possibilities for intelligent selfhood and imaginative exchange have been crowded out. A system of professional practice repeatedly replays the boring binary opposition between a white male mode of subjectivity dressed up in transhistorical robes and a familiar variety of different, formerly repressed subject positions—African American, female, gay and lesbian, (post)colonial—that make up the cultural politics of identity being played out now in the profession, usually under the name of cultural studies on a global scale. I find this binary opposition boring, because, like all such oppositions, it is simplistic and reductive. But it becomes deadly when it is applied as a framework for reading and reflecting on the formal features—conventional and innovative—of literary works that experiment with and perform new modes of human subjectivity. In their stylistic choices, structural configurations, and intertextual resonances, such literary works dramatize their imaginative critique of all normative critical prescriptions, whatever the informing model or motivation. *The Edge of Night* exemplifies this project of literature. But how did we get to this situation in the profession, which Lentricchia can address only by leaving it to do literature himself?

The other day, over lunch, I asked a recently retired colleague of considerable professional standing why he had originally become a literary critic. He responded that when he started, it was assumed that literature gives people who read it carefully access to different points of view, other selves, and their worlds repeatedly in the making. These embodied, but unfinished, perspectives are, to be sure, imaginative idealizations, but they are open to a critical appreciation. "What about formalism?" I asked. He looked benignly on my stupidity and responded, "Even the New Critics practiced criticism—no matter what they may have preached —as if literature, precisely through its formal perfections, enlarged, in a memorable way, the experience of readers and so made possible a basis for recognition and respect between different people." Literature, in short, was once thought to be an imaginative form of ethical significance worthy of remembrance. In a Cold War era of domestic witch-hunts, as the first- or second-generation offspring of immigrant ancestors began to enter the profession, and as the civil rights movement began to gain momentum, this vision of literature in liberal culture could, and did, have socially progressive consequences, I believe, within and, shortly, without the profession.

It has been some time, however, since this ethical vision of literature has prevailed in the profession. As long as literary study was generally insulated by educational principle and economic circumstances from the harsher realities and bottom-line mind-set of the global marketplace, such liberal humanism could be largely entertained and, to a degree, practiced. However, once universities and colleges no longer saw an expanding pool of students but instead faced steadily dwindling or just uncertain enrollments, increasing costs, and a labor supply more and more in excess of current and future needs, competition for positions, for status, for professional influence—for just about everything—became fiercer and fiercer. Every move, on everyone's part, then became calculated to cultivate the main chance. Fewer and fewer good professionals could read and write primarily for other reasons. Skeptical, disillusioned, and even cynical views of literature and literary study, whether imported or homegrown, found an audience ripe for their poststructuralist, deconstructive, and New Historicist performances of cultural despair dressed up as liberating symbolic gestures from what we must see as an escapist, canonical, and so exclusionary institution of literature, the principal ideological illusion of a decadent and repressive culture. Now in our post–Cold War era, a cynical reason prevails in the mode of ritualized postmodernist postures standing against grand narratives of any kind, ironically enough, and standing for so-called marginalized positions and language games of every kind, most still underwritten by the university in global America.

Because material conditions make possible both the idealized and the disillusioned views of literature, only another change in such conditions, for better or worse, can make yet another view arise and prevail. And I see such change—for the worse—coming. It is now harder to get a tenure-track job than at any other time in the history of the profession. It is now harder for graduate programs to support as many students as they once did, even as more candidates for graduate school than ever before are applying for fewer and fewer entry positions, due to the mistaken belief that because more than half of all professors will retire shortly, schools can choose to make up their losses with permanent, rather than temporary, replacements. Schools cannot afford such a choice. They will make do with at best one in three or four permanent replacement lines and make up the difference, as they have done so far, with adjunct lines, greater use of computers in the classroom, larger sections, and so on. In essence, the profession is becoming a lot like professional sports: a few "irreplaceable" superstar "free agents" and a mass of interchangeable "utility" or "role" players, most of whom do not have, and cannot get, long-term contracts (i.e., tenure).

As chapter 6 spells out further, this means that two professions are developing: a proletarian service profession and its aristocratic and alienating ideal image. The elite few who make it big time, to "the show," the highest reaches of the circuit of professional fame, perform this "glamorous" role of professional success for the envious mass. The latest fashion for celebrating difference, otherness, history's and society's victims, is the sign of this emerging situation. Most in the profession now begin to feel the imminence of the social death, the total nonrecognition, this professional situation will solidify. And so they reflexively identify with those—women, African Americans, Native Americans, postcolonialists, gays and lesbians, and so on—who have suffered similar, or worse, social deaths and yet have risen again to demand recognition as themselves via an elite few who are now making it professionally and can impersonate their desire for representation. Meanwhile, those of an earlier generation who have already made it professionally and played a similar role for a different constituency have now taken to admonishing those who celebrate multiculturalism for their "political correctness." These stars of an earlier generation condemn their multicultural heirs for the failure to see how professional change does not necessarily entail either social change or real economic transformation. The established professional aristocracy, and those who still aspire to its ranks, are beginning to be worried as the lower orders and their emerging stars now repeat the earlier generation's original gestures of disillusioning or (so-called) liberating critique by turning the earlier critical thrusts back against the established professional aristocracy itself, in order to ensure that, in similar fashion, the few new multicultural stars secure the emerging regime.

In "Why Literary Criticism Is like Virtue," Stanley Fish argues that "the effects of one's actions will always be confined to their disciplinary settings even when those settings receive some grandiose new name like Cultural Studies."[2] He concludes by repeating an old familiar point of his: "Disciplinary actions have disciplinary origins and can only reasonably aim for disciplinary effects" (12). Fish attempts here to disabuse multiculturalists of their irrational belief that they are not literary critics but practitioners of cultural studies whose work of critique can change the world. Fish has made a career out of dashing larger hopes by throwing on them the cold shower of a cynically professional reason. Ironically, however, Fish's assumption that literary criticism is like virtue by being its own—self-limiting—reward, rather than being an empowering revolutionary critique, positions the profession as a purely formal discipline entirely focused on its own protocols of self-presentation, via textual analysis and literary historical contextualization, even when it makes more socially representative claims.

I disagree with Fish's conception of rationality underlying his argument—it is too narrow and instrumentalist—but I agree with him that cultural studies, working from within a disciplinary setting, cannot change the larger world. But the real problem with Fish's argument—aside from his dubious and diabolical alignment of literary criticism and virtue—is that it does not really disempower his multiculturalist rivals and their championing of otherness and the moral superiority of victimization. Instead, it opens the door wider to their critical thrusts against the established professional aristocrats who, like Fish, can only claim now to practice literary criticism as its own reward and who can offer no terms of rational justification for their activities not drawn from the openly self-congratulatory clichés of these very activities. Is literary criticism really like virtue, or like the pure activity of Aristotle's God, thought thinking itself, or like some Kantian moral end in itself? As it turns out, Fish reduces his analogy between literary criticism and virtue by admitting that, for him, he just likes doing it. The original and continuing vocational imperative of literary criticism can only be, for him and, he claims, for others, not a matter of free choice but merely a question of fortunate taste:

> If you ask me why is it a good thing to explicate *Paradise Lost,* I can do nothing better or more persuasive than do it, spinning it out in directions at once familiar and surprising, ringing the changes, sounding the notes in the hope that the song is one you know or that it will be infectious enough to start you singing. Literary interpretation, someone has recently said, has no purpose external to the arena of its practice; it is the "constant unfolding" to ourselves "of who we are" as practitioners. The only "value of the conversations is the conversation itself." That's all there is, even when we try to enlarge it by finding in it large-scale political and cultural implications. I say again, that's all there is, but it's enough for those who long ago ceased to be able to imagine themselves living any other life. Last year, an old friend whom I hadn't seen for a while called me to catch up. "What are you doing this summer?" he asked. "Writing on *Paradise Lost,*" I answered. "But that's what you said thirty years ago," he responded. "Right," I replied,

"yet once more"; and if I had thought of it I would have borrowed a line from my friend David Lodge, who borrowed it from George and Ira Gershwin: "Nice work if you can get it." (16)

(I assume that the remark about the conversation of the discipline being its own end comes from Richard Rorty; about the old friend at the end here, I can't even begin to speculate.)

Given such a failure by Fish and his critical generation to provide broadly rational and ethical grounds for literary study, which incorporate whatever aesthetic grounds there are, multiculturalists, misreading their model Foucault and secure in their new standing, can all too easily declare the discipline to be an irrational luxury, practiced by a dying class of self-indulgent white male aesthetes, whom, given the intolerable injustices without and within the profession, global America can no longer afford. Literary study, therefore, must be replaced by a more representative and responsible practice, whether it is to be called cultural studies or something else. This is the kind of thing multiculturalists can now say persuasively, thanks to Fish's and his generation's failure to mount a systematic defense of literature and its study. That I think this multicultural critique is essentially a reflection of the resentful alienation of the many, as now led by their self-elected shepherds, in the face of the happy alienation of the fortunate few stars of the critical establishment, whatever their current orientations, could, of course, go without saying, but I'm saying it anyway, for clarity's sake.

Stanley Fish and company—and, indeed, literary study—are thus without any general rational and moral grounds for "doing what comes naturally," which is, for them, "business as usual." Due to an original vocational imperative based on a fortunate formation of their taste, and still supported by their somewhat fading star status, they are, for the time being, still permitted to repeat themselves by doing *Paradise Lost,* or whatever, yet once more. Meanwhile, multiculturalists have elaborated a conceptual framework of wholesale critique of canonical literature and the profession that "pre-reads" any practice of literary criticism, including all efforts to provide rational justification for the profession and its canon, solely in light of the bad example of Stanley Fish and company. Consequently, all would-be devotees of literature, of whatever generation, are automatically consigned, in advance, and without serious thought, to the status of self-blinded dupes of the larger culture's ideological apparatus. Consider the possibility: one can be reduced to the self-congratulatory, always already knowing program of resentful critique disguised as a multicultural agenda of universal social liberation contradictorily based on a narrowly construed imaginary identity politics founded on the problematic basis of personal experience. To what identity formation, by the way, would a Stanley Fish belong—literary critics who always wanted to be lawyers?

However that may be, in an interview with Edward W. Said about his book *Culture and Imperialism,* one of the interviewers characterizes this current professional situation in a typically telling fashion, capturing its truly vicious ironies:

> There are cases in the profession where the exclusion of literature is almost programmatic. The perverse logic of the so-called canon debate has reached the point now that if, for example, I were to go to a graduate course with your book (which I probably will next year), one of the first questions I expect a student will put to me is, "Why do you think of this book as an oppositional text? It starts with T. S. Eliot." I have problems with persuading some of my fellow faculty members that it is important to continue teaching criticism courses with Plato, Aristotle, Dryden, and Kant, which for them seems a waste of time. They would say, "Why don't we start with something more urgent, Like Derrida?" It's not that I disagree with you about the importance of literature, far from it. But I see a rather bizarre situation: Your book demonstrates the very rich potentialities of literary reading, but, at the same time, it is going to be read by oppositional critics, who might be generally sympathetic with your position politically but who are caught in a web of logic that does not allow them to confer upon certain texts the value you do. At the risk of exaggeration, I would say that there are people in the profession who are not even trained to read the texts you read in the way you read them.[3]

The major irony of this situation is enormous, indeed, almost overwhelming. Here is Said, whose *Orientalism* has almost single-handedly made the oppositional critique of multiculturalism possible, who is asked, by a knowledgeable and sympathetic interviewer, to justify his latest book, before the fact of its reception by professional oppositional critics who owe their stance to him. Said is asked to provide such justification because *Culture and Imperialism* dares to read, contrapuntally, for the aesthetic and political forms and values of canonical texts. Unfortunately, neither in this interview, nor in the fine conclusion to *Culture and Imperialism*, nor (as we have seen) anywhere else, does Said, who essentially possesses a brilliant essayistic mind, provide a fully comprehensive defense of literature and literary study, as he understands the former and practices the latter. Instead, much as Fish does in his very different manner, Said just performs his preferences here and in his book. Said usually does so magnificently well, but exemplary status alone does not make a systematic argument, however importantly it may contribute to one.

Although I do not plan for this chapter to be the occasion for producing such a systematic defense, I do want to do two things now that I've highlighted what is missing in current debates. The principal thing I want to demonstrate is how Frank Lentricchia's *The Edge of Night* significantly addresses this situation. But I also want to sketch a framework for evaluating literary and critical judgment, in which we can better see what Lentricchia and, I hope, others are doing, so that we can measure how much more must be done if we are to provide an adequate justification of literature and literary study. What immediately follows, before my turning to *The Edge of Night*, is a quick outline for a standard of judgment.

I propose (as in chapter 2), following Foucault's understanding of the classical *epimeleia heauton*, or "care of the self," that we analyze the rapport à soi, the relation to oneself, in the work of any writer.[4] Because the relation to oneself is a complex, reflexive relation to a composite, socially produced and performed self-project, my proposal avoids the charges of abstract individualism and pure narcissism. At the same time, my adoption and adaptation of Foucault's understanding of this rapport à soi is broad enough to encourage flexibility and tact in its application, even as it calls for making sharply drawn discriminations among kinds of judgments.[5]

The rapport à soi—I repeat myself here for convenience's sake—consists of a fourfold grid of ethical contingencies: (1) the problematic material to be worked on, or the ethical substance, as defined by the traditions the writer draws on; (2) the strategic rationale given, and the mode of subjection proposed, for working on the ethical substance; (3) the self-forming ascetic activity itself or the practice of discipline; and (4) the goal, the kind of being that this aesthetic project of ethical self-stylization has for its ultimate end. The ethical substance, for any writer, is the material of personal and cultural memory drawn from what I call the collective archive of written and oral stories and examples. The mode of subjection, the strategic way of producing a certain kind of subject position, is the intellectual rationale for the transformation of this material into another text. In the literary critical context, the ascetic practice of self particularly entails the professional disciplines of the scholar-critic-theorist-teacher: those slowly acquired, second-nature habits of reading/writing/listening/responding that a critic (and, in some related fashion, any writer) performs on, and as, the self for others. Finally, and I speak primarily of the critic here, the ethical goal is the kind of aesthetics of existence, of being open to becoming repeatedly other than oneself, which requires the repeated overcoming of resentment by a noble ideal of magnanimous self-mastery. As we will see, Lentricchia brilliantly exemplifies this fourfold rapport à soi in his imaginative avowal of his own life.

Thus Fish and Said, in their very different, yet representative, ways, fail to provide a defense of literature and its study against the reductively resentful critiques of what are often their own epigones in multiculturalist drag, who want to replace literature with its historical context as the object of analysis and want to change the name of literary study to that of cultural studies, automatically ignoring or condemning in the process the formal aesthetic dimensions of texts, canonical or otherwise, which can make for a subtle and complex critique not to be missed without losing significant food for thought. The aim should not be to dismiss canonical texts and their aesthetic analysis. Rather, it should be to equip ourselves for seeing how formal innovations and achievements in canonical and noncanonical texts compose an aesthetics of existence, a potentially exemplary rapport à soi, within the collective archive of culture, from which we can draw our fine inspiration and object lessons, our cautionary tales and life profiles for emulation in our own projects of self-invention. Failure such as Fish's and Said's is representative of the profession's general failure to recall what literature has been in other circumstances, so that we can reenvision what it can be in our newly emerging condition. Frank Lentricchia's *The Edge of Night* performs this double act of the historical and revisionary imagination. By saying this, however, I mean only to suggest that *The Edge of Night* is a work of high literary art that can fuel a comprehensive reflection on the grounds of literary study. By being literature, *The Edge of Night* performs its own defense, even as Lentricchia, by becoming an author, does likewise for his original choice of vocation, literary study. This complex defense can then be critically developed, a task I hope to begin here. In short, I am revising a point that Lentricchia makes elsewhere about T. S. Eliot: "Looking back at the early days of his poetic development, in the first decade and a half of this century, T. S. Eliot reflected on the literal and anxious truth of his poetic origins when he said that there was not 'a single living poet, in either England or America, then at the height of his powers, whose work was capable of pointing the way to a young poet conscious of the desire for a new idiom.'"[6] I would revise this statement by changing the references from poetry and poets to criticism and critics, and by claiming that in Lentricchia, especially with *The Edge of Night,* we do have an example capable of "pointing the way" to "a new idiom."

The Edge of Night could be considered a companion volume to *Modernist Quartet,* Lentricchia's contribution to the recent Cambridge History of American Literature series. T. S. Eliot's hypersensitive figure, so important there (as the title suggests), permeates *The Edge of Night,* but then, significantly, Yeats's contrasting heroic figure appears only in the latter volume to mitigate Eliot's ironic contagion. The question of the tragic cost of making a public persona and achieving fame, the solemn central theme of the Frost chapter in *Modernist Quartet,* also appears in *The Edge of Night* apropos the critic's identity, but with comically absurd overtones. The relation of aesthetic and political matters, as in the Pound chapter in *Modernist Quartet,* also informs *The Edge of Night,* but in terms of the critic's choice of vocation and the manner of working. In *The Edge of Night,* the question is, To what degree does the critic's work absorb the whole person the way his ancestors' manual labor did, to what degree did their labor, like criticism, alienate the worker, and why? Similarly, the problematic issue of gender identity involved in this choice of work appears in the Stevens chapter of *Modernist Quartet* as part of a distanced, impersonal analysis; but in *The Edge of Night,* this issue is immediately center stage and quite personal. As Lentricchia reminds us in both books, doing literature or literary criticism is a mode of work that has often been looked on in America as less than a "real" man's job. The primary difference between *The Edge of Night* and *Modernist Quartet*, however, lies in the former's literary shaping of all the particulars—personal and professional—of the critical life. The latter volume can only deal with them, if at all, via the projected allegory or symbolic mask plays that the critic performs by making his chosen authors impersonate, partially, the figures from his life in criticism's analytic scenes of judgment. This is to be expected, after all, since *The Edge of Night* was originally called *Memory and Other Crimes: An Autobiographical Experiment*. The immediacy and particularity of the imaginative processes as they form and reform the narrating persona "Frank Lentricchia"—everything (and more) that for generic reasons could not become the explicit matter of the scholarly *Modernist Quartet*—do compose the principal subject of *The Edge of Night*.[7]

The particular and immediate, the terrible beauty of contingency—this is the radical phenomenon explored in various ways by *The Edge of Night*. At every level of analysis—textual, structural, personal, professional, historical, philosophical—the beauty of contingency composes the ethical subject to be worked through. Let's start at the philosophical level and work our way from there.

> Is it becoming obvious to you that I'm a somewhat uneasy Italian-American aesthete who finds Walter Pater, unofficial mentor of Oscar Wilde, almost sufficient? "Of this wisdom, the poetic passion, the desire of beauty, the love of art for art's sake has most; for art comes to you professing frankly to give nothing but the highest quality to your moments as they pass, and simply for those moment's sake." When I experience art, I feel good because I feel the specificity of the moment, the act, the image, the scene, but before and after I don't feel too good, so I seek out more experiences of art's particularity because art is the only place I know where to find deliverance of the specific from the habits of abstraction. Pater means "art" in the traditional sense, a good enough sense. But if I limit myself to what he intends, I don't feel good that often. That's why I look for the beautiful everywhere, why I coax and stroke it when I find it stirring in front of me. And I do mean "in front of me," in a restaurant in Little Italy, 146 Mulberry Street (honor to the site), at Angelo's (everything's in a name). Art as stubborn specificity, as untheorizable peculiarity. Art for life's sake. (89)

The ethical material to be shaped is the stubborn specificity of art in life, art for life, of the beautiful wherever it may arise. The mode of subjection, the work rationale, is the quest to deliver this beauty from the habits of abstraction. The ascetic discipline practiced on the self in this regard is the imaginative recording of these occurrences, drawing on the personal and collective archives of memory and desire for improvised resonances and frameworks. The goal of Lentricchia's spiritual exercise is to "feel good," to become a being absorbed by, and in, the stubborn specificity, the untheorizable peculiarity, of the beautiful as it contingently emerges and elaborates itself there before him and, in his pages, before us. The intellectual commodification of life and of the critic—by the culture industry that robs us of the beauty of contingency by giving us the always already known—is the evil from which Lentricchia would save his beauty. Because a part of Lentricchia's soul is the product of this intellectual process of cultural commodification, it is as if Faust would save beauty from this cold-beast part of himself, even as the beauty of contingency is clearly recognized as representing his own capacity for imaginative receptivity and response, or the best part of himself, or at least his better half. What *The Edge of Night* proposes to do is to renegotiate the union of these parts, to set the marriage of Lentricchia's two minds—the critical and the imaginative—on a new basis, to revise his rapport à soi. This is one reason why the theme of marriage haunts the book.

If there are not ultimately meaningful origins and ends, if from accidental conjunctions inescapable personal habits and monumental cultural forms equally arise and together act like tragic fate, then the goal in life is to cultivate the specific contingent moment in all its precarious openness as often, and for as long, as possible in order to feel the passionate pleasure of being fully alive, that dangerous beauty of being in the world that we used to call imagination. Without religious or metaphysical or clear and distinct guarantees of any kind, each and every one of us exists as if "at sea," flowing along with whatever currents—historical, psychological, discursive—are now at play. We can seek to appreciate the emerging beauty of each moment's novel, improvised performance as flux develops repeatedly into form to become flux once again, or we can definitively prejudge each future moment via a programmatic agenda of abstraction and doctrine. What makes Pater's "art for art's sake" or Lentricchia's "art for life's sake" not a philosophical prejudice of this kind is that specificity, particularity, even peculiarity may resist even the aesthetic of flux and form, which is an aesthetic that is deliberately not held in any other way but lightly. The appreciation Pater recommends and Lentricchia practices constitutes an act, and it takes one of the changing forms of art, so as to give the pleasurable gift of imaginative passion to others.

Historically, the implications of this "aestheticism" are profound. Family, class, race, gender, culture—all mark in particular, contingent, yet ineradicable ways the imaginative matrix for any individual act of appreciation. It matters that Frank Lentricchia comes from an Italian American background of working-class people, whose men and women alike toiled with their hands at trades and in factories to support the family and to make possible the realization of their intellectual aspirations through him. This background enables Lentricchia to see reading and writing as "a medium of kinship" for different peoples (110). In an otherwise hopelessly fractured modern culture, all these specific marks or determinations of ethnicity, gender, and so on make up the historical landscape of self in *The Edge of Night,* which Lentricchia critically appreciates as this "medium of kinship."

Consider, for example, the book's opening section, "September 1992," which climaxes with Lentricchia envisioning his maternal grandfather, Tomaso Iacovella, great storyteller and cultivator of giant cherry trees, playing Lady Gregory to his paternal grandfather, Augusto Lentricchia, man of ice, erstwhile baby-sitter of our author and self-disciplined, if secret, journal keeper and unsung poet, who could have been the Yeats of his clan. "Now I shall write out," Lentricchia declares, "my desire for a dead man. This is what I want. That he, Augusto, could have been his, Tomaso's Yeats" (34). Lentricchia then carefully specifies all the stubborn, untheorizable details of this imagination, including "a little writing table" on "the second floor back porch," with special access and a key to a secret inner cellar below the cellar in the old house. Here would be all the "resources of writing, reading, and bodily nourishment, and a pallet for when he needed to sleep." Lentricchia envisions all this so that Augusto might be "lost" in "life's, not Augusto's, self-delight," in "life's self, which was the world of Tomaso" (35). The aim would be a unified being, as in the vision of Homer and the heroes he sung, which Yeats revises in the "Ancestral Houses" section of *Meditations in Time of Civil War:* "And then from Augusto would spring, as it had sprung from Homer, the abounding glittering jet, expression pouring forth, piling high upon itself, the lines he would most like, lines that were part of the quiet and self-delight of which he himself was only part" (35). Lentricchia even envisions a happy death for his chosen hero:

> And let it be his death room, the second floor back porch, let it be detached and boarded up, and let him be buried in it between the fig and the cherry tree, and upon the grave let there be placed a sprig of cherry, one fig, and each day, one mushroom, one for every time he could press back, almost without knowing he was pressing back, almost without pain, his urges for marriage and fatherhood. Let it all be. Augu, Edge 'a Night. (35)

Lentricchia believes that, freed from the responsibilities of marriage and fatherhood, at least for a while in his own mind, Augusto could have had a real chance to put his talent to the test. (This belief prepares for the next section of the book, when Lentricchia recounts his visit to a Trappist monastery, Mepkin Abbey, to discover, if he can, the discipline of authentic recollection and loss of self so necessary for a writer to learn to practice.) The final line of this scene, "Augu, Edge 'a Night," provided the second title for the book before settling on the less ethnic *The Edge of Night*, and it is what Augusto's wife, Paolina, would say every afternoon to call him from his brooding so that together they could watch the old soap opera, now long canceled, of this name, even as Lentricchia now calls his grandfather, as his ideal reader, to watch his accomplished grandson's own *Edge of Night*.

In this scene of judgment, Lentricchia uses the literary tradition to give resonance to the personal life, even as the personal life renews a traditional topos, that of the muse-mentor and poet-pupil, in an original way. By uttering this final line, by spontaneously improvising this repetition, Lentricchia plays both the role of Tomaso as Lady Gregory and that of Paolina, his paternal grandmother, to the finely tortured, yet stoic, Augusto Lentricchia, thereby imaginatively avowing the magnanimous return of the favor of nurturing to one of its primary sources. The being of the beloved spouse speaks through Frank Lentricchia to offer up this vision, and indeed that of the entire coming book, to the memory of this grandfather's unfulfilled desire for sponsorship, as that desire is now being realized in the all-absorbing work of his grandson's hands. In this intensely overdetermined manner, historical particularity incorporates a radical contingency and mobility of identity transgressing rigid categorizations of generation, class and cultural status, and gender. Lentricchia recognizes here the force of desire that cuts across, and cuts between, the lines of one historical matrix and another. Aesthetic liberation is this writing/reading/responding that makes up the imagination in action. Such textual work is "a medium of kinship" that, originating in a historically particular site, moves on to produce, thanks to language's uncontrollable figurative inventiveness, specific representation openings at other historically contingent sites of enunciation. If temporal differences both matter and yet are overcome, why not other differences of culture, class, race, and gender?

Professionally speaking, such historical aestheticism finds few echoes nowadays. So Lentricchia returns, in another section, to the figure of his high school Shakespeare teacher, Senatro D. LaBella, to dramatize how the latter's performance of the plays—to the point of their bodily impersonation before his students' wide eyes—gives the plays as gifts to his Utica, New York, Italian American students. This kind of gift giving is an act of the medium of kinship. Acting, in all its forms, is a crucial mode of being for Lentricchia. Senatro D. LaBella's beautiful act is one of giving cultural resources to students in need, who want to possess what their ancestors were denied access to and what their more privileged contemporaries assume as their birthright. These students want to make it in modern America. And by "making it," Lentricchia means being capable of envisioning for themselves in their own complex terms the fulfillment of their most imaginative desires, a spiritual fulfillment beyond their growing alienation from social origins that always dogs such cultural aspirations. In *The Edge of Night*, Lentricchia cites T. S. Eliot's authoritative critical comment on this matter from *Notes towards the Definition of Culture*: "To be educated above the level of those whose social habits and tastes one has inherited may cause a division within a man which interferes with happiness" (100). Lentricchia then shows how Eliot, in *The Waste Land*, imagines, for a moment and to the contrary, a harmony of classes and tastes realized by the mandolin's music in the pub by the Church of St. Magnus Martyr, with its magnificent Ionic columns of inexplicable white and gold; and so Eliot, too, holds out the possibility of creating a culture like the one informing Shakespeare, which would transcend the alienating divisions between "high" and "low," "elite" and "popular," classifications.[8] Although Lentricchia later does come to credit Eliot's critical caution concerning the utopian conception of now producing a great literature such as Shakespeare's on the model of Marie Lloyd's music hall performances (my "empire burlesque" *avant le lettre*), he nonetheless gives the definitive rejoinder to such cultural despair in the following vision of the meaning of LaBella's act of giving.

> Shakespeare is a secret. LaBella tells us the secret. The secret is good but the man who tells us is better than Shakespeare because he makes it possible for us to learn new secrets on our own. He is a teacher, Senatro the Beautiful. . . . When he taught us, we couldn't separate Shakespeare from LaBella. Shakespeare didn't exist for us except in LaBella, inside him, flowing forth on that burnished voice. It has never occurred to me that such knowledge, of Shakespeare living in the flesh and voice of my teacher, would divide me against myself and my background, that it would, in Eliot's words, "interfere with happiness." I know what Eliot is implying. No one should be able to stomach the idea. (102–3)

A critic can see the specters of several theoretical debates informing this passage. Lentricchia, like Kant, chooses the man of taste, LaBella, who stands for beauty, over nature's favorite, Shakespeare, the genius. Like Schiller, Lentricchia recognizes the divorce between the naive and the sentimental, the immediacy of origins and the self-consciousness of achieved aspirations; but unlike him, and like Hegel, Lentricchia believes in the possibility of a knowledge sublating such divisions, a science of the concrete, if you will. Finally, unlike Plato, Lentricchia celebrates the superiority of the rhapsodic impersonator of poetry as the best teacher. Despite these specters of past debates, however, the real concern here is the memorable, particular impact of this person, LaBella, on Lentricchia and his fellow students. It is the particular imagination of this real person and his world that counts in *The Edge of Night*, counts as *the* form of agency.

Acting a selected role requires, as a necessity, the rhapsodic identification with, and risky exaggeration of, a previously unknown or fugitive spark of impulse in yourself that is occasioned by another's influential imagination. Reading, writing, performing onstage, teaching, working freely with one's hands in a master-and-apprentice relation—all are modes of acting in this sense, and acting abolishes, in the instant, the habits of alienating abstraction and prethought thinking amid a life's untheorizable peculiarities, even as this vision of acting lays itself open to (self-)accusations of defensive deception, as in *The Edge of Night*'s final two paragraphs:

> Forget who I am outside this doing this, for which I have no name. Because this is serious, because this is how I love. With apologies to my family, I offer you my bliss. Without apologies.
>
> I remember taking my parents on one of those Hollywood studio tours, years ago. In the middle of it, my father, who's about Fellini's age, shook his hand in a quintessential Italian gesture which I cannot describe with justice, and he said: "*Madon,*' Frank, the fakery!" (182)

There is, however, a dark side to this rapture of agency. It is rage. It is the rage that results from repeatedly inhabiting and losing oneself in all the processes of existence: work, other people, the imaginative forms of desire. It is the rage that arises to collect the self from its scattered sites of enunciation. It is the rage that makes a monastery, such as Mepkin Abbey in South Carolina, an attractive place to stay for a while, because its rituals discipline time and space for the recollection of self. It is the rage that, as imagined violence, would like to fillet a stupid New York City editor's head for thoughtlessly saying that readers would need to crawl into Lentricchia's skull to see what he was really like (5–6). Here is Lentricchia's catechism of rage:

> "How would you describe it?"
> "As the achievement of intimacy. The ice melts."
> "You like it?"
> "Yes."
> "When you vent it on the innocent, you like that?"
> "Yes."
> "As much as when you vent it on the guilty?"
> "No difference, when I vent it."
> "You cannot tell the difference?"
> "You deaf?"
> "But afterwards, the distinction is known to you?"

"Yes."

"And how do you feel afterwards, about the innocent?"

"Guilty. But not right away."

"I do not mean to imply that you should vent it on the guilty. Not even the guilty deserve what you vent."

"Of course."

"But will you vent it again on the innocent?"

"Of course."

"On the innocent?"

"You deaf?"

"You know that they are innocent before, and after, but during you do not know?"

"During is a pleasure. During is during."

[Pause]

"During is during."

"Yes."

[Pause]

"But what do you intend to do, for the future, in order to protect the innocent?"

"Nothing."

"I cannot accept that, I cannot accept nothing."

"You want something to accept?" (121–22)

Rage, in this manner reminiscent of Robert De Niro in *Taxi Driver,* is one part of what later, citing the baptismal rite, Lentricchia recognizes as Satan's seductive "glamor of evil" (174). This "glamor of evil" is the self-presentational power that real or imagined violence, fueled by rage, can secure, granting for the moment a purely formal existence and identity as "that dangerous man," or "the Dirty Harry of literary theory," or a fallen archangel who would rather reign in hell than serve in heaven. Rapture and rage are modes of ruling and resentment, establishing the emotional parameters of Lentricchia's experience, because rapture means the blissful loss of subjective mastery in the beloved object, and rage requires at least the imaginative obliteration of the object, of whatever sort, in a potentially self-destructive declaration of the subject. Arias of anger, virtuoso performances of loving perception—such are the antipodes of Lentricchia's planet.

Rapture and rage are alternative modes of ecstasy, that standing outside of oneself in the place of the other that is either a tender belonging with the other or the other's resentful obliteration in a jealous belonging to oneself alone that would secure such solitary status. The formal dialectical composition of, and ironic balance between, rapture and rage constitutes the ethical work of *The Edge of Night,* much as it does Shakespeare's *Othello.* Lentricchia knows and highlights this allusion in a wild fantasy scene near the book's conclusion. He envisions himself in the guise of "the multicultural avenger," who finally makes a brutal southern bar bigot pay, thirty years after the event, for rejoicing in John F. Kennedy's assassination, since this president promoted civil rights:

> I stand at the foot of his bed, attired in a sleeveless white gown of grand flowing robes, sporting an expensive Afro toupee, my skin darkened in the tanning beds to a commanding and gleaming swarthiness, my large gold earring glinting in the fierce arc lamp that I bring here for this occasion, for this his final entertainment, brilliant light sculpting me out of the darkness, a statue, a photograph, a movie, an opera, and I say, huskily, as his eyes open, "Desdemona, the time has come to consummate our marriage." He nods, he winks, he says: "I just dreamt of Kennedy . . . who got what he wanted. . . ." In response, I croon out of the black heart of my soul, Has anyone here seen my old friend Martin? And then I say, I am the multicultural avenger, the Black Italian-American Othello, and in my aspect you behold all that is best of dark and bright. Quick, make clean your loins, for Othello has found his occupation. And now he knows (oh, yes, God is real), he knows at last that he has met a serious character (yes, Jesus, the road has been rough). (165)

Subsequently, Lentricchia as Othello makes sexually inventive use of a Texas chain saw to (s)lay this blubber mountain of a Desdemona in drag (166). Significantly, he introduces this entire scene of judgment with the following lines from *Othello* 5.3.301–2: "Will you, I pray, demand that demi-devil / Why he hath thus ensnared my soul and body" (163).

In many ways, the pattern of *The Edge of Night* as a whole is like that of this scene—an exorcism: a past moment of traumatic crisis is revisited and revised, worked up, through, and out of a present moment of (self-) critical reflection via imaginary scenes of intense immediacy. Like *The*

Waste Land's pastiche of Shakespearean tragedy, the book has a five-part structure. There is a prelude entitled "September 1992," a conclusion entitled "August–December 1992," and, in between, three parts, two of which repeat this three-part division, in mise en abîme fashion, the last one of which comes to a precarious open-ended formal balance (but no definitive formal—or thematic—closure), much like in *The Waste Land* with its contradictory final statements that the redeeming reign has already, and has not yet, fallen. This precarious balance in *The Edge of Night* occurs in this third of three middle divisions, *before* the conclusion, of which there are two versions, so that unlike *The Waste Land*, Lentricchia's work does not strive for definitive New Critical organic wholeness. In *The Edge of Night*, this precarious balance of the third of the three large and marked middle sections rocks between the final fantasy of the multicultural avenger and Lentricchia's dual vision, immediately before this scene, of his experience with children: his bitter sense of regretful failure with his own children, whom he would give their separate voices of justified accusation here, and his ironic success with some Irish children whom, despite his jet lag, he drives safely home. Much of this penultimate scene, and indeed of the book, has the quality of Robert Lowell's best confessional invocations.

This is nowhere truer than in the final version of the conclusion, "August–December 1992," which reflects on his failure to put a definite end to the book, even as he finally admits his second marriage has now come to a definite end, a confession scarcely veiled throughout the rest of the book, and one that the prelude, "September 1992," foreshadows in his mother's lamentation to his wife, recalled from an earlier time, about the Lentricchia men composing "the genealogy of ice" (23), volcanic rage's terminal state. The book's temporality is thus, as Blake might say, that of a single pulsation of an artery, as past and future inhabit, in an overlapping manner, this expanded present of the writing self, which, unlike romantic or modernist aesthetic moments, perhaps, would remain formally and thematically open: "*Madon*,' Frank, the fakery!" (182).

The figure of T. S. Eliot haunts *The Edge of Night*. The book opens by remarking on Lentricchia's inability to finish *Modernist Quartet* because of his wrestling with this demon. (Lentricchia has subsequently finished this book of criticism.) The middle sections reflect periodically on Eliot's many critical injunctions about alienation caused by differences between social origins and cultural aspirations; about the possibilities of a truly popular great literature, such as Shakespeare's drama; about how self-reflection makes all of life a stage for the various self-conscious and so always potentially comic roles we act out; about the dialectical relationship between tradition and individual talent, which Lentricchia originally revises into his conception of culture as "a medium of kinship" (110); and about how writers and readers, of whatever origins and aspirations, even T. S. Eliot and Frank Lentricchia, may become, for critical moments, "kinsmen." (A central section of *The Edge of Night* about Lentricchia's "critical allegiances" was published as "My Kinsman, T. S. Eliot.")[9]

As I have already suggested, the very structure of the book, especially in how it ends, owes much to *The Waste Land,* even as Lentricchia transforms this text in the ways I've suggested. I think the book's most important, and pervasive, connection to Eliot, however, lies in the conception of literary practice as repeated self-surrender, what Eliot, in "Tradition and the Individual Talent," calls the writer's "extinction of personality" and "continual surrender" to something larger and "more valuable," the medium of the culture's language and its catalytic transmutation of purely personal experience into memorable public language.[10] This vision of culture, particularly literature, as an ascetic discipline of aesthetic perfection, joins Eliot to Lentricchia, ironically enough, via the Pater of the infamous conclusion to *The Renaissance* and its celebration of the poetic passion and "art for art's sake" cited earlier and revised by Lentricchia into his formula of "art for life's sake." It also joins Lentricchia with Foucault's late work and his "aesthetics of existence," as I have discussed earlier. But perhaps the conception of literature that informs *The Edge of Night* most tellingly is that explanation in the epigraph to the book's now-discarded conclusion:

> 'Tis to create, and in creating live
> A being more intense, that we endow
> With form our fancy, gaining as we give
> The life we image, even as I do now—
> *Childe Harold's Pilgrimage*[11]

Literature is the creation of new beings, new identities, new names that will live. This is why Lentricchia, in adolescence, gives himself the new name "Frank," after being known as "Francis," his baptismal name, or as

"Franny," his playground name. (There are other plays on his name, and all serve to compose the singular invention of Lentricchia's "Frank-ness.") What's in a name? Social life or social death, depending on one's circumstances and strengths, as the following reflection poignantly underscores:

> My best friend in grade school was a black kid named Nelson Brown, angular, tough, nasty elbows. We called him Nellie. I think I felt close to Nellie because, like me, he had a girl's name, only, unlike me, he didn't seem to mind, because if he did he would have been called something else, whatever Nellie wanted, who was going to argue with him? Nellie and Franny. Inseparable. (99)

They are inseparable still, as the scene of "the multicultural avenger" clearly, and with perverse generosity, Byronically dramatizes.

Literature is this imaginative giving that is also a gaining, since it produces creations that live a more intense life than we—writers and readers alike—share in common. Criticism, then, should essentially be the appreciation and general dissemination of this gift of imaginative life. Whatever else it is, or performs, criticism should begin in such appreciation and aim for such dissemination, even if it means cutting the monumental figure of the famous critic, the elite expert, down to human size.

This is why *The Edge of Night* is often so poignantly funny at its author's own expense, as in the following paranoid, and absurdist, scene worthy of a Pynchon or a Beckett. To set this Irish scene, you need to know that Lentricchia has been told that the only real crime in Ireland is theft from tourists of things left lying about in hotel rooms or rental cars, and that he has a long, deep-seated dread of losing any manuscript he has, as in this case, just begun:

> Each morning of my sojourn in the west of Ireland it happens. In my bed and breakfast, arise, pack the few things I've removed from my luggage the night before, check the manuscript [of *The Edge of Night*] in the small bag: take it out, look at it, make sure all the pages are there, in order, put it back in, zip it up in its special side compartment. Go to the dining room, making sure to lock the door of my room. Try it after I lock it. Rattle it. Return, after breakfast, brush my teeth, put away the toiletries. I can't remember. Check the small bag. The manuscript. Ready. Go to the front desk with the big bag and the

small bag. Put them down in front of me, between me and the front desk. Pick them up, return to the room, check to see if something was left behind. Return to the front desk with the big bag and the small bag. Put them down in front of me, between me and the front desk. Pay the bill. The car. Put the bags down in front of me, between me and the trunk. Open the trunk, put the bags in. I can't remember. Check the small bag. The manuscript. Close trunk, start car, shut off motor, go to trunk, I can't remember. The small bag, the manuscript. Shut trunk, try it, with a violent upward jerk, trying to remember. I think I remember. Start car and motor down highway. Pull over. The trunk, a violent upward jerk. Am I remembering? Start car, shut off motor. The trunk, I can't remember, the small bag, the manuscript, the pages, in order. Shut trunk start car I can't remember. Is it safe? Do it again, can't remember. Drive off in despair, not remembering. (81–82)

This scene, which repeats itself with novel variations, is touchingly comic in a postmodern manner, and I believe it has been given to me for my appreciation and dissemination to others.

What are the chances that criticism can generally be seen and practiced as a literary art? I don't know. But I become hopeful when I see a major critic, who remembers his origins, aspires openly to, and successfully performs, the literary author's role, as Lentricchia does in *The Edge of Night*. It is not that I believe many now would, or should, or even could, follow his example of embodying the subject of his career. It is only that such an example testifies to a pervasive, if largely unexpressed, dissatisfaction with the ruling critical dogmas. Before a full-scale systematic defense of literature can be developed, however, we need to recall clearly what literature has been and to envision specifically what it can be. And if most of the so-called literary critics and creative writers can't help us now with this twin project, then, as Lentricchia frankly suggests, those of us who still care will have to do it for ourselves and commit the crime of literature yet once more: "My allegiance is not to a literary theory but to the sum total of my liberating literary experiences, and, I have told you, have I not, what I want liberating from?" (88)

What follows is a critical reflection on that toward which Lentricchia has been moving.

Virgin Interval: The Place of Literature in Global America

A scene in Lentricchia's novel *The Music of the Inferno:* a group of men sit down to eat dinner around a large table in the cellar of a Utica bar.

> Laughter all around. Then a vigorous attack on the meal . . . An outsider would remark on the exceptional level of sound emitted, not related to conversation. The lip-smacking, the teeth-sucking, the numberless indefinable mouth-noises that accompany the chewing, the swallowing, the savoring. When they talk, they do not talk about death and related Utica themes: the forty percent decline in the city's population since the mid-fifties. The increasingly rare sightings of persons (of all races) between the ages of twenty and forty. The sooty air that they are forced to breathe. The calamitous departure of the textile mills. Followed by the departure of the three General Electric plants. Then the closing of Griffiths Air Force Base and the opening of the Marcy Detention Center for the Criminally Insane. Followed by no more arrivals. These men have grown weary of the incessant chatter of death.[12]

This is the landscape of abjection, the abjection of America, which means, both and at once, the abjection of what America once was (or was thought to be), and the abjection enacted by America on itself. Both victim and victimizer, in other words. And wherein lies the reason for this complex, albeit self-destructive fate? Although it is never stated outright here, it is clear that history is to blame—particularly, the history of globalization, the transference from an American Cold War national focus to an internationalist global framework, a passage from a heavily invested national narrative to anonymous tales of displacements and departures without returns or of new arrivals, which participate in a worldwide circulation of resources to new markets without end. (The differential interplay ensures, of course, the taking of profits.)

To put it another way: every element of the Cold War liberal national security state that reached the height of its power and development in the early 1960s—the military-industrial complex, the manufacturing basis of upwardly mobile middle-class aspirations, the ethnic hierarchies of former immigrant populations, the committed presence of young urban professionals—the state's warehousing, for care and correction, of deviants and criminals out of sight, and so on—has become displaced, either transferred elsewhere, to a world elsewhere, somewhere else around the globe where it can be done more cheaply, or foregrounded in the city as the service job substitute for a skilled career. Just as formerly working-class first-generation ethnics were making it, the scene changed rapidly and completely, everything being transferred to the domain of free-flowing capital and its ever-provisional investments in local realities. The American culture of the Cold War national security state was an ersatz one. In fact, all cultures—"here and abroad," so-called elite or popular—are ersatz, provisional, improvised, made like the new roadways, housing developments, parks, and shopping centers that multinational corporations bring with them when they invest in an area—East Timoor or East L.A.—made like these things, to be disposable. The mode of existence of global capital, in short, is becoming, has become, the mode of existence ruling the world. There are no safe havens.

In this new world, what are the always-already-outmoded-to-begin-with laborers—high tech or low service—to do? Here's the rest of the scene from *The Music of the Inferno:*

> They talk about the unbelievable weather. They talk about the current mayor, recently quoted in *The New York Times* as saying, "I'm the bum mayor of a bum town." Then settle on [Sebastian] Spina's appearance on yesterday's late night news, and his claim that the fires and the street sign "desecrations" . . . were linked. Theories emerge: an undeclared anarchist movement; minority self-loathing [since the street signs are all ethnic names]; disgruntled firemen; slumlord arson; and, inevitably, someone among the numerous homeless insane who'd poured from the asylums when Washington and Albany became fiscally responsible. No consensus develops. (85)

In other words, we have recourse to the postmodern culture of representation, with its mixtures of spectral possibilities and virtual realities, which proliferate and circulate ceaselessly would-be celebrity images of our own abject felicity. (As I write this, the number one nonfiction best-selling hardback is *The Rock Says,* and number three is his wrestling colleague Mankind's *Have a Nice Day: A Tale of Blood and Sweatsocks.*)

The abjection of America and global transference—these historical processes are forces, the lack of which exists in doubled or redoubled modes. To divest one's identification with one's "locale" (whether based in family, tribe, or nation) from that locale and to displace, simultaneously, that identification to the global system of capital—this double movement corresponds to and completes the abjection of and by America, a similar double movement. These twofold processes of abjection and transference appear in the portions of the culture of representation we know best, namely, literary study, as multicultural hyphenation and hybridity. The politics of identity and recognition shaping multicultural agendas of canon reformation, affirmative action in hiring and promotion, and political correctness in personal decorum are making the representation of America safe for its latent abjection and technological transference to the realms of global capital. "Literature," to use the name for the entire modern institution of production, distribution, and evaluation of imaginative written works, in this sense takes its place in the new global America as the legitimate space of democratic legitimatizing representation. (This is one major reason why everyone, even the literary critic, fancies himself or herself an imaginative writer of some sort or other.) Rather than witnessing the death of literature in America, we are seeing its differential spread everywhere and anywhere, as part of the perpetual flight of "America" technologically and culturally around the globe.

This global situation explains the situation of the profession of literary study: its (re)turn to a demotic ethics of self-fashioning (every critic his or her own memoir); its proletarianization generally into a service-learning function of the university; its renewed attention to pedagogy, student competencies, outcomes-based instruction, pragmatic professionalism, and vocationalism; and its frantic eagerness for infiltration of the on-line virtuality of the Internet. By saying this, I do not mean to suggest that local politics and political struggles between various "Lefts" and "Rights" play no part in these developments. Of course they do. But they do so in terms of an already established horizon, framework, and set of possible alternatives. Just as Lentricchia's *Music of the Inferno*—the local politics, the interface of conspiracy theories, celebrity media, and political careerism—matters (but it does so only in the institutional matrix of imaginary compensatory function I am calling the culture of representation, as it operates in the context of the new global America), so it is true, too, for these politically moderated recent developments in literary study, with respect to the profession's place in the larger world.

What I am proposing is that "literature," in its academic and commercial modes (which are, by the way, getting harder and harder to tell apart), is playing the role of host and place assigner for the cultural in the new representation of global America.

I had occasion a couple of years ago to visit Friend's Hospital in Philadelphia. This is what used to be called an asylum. The woman I was to see, an ever-returning patient there, came down the corridor to meet me as I arrived. She had emerged from her room at the corridor's far end, and she was dressed up in a fine, freely flowing skirt of green prints, abstract designs of different shades, all light in tone and airy. As she moved gracefully toward me, she waved hello to other patients in their rooms, to hospital personnel of different sorts (including "part-timers," usually former patients), and opened her arms both to greet me and to show me (into) her world. Hostess of her own abjection. This is literature's position in the world.

What can I mean by this? The place of literature in global America is to give a space of representation to a virgin interval, to a provocative blank in the culture of representation, into which the imaginary idea of oneself may be traced, so that one can become as such a "radical" performance artist as part of the multimedia literary archive, which now may or may not appear to be life, as in an asylum. Literature, in short, is what, in an essay bearing this title, Jacques Derrida describes as *Khōra*.

What is Khōra? As Derrida recalls for us, it is the name for the space or receptacle or matrix in which, in Plato's cosmological dialogue *Timaeus,* the Demiurge constructs, on the basis of formal paradigms, the moving image of eternity, or the world as we perceive it. The figures of speech Plato uses to represent this open field or space of the world—mother or nurse—supplement and confirm the system of figures, that of father and son, which presume that the authentic pedagogical relation of mentor and student permeates the structure of reality. But as Derrida never tires of saying in this essay, Khōra, like his own concept of *différance*, is aporetic; that is, it desires what it names even as it names it as an ironic denial.

Khōra receives, so as to give place to them, all the determinations [of representation of thinking], but [*Khōra*] does not possess any of them as her/its own. She/it possesses them, but . . . not as properties, she/it does not possess anything as her own. She/it "is" nothing other than the sum or the process of what has just been inscribed "on" her, on the subject of her, on her subject, right up against her subject, but she is not the *subject* or the *present* support of all these interpretations, even though nevertheless, she is not reducible to them. . . . This . . . provokes *and* resists any binary or dialectical determination—any [definitive canonization or revision].[13]

Consequently, Derrida concludes here, with respect to Khōra as the matrix for the culture of representation, "Everything happens as if the yet-to-come history of the interpretations of *Khōra* were written or even prescribed in advance, in advance reproduced and reflected in a few pages of the *Timaeus* 'on the subject of *Khōra* herself' ('itself')" (99). To speak from this space of Khōra, *not to be* Khōra, for Khōra both is and is not and is either nothing or an excess of being, since only it is from here that one can answer to a name, now and again; to speak from this no-place, which is what Socrates does in this dialogue especially; to pronounce or declare from this spectral utopia is to play host to the culture of representation, to hug it as with a democratic, Whitmannian embrace, assigning (and serving) perpetually in advance, as it were, all the places for all those participating in the conversation around the table. Khōra—receptacle, imprint bearer (wax), mother or nurse—is really the "necessity (*Khōra* is its new name)," which is "neither generative nor engendered" but nevertheless "precedes" and "receives" all "the images of opposition (intelligible and sensible)" constituting the culture of representation (126). Khōra performs the role of this necessity as if ever "so virginal." It appears "that it does not even have the figure of a virgin any longer" to be characterized with (126). This necessity in and of the scene of reading regulates any individual artistry and even all collective legislation for the space of representation by shaping a priori the folds of the text as a textual repetition, *en abîme*, of the other logic of inscription that determines the logics of reason and passion alike.

This always already framed and configured yet ever virginal space of representation receives inscriptions and gives them their places vertically in advance in a variety of spectral topologies. A global America *as literature* plays this part of Khōra in all the theaters of our world, whatever lines we may recall or improvise at any particular interval: "This history [of Khōra and her/its readings] wipes itself out in advance [repeatedly], since it programs itself, reproduces itself, and reflects itself by [and in textual] anticipation(s)" (99), without end—or predictable purpose. Apparently, in the global system of representation, each image bears for now the imprint "Made in USA."

PART TWO

● ● ● ● ● ● ● ● ● ● ● ● ●

Globalizing Literary Studies

4

Redesigning the Lessons of Literature

●●●●●●●●●●●●●●●●●●●●●●●●●●●●●●

In this chapter, I want to compare my project for an ethics of reading, ultimately derived from the practice of literature, with a semiological, a neo-Marxist, and a rational-choice conception of criticism. To this end, and in anticipation of my argument later in the book (especially chapter 10, on Henry James), I elaborate on the innovative dimension of formal experimentation with technique, via an example from James, to perform this comparison as imaginatively as possible while being fair to my representative critical foils.

Henry James's 1888 novel *The Reverberator* concerns, as its satirically resonant title may suggest, a new medium of manufactured popular taste, the scandal-mongering tabloid now so common in our world. The kind of relation between the modern subject and language that results from such new media's cultural work is the critical question defining the novel's principal theme. The novel stages, as an initial sketch of this relation, a familiar opposition of representative characters, an opposition between the vulgar producer of stereotypical and sensational representations, George Flack, a society gossip columnist stationed in Europe, and the refined consumer of rare and exquisite impressions, Gaston Probert, a connoisseur of singular visual images. Between them, Flack and Probert appear to embody radically conflicting social types and lifestyles. In terms of our last chapter, they may be seen as standing in for the professional and the aesthetic sides of the split subject of criticism.

Flack, on the one hand, is not really "a specific person" at all. This is because he has "the quality of the sample or advertisement, the air of representing a 'line of goods' for which there is a steady popular demand."[1] One cannot think of him as being "individually designated." Instead, he seems more like "a number, like that of the day's newspaper," a high number, in fact, "somewhere up in the millions" (14). Just as every copy of the newspaper answers to its generic name, however, so Flack is quite adequately marked by the general epithet "young commercial American" (14). In short, Flack can only represent his mode of work, the newspaper, "and the newspaper . . . represents . . . all other representations whatever" (22) for the time. The relation between language and this modern subject is purely instrumental. (The computer or the perpetual virtuality of the Internet might be the contemporary parallel.)

Probert, on the other hand, is American, too, but partially of French ancestry and French raised. He is a more individually distinctive type, although no less a modern subject than is Flack. Probert has the advantage of a comparative education—in America, in France, and in other European countries—and Flack has only his elementary American education and his practical newspaper experience. The education of Paris particularly opens Probert up, even renders him morbidly sensitive to impressions of a novel aesthetic order: "The society of artists, the talk of the studios, the attentive study of beautiful works, the sight of a thousand forms of curious research and experiment, had produced in his mind a new sense, the exercise of which was a conscious gratification of which, on several occasions, had given him as many indelible impressions" (45). Particularly "things that happened through the eyes"—perhaps, Probert recalls, as much as "half a dozen visual impressions"—give him "the experience of the eye" (46). This is the new critical sense that, within the general commercial society, the appearance of an adversarial aesthetic culture, a bohemian avant-garde ethos, makes possible. Probert thinks of himself as a new, more distinctively individual type of person, thanks to this "experience of the eye." For Probert, in short, it is as if he has "a sensitive plate" in his brain, highly polished by the separate sphere of aesthetic culture, which exists solely to register and develop novel impressions of this "modern sense," in which he "revels" (46). The relation of language to this modern subject is purely aesthetic. (The professional antiprofessionalism of the self-hating critic or computer expert might be today's parallel.)

The Reverberator begins with this simple polar opposition between vulgar American commercial culture and cultivated international aesthetic culture, but the novel concludes by putting all its initial oppositions radically into question. Flack, producer of tabloid sensation and scandal, first consumes the secrets of aristocratic society as his raw material before he can process them in coarse stereotypes for popular dissemination, much as Probert first produces his already rather conventional impressions and associations out of the aesthetic culture— traditional and experimental—he then consumes even as he conveys them to others before he defensively condemns his alter ego, Flack.

Flack and Probert, then, are the popular and high cultural middlemen for the (re)production, distribution, and consumption of the modern image in the culture of representation, the forerunner to our own postmodern society of the spectacle and the global American culture of the simulacrum. But by practicing a double negation—of Flack the philistine reporter and of Probert the refined aesthete, exemplars of complementary aspects of modernity—the novel outlines its author's (and ideal reader's) implied in-between yet transcendent, neither/nor, and ironically free-floating international (if not godlike) perspective and status. This intratextual move of double negation—canceling out philistine and aesthete and their respective ideologically opposed but in fact materially interpenetrating spheres of modern culture—performs, of course, the ironic strategy that has subsequently constituted the intellectual position of the comparative literary critic as a professional academic. The modern critic, again and again, following the lead of such modern authors as James, repeats this formative institutional reading.

Three comparatively recent books—Wlad Godzich's *The Culture of Literacy* (1994), John Guillory's *Cultural Capital* (1993), and Mette Hjort's *The Strategy of Letters* (1993)—all bear witness to, from their different vantage points, the theoretical, institutional, and strategic obsolescence of this ironic position of modern literary studies, an outmoding that accounts, as we saw, for Lentricchia's turn to fiction. The changes that have overtaken the profession—indeed, the humanities and the university—in the United States and Europe have been profound and overwhelming. Newer media of representation have emerged: radio, film, television, computer networks, virtual reality games. Each in its turn has redefined, and all continue to do so now all the time, the human subject and its representational relation to language, so much so that the polarities of instrumental and aesthetic, and even the idea of literacy itself, as we have known it, the ability to read and write in a (self-)critical fashion like a Henry James or at least like one of his characters, no longer appear to matter, even where literacy and such polarities still (partially) exist, as in the university.

The same media developments have accompanied political and economic changes of global magnitude. The dominance of world affairs by the multinational corporation, the fall of the Soviet empire, the so-called new world order of universal free trade and unrestricted movement of capital no matter what devastating consequences to host or former host locales—all these changes have resulted in the downsizing of the workforce (in education, too), the drive to increase productivity and competitiveness (and profit), and the selective Western administration of the conditions of life around the globe, a worldwide "quality of life" symbolized by an American soldier's wry comment, captured on CNN, that we invaded Haiti to make it safe for MTV.

The most profound change has been the effects of all these developments on the liberal welfare national security state of the Western "democratic" countries. The conservative agenda to dismantle most aspects of this state, combined with the radical academic agenda to oppose, on good poststructuralist grounds, all centralizing state apparatuses, has meant that the traditional institutions for national identity formation, such as education, have been called radically into question and systematically cut in their budgets. Conservatives and radicals alike, whatever their different reasons, have joined hands, as it were, in a common effort to dismantle and discredit the state—the "Right" slashing social programs, the "Left" forcing significant reductions (until "9/11" happened) in the defense establishment's workforce and its "welfare" for the defense industries. While conservatives justify their attacks in the name of an unregulated free market at home and abroad, academic radicals (whether represented by a Fish or Said) justify their attacks in the name of permanent "exile," a "nomadic," largely imaginary state of ideal opposition to any and all existing states as imperialistic entities, for the sake of performing their free-floating formal strategies of pure oppositionalism on the international stage of professional criticism.

Meanwhile, in a self-contradictory gesture of total resistance to every totalizing formula, the institution of literary studies has also redefined its object—the literary work of art as canonical monument—right out of existence, and so, also, itself as a distinctive field or discipline. What has replaced both traditional object and field is neither a new object of study nor a new definable field. Instead, we have a multicultural approach or series of approaches such as "race, class, and gender" studies, which are contingent, pragmatic, relativistic, and yet absolute in their moral certainties, for which any and all "objects" or "subjects" may become items in a line of critical goods, or more grist for the careerist mill. And thanks now to composition studies and its disciplinary vocationalism and anti-intellectual ideology, even "the work" of functionally illiterate students, whose visual and computer powers may be quite high, as high, perhaps, as their pleasure in the spectacle of violent images, can also become the primary if ever provisional "object" of our new comparative and im-provised "subject" of study. I don't think this is what Foucault had in mind as "an aesthetics of existence."

The connection between the passing of the state and the passing of the modern-literate subject is intimate and yet often overlooked. Recall, however, that the rise of the nation-state and the rise of all the "disciplines" for training good citizens in the language, literature, and "norms" or "practices" of the nation go hand in hand. Consider, for a late example, the 1947 Christmas classic film *Miracle on Thirty-fourth Street*. Every character, especially the multilingual protagonist, Kris Kringle, is a literate subject of the American Cold War liberal state. And it is the post office, then a profitable and respected agency of the federal government of the United States of America, that "proves" that Kris Kringle, an eccentric, do-gooding old man from a Great Neck, Long Island, old-age home, is the one and only, the bona fide Santa Claus, as he had claimed all along, despite being expertly tricked by a spiteful Macy's personnel psychologist into Bellevue. A postal sorter, noticing that one of this year's letters to Santa Claus is addressed to him not at the North Pole but at the courthouse, and then reading in the newspaper about the legal battle in the New York State Supreme Court over Kris Kringle's commitment, decides to send all the Santa Claus letters in the city's dead letter office to the courthouse. The postal worker thereby solves his own space problem and Kringle's identity and sanity problems. Because it is illegal to intentionally misdirect the mail, and because mail gets delivered without question, this action must mean that the post office believes that this man really is who he says he is. The film is appropriately and revealingly framed by the initial image of a huge American eagle float in Macy's Thanksgiving Day parade and the climactic courtroom scene of innumerable official U.S. Postal Service mailbags being opened and showering their contents onto the judicial bench, as the judge pronounces his verdict, which is: Since the United States Government has now certified that this man is the Santa Claus, then this court will not dispute its action.

The federal government's power to confirm authoritatively an individual's identity claim—no matter how bizarrely imaginary or even "mad," and however materially based, over-the-counter claims of public safety or other local concerns and "norms" made by provincial authorities—thus demonstrates the theory of the modern liberal state in fable form, a theory that can wed the most imaginary, "self-made" inventions of individuality to its own "disinterested," above-the-fray, regulatory function and position of authority. The modern state is the ultimate judge, for better or worse, of the reality of the identity of its subjects. In fact, the more outré or beyond the local conventions an individual identity claim may be, the more it can serve, in certain circumstances, the interests of the state in exercising its power. Such imaginary identities act as perfect ideological masks of, and legitimating occasions for the transcendent pseudo-nonposition of, the modern liberal state. The subsequent civil rights, feminist, and gay and lesbian movements for the free expression of their identities, as well as the identity politics within academe, all have depended, strategically, materially, and legally, on the power of this Cold War liberal state to authorize their identity claims, however literally assumed these imaginary identities may be. In the academy, self-stylization, from Lionel Trilling to Andrew Ross or Jane Gallop, is not really as far out as it first appears given this broader comparative perspective on the role of the state in individual identity formation. The demise of this state, engineered by conservative budget cuts and radical delegitimation crises alike, means the end of the liberal imagination—or, to put it in more current theoretical parlance, the death of the professional imaginary of modern literary studies. In short, the masquerade ball is really over, baby.

Unless, of course, we take our cue from the opening James example and reflect on the fact that there (what Foucault would term) the author function (also, given James's prefaces, clearly the ideal reader position) arises from the careful consignment of the characters to their respective fates and already appears as a more radically transcendent position barely confined within the work, a truly internationalist position from which can be seen both the oppositions between national types and their proposed sublations as needlessly confining. As such, this aesthetic situation is a perfect emblem for a once utopian internationalism now being materially realized by global capital. If we see this reading as a plausible extrapolation of the Jamesian visionary project, then the nation-state regulation of imaginary identity via professional criticism can be depicted as an ideological constraint on the inherently progressive trajectory of an emerging global prospect on identity formation. Modernist authors, in particular, and the institution of criticism they empowered, would then define in imperialistic spectral outline the new prototype of intellectual identity within our latest postmodern new world order. This order may not have the shape of a market, or have the function of a world state, but may act like a global fiction, or simulacrum of simulacra, in ways and with consequences we can neither absolutely foresee nor automatically categorize based on any a priori knowledge.

In many ways, this skeptical yet speculative conclusion defines the gist of Wlad Godzich's *The Culture of Literacy*.[2] Although all of the collection's essays have previously appeared, the majority as introductions to volumes in the famous Theory and History of Literature series that Godzich has edited for the University of Minnesota Press, the essays' overall impact, in light of this volume's new long introductory essay (much of which I have just put in my own terms), looms larger than the effect of some other recent collections, which are mere miscellanies of dated work, with perfunctory prefaces tacked on, as if cynically apologetic afterthoughts.

This is because Godzich's vision is remarkably prescient, being persistently comparativist. I know of no more erudite multilingual critic. The essays collected here demonstrate Godzich's unique mastery of theory. Deconstruction (à la de Man and Derrida), reception theory (à la Juass and Iser), "old" and "new" historicisms (à la Huizinga and the Annales school, as well as ersatz American replicas of Foucault), Marxist critical theory (à la Benjamin and Bakhtin), poststructuralist and postmodernist cultural semiotics (à la everybody else), just to name a few of the theoretical modes and figures from the volume's great riches—all these Godzich handles, with masterful care, in light of comparative philosophical and literary traditions, Western European, American, Eastern European and Russian, and "emergent" (about which term more shortly), in a manner that takes one's breath away. The introduction and the concluding essay, "Emergent Literature and the Field of Comparative Literature," represent the dominant contest in the volume as one between a Kantian aesthetic and a Hegelian historical problematic. Mark Tansey's cover painting, *Derrida Queries de Man* (1990), captures this contrast beautifully. It depicts Derrida and de Man, as if either dancing or struggling, like Holmes and Moriarty or Victor Frankenstein and the Monster, at the Wagnerian edge of a sublime abyss and Swiss Alpine falls, with their towering mountain made totally out of nearly illegible traces of theory's last decade of controversial babble. To simplify this dominant context drastically: A Kantian problematic would emphasize the inherent aporetic limits on human reason and so, often despite itself, as Heidegger shows, make a place for the appearance of the contingent, the pathological, the material, the pure givenness of human experience, however ultimately not subject to the structures of knowledge, because ultimately unknowable, such experience turns out to be, especially as aestheticized into the sublime and as "religionized" into supposedly plausible leaps of faith. A Hegelian problematic would dissolve all such limits of the unknown reason in the repetitive historical sublation of the past by the future in an absolute presence of the present moment as the perpetually imminent end of history. Whatever is will be perfectly all right once it finally becomes what was. De Man and Derrida, as do we all in Godzich's view, dance the last tango of theory by the chasm that separates and defines these problematics. To invoke my James example again: Gaston Probert or George Flack is still the choice—or so it appears. To translate these different philosophical problematics into political terms would mean an anarchic aesthetic individualism versus a new world order, à la Francis Fukuyama, beyond any one nation-state. Anarchic aesthetic individualism reaches its highest form and then self-destructs in the modern culture of literacy, the decadence of the liberal imagination, as underwritten by the perfection and passing away of the nation-state. Meanwhile, the new world order of things, the postmodern stateless international culture, promotes pre-fabricated and fragmented group identity types, contingent and hetero-geneous, based on a wholly visual and not a verbal literacy, as befits the global media society of the simulacrum. In short, over the gulf that divides Kant from Hegel, Andrew Ross and Homi Bhabha shake hands. A Bedouin, in traditional garb and designer jeans, carrying a CD boom box playing Gregorian chants, atop a camel with an ad on its backside for cheap flights to Mecca: such are the unreal scenes of our lives that Ross and Bhabha have made a career of exploiting in the academy.

What should a serious critic do, however, given such circumstances? Henry James famously defined reality as "that which one cannot *not* know." And what Godzich reveals to us is just such an unavoidable reality. Should one then aspire to become (to exploit James once more) a George Probert or a Gaston Flack? That is, should one sublate the American replica of Hegelianism, pragmatism, and the continental avatar of Kant-ianism, postmodern aestheticism, into a semiotic two-step, or buck-and-wing, within the ever-spreading culture of the simulacrum with its endless repetitions of images of images without any exemplary models, agreed-on paradigms, or first principles at all? Whereas the classic essays discussing de Man and Derrida ("Caution! Reader at Work," "The Tiger on the Paper Mat," and "The Domestication of Derrida"), which form the volume's central chapters, argue by their supreme example for the effective standards of the culture of literacy, and so against any post-modern hang gliding, some of the volume's final essays ("The Semi-otics of Semiotics," "From Eye to Ear: The Paths of Allegory in Philo," and "Emergent Literature and the Field of Comparative Literature"), in light of the introduction, several other chapters, and the book's self-description on the back cover, ironically, even self-parodically, perform a very different argument. It's as if the Kantian and Hegelian, aesthetic and historicist, problematics remain intentionally unresolved (because unre-solvable?), in terms of their counterpointing argumentative and perfor-mative thrusts. To put it another way, it's as if Godzich inhabits the position of a Gaston Flack–type critic, after all: that position of my composite imaginary metacritic, my theoretical reporter of our would-be apocalyptic epoch's cynically pragmatic aestheticism. (This is a critical position that "empire burlesque" must inhabit.)

Observe, for example, how the last line of "The Semiotics of Semiotics" brings one violently up short: "Rather than helping to preserve the remnants of representation within the mode of repetition that is ours, semiotics can accelerate the demise of both" (216). Packed into this curt sentence is an elaborate argument to which I can only do partial justice here.

Borrowing from Jacques Attali's analysis in *Bruits: Essai sur l'économie politique de la musique,* Godzich argues that there is a radical difference between the culture of literacy and our moment, between modernity and postmodernity, between liberal capitalism and late capitalism. This radical difference testifies to a great shift from a Platonic metaphysics of productive presence to a postphilosophical (Deleuzian or Lyotardian) repetitive practice of difference. And this shift arises out of the global difference between the economic and cultural modes of production for representation and for repetition, respectively. Under the reign of representation, each kind of work relates to every other labor mode in terms of the central model of alienated work and the surplus value theory of labor. And for each mode of production, there is a model or paradigm or idea according to which raw material of some sort gets transformed by the exercise of labor power into a new object, the commodity, to be sold at an unfair profit, far beyond any costs of "fair return" on investment, extracted from the workers' hides. Each object or commodity produced in this general economy synecdochically represents in its own way this archetypal productive process—a productionist aesthetics, as it were—under the reign of representation. It's as if liberal capitalism, in the adoption and adaptation of Fordism's assembly line factory model for all forms of production, materializes the dream of Platonic mimesis, especially given a revisionary Marxist perspective.

But we now live largely under the regime of repetition, by which Godzich means increasingly a mode of production with no central archetypal model of exploited labor and surplus value or strict class or any other kind of synecdochical representation. Consider the "class" of producers, for example, who fabricate new "designs." A new patent, computer program, musical composition, fashion line, or architectural style, or a new method for critical practice, or a technical innovation or invention that changes production—all require the repetition of certain procedures of performance, certain rules for realization and construction, always with an improvised difference. This is the mode of repetition in production, and as Toyotoism's success makes clear, it has progressively redefined our lives.

Strictly speaking, these inventors build into their designs the potential for our sharing in their new creation via a margin of improvisation, or repetition with a difference. Such inventors or "designers" of new productive modes are not simply capitalists, not workers, not predetermined representatives of a fixed class or an ideal social type, and the work they do is not simply like that of traditional artisans or of any other artist. Like Bill Gates, they constitute a new class, that of "designers," for a new general economy of production, repetition, for a new culture, that of the simulacrum: "The simulacrum is not a copy of a copy; rather it is a thing that no longer resembles a model; it only resembles other simulacra, and it enters into unholy alliances with them. It may produce an effect of resemblance, but this effect is external to it [as a kind of parody] and the result of means [often radical in critical intent] specifically mobilized to produce that [ironic resemblance] effect. It is not, in any way, the result of its internal [aesthetic] properties. The links between the copy and the simulacrum with the commodity under representation and repetition become apparent" (214). This difficult passage from a 1985 essay, however much it may sound like Baudrillard or even Žižek, performs what it argues regarding the simulacrum. It actually derives, with significant differences, from Deleuze's analysis of Platonic and postphilosophical epistemology and metaphysics in *The Logic of Sense*.

I can explain what Godzich has in mind here by reference first to my own James example and then to Godzich's example from Attali, but before all that, I need to recall Plato's quarrel with poetry. Poetry produces its fictions out of other poetry and its fictions. That is, simulacra breed simulacra, by inspired or contagious repetition, horizontally, democratically. The idea or Form, the Great Archetype, on the other hand, produces a material image that is a defective reflection in material reality of the eternal ideal perfection. Model and copy stand in a hierarchical and authoritarian representative relationship. Fordism and Toyotoism, Plato and Derrida, encapsulate all the productive differences of representation and repetition.

George Flack, to return to my original James example, is a gossip columnist, a representation of a familiar type, working at the modern newspaper, the source of all representations. He is a Grub Street hack, only American style. He works to gather raw material for his column, the secrets of high society. He transforms this material, according to the well-established conventions of his trade, into sensational stories about the scandalous lifestyles of the rich and famous, a line of goods for which there is an ever-growing demand. And he does all this for a salary worth considerably less than the profit he brings in for *The Reverberator*'s owner. Flack, however prototypical of certain recent developments, remains essentially a creature of representation.

Gaston Probert, the internationalized aesthete, is, however, for his time a new design, a Henry James "program" for the character with a new aesthetic sense, "the experience of the eye," the new imperial organ of all pleasure, which makes Probert virtually a fragile new species of human being, and certainly makes his fictional lifestyle, like those of other "designs" for the aesthete, a composition to be repeated, that is, a theme to be formally realized by others. It is like the way a musical composition is realized and repeated with differences by music publishers, orchestras, recordings, radio, and listeners, often in performative circumstances and ways radically different from, and unrepresentative of, any possible original Idea that even the most masterful composer may have had in mind. Probert is a virtual creature for inventive repetition and sampling. Of course, once the new mode of production, the technical innovation, the latest design or program or practice becomes no longer competitively effective, it's "out," and another protocol must be invented by this new class of "designers," who are, recall, neither traditional artisans, nor capitalists, nor workers, but rather novel agents of change.

For Godzich, semiotics, as it reflects on its role of assigning meanings to such new developments in the culture of repetition, has the best chance, by virtue of its position and work, of critically analyzing, without nostalgia, the consequent loss of representative meanings in our time, and of stoically refusing to celebrate the remains of the culture of literacy's day in the sun. Godzich exemplifies this crucial difference between a scientistic or uncritical semiotics busy restoring representative meanings and a semiotics critically self-reflective of our historical moment and its genealogy in a way that further helps to unpack his dense argument.

A September 28, 1982, *New York Times* article in the "Science Times" section describes semiotics as a new science of reading otherwise opaque, radically heterogeneous, and surreal signs and making sense of them for us. The case in point adduced is that of the then latest phenomenon of trendy New Yorkers wearing expensive cowboy boots in clubs and offices. "What does it mean when a man wears cowboy boots, even though he lives in a city?" (194). This is the way the article puts the question to a representative sample of expert semioticians. And Godzich argues that their proposals for "rational" explanations for why rich urbanites "really" wear cowboy boots (such as that this fad represents the revival of the old American myth of the Western free spirit ever in revolt against Eastern bureaucratic elites) not only are banal semiotics, American studies clichés, but also possess the model-copy, myth-avatar structure of representation. Such scientistic semiotics do not critically reflect on the new role that official cultural organs such as the *New York Times* have assigned to semiotics, namely, to restore meaning otherwise lost in the purely free play of contingently related, empty simulacra. Gratuitous hollow signs "poetically" define our cultural economy, and they are not at all like the spiritual symbols of an earlier age, such as the cross in medieval Christianity tied to a comprehensive and systematic allegorical reading of all beings. Wearing cowboy boots in Soho has more to do with *Urban Cowboy*'s style than with the Western myth of the rugged individualist. A critical semiotics needs to refuse any therapeutic role and choose a critical one by, for example, reading the differences in the production and circulation of signs, including contemporary and traditional religious practices, in light of their comparative histories. And this is just what Godzich attempts to do with his use of Attali on the culture of representation (or literacy) and that of repetition (or the postliterate simulacrum). To Jamesize a bit: Neither a George Flack, nor a Gaston Probert, neither a newspaper hack, nor a spectatorial aesthete, nor any (facile or simple) combination of such types does Godzich prefer or recommend. But are such roles or their composite spectral simulacra so easy to sidestep, after all?

I think the haunting nature of this question accounts for the vehement last line in "The Semiotics of Semiotics" already cited. And yet the vehemence infiltrating this line, as well as the rest of the final paragraph, makes one feel that Godzich is performing fantasmatically a Samson Agonistes–like feat of sublimely bringing down both the monumental Golden Idol of Representation (Flackism) and the ironically simulacral Temple of Repetition (Probertism) via his Last Judgment manner, the

Redesigning Literature for a New Age ••• 107

rhetoric of which continues to resonate with such haunting specters. If this is so, it would make Godzich, I think, too much like my imaginary composite figure, Gaston Flack, apocalyptically cynical reverberator of our tabloid moment.

What finally secures Godzich from succumbing blindly to this fatal design is the lesson he learns and presents in his reading of Philo's allegorical method of Old Testament interpretation. Even as a title, "From Eye to Ear: The Paths of Allegory in Philo" can be read as an ironic injunction to all post de Manian readers. This becomes especially clear when we read and understand the conclusion to one of the essay's final paragraphs: "It is Pharaoh who, blind to God, takes Moses for God and Aaron as his prophet. Any form of thought that limits itself to two terms will seek to build two-stage processes that will admit of reiteration, in the hope of ensuring its self-promotion, but this is a hope that is not to be fulfilled, and a lesson that allegory [with its contagious simulacra and unreachable anteriority] will remember" (230). Read self-referentially about the critic, there could be no clearer warning for how the twofold argument of "The Semiotics of Semiotics" and its reiterative performance, like the argument and performance of the whole volume, should be taken as an aporetic, rather than apocalyptic, allegory.

Like the introduction, the vision of which I have already discussed and which contains the most succinct and accurate history of twentieth-century critical theory I know, the last essay in *The Culture of Literacy,* "Emergent Literature and the Field of Comparative Literature," is also a little masterpiece. It brings together a sustained critical reflection on what "a field of study" is and what it has meant with respect to comparative literature; theoretical analyses of Kant's position on the aesthetic subject in *The Critique of Judgment* far superior to anything either Paul Guyer or Lyotard had done; and a philological and literary historical understanding of South African writer Ezekiel Mphahlele and his work about negritude. All this conclusively demonstrates Godzich's proposition that "givenness is agency." "As such," he continues, "it never gives itself but is figured in that which is given, and it is knowable only through its figurations: God, nature, history, consciousness, the state, language are some of those that have historically been proposed" (286), and, of course, have been proposed not merely in ultimate legitimation of the field of comparative literature but of much else besides, such as the entire culture of literacy.

What Godzich now proposes, in conclusion, as the most appropriate object of study to reconstitute this field as a serious "post-state" semiotic discipline is "emergent literature." Godzich does not mean by this fine phrase the supposedly undeveloped literature of patronizingly dubbed "developing natives"; rather, he means the literature of people anywhere around the globe that by its particularly resistant and probing figurations of their givenness implicates in a cross-cultural critical dialogue our own always already, all-too-readily unquestioned figurations for our givenness. That is, if we can only learn to listen again, as well as to see, the lesson of "emergent literature" may renew, comparatively speaking, us all. *The Culture of Literacy,* for this essay alone, is the most important book of criticism to appear in some time because this essay, even more clearly than the others, designs a conception of aesthetic agency as real intellectual work fitting for our radically provisional movement. I will take up this topic at greater length in the next chapter.

My other two books for comparative analysis, John Guillory's *Cultural Capital* and Mette Hjort's *The Strategy of Letters,* are also important. Guillory analyzes the current canon debate via Pierre Bourdieu's concept of cultural capital.[3] Guillory then provides case studies of earlier canon debates—the romantic "revolution" against the reign of poetic diction, the formation of the New Critical canon of masterworks of ironic genius, and the function of critical theory in professionalizing literary study. He concludes with an extended discussion of the discourse of value from its twin origins in Adam Smith's general economy and Kant's theory of aesthetic judgment, both of which were contributions to moral philosophy at the time, to the long separation of economic and aesthetic ideas of value, whose intellectually debilitating effects can still be traced in both Barbara Herrnstein Smith's and even Bourdieu's very different works on the question of value, not to mention the effects on other social philosophers and economic theorists such as Jon Elster.

Cultural Capital, a winner of the René Wellek Prize of the American Comparative Literature Association, argues that the current canon debate has been conducted in terms that are intellectually reductive, historically uninformed, and sensationalistically distracting. The realities of contemporary literary studies have gotten lost in the shuffle. These realities, for Guillory, are financial and symbolic capital flight from the humanities and the university, the substitution of method for study, the irrelevance of literacy, materially and symbolically, in our culture, and the rigid institutional hierarchies for the delivery of less and less distinctively disciplinary objects of knowledge such as "texts," in favor of the delivery of detritus from popular culture. Like *The Culture of Literacy, Cultural Capital* focuses on de Man to mark the change from the mentor-student mode of professional initiation to a more impersonal transference of mastery to the new method of program of critical production. Unlike Godzich, however, Guillory reads this transference from the person of de Man, the master, to the technical innovation of deconstruction, the method of mastery, as an ironic displacement that reinstalls the master figure of de Man, in accordance with the new professional class structure of theory in literary studies. De Man, in his reading, is the American critical designer and bureaucratic Czar of Deconstruction, so to speak.

Godzich would see this conclusion as one that de Man's work, when read cautiously, would preclude. Nonetheless, Godzich would also endorse for more general historical reasons the change Guillory sees in professional initiation practices from personal mentor relations to impersonal market mechanisms, such as the drive of repeated technical innovation for the latest theoretical method, critical program, or intellectual practice. The general shift from representation to repetition in all modes of production takes this form of intellectual fashion, style, or fad in literary studies. Guillory stresses the personal authority of de Man because he sees it as a mask for the much larger changes going on, which like the current canon debate distract our attention and so must be struck through. In the end, Guillory wants to recuperate along neo-Marxist lines the concept of aesthetic value, and to do this, he must debunk de Man, the greatest critic of aesthetic ideology and the bad conscience of any nationally based criticism. Guillory is often successful in reading de Man's criticism closely, especially his most manifesto-like pronouncements such as "The Resistance to Theory."

Guillory's solution to our fate is less satisfactory in the end than his sustained analyses of the various topics already mentioned. Particularly devastating, along the way, is his analysis of Barbara Herrnstein Smith's quintessentially contingent, relativistic position on aesthetic value, the details of which I recommend to the interested reader. But his conclusion, following Bourdieu, is conceptually disappointing, even as it is modestly put: "The point is not to make [critical] judgment [of aesthetic value] disappear but to reform the conditions of its practice. If there is no way out of the game of culture, then, even when cultural capital [i.e., materially rewarded intellectual power and symbolic status] is the only kind of capital [in our postmodern world], there may be another kind of game, with less dire consequences for the losers, an aesthetic game. Socializing the means of production and consumption would be the condition of an aestheticism unbound, not its overcoming. But, of course, this is only a thought experiment" (340). Yes, one wants to respond, a thought experiment appropriate, as is the design of a new video game, for the legible babble of the Internet, but hardly any effective answer to the problem of literary canon formation or any of the other problems of literary studies that Godzich so well exhibits. At this point, I think I see the ghost of Gaston Probert beckoning George Flack from the wings.

Mette Hjort's *The Strategy of Letters,* a first book, argues convincingly that although "strategy" has been a term riddling the rhetoric of poststructuralist theory and critical practice generally for twenty-five years or more, there has been in literary studies precious little sustained conceptualization of what "strategy" may mean, particularly with respect to literary agency.[4] Hjort's introduction and first three chapters both analyze this failure and supply an extensive discussion of strategy from von Clausewitz to Elster, from Gregory Bateson to Foucault. For Hjort, strategy necessarily implies at least a measure of rational free agency, in a social context of agents each calculating the probable effects of actions on others, matching means to ends, and envisioning contingent scenarios in light of deeply held beliefs and values, as well as of the models of strategic action embodied in literary works, especially works of dramatic art. The last three chapters discuss literary texts, drama, and autobiography, ranging from Molière's *Tartuffe* to Ludvig Holberg's memoirs, with many discussions of the controversial circumstances, provocative manifestos, and critical commentary surrounding all the works covered. Hjort's major contribution to the theory of literary agency involves her claim, persuasively argued, that strategic thinking entails a passionate dimension. Particularly in the theater, the contagious quality of social emotion, artfully parodied and orchestrated by the drama, reflects the role that social emotion plays in any strategic situation where beliefs about choices and consequences of actions are conceived and calculated. (This idea will be developed in chapter 6, using Jon Elster's work.)

The social emotion Hjort focuses on, euphoria, and her conceptualization of its mode of communication, contagion, are appropriate to the theater especially; whether other literary genres are so readily defined in these formulas is a question for her subsequent work. In any event, Hjort needs to add the social emotion of euphoria and the contagious conception of communication where the strategies of literary agency are concerned, in order to provide the appropriate framework for her extensive discussion of the problem of self-deception—of characters, authors, and nonliterary agents—that concludes *The Strategy of Letters*.

Hjort examines at length the memoirs of Ludvig Holberg, a Danish writer who practically by virtue of his self-deceiving self-representations makes himself into a major nineteenth-century figure for his fellow countrymen and many on the international scene, as well. How Holberg does this in all its comic detail—with a narrow patriotism promoting his legend—is brilliantly illuminated by Hjort. In essence, Holberg gets his contemporary readers to produce in the theater of their minds the allegory of his great genius that his self-deceiving figures for himself outline for subsequent realization. Although this sounds like "an aesthetics of existence," it is clearly not an ethics of reading suitable for global America.

Performing such self-deception intentionally, strategically, is of the essence of the aesthetic for Hjort, and seeing through this strategy is, for her, of the essence of critical judgment. Her discussions of Kant on aesthetic judgment and Freud, Donald Davidson, and others on the psychological and epistemological problematics of self-deception are effective and useful. I concur with her conclusion on this subject: "Self-deception, I want to argue, can only be properly strategic if intentional. When self-deception is unintentional, it is motivated and hence purposive, but not strategic. Agents behave strategically when they knowingly set out to manipulate themselves into believing the opposite of what they sincerely believe to be true, and when they do so because the desired belief seems advantageous" (220). Freud would analyze such strategic self-deception via the now questionable theory of repression, Donald Davidson via his untenable mechanistic theory of "mental partitioning," as if the conscious ego could be split into equally conscious compartments with mutually incompatible contents. Hjort is excellent on why such theories of what Gregory Bateson first conceptualized as the double blind of self-deception are evidently inadequate in these various ways. Her solution is gestalt based. A focal belief and a background belief may be consciously held at the same time, no matter how contradictory, without cognitive or emotional dissonance until both beliefs happen to be brought into the same field of conscious scrutiny. Holberg may consciously know in the back of his mind that his works strategically express patriotic and nationalistic sentiments for purposes of career advancement, even as he may consciously focus in his commentary about his works just on the patriotic and nationalistic motives so as to better gain his readers' support for his claims of greatness. One conscious belief is part of the more distant background, the other part of the immediate figure, together making for strategic self-deception. The repeated lesson of such self-deception, despite all global changes and cultural capital flight, remains literature's permanent curriculum. How this imaginary model of strategic self-deception might be applied to the criticism of our moment, I leave for other chapters in this book.

Hjort's book is valuable in itself as a coherent and comprehensive study of the strategy of letters and of literary agency. Literary agency, in Hjort's view, is the contagious representation of social emotion performed for strategic purposes. These purposes are equally rational and passionate, being infused with pragmatic calculations and ideal beliefs, as well as based on ethical assumptions. However compromised these may become by the contradictory contagions of self-deception, and whether the case concerns a Holbert or a de Man or that fiction writer fabulously enshrined as "the Master," it is in this critical form that, as the self-demystifying process of self-deception, literature itself repeatedly informs any strategy of letters we choose to perform and care to read, especially now in global America.

5

The Return to Ethics and the Specter of Reading

As for me, I do not see, at least for now, what criteria would
allow one to decide what one should fight against except perhaps aesthetic criteria.—Michel Foucault to Paul Veyne

●●●●●●●●●●●●●●●●●●●●●●●●●●●●●●

For many years now—or so it seems—American literary study
has focused on an oppositional ideal. Cornel West has dubbed it
"the new cultural politics of difference."[1] This oppositional ideal
virtually requires, as if it were a latter-day categorical imperative for
American critics, a formal maxim to direct critical practice. It would go
something like this: that the self-representations, in all cultural media,
of previously marginalized and repressed subjects within America and
from around the globe be incorporated into the canon of what gets
taught, whether or not such works of so-called minority voices were
originally written in English and no matter what historical period may be
in question. This new oppositional ideal (or critical categorical imperative) entails, of course, the assumption of certain value judgments, even
as it empowers explicit claims for social justice and for the practice of a
"new cultural politics of difference" in American criticism, pedagogy, and
employment.

Meanwhile, outside the academy, despite the closeness of the last pres-
idential election, the neoconservative domination of the popular media,
its power to set the political, social, and cultural agendas and terms of
debate, continues unabated. Here and there, this neoconservative popular media tide is challenged—weakly, to be sure—by the few public fig-

ures still willing to identify themselves as being "on the Left." Meanwhile, too, in ways I don't pretend fully to understand, many developments—technological, economic, and geopolitical—are looming large on the horizons of world history. These emerging changes promise and threaten radical transformations in the lives of most people on the planet, for better and for worse. The disintegration of old hegemonies, the renewed outbreaks of genocidal ethnic and religious rivalries, the new world order of triumphant capitalism, the global information superhighway—all these occurrences and more not only complicate any perspective one may embrace now but also put the academic and even the larger American cultural contexts in an uncertain light, and, perhaps, a truly diminishing one. Although the spectacle of the post-"9/11" war on terror may be patriotically impressive, it clearly fails to hide America's new vulnerability.

Of course, it would be easy to say in return that as specific intellectuals working at our particular sites in the American academy (or elsewhere) and doing our different histories of the present with the new tools of capitalism at our disposal—PCs, faxes, e-mail, the Internet—we are thereby actually in touch with an emerging international intellectual culture not based on any single racial, national, or linguistic foundation. And so we are in fact part of an equally new, free-floating, and free-wheeling global oppositional formation, a radical being-in-the-world, ready to fight the good fight for—well, for including previously excluded subjects and their self-representations in the academy and in the canon, even if such inclusions mean the displacement (wholly or in part) of "purely" Euro-American subjects, those old literary masters, and their self-representations.

I find such a claim to be a self-congratulatory promise to do not very much. Now, please, don't get me wrong: I'm not one who thinks that including women, people of color, and gays and lesbians in the canon and in the academy is simply incarcerating them in the disciplinary society of seductively empowering confinements. For example, I think James Baldwin's *Giovanni's Room* should be taught. I learned more about love and its vicissitudes from it than from Shakespeare's sonnets. But given the larger national, and international, frames of reference, incorporation into and reconstellation of the literary canon tends to lose the savor of great victory.

One reason for this is the general sense of teaching today. Teaching the canon used to mean transmitting a cultural memory and heritage from one generation to the next, but now it most often and clearly means the discovery of both a pervasive cultural amnesia and a sensationalistic trivialization of everything, regardless of which text or writer, established or newly established, may be at issue. For one recent, well-received example of sensational trivialization, consider Carole De Chellis Hill's postmodern "metafictional" novel *Henry James' Midnight Song* (1993), which casts as potential psychopathic serial killers of women both Sigmund Freud and Henry James. This kind of popular feminism we should, perhaps, forget.

Students and colleagues alike appear to be suffering a surfeit. They are fed up, unable to take in and retain one more sweeping critique of the privileged Western white male global oppressor, one more theoretical celebration of the other, or, especially, one more "intersectional" or "hybridic" reading of "passing" between class, race, and gender subject positions. It is clear that both students and colleagues around the country have already lost interest in, "tuned out," the old masters and their major works, and scholarly industries, as well. Consequently I think the new turn to "self-writing," or "moi criticism," as it has been called, by such different leading figures as Henry Louis Gates Jr., Cathy Davidson, Frank Lentricchia, and Jane Tompkins, just to name a few select "stars," represents a response to this pervasive sense of surfeit on all sides. Despite the alleged demise of the literary subject as a privileged genius, this latest phenomenon of "self-writing" should not be attacked for self-contradiction on the part of poststructuralist critics who should know better. The self these critics write about, like everything else, is clearly presented as a product of the unrealization, sensational trivialization, and cultivated unmemorability of contemporary life. This "unreality principle" is what, I suppose, postmodern society, as the cultural logic of late capitalism, serves up as its popular and professional commodified goods.

To promote her memoir *A Life in School,* Jane Tompkins sizes up the "unreality principle" of the professional side of things in an interview in *Lingua Franca:*

Everybody walks around with this huge invisible superstructure around them—their reputation, their ideology, their latest book, their position on this and that. You know, blah, blah, blah. . . . Somehow or other higher education has evolved so that it puts students [and faculty alike] in touch neither with the world out there nor with themselves in here . . . and I think it needs to move in both directions.[2]

Each of us, then, is a micro-unreality machine, a small- or perhaps big-time operator of a professional imaginary. While my own full formulation of this phenomenon would be somewhat different, I suspect, I can accept hers, for now. I have learned how my former teacher and onetime colleague usually spots an important trend before anyone else does.

In light of Jane Tompkins's last remarks, I do see two new developments. One is represented by this latest turn inward to the personal, to memoir, autobiography, personal essay, diaries, anecdotes—in short, to "life writing." The other is represented by a turn outward, by those attempts to broaden the nature, scope, and terms of critical debates by bringing into focus all the things that are happening around the globe and those figures who have had a hand in making them happen. At the risk of sounding professionally self-serving, I can most easily refer, for one example of this last turn, to a special issue of *boundary 2,* vol. 21, no. 1 (spring 1994), coedited by Rob Wilson and Arif Dirlik, entitled "Asia/Pacific as Space of Cultural Production"; and I can also refer, for another example, to *The Culture of Literacy* (1994), by Wlad Godzich, one of *boundary 2*'s editorial board members.[3] As we have seen in the last chapter, the book's introduction masterfully takes on, among many other important matters, Francis Fukuyama's influential "end-of-history" foreign policy position and the role of multinational corporations in promoting simultaneously the demise of the strong nation-state, the spread of multicultural vocationalism, and the proliferation of "postliterate" nonverbal media. In sum, then, these two latest critical moves—both inward and outward—are emerging in the present scene. They appear to be constituting the current version of the familiar private-public division into different spheres of agency, one "privately" reactive, the other "publicly" proactive, both moves staged, of course, hyperactively in varying professional venues and arenas.

Here is where the call for a return to ethics comes in, I think. Prominent in this development has been Slavoj Žižek, especially in *Tarrying with the Negative* (1993). But we see it, differently to be sure, also on the popular front, with the much heralded publication of James Q. Wilson's *Moral Sense* (1993)—much heralded by William Bennett, George Will, Charles Murray, and company, some of whom *Newsweek* dubs the "virtuecrats." (The book was also a *Reader's Subscription* selection.) We can see the return to ethics as well in the new scholarly edition of Francis Hutcheson's eighteenth-century classic *On Human Nature* (1993), which discovers and champions this supposedly natural and universal moral sense. More immediately, in Anglo-American philosophical circles, we see it in projects such as Richard Shusterman's *Pragmatist Aesthetics* (1992) and Richard Schacht's collection of essays, largely by Anglo-American figures, entitled *Nietzsche, Genealogy, Morality* (1994), which discusses *On the Genealogy of Morals*. There is a new Princeton paperback, *A Spinoza Reader* (1994), which includes *The Ethics*. Beach reading? Also from Princeton, to cover the classical sources of future debates, there is Martha Nussbaum's *Therapy of Desire* (1994). Finally, to keep this list short, there is the multipurposed Blackwell reference work *A Companion to Ethics* (1991), edited by Peter Singer. Amid all this activity and texts (and so many more could have been cited), there remains the Habermas industry as it continues its master's long-running debates about modernity and the ethics of communicative action, particularly in composition theory circles. In this context, to be fair, I'd like to recall J. Hillis Miller's *Ethics of Reading* (1987), a deconstructive approach to the subject, even as I also like to imagine Barbara Herrnstein Smith, author of *Contingencies of Value* (1984), smiling knowingly, pragmatically, on all the current axiological scenes of instruction. Perhaps the John Rawls of *A Theory of Justice* (1973), the Luce Irigaray of *An Ethics of Sexual Difference* (1993), and the Jean-François Lyotard of *The Differend* (1988) are joining her for drinks on her porch? Ideally, of course, the John Caputo of the opportunistically oppositional *Against Ethics* (1994) should serve them.

Why this return to ethics? Has the late, often berated (when not ignored) Foucault, the Foucault of volumes 2 and 3 of *The History of Sexuality,* the Foucault of *The Use of Pleasure* (1984) and *The Care of the Self* (1985), the final Foucault of my epigraph, simply been there ahead of us all? Well, none of us could tell, apparently even if that were the case. This is what one authoritative commentator has to say: Foucault's aims in his last studies, according to Arnold Davidson's entry in *The Cambridge Companion to Foucault* (1994), "have been widely misinterpreted and even more widely ignored, and the result has been a [general] failure to come to terms with the conceptual and philosophical distinctiveness of Foucault's last works."[4] In other words, including those in chapter 2, whatever Foucault was saying, many of us still can't hear it, and so we can't know how the present return to ethics may relate to Foucault's last work. Given my critique in that chapter, it should come as no surprise that I concur with Davidson's general judgment about the currently pervasive ignorance of what Foucault does in these books.

I believe that the private-public division of critical agency into inward personal criticism and outward global criticism, into "moi criticism" and Godzich's fourth, Kantian-stylized "Critique of Political Reason"— problematic turns away from perceiving the actual situation of the profession and its material crises—potentially represent unchecked flights either into the abysmal psychology of (mis)identification and specular narcissism or into the labyrinthine corridors of power politics in which very few, if any, of us possess the creditable, mandarin expertise. I believe the return to ethics represents an attempt both to check these flights from the professional situation and to cultivate a sensible middle ground for engaging in the quotidian give-and-take of dialogue on matters of intellectual conscience and professional judgment in a time when a very bad job market is just one major sign of our problems.

Let me give a relevant example. In the spring of my first term as chair of my department, I took over a search for an assistant professor in African American literature. When our first two choices, both of whom were African American women, got offers we couldn't match, we were prepared to go to our next choice, who was ranked in a virtual tie with our second African American choice. But because this candidate was a white male, and despite his being a distinguished African American professor's most highly recommended student, a product of this professor's African American Center, our dean made it clear that funds for this position, which had been approved by central administration, would be frozen by our provost until a more suitable candidate could be found next time around. What was I to do? What can anyone learn from this scene of instruction?

The reigning psychology is that of Lacanian *méconnaissance*, misrecognition, what, as I already mentioned, I prefer to call (mis)identification. And the reigning politics is an oppositionalism that sees critical resistance to any normalizing power as a sign of liberation. Here was administrative power itself, via the dean and provost, imposing a *norm of diversity* in the most contingent of terms. (Diversity is much desired by my department, let me add.) Nonetheless, I—for one—could have been made furious by such administrative action. And neither personal criticism, which I suppose I am indulging in now by recounting this anecdote, nor global criticism, Kantian-styled or not, could relevantly address this everyday situation in the workplace. Perhaps the return to ethics may provide the resources needed to handle such situations and their many problematic equivalents in our workplaces?

I handled this situation by both officially acceding to the dean's fait accompli and actively making this administrative fiat as public as possible. I even informed the candidate's famous professor and dissertation director, who promised to write what he called "a national essay" about the incident, since it was, he claimed, part of a disturbing trend toward "ghettoization" in the profession. As far as I know, and I could have missed it, I suppose, he has not written his "national essay," and this is one reason why I have decided to relate the incident here. My belief is that making what we do as public as possible will bring the greatest available potential of ethical pressure to bear on any professional situation. This assumes, perhaps wrongly, and even unjustly, that all people, even administrators—or *my* administrators, at least—really care about being put in a shameful position, or about being made to bear the assumption of guilty deeds in other people's eyes.

One of the things any return to ethics must do is to recall for us a distinction central to Nietzsche's critique of morality, and so something we must face if we want to return to ethics at all. You will remember that *On the Genealogy of Morals* (1887) makes much of the ascetic priests' will to represent themselves as, rather than actually being, the bearers of justice. As Nietzsche puts it, it is not that they are, in fact, just, or that they perform just acts; it is that they simply desire to represent justice, to "incarnate" in themselves and their purely formal rituals of *ressentiment* an absolute difference as if they had made themselves into sublime moral emblems vis-à-vis both the people and the noble minded.[5] In this way, they better betray the people into a plastic resentfulness, ever at their disposal, and so can better seduce the noble minded into a self-destructive pity for all the truly meaningless suffering of others. That is, in the hands of the ascetic priests, moral representation is just another name for a poisonous power trip. I do not think anyone aspires to such status. In any case, not communitarian ethics, not deontological or duty ethics, not Foucault's "aesthetics of existence" (his ethics of self-stylization), not Alasdair MacIntyre's "after virtue" ethics, and not any other kind have so far answered successfully, in theory anyway, to my knowledge, Nietzsche's critique.

But perhaps any return to ethics needs, first of all, to be a return to the ethical imagination informing, and being formed by, aesthetic practices and art. This is a view Nietzsche himself suggests near the end of *On the Genealogy of Morals* when he invokes the aesthetic morality, the good conscience about the lie, about fiction, among the ancient Greeks—before Plato. By invoking "the ethical imagination," I do not mean simply to follow Lionel Trilling's conservative example of more than fifty years ago, in *The Liberal Imagination* (1950), even as my proposal for an aesthetic morality does indeed echo his similar invocation of what, with particular respect to Henry James, the subject of chapter 10, Trilling calls "the moral imagination." To suggest a difference between Trilling and today's academic scene, let me discuss not Trilling or Foucault but a fine work of a generally unknown contemporary poet, Jack Gilbert.

Jack Gilbert is the author of the collection *The Great Fires: Poems, 1982–1992* (1994), and two other poetic collections, *Views of Jeopardy*, the 1962 winner of the Yale Younger Poets Series, and, from the 1970s, *Monolithos*, a collection that, like the earlier one, was nominated for the Pulitzer Prize. A limited edition of another, smaller collection, *Kochan*, was published in 1990. Most of Gilbert's poems mourn his wife, Michiko Nogami, who died from ovarian cancer in 1982 at the age of thirty-six, and they are now incorporated into *The Great Fires*, which carries a dedication to her. The collection contains many elegies, often in unrhymed sonnet or truncated sonnet forms, as well as odes and haiku. There are even what Jahan Ramazani, in *Poetry of Mourning* (1994), calls self-elegies, or imaginings of the poet's own death, a peculiarly twentieth-century variation, Ramazani argues, on the traditional mode (although I think Geoffrey Hartman, for one, has shown that Wordsworth representatively worked on his own self-elegies).[6]

Gilbert is a well-traveled American who has lived in various places in the United States—San Francisco, Maine, Pittsburgh (where he was born and raised), Florida, and New York, among others. He has lived abroad, as well, in Paris, Madrid, the former Yugoslavia, Rome, pre–civil war Lebanon, and Japan. For the last fifteen years or so, he has lived on a small island in the Aegean, which he does not name. Although these other places, especially Pittsburgh, do appear in Gilbert's poetry, the Aegean island is the imaginative scene for, and its inhabitants the subjects of, most of the poems in *The Great Fires*. The title poem's concluding lines sum up the volume's passionate subjects and its contingent perspectives: "Isaiah said each man walks in his own fire / for his sins. Love allows us to walk / in the sweet music of our particular heart."[7]

The poem I want to discuss, however, is not particularly a hymn to contingency or directly an elegy to dead love; rather, it is a poem primarily about thinking, about its ethics, about its weird ecstasy:

Haunted Importantly

It was in the transept of the church, winter in
the stones, the dim light brightening on her,
when Linda said, Listen. Listen to this, she said.
When he put his ear against the massive door,
there were spirits singing inside. He hunted for it
afterward. In Madrid, he heard a bell begin somewhere
in the night rain. Worked his way through
the tangle of alleys, the sound deeper and more
powerful as he got closer. Short of the plaza,
it filled all of him and he turned back. No need,
he thought, to see the bell. It was not the bell
he was trying to find, but the angel lost
in our bodies. The music that thinking is.
He wanted to know what he heard, not to get closer. (17)

The title of another poem in this volume, "Music Is the Memory of What Never Happened" (58), may cast some ironic light on what music means to Gilbert. And lines from another poem, "Thinking about Ecstasy," may clarify the self-reliant ethic of thinking, its stubborn perversity, that shapes any occurrences of the ecstatic moment:

If ecstasy means we are
Taken over by something, we become an occupied

country, the audience to an intensity we are
only the proscenium for. The man does not want
to know rapture by standing outside himself.
He wants to know delight as the native land he is. (73)

The Emersonian strain, as well as the anti-imperialist note, familiar from
my earlier discussion of Lentricchia, resonates in these lines, especially
in the last line. Apropos Emerson, I am thinking particularly of his
notorious comparison, in "Experience," of his dead son and namesake,
Waldo, to a beautiful lost estate. Also in "Experience," there is the trope of
an ideal self as the ever new, unapproachable America. But there is a long
and various history of his trope in American poetry. The revisionary
imagination appears as this figure of the internalized, daimonic landscape of the self, which Emerson originally borrows, I found, from Plu-
tarch's "In Consolation of His Wife for Their Lost Daughter," and some
of the latter's other moral essays that repeat this classical topos.

In any case, the Emersonian echo does provide a clue to how we can
hear the concluding lines of "Haunted Importantly" and its generally
clipped, fragmentary parataxis. Emerson's "The Poet," following Shelley's
"Defense," which also informs so much of poetry to come, presents
poetry as the overhearing and transcription of the already-being-uttered
grand cyclic poem of life. "Haunted Importantly" dramatizes this position in nearly Stevensian meditative form, to be sure, and in its own way,
too, as we will see. And one of the volume's final poems, "The Lives of
Famous Men," recalls the relation between a revolutionary literary fame
and the bell image in the romantic tradition, in a way that suggests how
central that image is to *The Great Fires:* "Yes, yes, I say, / and so go on
pulling at the long rope" (87), even though the lyric subject here knows
no fame of any kind, not even Hart Crane's once problematic notoriety,
and is in despair at living without his beloved wife. Nietzsche, you will
recall, uses the bell image differently in *On the Genealogy of Morals:* to
highlight, ironically, the belatedness of all men of knowledge vis-à-vis
their experiences.[8] And finally, another concluding poem, "The Edge of
the World," underscores the necessary, even fatal, sense of solitude haunting the poet's relation to modern society. On his island, late at night, the
poet searches the shortwave band, what he calls "the skirl of the Levant,"
and finding something at last coming in clearly, he hears "Cleveland

playing / the Rams in the rain," which makes him "feel / acutely here and everybody else somewhere else" (82). Perhaps this peculiarly American social solitude at play is what the information superhighway and the Internet are concretely to bring now to all the peoples of the earth?

"Haunted Importantly" is a self-haunted poem, clearly, and though unrhymed, it is also a poem haunted by the Petrarchian sonnet form's fourteen lines of octave and sestet, with the famous two-part argument and reversal, or *volta*, structure, that little peripeteia of thought. The shift from the quest for the source, or re-source, of the haunting sound to the sudden return from that romantic quest for immediate vision clearly enacts this volta. And the subliminal ironic variations on its central theme of quest get played out by the unrhymed, perfectly positioned end words and carefully selected enjambments—all of which ghostly formal play I will spare you, except for mentioning one combination of an end-stop line and an enjambment: "No need," and "the bell / he was trying." I indicate this kind of formalist matter here to give the reader the gist, to suggest the disciplined aesthetic basis—down to the syllable—for the poem's ethics of thinking, a literary ethics to be sure, and its strangely immanent ecstasy. Similarly, the evident use of free indirect discourse via the woman named Linda, the reflexive impersonal stress on perspectival changes, and the shifting points of view—that of the "he" of the poem, the poetic narrator's, and ours—also embody this ethics on a more evident structural scale.

The story the poem narrates is the romantic quest for the adequate knowledge of thinking's authentic responsiveness to the world's immediacy, thinking's capacity for both reception of and reflection on sense experience, and thinking's connection to, its incarnation in, "our bodies" (17), however angelic or unangelic we imagine that intelligence to be. What makes this poem modern, even postmodern, or more generally of our time, is not only the subtle revisions in, and tropes on, the prior exemplars of the sonnet form or of romantic poetic thought. Is this poem's lost angel à la Blake or Rilke, or even earlier figures? Nor is it only the insistent immanence of thinking in the world about the world, and thinking in and by the body, however much the world's edginess cuts into the body. Rather, it is the poem's attitude of listening, of desiring to listen, to multileveled, resonant histories—what else are "the spirits singing inside" the church, the night bell in Madrid and that city's tangled streets, the injunctions by the companion to listen, all about? Most of all, what makes "Haunted Importantly" of our time is its movement of return, a movement of intentional self-dispossession, an ascetic fulfillment of the psychodynamics of mourning, perhaps. But it is the pragmatic result of this process, not its precise analytic status, that concerns me here. Rather than subject the bell to the acquisitive gaze, as a transitional object, defensively, protectively holding the self from both its still too raw feelings and a hostile world, the poem allows the bell's truly uncanny tone, its resonant chord of many remembrances, to fill the speaker with its complex witnessing to the world. The poetic speaker wants to know finally "what he heard," not to "get closer." He thereby resists the lure of that false intimacy of unthinking assimilation of objects and people that marks the careless innocence of Americans, especially when they are abroad. The scholar in the poet listens to the spontaneous speech of the world. This poem's active return to thinking, however problematic, embodies the aesthetic precondition that I, perhaps indeed after Foucault, now conclude is necessary for any serious critical return to ethics: "The music that thinking is" (17).

Human and All Too Human: Two Styles in Critical Ethics

The return to ethics in academic criticism, unfortunately, has resulted in the further erosion of the power to read carefully. What do I mean by such a stark assertion? For some time now, no matter what the object of analysis—a text (literary or not), a film, a cultural narrative, a historical event—critics have done less and less reading. And by reading I mean the comprehensive analysis of the complex interplay of themes and figures animating the often intricate structures of the object of analysis. That is, there are increasingly fewer attempts to treat even the usual literary objects of analysis as integral works of imagination. No one seems willing, or perhaps is still able, to follow the twists and turns of an argument, to trace the complexities of the imaginative profiles a work makes, to place statements in their full contexts, including that of an intellectual career. Too often, in recent criticism, it feels as if everything were already known in advance about the work brought forward for what turns out to be an inadequate discussion akin to shadowboxing with sound bites. Or at least this is how it usually appears.

By saying this, I don't mean to suggest we should hug close our nostalgia for either New Critical organic wholeness or deconstructive rigor mortis. Rather, I hope to point out what we are losing by doing criticism as if it were solely a cut-and-paste operation that did not derive from philology. What we lose, in short, is the contingency of reading, the sudden surprising discovery, the self-overcoming moment, when the critic has to recognize his or her education by the text, as the hole in the argument gets filled, the aporia is recognized, the structure of images does or does not subvert itself, and, yes, all those allusions the text is making do anticipate perfectly and rebound ever more sharply the reader's— the author's or critic's—most precious barbs. In sum, what the initial return to ethics has fostered, ironically enough, is the erasure of the authentic ethical moment of self-judgment from recent critical practice.

Before turning to an example of this latest critical disaster, I want to present, in fairness, at least some indication of a critical ethics successfully at work. And in anticipation of chapters 7 and 8, I select as an instance of the kind of critical ethics in reading worthy of the name, Jacques Derrida's *Archive Fever: A Freudian Impression* (1996).[9]

Most of Derrida's book reads Yosef Hayim Yerushalmi's controversial study *Freud's Moses: Judaism Terminal and Interminable* (1991). In fact, Derrida gave the argument of *Archive Fever* at a conference where, but for a sudden illness, Yerushalmi would have been in attendance. *Archive Fever* singles out for particular emphasis the imaginary letter appended to Yerushalmi's book, which he provocatively entitles "Monologue with Freud." Yerushalmi argues there that *Moses and Monotheism* (1939) is either Freud's climactic exercise in personal bad faith and ethnic self-hatred or a perversely esoteric justification of the Jewish religion of his father. This uncanny argument is not now my concern. What is, is Derrida's specular postscript to *Archive Fever,* which reflexively concludes the reading of Freud's earlier essay "Delusions and Dreams in Jensen's *Gradiva*" (1909), which occupies the last half of *Archive Fever*. The first half of the book traces the literal etymology and philosophical genealogy of the word "archive," about which I will say little or nothing here.

Derrida, in essence, is reading Yerushalmi's critique of late Freud via Freud's earlier reading of Jensen's novel *Gradiva*. In doing so, Derrida constructs a haunted fun-house labyrinth of glass, so as to capture the phantasmagoria of spectral authority he first discusses at length in *Specters of Marx* (1994). This allegory of reading allows Derrida to stage the dramatic recognition of his own bout of archive fever. By this term, Derrida means that critical desire to incarnate definitively in one's own text the general law for any revisionary practice. It is as if one were, regardless of the work read or how it is read, the work's first reader. This is the trope I will use to refer to the critical desire for absolute priority and so final authority. Think of it in this way: being there at the creation would count the most. Such knowledge would indeed have been a destiny.

Derrida's ecstatic (self-)analysis in his postscript is accomplished through a reading of Hanold, the protagonist of Jensen's 1902 novel, and his archive fever. Hanold madly dreams of discovering the living embodiment of Gradiva, a young woman who perished in Pompeii's destruction and whose identity Hanold's archaeological science of digging, tracing, and deciphering has apparently reconstructed. It is as if Gradiva, whose strange gait appears depicted in an artifact that has survived the volcano's wrath, is a figure for the muse of all would-be first readers, especially those, like Foucault or Yerushalmi, with an archaeological bent. Derrida's reading, it must be noted, reflects critically on Freud's reading of this archaeological fiction and also on Yerushalmi's historical critique of Freud's *Moses,* which Freud intends, after all, to be taken in part as a fictional romance of origins. Most importantly for my purposes, however, Derrida's reading reflects critically on his desire for priority in interpretation as it mirrors Yerushalmi's historicist critique of Freud's similar desires. This critical desire to assume the position of the first reader is, in Derrida's imaginative reading, the contingent invention of a repeated textual experiment, ultimately out of his or any one scholar's masterful control:

> Now here is a point which is never taken into account, neither in Jensen's reading [of his own fiction] nor in Freud's, and this point confounds more than it distinguishes: Hanold has come to search for these traces [of Gradiva's existence] in the literal sense. He dreams of bringing her back to life. He dreams rather of reliving. But of reliving the other. Of reliving the singular pressure or impression which Gradiva's step, the step itself, the step of Gradiva herself, that very day, at

that time, on that date, in what was in-imitable about it, must have left in the ashes. He dreams this irreplaceable place, the very ash, where the singular imprint, like a signature, barely distinguishes itself from the impression. And this is the condition of singularity, the idiom, the secret, testimony. It is the condition for the uniqueness of the printer-printed, of the impression and the imprint, of the pressure and its trace in the unique *instant* where they are not yet distinguished the one from the other, forming in an *instant* a single body of Gradiva's [eccentric] step, of her [uncanny] gait, of her [distinguishing] pace, and of the [unique] ground which carries them. The trace no longer distinguishes itself from its substrate. No longer distinguishing *between themselves,* this pressure and this imprint differ henceforth *from all other* impressions, from all other imprints, and from all other archives. (98–99)

As you can see, I think, from these final sentences, the dream of a first reading, once personified, gives birth to the dream of becoming in that mythic instant the first reader, Gradiva's favorite offspring, between whom all lines of demarcation of identity of whatever kind blur, intersect, and reform around a new composite yet singular structure: "No longer distinguishing *between themselves,* this pressure and this imprint differ henceforth from all other impressions, *from all other* imprints, and from all other archives." I would add that such a figure of "the first reader," as a discursive and psychic reality is, like Foucault's "oneself" or Ricoeur's (see chapters 2 and 10, respectively), a split identification of force and inscription.

More typical of our recent critical ethics, unfortunately, is Geoffrey Galt Harpham's "Imagining the Center," the leadoff essay in a collection edited by Dominic Rainford and Tim Woods, entitled *Critical Ethics: Text, Theory, and Responsibility.*[10] As Harpham's biographical note reminds us, he is professor and chair of the Department of English at Tulane University, the author of four books, *On the Grotesque* (1982), *The Ascetic Imperative in Culture and Criticism* (1987), *Getting It Right: Language, Literature, and Ethics* (1992), and *One of Us: The Mastery of Joseph Conrad* (1996). He is also the author of the new "Ethics" chapter in the second edition of *Critical Terms for Literary Study* (1995), edited by Frank Lentricchia and Thomas McLaughlin. I summarize Harpham's accomplishments in part because he makes an issue of professional eminence, a term he uses repeatedly, for critical purposes, throughout "Imagining the Center."

The essay falls into five movements. Its opening and closing movements are comparatively brief set pieces touching, respectively, on Kant's "An Answer to the Question: What Is Enlightenment?" and Václav Havel's "The Hope for Europe." For Harpham, Kant exhibits the problem facing contemporary critical intellectuals, and Havel, the best solution. As Harpham puts it, the problem is "crystallized" in Kant's "notorious injunction to 'argue as much as you like, but obey' " (37), by which Harpham intends to indict the familiar ethical disconnection in academic life between what critics avow in theory and what they do in practice. The solution, according to Kant's critic, is best indicated by Havel's power to imagine and inhabit the center, to choose to participate fully in the processes of governance, and so to propose specific and immediate projects and policies of change. The witting or unwitting hypocrisy of critics who use their professional status of symbolic eminence to luxuriate in the imaginary revolutions of their theoretical polemics, while steadfastly evading and disdaining the coils of the real politics of our lives—such hypocrisy, though curiously left unidentified as such, is the unnamed but pandemic condition typical of our profession that Harpham's critical ethics would expose, judge, sentence, and execute. The three central movements in Harpham's essay discuss, in turn, Edward W. Said, Homi K. Bhabha, and Christopher Norris, as case studies, not so much in personal imperfection, of course, as in a professional bad faith representative of the intellectual ethos, the critical culture, sustaining all of us nowadays. While I myself share some of Harpham's critical judgments about such figures, what I hope not to share is his apparent ignorance of the critic's first duty: "read the text closely."

Harpham's formulation of self-congratulatory bad faith goes as follows: "Kant's [injunction 'argue as much as you like, but obey'] . . . expresses not only the reigning cliché in the self-description of the modern intellectual, especially literary intellectuals—that they think for themselves and are answerable to no one—but also, in its forthright compact with the authorities, a blurted confession that today's intellectuals would make if only they had the insight and the honesty" (37). In other words, as Harpham elucidates his point for us, "critique is acceptable or even possible only when it occurs within a politico-conceptual space demarcated and secured by the police. Thus constrained, 'free' thought must be a kind of group hallucination, an agreed-upon game with a conservative programme that remains hidden despite its manifest success. This programme . . . is a truth, denied by many, but disproven by none" (38).

The presence of Bhabha and Norris in the essay is purely strategic. They allow Harpham to deploy a generic image of critical theory and its formative influence on postmodern and modern Enlightenment critical modes alike that can be made to appear solely derivative of Kant's position, no matter what, in this instance, Bhabha's postcolonial and Norris's moral intentions may be. By cornering Said in a conceptual space defined by always already bankrupt post-Kantian positions, Harpham can move in for the kill. Whether Harpham's instrumental portrayal of Bhabha and Norris is correct concerns me less than does his reductive reading of Said, who all too clearly is the object of Harpham's brand of critical ethics throughout "Imagining the Center."

First of all, Harpham uses only a few statements from Said's *Representations of the Intellectual* (1996), his BBC-broadcast Reith Lectures, and Harpham uses these few statements to stand for the purported inconsistency, hypocrisy, and, ironically enough given this public venue, academic insularity of Said's theoretical position and critical corpus. (About such self-defeating tactics, more shortly.) Harpham also ignores the shape and diversity of Said's considerable career. Similarly, he overlooks the unfolding of Said's argument in this book. In both cases, that of Said's career development and that of his unfolding argument here, Harpham fails to read Said's language carefully. In short, whatever Said's recent limitations, a critic ought to give this text its due.

In recounting Said's account of his fifteen-year relationship with an unnamed Iranian intellectual and wary supporter of the Ayatollah's theocracy, for example, Harpham laments, as so much overintellectualized fastidiousness, Said's surprise at his Iranian friend's decision, when faced with the choice of supporting Iraqi fascism or U.S. imperialism, to opt for the latter, rather than doing what Said thinks he and many others should have done, and say "a plague on both your houses," since for Harpham's rather whiny portrait of Said, *there have just got to be more choices than this*. Here, first, in his own voice, is Said: "This decision [by my Iranian friend—to support imperialism over fascism] is unnecessary. . . . It would have been quite possible and indeed desirable on both intellectual and political grounds to reject both fascism and imperialism" (41). Now here is Harpham's ventriloquized complaint: "Said is surprised, that is, that nobody had thought of the intellectual's way out, which is not to choose at all but to construct another set of choices, more abstract, more nuanced, more undecidable than the original ones" (41). I think Harpham strongly implies by his language a certain reductive conception of critical theory as the culprit informing Said's position. Although Harpham goes on to quote Said on this matter and does report that Said openly confesses his own serious second thoughts concerning this possibly glib criticism of his Iranian friend's position—"Not being a joiner or party member by nature," Said reminds us, "I had never formally enlisted in [any government's] service" (41)—Harpham nevertheless blithely continues his argument, branding Said an irresponsible intellectual "star" in the academic celebrity system, who has never had to suffer any real risks at all: "What risks has Professor Said run?" Harpham asks in mock surprise and true ignorance (39).

As I have indicated before, whether Said is right in this instance or in any others is not now my concern. What is, is Harpham's moral failure to read what he himself cites. Immediately after Harpham quotes Said's remarks about not being "a joiner or party member by nature," Harpham also quotes Said's rueful confession that immediately follows: "I had certainly become used to being peripheral, outside the circle of power, and perhaps because I had no talent for a position inside that charmed circle, I rationalized the virtues of outsiderhood" (41). This statement, from the last chapter of *Representations of the Intellectual,* is an important ironic revision of Said's position in the book. As such, it is a major qualifying turnabout in Said's career-long elaboration of his view of the critical intellectual as being at his or her best when an exile, an outsider, an amateur. Harpham knows this, of course, because he reflects on this view, which Harpham disdainfully terms a mere theory, as he begins his critique of Said as an "eminence," and so really an insider virtually all along. In short, Harpham's so-called critical ethics barely hides a resentful rage to become the first reader of Said's alleged moral hypocrisy and intellectual irresponsibility, an inquisitional rage that blinds him to what his object of critique is now literally saying for all to see. Perhaps what may inspire this rage of resentment may be precisely the fact that Said is performing a self-critical return on himself here, so that Said, not Harpham, would always have been in the position of his own first reader.

However this may be, the point I want to make is that Harpham's potentially salient critique of Said as a representative figure of the contemporary critical intellectual misses its mark by failing to read the contradictory traces of global America's imprint on his life and career. What follows is my admittedly sketchy outline of such a closer reading.

The Aporia of America

Two passages in Said's memoir *Out of Place* define best what I mean by my title. The first passage, which I have quoted at length in chapter 1, presents a "routine" yet "emblematic" moment from summer camp in 1948:

> The rest of the time in Maranadook [Maine] was quite routine as I had stopped deriving any pleasure from the place, and none at all from my fellow-campers. . . . One later experience emblematized the peculiarity of a camp summer. . . . There was an overnight canoe trip . . . that involved portage from one lake to another in the bland Maine forests, as well as long trajectories when we rowed across vast blazing hot tracts of brown-water lakes. My canoe was manned by me in the stern and another camper in the bow. Comfortably stretched out in the space between us was a counselor, Andy, with a long Czech name, who in his shiny red bathing suit, moccasins, and smoking pipe sat for hours reading a book whose title and contents I could not decipher. The odd thing was that after quickly going down a page with his left index finger he would methodically detach the page from the book, roll it up into a ball, and toss it casually into the lake.[11]

This entire scene becomes, for a while, indecipherable to Said, a "moment" of "wondering what it could all mean," as our twelve-year-old culture critic looks back "at the line of bobbing paper casualties of Andy's destructive reading habit" (138). After discovering "no sensible or plausible answer," except that Andy "did not want anyone to read the book after him," Said puts it down to "an aspect of American life that was inscrutable," unreadable (138). However "routine," "casual," with its own paper "casualties," this nonetheless "emblematic" aspect of American life was,

Said remembers "reflecting afterward," that "the experience took its significance from the desire to leave no traces, to live without history or the possibility of return" (138). As if to confirm this reading of "one aspect of American life," Said drives "twenty-two years later" to where he thinks the camp once was, but all that is left of any "habitation," as if in fulfillment of Andy's destructive reading habit, are the deserted cabins, which had become a motel, then a retirement colony of some sort, then nothing, "as the elderly Down East caretaker" tells him. This "old fellow" has never heard of Camp Maranadook (138). Americans, unlike other peoples, apparently colonize provisionally (if repeatedly), until "nothing" remains.

In miniature, as it were, this episode from post–World War II American life, this "inscrutable" moment, provides the reading for America's ultimate impact on the rest of the world during the same period. The mixture of destructive innocence, meaningless intervention in nature, experimental entrepreneurship, and imperial expansiveness—the fate of Camp Maranadook after 1948 presages that of Palestine, and the world, in our era of globalization—all these critical elaborations of this otherwise inscrutable moment testify to America's careless power to abject itself and the domain it rules.

The second passage from Said's memoir, however, makes clear that our fledging culture critic and the family and class from which he comes (whatever the origins given on their passports) are, with respect to "the practice of self-making" (10), quintessentially American:

> Curiously, nothing [much] of my father's American decade [including his service in General Pershing's command in France, 1917] survived except his extremely lean retellings at dinner, and such odd fragments as a love of apple pie à la mode and a few often repeated expressions, like "hunky-dory," and "big boy." Over time I have found that what his stint in the United States really expressed in relation to his subsequent life was the practice of self-making with a purpose, which he exploited in what he did and what he made others around him, chiefly me, do. He always averred that America was his country. . . . so powerfully instructive was his story for the shape my youth took under his direction that I cannot recall ever asking anything like a critical question. (10)

To underscore this point, Said concludes (as well as opens) his memoir by spelling it out: "Well past the colonial period we collectively thought of ourselves as being able to lead an ersatz life, modeled on European summer resorts [and American summer camps?], oblivious to what was going on around us" (268). As this later passage puts it, Said's parents "tried to reproduce" their "Cairo cocoon" in Lebanon. Given their "peculiarly fractured status as Palestinian-Arab-Christian-American shards disassembled by history, only partially held together" by Said's father's "business successes," which nevertheless allowed the family "a semifantastic, comfortable, but vulnerable marginality" (268), who could blame them for this collective "practice of self-making with a purpose" (10)?

Here is the other side of America's power to abject itself and others, this being the "ersatz life" whose pathos lies in its "vulnerable marginality," its "out-of-placeness," its being a mode of life transferred from America and placed precariously and provisionally maintained, by self-conscious acts of will and discipline, as well as strategic acumen, in situations of "vulnerable marginality" elsewhere around the globe or even, as also he suggests tellingly, Said's memoir in academic America. Such "global transference" performs the spread of self-making as a personal and group enterprise to the former and current victims of global white male oppression. This latter is, of course, American modernity's destructive habit of reading and revising itself and its world into and out of existence, deliberately without leaving traces behind, because it has no other goal beyond itself than itself.

It is my argument that this "aporia of America," this modern dilemma of open-ended, destructive revisionism, as one's fate and opportunity, now defines the future of literary study. By saying this, I mean that critical reading as "the practice of self-making without a purpose" has become the essence of the personal and institutional enterprise of literary study with no other higher goal than itself, than its own constancy, no matter what the provisional and replaceable goals of the moment, however laudable, might be.

Whatever literary study was before, it is now, and for the foreseeable future will be, the profession of abjection as an alibi for the practice of self-making with a vengeance, which is another way of saying with a purpose that is temporary and temporizing, the ghost of an authentic goal, the essence of a marginal and ersatz life haunting us all. Machination and lived experience are the specters that fill such a life; the one preys on us with repeated anxiety about one's "position," and the other teases us with nostalgia for the unknown, for those imaginary moments when one could have been taken unawares by life and so would have been overwhelmed by some enduring passion, of whatever sort. Here is, for the last time, Said on this final effect of the aporia of America, an effect he identifies as the constancy of the critic's self-conscious awareness, in the spectral figure of "sleeplessness":

> Sleeplessness for me is a cherished state to be desired at almost any cost; there is nothing for me as invigorating as immediately shedding the shadowy half-consciousness of a night's loss than the easy morning, reacquainting myself with or resuming what I might have lost completely a few hours earlier. I occasionally experience myself as a cluster of flowing currents. I prefer this to the idea of a solid self, the identity to which so many attach so much significance. These currents, like the themes of one's life, flow along during the waking hours, and at their best, they require no reconciling, no harmonizing. These are "off" and may be out of place, but at least they are always in motion, in time, in place, in the form of all kinds of strange combinations moving about not necessarily forward, sometimes against each other, contrapuntally yet without one central theme. A form of freedom, I'd like to think even if I am far from being totally convinced that it is. That skepticism too is one of the themes I particularly want to hold on to. With so many dissonances in my life I have learned to prefer being not quite right and out of place. (295)

When being out of place in this style, however, is the ruling style, as it now is in literary study in America, and increasingly around the globe, what then? That is, if being "out of place" really means being "in place," then the lesson Said and perhaps all of us have in fact learned is merely good old Andy's destructive habit of (self-)reading.

6

Class in a Global Light: The Two Professions

• •

The modern literary critical use of "class" follows Marx's transformation of the term (about which more shortly) and the much later appearance of a "leftist" intellectual agenda in the 1930s. Although much is often made of the class theme at that time, in America especially, none of the promising social critics of the 1930s went on to develop a general theory of class fully adequate for literary study in the contemporary world. Critics such as Lionel Trilling in *The Liberal Imagination* (1950), Edmund Wilson in *Patriotic Gore* (1962), and Kenneth Burke in *The Grammar of Motives* (1945) and his subsequent theoretical texts assimilate their local insights into the class realities of literary representation to larger moral, cultural, and philosophical concerns—the ethics of social manners, the history of national identity formations, and the symbolic grammar of human action, respectively. Class in America gets progressively incorporated, after the 1930s, into the practice of cultural criticism or theory without further thought; much as in the case of the neo-Marxist Frankfurt school of critical theorists such as Theodor Adorno and Walter Benjamin and their later followers Fredric Jameson and Terry Eagleton, "class" is subsumed by the intense interest in the relation of avant-garde or experimental art forms to ideology. The class work of Raymond Williams and a few other English social critics and postcolonial critics such as C. L. R. James has been taken seriously by more people only recently.

Consequently, despite today's rote invocations of "class" in the catchphrase "race, class, and gender," American criticism in particular has generally not kept in contact with the subsequent revisions in the theory of class, made in response to better empirical and logical analyses, within the relevant disciplines—the post-Marxist wing of analytic philosophy, radical social theory, and the materialist critique of political economy. These are the important heirs of the discourses whose matrix of concepts first made "class" possible as a serious term for Marx and any subsequent mode of intellectual study.[1] In what follows, then, I am attempting to reestablish that lost contact in a way that also addresses both the present function of American literary criticism and one major representative example of the past literature it still can profitably study.

Specifically, I will discuss "class" in three interrelated ways. First, I will describe the present scene in the university teaching of literature in economically material terms to disclose the academic institution's newly representative class structure. I choose the American academy as my site of class analysis because I know it best. It is where I live and work, for the most part. And in my experience and in that of the other faculty I know at my university and at other places around the country, the natural readership of this book should find the situation in the academy of interest, if not of concern. But more importantly, I pick the academy because it mirrors in a markedly hypocritical fashion the harsh economic truths operating at large. That this is the case is, or should be, felt as a scandal. The academy has always claimed to be a place largely free of such material constraints on its ideas and ideals, so that it could function as a separate critical sphere of adversarial culture, on the model, ultimately, of Socrates playing gadfly—but without penalty—to the polity. That the academy cannot do so, especially now, tells us a great deal about the real limits—past and present—of all so-called oppositional criticism.

The ultimate reason, however, why the academy is an instructive site for class analysis lies in its being a comic microcosm of economic developments in the larger world, such as the downsizing of the workforce, the increasing reliance on computer technology and innovation, the selective privileging of a global multicultural perspective (so as to penetrate different "markets" here and around the world), and the practice of making token celebrities of a few members of "oppressed" or "marginalized" groups. The ultimate irony of these general developments, as they appear in the academy, just may lie in the grand spectacle of (unwitting?) hypocrisy that results. Picture this: Stanley Fish, or Edward W. Said, or Cornel West is once again making an appearance on *The MacNeil-Lehrer News-Hour, This Week,* or *Nightline.* The media take these critics as spokespersons for an academy ostensibly "liberal" or even "radical" in its orientation, when actually the academy they speak for is, as they probably know, a class-divided workplace of the few critical stars and the mass of intellectual drones, all of whom, stars and drones alike, are encouraged, ironically enough, by these new circumstances, to embrace a leftish ideology of radical liberation while using the latest instruments—PCs, e-mail, the Internet—of a global capitalist rationality and in the latest style of the world media with its increasingly tabloid tastes and ethics. This makes for a scene of instruction with a vengeance.

The second way I will discuss class, then, will be in the context of Jon Elster's post-Marxist social analysis. This theory, I believe, can shed light on the academic situation, does possess a flexible coherence in itself, and may contain broader implications for radical change. Finally, I will exemplify Elster's theory of class, elaborated in light of current circumstances, professional and otherwise, by analyzing a 1903 novella by Henry James, *The Birthplace,* which, as James fully expected, no journal editor of his time dared to accept. This story, as we will see, delineates how class realities relate to the questions of truth and personal authenticity in what I take to be a prototypical postmodern setting of radical contingency and heterogeneous identities. What I mean by these last phrases Václav Havel memorably captured in his speech on receiving the Liberty Medal at Independence Hall in Philadelphia on July 4, 1994. He observed early on that "a symbol of that [postmodern] state [of mind] is a Bedouin mounted on a camel and clad in traditional robes under which he is wearing jeans, with a transistor radio in his hands and an ad for Coca-Cola on the camel's back."[2] And Havel concludes apropos such unreal scenes that "we live in [this] postmodern world, where everything is possible and almost nothing is certain." What follows here is my attempt to make "class" a little more possible for such an uncertain world.

The Two Professions: Multicultural Proles and Powerbook Radicals

Looking around the profession these days sobers the mind. For the 1993–1994 academic year, for example, the year I first became chair of my department, English literature departments produced 1,082 new Ph.D.'s, a figure approximately the same for each of the previous four years. Also in 1993–1994, English literature departments advertised in the Modern Language Association's Job Information List for 1,054 positions. The bad news is that only 60 percent of the advertised positions were tenure track: the rest were adjunct, non-tenure-track positions. (These and subsequent figures for job production and related matters are also typical for more recent years.) Not only did English literature departments produce twenty-eight more Ph.D.'s than the total number of positions available in 1993–1994; they also produced approximately 450 more Ph.D.'s than the available tenure-track positions, which was 632. The situation gets much worse when you add in the unemployed and underemployed Ph.D.'s from the previous four years. These are Ph.D.'s either unable to get any kind of college or university teaching position at all, a figure as high as 12 percent, or those Ph.D.'s teaching at an institution or a series of different institutions, on a one-year, usually renewable, adjunct basis. These adjunct positions are renewable at most schools for only up to five years, because of long-standing tenure policies. Finally, the number of Ph.D.'s from the last few years who are doing part-time teaching at a salary rate of $1,500 to $2,000 per course—that is, who do not even have a visiting or adjunct appointment, with a full course load at a somewhat decent salary —has been as high as 15 percent of the Ph.D. pool for the last four years. And while some gains in salary per course have been made, the basic situation remains pretty much as it has been for the last decade or so.

What this means is that the number of new and recent Ph.D.'s looking for one of the 632 tenure-track positions could have been as high as five thousand if all of them had still applied or hadn't become discouraged workers. And among this number of Ph.D.'s in the market, there are representatives of all schools and graduate programs, including the most prestigious institutions, such as Duke, Columbia, Princeton, and Harvard, with the most famous celebrity names for faculty, such as Stanley Fish, Edward W. Said, and Henry Louis Gates. Despite the spate of actual and anticipated retirements, which as predicted has been accelerating at an ever faster rate, hiring lines come in a ratio of one replacement position for every four or five positions lost to retirement, illness, or death. This is, of course, due to the chronic financial woes in higher education, much of them caused by now institutionalized conservative fiscal and social agendas.

To make matters worse, immediate prospects for university and college enrollments, overall, look to be rather steady state. But the best demographic projections for the long run strongly suggest that enrollments will balloon slightly and drop precipitously, at least among the traditional college-age population of eighteen-year-old students. Consequently, given this entire dismal situation, schools are making do by adopting a fourfold policy of survival: (1) making occasional and highly selective or "target" tenure-track hires; (2) raising faculty productivity by increasing course loads and class sizes; (3) shifting resources from expensive graduate programs to less expensive—in fact, profitable—undergraduate programs, with their extensive "service-course" components; and (4) appointing adjuncts and part-timers to these basic required writing and introductory courses, which "service" the university's general student body by teaching a bare-bones verbal and cultural literacy. As many as 40 percent of any department's total number of courses are staffed by non-tenure-track faculty, and at some schools, the percentage is as high as 60 percent. To speak of a crisis in the profession in this general context is to risk euphemism.[3]

I rehearse all these statistics because they outline the stark material conditions in current literary study for faculty and would-be faculty alike. Naturally, the kinds of hires made in these conditions acquire a powerful instructive status for all concerned. Whatever the anchoring subspecialty—Renaissance (or "early modern," as it is now called), critical theory, or composition and rhetoric—the primary specialty marking these rare hires nowadays is a multicultural distinction of some kind: African American studies, gender studies, cultural studies, or postcolonialist studies.

I don't think this is simply political correctness at work. Such a hiring pattern is part of a continuing sincere effort to make the professorate more representative and more responsive to the heterogeneous constituent groups of students it serves. Nonetheless, in some instances, and perhaps in a growing number, these hiring practices represent a reflex response on the part of administrators to the setting of implicit affirmative action "targets." University and college affirmative action officers scrutinize all the paperwork for any proposed hire in light of the number of women and minority candidates, first in the original pool of applicants, then in the group whose credentials are selected for review, and then among the finalists actually interviewed. Ideally, a department will land a woman or a minority candidate, virtually all of whom, for reasons I will analyze, now embrace a multiculturalist identity politics; but at the least a department will have good overall numbers for the selection process, even if it finally hires, as the product purchased, a white male doing neo-Marxist critiques of popular culture.

This hiring scenario constitutes a powerful scene of instruction for new Ph.D.'s, struggling graduate students, and literature majors. The ethos of multiculturalism, its mind-set, which celebrates the emergence of excluded identities on the professional and world historical stages, appeals, for more than fashionable reasons, to those facing the loss of the full intellectual life because of permanent professional non- or under-employment. Multiculturalism has, in this scene, an inspirational or edifying function. In such a bad labor market, it is truly the ideology of the oppressed. As already noted, however, multiculturalism as a cultural ethos of the profession gains in formative power by being reinforced at the material level of the institution, with this depression-style labor market. This hiring pattern then takes on an indelible weight, especially as graduate programs shrink, reduce their course requirements to speed fewer people to the degree, and also diversify their offerings even further —all of which many graduate programs are now doing to "downsize" into "lean and mean" professional-making machines.

The way graduate students and undergraduate English majors geared up for graduate school speak of this endemic situation in the profession should truly become instructive for professors. Students now speak of a "choice" in "profession styles" between "the archival dig" and "the cookie-cutter take." The former style of work entails a lot of library research, a lot of time sifting evidence, considerable thinking, and many rewrites to get everything about one's argument—the evidence, the thesis, the genealogy of theoretical concepts—just right. "The archival dig" is something students speak of with a resentful nostalgia for the unknown, as a critical luxury that they have only heard about and associate with the profession up to the death of Foucault, this scholarly style's finest exemplar. Students cannot know the archival dig firsthand because they must always already be doing papers for conferences, getting essays circulated and published, and generally networking and promoting their names. Consequently, the "cookie-cutter take" is the only style of criticism they can afford to practice. It consists of the quick-fix fabrication of a distinctive-sounding framework, whose sole purpose is to put one's marketable stamp on the object of analysis, whatever it may be: text, film, current event, and so on. The cookie-cutter take is the critical equivalent of a Robin Williams comic improvisation: speedball word-salads for a postmodern profession. To put it schematically, the archival dig is traditionally historical, documentary, theoretical, and text centered; the cookie-cutter take is criticism in the present tense, free-floating (like anxiety), cynically pragmatic, and indiscriminately omnivorous. Any object can become the material for receiving the stylish cut, which makes everything one does look the same, like designer-named fashions.

I call this class of adjuncts and graduate students "multicultural proles" because they are, for the most part, a professional generation condemned to the worst conditions ever in the U.S. academy, even as they espouse, for mixed motives, the multicultural line. Proles they certainly are; whether they are, as a class, that multicultural in fact (as opposed to in theory) remains to be seen. The very few who do succeed in obtaining tenure-track positions, and the very, very few who, best exemplifying this line, actually ascend to the heights of professional stardom, can only act in ways that must secure and extend the current situation well into the foreseeable future. In the rare but spectacular successes of multicultural stars, multicultural proles—gypsy-scholars and soon-to-be gypsy-scholars— ruefully see their own alienated majesties returning to them.

It used to be the promise of higher education, and particularly of literary study, that students, whatever their familial and national identities and circumstances, could assume with the proper work professional and larger cultural identities of their own imaginative choice and revisionary devising. However initially alienating this practice of education may have been, students now see that if they possess the politically correct "original" identity, or can cleverly appropriate or opportunistically affiliate themselves with one or another such identity—that of some so-called or actually oppressed or marginalized group—then they at least have a chance of selling themselves in the job market and so can enter the distinctive hierarchy of the academy, a situation remarkably akin to those of other professions. Often, those few who will not or cannot perform in this fashion end up, in the academy, teaching in "intellectual heritage" or "great books" humanities programs where multicultural texts and politically correct attitudes are usually less prominent and rather less in demand than they are in departments of English and other literatures. To teach Plato and the Bible and Shakespeare for most of a semester is, to these few adjunct instructors, worth the addition of a week or two on the Koran, and certainly better than a semester of teaching the new *Heath Anthology of American Literature,* with its many bloated entries for writers whose works may be fashionable but the aesthetic value of which leaves something to be desired for such recalcitrant adjuncts.

I call the rising multicultural stars of "the cookie-cutter take" critical style "powerbook radicals" (after the laptop computer) because it is among these newer members of the changing professional elite that I observe the greatest reliance on personal computers and the Internet and the related emergence of a new theoretical posture of globalism in cultural matters. This theoretical globalism of the professional "Left," ironically enough, aligns itself, wittingly or not, with the new postliterate global economy of sensational media images dominated by the multinational corporations. Powerbook radicals, as they aspire to represent the world at large in some diversifying sense, will prove to be either the postmodern reincarnations of the Renaissance genius, or, in their ersatz cosmopolitanism, the first instances of the institutionalization of the global dilettante as the latest figure for the New Historicist oppositional critic. With little or no training in any other discipline or knowledge of other cultures, powerbook radicals use the latest technology to speak authoritatively about the new world order, to rail against this system, and to envision utopian alternatives to it in the virtual worlds of their computer terminals, even as their use of these new machines of instrumental reason fosters the extension and profitability of the very global economic system they claim we should all desire to overcome.

Two dangers facing the multicultural proles should be glaringly evident, but a couple of anecdotes will spell them out conclusively. One is the danger of students' sacrificing the quest for knowledge to expediency. A brilliant graduate student I know, a young gay man who does queer theory, among several other things, asked me recently whether he should "commodify" himself solely as a queer theorist, since there was a steadily growing demand for this intellectual commodity in the job market. Shouldn't he worry about "learning anything else" until after he secured a position on this potentially constraining basis of pure identity politics? What could I say? I listened as he decided to go, as he put it, "the commodity route." Given the general state of affairs, I could not realistically advise him to do otherwise. Similarly, I was at a loss with another student, although a little less of a loss, as it turned out. The danger represented for this second student, a black woman from the Caribbean, has to do with the wholesale appropriation of another people's cultural experience—an academic imperialism committed, perhaps sincerely, perhaps opportunistically, in the name of global liberation, but often committed ignorantly in any event. This student from the Caribbean lamented recently that when she went to the Modern Language Association of America convention sessions on Caribbean writers, all the speakers were, as she characterized it with bitter irony, "young white women in short black leather skirts"—feminists who reduced Caribbean women's texts to generalizations about the necessary destruction of patriarchy everywhere. After listening to her story, I suggested that she revise for publication her paper on the positive cultural work of oral narratives, performed at ritual festivals in Trinidad, which tell of the desired return of authoritative male figures, in the historically specific context of a society whose family structures had virtually been annihilated by slavery and its long aftermath. This paper has at least a chance of doing some important corrective work, if it ever does get a fair hearing. It may be that the trivializing sort of professional strategies this student witnessed at the MLA convention will always be with us, but I believe that the present situation in literary study typifies a contemporary mind-set of cynical rationality, one the academy always used to say it tried to oppose, and may yet again. That the present class structure of the profession need not persist, I hope to demonstrate in what follows.

Toward a Post-Marxist Theory of Class

Traditionally, in Marxist and related strains of theoretical analysis, there are five distinct classes in modern society. The three primary classes are the aristocracy, which represents the vestigial past, the bourgeoisie, which represents the potent if soon-to-pass-away present, and the proletariat, which represents the promise of the future. The two other classes, the petite bourgeoisie and the lumpenproletariat, are liminal hybrids and have often puzzling links to the primary classes. I will discuss all five of these classes, briefly, in their order of priority as primary and secondary phenomena. Marx, by the way, defines a class pragmatically via what means of production, material or mental, its members own.

The aristocracy is the original landowning class, the so-called nobility whose forebears conquered the lands their heirs inherit as huge estates by right of the laws they instituted often over the stifled objections of the native inhabitants who "lost" the lands. The bourgeoisie is the class owning the commercial, financial, and manufacturing means of production. This class attempts to assimilate all forms of labor—manual, artisan, and intellectual—to the standards and practices of one or another mode of its means of production. This is the notorious "bottom-line" mind-set. The bourgeoisie profits by driving down the costs of production, which includes paying workers the least amount their mere subsistence requires. It also profits by then extracting for itself the savings gained by cost cutting, more efficiently organized labor forces, and technical innovation. This is the surplus value of labor, since this profit is beyond a fair return on investment and is ultimately had at the expense of the exploited and alienated workers, who must sell their creative power to these "others" just barely to live. The bourgeoisie appropriates this surplus value of labor for its exclusive use, either in reinvestment or in the accumulation of luxury items. Marx derives his analysis here from the late-eighteenth-century English political economist David Ricardo.

The proletariat is the class whose members own nothing but their physical labor power, which they must sell individually to the bourgeoisie capitalists for subsistence wages, even as their bosses tend to act together (as a monopoly, if possible) to drive prices for goods up as much as possible, as much as the market can bear. But the proletariat, as workers on the front lines of technical change, must receive instruction on the latest advances in order to maximize efficiency, and this means they must be made literate to begin with. By also being associated in large groups in the workplaces and cities and by necessity participating in the circulation of information for the distribution and sale of products in a consumer society, the workers naturally grow in knowledge, technical and professional expertise, and communication and organizational skills. Their capitalist "masters" thus breed ironically in their proletarian "slaves" the basis for their own eventual undoing. Once the proletariat can recognize itself as a class and starts to unionize and agitate for political change, that is, once the workers, too, choose to act in concert, then they pursue their own interests passionately. But since the proletariat constitutes the vast majority of people within the capitalist world system, and is on the cutting edge of technological change, it represents, as a class, especially through its intellectual vanguard, the promise of a better, more just future for all, once private property is abolished and exploitation has been replaced by mutual recognition, respect, and communal cooperation, after the inevitable blood revolution occurs.

The petite bourgeoisie is the class of small self-employed farmers, businesspeople, and professional service providers, such as teachers, nurses, journalists, and government employees. These people believe in, and try to practice, the ideology of radical individualism and the self-made man, and tend to side in political disputes with any one of the primary classes, depending on their pragmatic estimate of the advantage to them of doing so. And the lumpenproletariat, what Marx calls "the scum of the earth" (as opposed to the proletarian "salt"), is the class of totally alienated, unemployed, and unemployable street people, the deranged or chronically malcontent rabble who provide the raw materials for molding by the demagogic authoritarian populists from Napoleon to Hitler into counterrevolutionary tools and dupes, urban armies of thugs and would-be assassins, the protofascist mother lode.

This traditional Marxist theory of class presents several problems. First, it is time bound. It can persuasively appear to account for human history, on the basis of class warfare, up to its own period—from the middle of the nineteenth century to the early twentieth. At this point and even more so subsequently, its class categories and characterizations can too easily become fixed stereotypes, especially in the context of the incredible fluidity and radical contingency of a postmodern world. Second, as a grand narrative of humanity's past, present, and future, this time-bound theory aspires to explain everything totally, and as such, like all other time-bound grand narratives, religious or secular, it sounds suspiciously like a coercive myth. Third, as a collapse of virtually all Marxist societies and the simultaneous embrace of liberal democracy and authoritarian populism by all classes apparently everywhere makes clear, the predictive power of this traditional Marxist theory of class leaves something to be desired, to say the least. Fourth, this theory also leaves uncertain the exact relationships between its general assumption of historical necessity and its specific strategic reliance on individual and collective free choice. Fifth, even sympathetic Marxist political economists and social theorists from Ernst Mandel to Jon Elster now seriously question Marx's use of Ricardo's surplus value theory of labor. Last, the way Marx uses class in different historical and cultural contexts makes it hard to distinguish a class from a "caste," an "estate," a "guild," a "status group," or a "profession."

In this context, then, the best theoretical definition of class that I've discovered appears in Jon Elster's *Making Sense of Marx* (1985): "A class is a group of people who by virtue of what they possess are compelled to engage in the same activities if they want to make the best use of their endowments."[4] For example, when capitalists each act to keep costs down and also act in concert to drive prices up, despite antitrust laws against monopolies, they are acting as a class in this situation; that is, they are constituting by their action a collective agent or actor on the historical stage, with a prescribed script or scenario, which does allow for tactical improvisations, if necessary. Elster's definition suggests that "class" is an ever emergent, albeit repeatable, phenomenon. A class emerges as a collective actor on the historical scene because the people forming membership in the class possess the same or very similar "endowments"—a broadly conceived term for their material and symbolic property or "capital," their "know-how" and power position in society. These individuals perceive, whatever their differences and rivalries in the short term, long-term common interests, and they believe and act on this belief, in response to historical conditions, because certain courses of action will preserve and maximally enhance their holdings and positions. This sense of class as a repeatedly emerging phenomenon makes it particularly appropriate for a postmodern world economy and the improvisatory cultural logic of late capitalism. Its downsizing—sudden, radical, and destructive—is a pervasive phenomenon we see in the profession of literary study now all the time. Elster's flexible empirical sense of class, which evades Marx's more abstract and static structural formulations and stereotypes, is a major reason in favor of Elster's definition.

Another reason is equally important. Elster's "methodological individualism" makes the empirical assumption that groups are composed by individuals who are rational and self-interested. They act accordingly by making rational choices among available options when faced by historical necessity. As he moves from the individual level of agents (or "actors") and events to the always provisional but also always emerging collective level of historical action, Elster maintains this principle of "rational-choice" theory and argues that individuals in groups are persuadable with respect to the perception of both their real personal interests and their commonality of interest with others. Rhetorical persuasion, precisely because all identities in a postmodern world are heterogeneous and constructed, is central for Elster to the formation of any collective agency.

In addition, given his definition's invocation of the "best use of their endowments," Elster can also discuss the making of value judgments—practical, aesthetic, ethical—insofar as all these kinds of value judgments implicate standards and criteria engaging a full array of cognitive, cultural, and political assumptions and beliefs, which function as reasons for making one or another choice. Elster's versatile post-Marxist theory of class sees a group ever in formation and reformation, whose members are rational and self-interested agents who can choose among different options when responding to perceived historical conditions and in light of both short-term satisfactions and long-term individual and collective interests. In light of my earlier analysis of literary study, this highly nuanced sense of class makes Elster's definition particularly useful for understanding the profession, as I will try to show shortly in this section, as well as in this chapter's final section.

A class, when analytically conceived, appears as a collective actor on the historical scene. This appearance arises by virtue of its members' "endowments." These are what people possess or own: some means of economic and cultural production and reproduction, such as general knowledge, technical expertise, physical labor power, or the machinery of capital formation, circulation, and distribution. Signs of privileged class position—the right clothing, a good house, a luxury car, and so on—are just that: signs of power, but not the power itself, of course, which lies in the capacity to produce socially valuable goods and services. As a result of how a group of people have to act in concert to make the best use of their endowments when facing particular historical circumstances, a class emerges to select one of several real options in a symbolic setting in which its members reciprocally recognize their rational, self-interested, and necessarily mutually respectful because overlapping intentions to keep possession of and significantly enhance their endowments. This symbolic setting or recognition scene is the story, the narrative, that the members of a class tell and repeat, with revisions, about themselves and their group-in-(re)formation. Class in this fashion promotes strategic critical recognitions and at least a wary respect. It thereby has an educative civilizing function, ironically enough, even as the class in question plays its part in the social war for more power, better position, and greater influence.

To summarize: Elster's rational-choice post-Marxist approach to the idea of social class—an idea he traces from Marx through Weber into later writers—assumes that social situations, as Anglo-American philosophers like to say, are rule-governed "games" with their own conventions, in which the presumption is that the participants in a game think themselves to be rational agents seeking to maximize their interests vis-à-vis each other, but who can and also do act in concert when they are persuaded to see that their interests overlap and are threatened or can be maximized by cooperation. This rational-choice model thus begins with the empirical experience of individuals who, whatever their circumstances and positions, act as if they are intelligent free agents. This analysis then moves to the more general level of ever-emergent collective agents also acting to choose freely from a contingent range of possible courses that they are forced to confront by specific historical developments, among which not least in importance are the consequences of past actions.

The greatest advantage of Elster's making sense of class inheres in how it frees us from thinking about classes as fixed and selectively privileged as the symbolic capital of Marxist intellectuals. Micropolitically, via Elster's revision of Marx, we can define individuals and the groups they strategically form and repeatedly renew in terms of what particular possessions or endowments are concerned in any particular context. No endowment, however comparatively small in the grand scheme of things, can be beside the point of discussion, negotiation, and care, if only for tactical purposes. Yet at the same time, macropolitically, we need never lose sight of the large-scale and historically institutionalized structures of endowments striating a changing social scene. For example, the connections between employment practices in the academy with those in other professions and in the corporate world stand out in this broader horizon. In short, we can use the old names for classes strategically, pragmatically, with a certain ironic, even (self-)parodic lightness, if the need arises: global America as empire burlesque, for example.

Let's look, in this light, at my opening analysis of "multicultural proles" and "powerbook radicals." Strictly speaking, from a conventional Marxist perspective, both of these groups should be seen as parts of the same whole, the class of professional intellectual workers, a crossbreed of the petite bourgeoisie who are, in theory anyway, self-employed service providers—teachers—who contract to sell to the university their expertise for its use, and many of whom have organic ties to, and ideological affiliations with, repressed or marginalized peoples. But in fact, as I've already stressed, only multicultural proles are in the position of acting like intellectual workers in this mixed-breed or hybrid sense, whereas the powerbook radicals are in the position of acting like an official "outlaw" caste. These critics compose a professionally elite version of the old lumpenproletariat, as shaped by the demagogic forms and norms of the current academic celebrity machine and our sensationalistic corporate media culture. One of the markers of postmodern society, as we saw with John Guillory's *Cultural Capital,* is precisely this substitution of impersonal machinelike or semiautomatic systems of cultural (re)production for the personal relationships of professional mentorships and the wholesale social pathologies of the leader and the cult of personality. This substitution of impersonal mechanisms of popular media images for more personal modes of literate cultural transmission—celebrity icons instead of personal masters—is the hallmark for what, as we also saw in chapter 4, Wlad Godzich in *The Culture of Literacy* considers our "postliterate state" beyond a now clearly passé modernity.[5]

However this may be, the most important consequence of Elster's making sense of Marx on class lies in the threefold diagnostic question his new definition entails: What are the specific circumstances, the historical scene, in which collective actors can make their appearances as distinctively recognizable figures? How can this phenomenon be most convincingly analyzed in a creditable account of those circumstances when they do arise—that is, how can one most usefully tell their story? And finally, what can one do, if anyone wants to do so, to promote most effectively the wedding of these collective actors to these stories about them, with respect especially to improving the prospects of radical change? In short, Elster on class encourages us to think of ourselves—intellectuals or otherwise—as the real authors of such possible visions of radical change. In this way, each of us may come to join one another in a mutual act of revisionary telling.

If the emergence of multicultural proles and powerbook radicals constitutes an opportunity for such collective authorships, perhaps what needs to be envisioned in this case, in order to promote radical change, is a scenario in which adjunct faculty and graduate students are successfully unionized by strategically proposing to them the goal of abolishing current tenure practices. (This first step of unionization, including graduate assistants, was accomplished in 2001 at Temple.) If we mean the most radical change of all, the abolition of tenure itself, such a move could establish a new free-for-all competition for positions based on market standards. This would tend to proletarianize in appearance and in fact the entire profession and so destroy the present system of academic hierarchical distinction. One class of truly miserable intellectual workers would result. They could then act perhaps better in concert as one collective agent with and among other such collective agents in the world at large, perhaps even in the long-term interests of most people. This is a familiar vision, originally renewed for literary study in Frank Lentricchia's *Criticism and Social Change* (1983).

The powerbook radicals, masters of the Internet and the information superhighway in my scenario, could then play the role of international organizers and global communications experts rather than, as now, merely the role of our ever-returning alienated majesties, those professionalized puppets of the celebrity image-making mill. Of course, we could choose to envision less radical change with respect to tenure practices, such as de-emphasizing sheer quantity of written productivity, including experimental collective work via the Internet, and reemphasizing teaching effectiveness. I prefer the more radical vision, the abolition of tenure, since I do not believe it works to protect "free speech," whatever that may be, but I do see how it works to sustain an outmoded academic hierarchy of purely invidious distinctions. But this is just one man's opinion.

Since, as intellectuals, our endowments are various "knowledges," and since what we possess or own is professional expertise in the production, circulation, and regulation of cultural or symbolic capital, including certain socially accrediting discursive practices such as reading, writing, and critical thinking, we could be properly compelled, in the light of my visionary scenario and by virtue of such endowments, finally "to engage in the same actions," for the radical benefit of all. If we "want to make the best use" of our powers, we must begin to see what is there to be seen, necessities and possibilities alike. Or so I prefer to think.

"The Biggest Show on Earth": The Case of *The Birthplace*

The Birthplace (1903), by Henry James, tells the story of Morris and Isabel Gedge, a long-suffering, not very financially successful married British couple. As Mrs. Gedge pointedly remarks, they have "no social position."[6] In fact, from a classical Marxist perspective, they are generally self-employed professional service providers, or intellectual petite bourgeoisie. From Elster's perspective, they have not yet found their other class members, as such. That is, they do indeed have "no social position."

For a brief period, the Gedges ran "a small private school of the order known as preparatory" (109). One of their pupils, Mr. Grant-Jackson's only son, had once fallen ill, had been near death, and the Gedges, especially Mrs. Gedge, had nursed the boy back to full health while his parents were traveling in America. As the story opens, years have passed since this incident, and Mr. Gedge has failed at a series of practical enterprises. He has ended up "in charge of the grey town-library of Blackport-on-Dwindle," a provincial library the Jamesian narrator characterizes archly as "all granite, fog and female fiction" (110). I suppose, in good dialectical fashion, the latter sublates the granite and the fog in its stony amorphousness.

However that may be, in a romantic development as if drawn from this very predetermined female sentimental fiction, James's story has Mr. Grant-Jackson, now so many years after the fact, suddenly intervene to repay his debt to the Gedges. He does so by using his influence to get them appointed as the caretakers or "wardens" for the cottage museum and birthplace, "the early home of the supreme poet, the Mecca of the English-speaking race" (110). Although in characteristically late Jamesian fashion, the tale never mentions the names of Stratford-upon-Avon or Shakespeare, these real if spectral presences, among others, loom over its telling.

Thanks to Mr. Grant-Jackson's belated influence, Mr. Gedge will no longer sell his labor power and intellectual resources to service provincial tastes. Now he, along with Isabel, will sell their labor, for only slightly more total income (but with the rent-free use of an adjoining cottage), to service "the Mecca of the English-speaking race." To this birthplace of pure genius itself come "types, classes, nationalities," expressive of "manners, diversities of behavior, modes of seeing, feeling" unknown to Blackport-on-Dwindle, and so this fabulous spectacle constitutes the mode of mental travel for Mr. Gedge, "an untravelled man" (125).

To this traditional center of an imperial culture, from provincial, colonial, and even, as we'll see, postcolonial margins and peripheries, come these hordes, all of which the Gedges are to teach and delight as they uncritically retail the antiquarian details of the monumental genius and his humble, pedantically preserved birthplace. Ironically enough, as in the case of a certain Mr. and Mrs. B. D. Hayes, a young couple key to the tale's crisis, most of the pilgrims to the shrine are indeed postcolonials —American—because they can most afford to indulge their curiosity. Indeed, these Americans combine with their curiosity an ignorance of class and its constraints on free expression that makes, for the Hayeses at least, Morris Gedge's position as the caretaker of genius and the warden of the birthplace an interesting case.

But an acute problem has arisen for Morris Gedge by the time he meets the Hayeses. He has begun to realize that "the Body," or "the Committee" (as it is also called), which runs and oversees the birthplace and for which Mr. Grant-Jackson acts as mouthpiece, has expected Morris Gedge and his wife to play only one role. They are to enthusiastically give the vast, anonymous numbers of "They" who visit the birthplace the same glorious legend of sublime genius amid the details of everyday life, all of which details are, as all concerned know, most likely founded on absolutely "Nothing" at all (125). This professional requirement for the Gedges to misrepresent, to lie, affects them differently, which complicates and increasingly exacerbates Morris Gedge's problem. In true comic foil fashion Mrs. Gedge reasons, self-interestedly (and circularly), that since next to nothing really is, or can ever be, known for certain about the genius of the English-speaking race—note, by the way, how race here is principally a linguistic being, and not a biological fact— then nothing can ever be known for certain. Consequently, she concludes, any and perhaps all the details that she and her husband spout for the crowds may perhaps be contingently, accidentally true after all. Mr. Gedge, however, cannot accept his wife's casuistry, her pragmatist reasoning, and fledgling contingent theorizing. Instead, he grows more irritable, restless, and resentful. No negative capability for him! During the days, he recounts to the gaping public, with rising sarcasm punctuated by knife-thick, increasingly prolonged silences, the phony details of the legend. During the nights, he haunts the birthplace to feel the authentic absence of genius all the more palpably and so be in better possession of the truth he does know.

This growing double split between the Gedges and within Morris Gedge, between the public performance demanded by the profession of caretaker and the private sensibility, one in his case that had never been uniformly whole, clearly represents the unhappy consciousness of alienated labor, the alienated being of the worker: "One of the halves, or perhaps even, since the split [in Morris Gedge] promised to be rather unequal, one of the quarters, was the keeper, the showman, the priest of the idol; the other piece was the poor unsuccessful honest man he had always been" (127). Gedge calls the former public and professional part of the self interchangeably "the showman" and "the priest," and what this part performs he usually perceives as being the master-of-ceremonies role in "the Biggest Show on Earth" (144), a circus- or carnival-huckstering role of routinely retailing the legend to the masses. He calls the latter private and resentful part of the self "this primary character" (127), the idea of which makes him shake in his shoes. His wife insistently cautions him to be politic.

Why all this fuss? I think the reason for the difference in Morris Gedge now lies in his change from being simply a cultural worker (schoolmaster, provincial librarian) to his being also a cultural investor or unwilling symbolic speculator. Gedge not only sells his labor power and expertise in certain discursive practices, just as he did before, so as to purchase basic commodities of existence such as food, clothing, and shelter; he must also now speculate, according to a conventional corporate design, in the genius-legend market, actually performing and professionally investing in the commodified formulas and ritualized forms of this genius-legend's "facts" and museum souvenirs. He thus spends the symbolic capital of his discursive intelligence, such as it is, to sell the commodity of genius and its ersatz and fetishized birthplace, all for the purpose of bringing in more and more receipts. In legal and contractual terms, as an agent for his principal, the corporate "Body" or "Committee," Gedge administers, as curator, the cultural capital of the symbolic myth of romantic genius for profit. In this fashion, Gedge has been transformed by his new profession from an intellectual petit bourgeois into a representative disciplined subject of speculative or modern consumer culture. As such, Gedge appears to have only two choices: follow his wife's advice and example and mouth the profit-making if absurd pieties, or leave his new position in this cultural capitalist class and return to his petit bourgeois status. Shades of Frank Lentricchia!

When, as part of "some supreme assertion of his identity," Gedge does revolt, and tells the truth about the birthplace as he sees it to the apparently sympathetic Hayeses, he feels he has finally found, among this small circle of friends, the core of "the good society" (140). Here is where Elster's definition of class comes in most handy. The idea of a new class improvising itself into existence in this fashion is something his revision of Marxist categories allows us to credit, even as his perspective allows us to use the traditional Marxist categories, such as petit bourgeois and so on, with more allegorical versatility.

It is now that Mr. Grant-Jackson, on the Body's behalf, dramatically reappears to warn Gedge that his prolonged and sullen silences during his wife's dutifully enthusiastic performances of the legend have been remarked by the public. (James's world still knew how to read.) These pointed silences would have brought the Gedges' dismissal this time if Mr. Grant-Jackson hadn't intervened, once again, in their interest, for old times' sake. As a result of this visitation, Gedge launches on a new course of action, one that may help to form the core of a new society, although whether it should be christened "good" remains to be seen.

Gedge's new chosen course of action is to embellish the legend with an inventive vengeance that would have made the late Oscar Wilde of "The

Decay of Lying" mighty proud, or the late Foucault laugh out loud in his grave. Gedge even risks going over the top with his new act:

> It was ever his practice to stop still at a certain spot in the room and, after having secured attention by look and gesture, suddenly shoot off: "Here!" They always understood, the good people—he could fairly love them now for it; they always said, breathlessly and unanimously, "There?" and stared down at the designated point quite as if some trace of the grand event [of the genius's birth struggles] were still to be made out. This movement produced, he again looked round. "Consider it well: *the* spot of earth—!" "Oh, but it isn't *earth!*" the boldest spirit—there was always a boldest—would generally pipe out. Then the guardian of the Birthplace would be truly superior—as if the unfortunate had figured the Immortal coming up, like a potato, through the soil. "I'm not suggesting that He was born on the bare ground. He was born *here!*"—with an uncompromising dig of his heel. . . . Mr. and Mrs. Hayes were at first left dumb by [this rehearsal of his now standard performance]. They had uttered no word while he kept the game up, and . . . he could yet stand triumphant before them after he had finished with his flourish. (151)

The Hayeses have now returned, two years later, after Gedge has perfected his act, to warn him that his wonderful reputation for improvising, elaborating, and ritualizing all these new "facts" has reached America, where his name in cultural circles is now all the rage, and so he may become perceived by "the Body" of suspiciously laying it on too thick. But the Hayeses have also returned to witness, given his sudden rapid transition from one extreme, truth telling, to its polar opposite, radical parody (or empire burlesque?) of the pieties of the genius discourse, the perfection of what the Hayeses hope is "a true case-study": "The case with an ideal completeness" (154). Gedge now understands that this "good society" of sympathetic friends depends on this purely and selfishly aesthetic interest in him as "a case." Such an aesthetic motive of the spectator means, for Gedge at this moment, that the Hayeses may not be real friends after all, since the Gedge as the potential perpetrator of a novel scandal due to this ironic emergence of his "critical sense" is not his "true" self but merely his self-parodically revolting mask—or so Gedge still believes (144).

Just at this final crisis point, Mr. Grant-Jackson does indeed return with another message from the Body. But although Mr. and Mrs. Hayes, Mrs. Gedge, and Morris Gedge himself now fear the worst, that his radical parody has been seen through, the questions of "real" knowledge, intention, and authenticity on all sides become purely moot. One may as well believe in free agency as not believe in it. What matters the most to the Body, and so to Mr. Grant-Jackson, whatever they may or may not suspect—and so, as well, ultimately to the Gedges and to those aesthetically curious young Americans, the Hayeses—is the good news about the greatly increased receipts that, thanks to its priest's greatest-show-on-earth performances, this "carny" church of genius, with its sublime side-show, is now bringing in. And it is the receipts, as Morris Gedge delights in suspensefully drawing out Mr. Grant-Jackson's point for them all, "The receipts, it appears, speak—Well, volumes . . . They tell the truth" (159). "Oh, *they* at least do?" Mrs. Hayes pointedly responds. So powerfully, in fact, do these receipts speak the truth that, as Mr. Grant-Jackson has just announced in private to Morris, the Gedges have received a substantial raise in their stipend. "They double us?" asks Isabel Gedge, with full dramatic irony. "Well—call it that," her husband says. "In recognition," he concludes (160). The sentence from his lips, "There you are," and its slight variation, "And there *you* are," sounds a pointed refrain as the tale ends (160).

The moral of this story could not be clearer: direct critique will not be countenanced by the powers that be, and indirect critique, via parodic ridicule of conventional discourse practices, will be supported, even encouraged, whether fully understood as such or not, so long as the status of the receipts in question speaks the only "truth" now known, their always potentially infinite because purely speculative increase.

Three formal features of *The Birthplace* bring home its prototypically late capitalist or postmodern "truth." The language of religion and its rituals ("shrine," "idol," "priest," "the Body") in combination with the language of the modern international corporation, of business ("the committee," "souvenirs," "selling," "receipts"), constitutes a broad range of topical, historical, literary, and romantic allusion. All this composes an ironic allegory, a tale of truth telling becoming radical parody, the circus of genius that represents James's own rueful fantasy about the fate, as a "genius" in his small way, awaiting him after his death. Given the poor receipts his later work did generate at the time of this tale (1903), and his long-ruminated twofold design for what became the *New York Edition of the Collected Works* (1907–1909)—for it to enshrine his reputation and to increase his writing revenues (it never did the latter)—this stylistic overdetermination of *The Birthplace* evokes more and more poignant resonances.

Similarly, the restricted point of view—the Jamesian narrator largely effacing himself in favor of the perceptions and the verbal habits of his protagonist, Morris Gedge—acts to produce a systematic structure of ever contingent, socially symbolic ambiguities. To take one major example: Gedge first sees Mr. and Mrs. Hayes sentimentally as representing, with him, in miniature, the utopian idea of the "good society" of sympathetic friends; then, in disillusionment with their aestheticism, he sees them cynically as the merely curious spectators of the ideal case study his story makes as he races perfectly from one polar opposite, truth telling, to another, parody lying. How are we as readers to credit his shifting point of view in this or any other instance of such a complex tale? Do we instead form our more independent, if still sympathetic, judgment of all these characters and their situation based on the presence in the text of suggestions of more complicated patterns of motivation? Like the stylistic overdetermination, this structural ambiguity of restricted point of view precludes any facile conclusion that *The Birthplace* is merely a despairing revelation, however blackly comic, of a genteel sensibility's defeat by crude commercialism.

Finally, however, a number of elements combine to balance any conclusion. There is the insistent refrain, with its elegant variation, uttered by Gedge literally as the tale's last words—"There you are" and then "And there *you* are!" (160). There is the subtly cruel manner in which Gedge creates and sustains for as long as possible the Hitchcockian suspense of the other characters; how he orchestrates the final scene of revelation about the truth of the receipts, the raise, and the general ironic reversal of expected tragic fortune. And there is how he delivers the infectiously comic turnabout for any and all spectators—"And there *you* are!" It is as if we all are somehow intimately implicated in the truth the receipts speak volumes of. We are all like Gedge: a defeated but still "revolting" protagonist who assumes the more creative role of "authoring" with James and us—or, if you prefer, "coauthoring"—this final scene of aesthetic and moral judgment in *The Birthplace*.

Supporting this perhaps innovative-sounding conclusion is the pervasive, even contagious pattern of formal, specular doubling in the tale. The Hayeses are an ideal version of the Gedges, as Morris Gedge would wish himself and his wife to be. His former jobs as schoolmaster and librarian are matched by his new profession as the instructive caretaker for the genius of the English-speaking race. Even "the Body" has another name: "the Committee." The church of genius is also the circus. As we have seen, Gedge himself is split and at least doubled by his changing responses to his new role, a process that his wife's final questions about their salary raise—"They double us"—resonate with ever widening implications. And most significantly, Gedge at the last does assume, albeit in a minor mode, the master's role of the suspenseful tale-teller. Morris Gedge, as radical parodist and especially as improviser of this final scene, thus mirrors and is mirrored by his (and our) author, "James himself," who is by now impossible to distinguish from the specter of the reader's critical imagination, a position I will develop fully in chapter 10.

In terms of Elster's post-Marxist theory of class, *The Birthplace* demonstrates the emergence of a new ironic collective aesthetic recognizing this new historical truth of receipts being the be-all and end-all, of being all in all. Such a truth subjects to critique all romantic idealism about genius, to be sure, as well as any sentimentally utopian notions of the good society of sympathetic friends, both of which positions depend on a practice of aesthetic spectatorship, of being above the fray of market conditions, which this story reveals is now impossible, even for beautiful, young, rich Americans. To confront his select, genteel audience of Anglo-American readers with this new reality destructive of aesthetic distance, critical disinterestedness, and mere ivory towerism, in a tale that both practices truthfully and parodies radically these very "virtues"—such is James's considerable achievement in *The Birthplace*.

The self-destructive form of this tale, which implicates characters, author, and readers (then and now) in its mordantly comic "truth," suggests the initial emergence of both a new reality—the total penetration of culture by capitalistic standards of value—and a new class consciousness among nouveau riche cultured dilettantes, professional intellectual workers, and culture-starved masses from around the globe. All stand discovered together here, ready to tell each other their stories.

Elster's theory of class can help us to recognize this conflicted collective self-discovery of a new class of speculative culture producer-consumers, a new class of intellectuals now grown older and yet facing another painful birth in the place where, for better or worse, multicultural proles and powerbook radicals currently play their assigned roles—the postmodern American university. "Types, classes, nationalities, manners, diversities of behavior, modes of seeing, feeling, of expression, would pass before him and become for him, after a fashion, the experience of an untravelled man. His journeys had been short and saving, but poetic justice again seemed inclined to work for him in placing him just at the point in all Europe perhaps where the confluence of races was thickest" (125). Perhaps, as poetic justice would have it, we are at the point in all the world, the American academy, where such an opportunity is now the greatest, an opportunity that includes our refusal of merely assigned roles and entails our assumption of the new role of a collective self-authorship—to take *The Birthplace*'s creative intention one step beyond itself—which will be performed by subjects as riven, mobile, and provocatively improvisatory as any of James's best: "So Gedge had the last word. 'And there *you* are!'" (160).

PART THREE

● ● ● ● ● ● ● ● ● ● ● ● ●

Analyzing Global America

7

Transference and Abjection:

An Analytic Parable

●●●●●●●●●●●●●●●●●●●●●●●●●●●●●●●●

I recently went to a noted critic's lecture on "globality." By this term, I learned, he meant not just the many diverse economic phenomena operating since the end of the Cold War on a world-wide scale, such as the radically unpredictable flows of capital invest-ments, financial trading, labor migration, political unrest, renewed ethnic warfare, nation-state instability, and uncertain internationalisms of one sort or another. No, not just these "geopolitical and economic develop-ments." Even more so, he meant by "globality" a new feeling or pathologi-cal affect, a new experience of existence, which makes the global condition more visible and recognizable to us than all the bundles of flowcharts could ever do.[1] This new "feeling global" is the experience all of us are having of being increasingly harried and harassed, from morning till night and too often all through the night as well, by the demands, the imperatives, of our work. Thanks to frequent-flier discounts, com-puter technology, the Internet, e-mail, on-line business transactions, cell phones, beepers, pagers, we are in principle never not reachable by, or assignable to, our work.[2] And choosing to be "out of touch" is now a decision fraught with the nerve-racking implications of office politics, to say the least. Consequently, this new kind of exhausting anxiety—

"globality"—testifies to the latest phase in late capitalism's penetration of every aspect, each nook and cranny, of modern life.

For a certain class, especially. What this critic is pointing to by the term "globality" is not so much a universal experience of being harried, harassed, stressed out, and exhaustively anxiety ridden, however widespread it may be or may become, as it is the exemplary experience of the class of intellectual workers not previously so exposed to, so haunted by, the realities of capitalist penetration: the American professional-managerial class. (I include in this class, by the way, the generation of so-called tenured radicals, with their multicultural imperatives and cosmopolitan aspirations, who occupy positions of authority in the academy: lit crit's "bobos.")

The point I want to underscore is that the systematic transference to a global economy from a Cold War superpower and nation-state model of world order means the social abjection of this critical generation in the American professional-managerial class. Professional life in academe is readily losing its distinguishing traits as a traditional profession. Academic life is becoming proletarianized. "Globality" is the feeling accompanying this transformation.

Let me put the point even more starkly by citing a classical statement from the first volume of Marx's *Capital*, on the subject of the typical condition of the laborer under a capitalist system: "The owner of money . . . meets in the market with the free labourer, free in the double sense, that as a free man [and not a serf] he disposes of his labor power as his own commodity, and that on the other hand he has no other commodity for sale, is short of everything necessary for the realization of his labor power."[3] By adopting in the 1980s an individualistic productivity model of professionalism in the university, we are now at the mercy of the changing market conditions, which increasingly reduce our state to one as abject as Marx delineates. Given the new world order of the global economy and the brave new world of information technology, communications, and biological sciences, not to mention the efforts to downgrade or to abolish tenure, to increase part-time instruction, to submit every aspect of professional life to productivity assessment and contingency calculation, to substitute administrative standards for the principles of faculty governance, is there any wonder that feeling global, so-called globality, is running rampant in academe? Globality is the pathos of this class's abjection.

Consider what has been happening at my school, Temple University in Philadelphia, a state-related institution.[4] Temple spent much of its capital during the 1980s achieving national status as one of the group of so-called Research 1 universities. It also invested heavily in its regional campuses while expanding its foreign operations, including campuses in Japan and Italy. Temple weathered two union strikes and a temporary downturn in enrollments and is now investing heavily in new technologies, especially computers, smart carts and smart classrooms, new instructional and plant facilities, and an urban enterprise zone called "Temple Town," an entire community with a trendy mall, an upscale University Inn, and a state-of-the-art entertainment venue and a sports arena.

Meanwhile, courses have been increased for all faculty, 58 percent of introductory courses are taught by graduate assistants and part-timers, and the union has accepted a plan to establish a two-tier faculty: the older, smaller, and shrinking tenured group and the younger, larger, and growing nontenured group, who would receive five-year contracts, renewable indefinitely. More of the university and more administrative and support functions have been reassigned to the (albeit technically enhanced) tenured faculty to perform. The strategies and tactics of the contemporary business world, in other words, have redefined the conditions of work at Temple—and, increasingly, virtually everywhere else in American higher education.[5] This is bringing it all back home with a vengeance. Those who are eligible are retiring early, those who can leave have already done so, and the rest of us are bearing witness to globality. Temple's board of trustees, for example, has approved a for-profit venture, Virtual Temple, the university on-line, whose curriculum and instruction are entirely beyond the structures of faculty oversight and governance, in administrative hands. Meanwhile, a hopeful sign: teaching assistants have formed a graduate student union.

My university, apparently like every other social institution in America these days, is acting like a transnational corporation. The Cold War liberal welfare state no longer provides the ultimate model of collective action, not even in theory.[6] And only work that advances the corporate interests of the university gains significant recognition and receives substantial support. The neopragmatism of Clintonian politics or Fishian professionalism has been a perfect fit for this recent moment.

When the transference of intellectual identity from a purely professional standard or code to the free-market global point of view coincides with (because it institutes) the abjection of the academic profession to the level of the service industry—Temple's new School of Tourism and Hospitality Management is a good case in point—then, it seems, university professors must join together on a national and an international basis to promote their interests, to say the least. But on what basis can they do so? There are no agreed-on values except those of self-interest and self-promotion. Collective endeavors are not truly communal; they are at best corporate alliances. There is no agreed-on language to make a powerful appeal for negotiating any system of values beyond rational self-interest, a situation that makes all associations provisional projects, not structural necessities. Such poverty of resources, along with constant technological innovation and outmoding processes, reduces academic professionals to the status of the "free" laborer described by Marx. This abjection of the American academic professional is, however, a great opportunity, on a global scale. What is needed is a new or revised vocabulary to speak about the emerging universal plight, without effacing or eliding the differences between the displacements suffered by, say, former West African peasants now living in tin shacks and cardboard boxes outside their cities and academic professionals serving as support staff, student recruiters, personal mentors, and "amateur" efficiency experts—anything but the scholars, writers, artists, teachers, and critics of society they trained themselves to be. The feelings of alienation, anxiety, and resentment can give food for similar thoughts. Just as in the last chapter we saw in Elster's rational-choice version of Marxism that any collective subject for intellectual workers can emerge in our global culture only fugitively, piecemeal, and thus repeatedly, with differential accumulations, so, too, I think that any critical vocabulary for analyzing and rectifying any current or foreseeable scene of instruction can be innovated only in a provisional and an improvisatory way. In any event, I want to suggest how a reading of Jacques Derrida's *Adieu: To Emmanuel Levinas* just might be able to supply us with the first words of that new more generally accessible vocabulary in our current moment of the War Against Terror.

Before doing so, however, I need to make two points: one concerning the terms "transference" and "abjection," and the other concerning method. I'll start with the latter first.

In the reading of *Adieu* that follows, neither an original intention of the text's author, nor a belated revision of the text's meaning, is the object of the analysis. Instead, the reading will follow one trace of the text's dissemination, a strand of the figurative chain, to bring out a style of critical performance, a practice of reading, neither strictly mine alone nor Derrida's nor Levinas's, which is yet adequate to our global moment of criticism by virtue of the language it puts into play for our mode of work, a language at once new and traditional that can enrich our current poverty with its imaginative resources. It must be such language—call it "literary," if you like—that remains the primary object of critical analysis and prophetic hope.

Of course, in their present sense, the terms "transference" and "abjection" have their genesis and genealogy in psychoanalysis. In chapters 8 and 9, I investigate some of those associations, but here I simply want to put these terms into play to characterize and trace a chiasmus, a criss-crossing movement in the rhetoric and stance of contemporary critical discourse. The move or shift to a global perspective, the adoption and adaptation of capital's point of view, whatever the supposed nature of the capital—financial, symbolic, biological—such a tactical positioning, no matter what the strategic terms, is what the term "transference" primarily refers to here. Similarly, "abjection" refers less to the psychological mechanism whereby the (m)other introject is self-destructively trashed for "her" apparent lack of the phallus than it does to the debasing fall in status whereby the realities of the global transference impose themselves specifically on intellectual workers. These social and aesthetic meanings of "transference" and "abjection" are not opposed to the psychoanalytic and moral meanings, just, I think, a bit more easily generalizable, more useful as figures of and for analysis.

• • •

Adieu: To Emmanuel Levinas collects both Jacques Derrida's eulogy of that title "originally delivered upon the death of his magisterial-teacher," at the cemetery in Pantin on December 27, 1995, and "A Word of Welcome," his opening lecture "given one year later, on December 7, 1996, in the Richelieu Amphitheater of the Sorbonne." The occasion was a two-day gathering entitled "Homage to Emmanuel Levinas: Face and Sinai," which was organized by Danielle Cohen-Levinas under the auspices of the Collège International de Philosophie.[7] I begin with the eulogy.

"For a long time, for a very long time," Derrida starts off, "I've feared having to say *Adieu* to Emmanuel Levinas" (1). Derrida is certain, as he says this, that his voice must be trembling (1). So why does Derrida begin in "fear and trembling"? Does he fear a sacrifice? A death? Whose? The already dead teacher's? His own? He tells us a few pages later that he fears and trembles in anticipation of "the death that 'we meet' 'in the face of the Other'—as *non-response*" (5). Derrida, in other words, dreads the teacher's nonresponse as a prophetic sign of a death, not that of the already dead teacher, nor that of his devoted student and friend (himself), but the death of the nonresponse we meet in the face of the Other— the socially symbolic death of the teaching, of any and all teaching, when it meets with nonresponse. Beyond debt or guilt, the "entrusted responsibility" of a legacy recognizes the first death in the face of the Other as nonresponse (6), and assumes the nonexistence to come of the final death, but works to disavow the future death of the legacy, not so much like a son preserving the purity of the father's message intact as like a parent entrusted with his own Isaac and awaiting God's word, as if it were *the unknown* itself (8). Such nonknowledge of the fate of the teacher's message at the hands of the disciple, not to mention at those of the ignorant, defines "the element of friendship or hospitality for the transcendence of the stranger, the infinite distance of the other" (8).

This is not to say that it is solely the processes of dissemination without reserve or return that the student stands in fear and trembling for. Derrida puts the issue thus: "If the relation to the other presupposes an infinite separation, and infinite interruption where the face [of nonresponse] appears, what happens, where and to whom does it happen, when another interruption comes at death to hollow out even more infinitely this first separation, a rending interruption [in the filiation, in the bearing of the legacy] at the heart of interruption itself?" (9). The literal death of the teacher and the symbolic death of nonresponse stand for each other like two halves of a metonymy, an allegory, a parable, albeit in a hierarchical relation of the greater and lesser degree of (in)finitude. As such, Derrida is driven back to begin again this source of his own sense of hospitality: "Each time I read or reread Emmanuel Levinas, I am overwhelmed with gratitude and admiration, overwhelmed by this necessity, which is not a constraint but a very genteel force that obligates and obligates us not to bend or curve otherwise the space of thought in its respect for the other, but to yield to this other, heteronymous curvature that relates us to the completely other (that is, to justice . . .), according to the law that this calls us to yield to the other infinite precedence of the completely other" (10). Rather than reject or expel, or incorporate via assimilation, this relation to the Other, whether teacher, lover, stranger, Derrida would receive the impression of the Other in its own elaborated or expanding space, whose borders are openly permeable each way.

Derrida explains such an experience of psychic and social imagination as the response to *un enseignement majestral,* "magisterial teaching," a masterful or lordly lecture style, a noble or knightly insemination. This teaching, itself already a welcoming of the scene of instruction, inspires "the figure of *welcoming,* a welcoming where ethics interrupts [formally all Socratic maieutics] and foils the ruse of the master who feigns to efface himself behind the figure of the midwife" (17). No one gives birth to himself or herself, except as and in a fiction. A teaching must find one first, before there is both ignorance and the unknown. The pedagogy of Socratic dialogue, Hegelian dialectic, pragmatic conversation, is ultimately that of the fiction of autogenesis. It is not truly a pedagogy, only a therapy: "For the *study* of which we are speaking [with respect to Levinas's magisterial teaching] cannot be reduced to a maieutics which would reveal to me only what I am already capable of, as Levinas says." Following his *Totality and Infinity,* "we might perhaps say . . . that maieutics teaches me nothing. It reveals nothing to me. It unveils only what I am already *in a position* to know *myself,* capable of knowing by *myself,* in this place where the self, the same . . . gathers *in itself* capacity and knowing, power and knowledge, and as the same, the same being-in-a-position-to, in the property of what is proper to it, in its very essentiality" (18). Derrida's point against maieutics, made via Levinas, concerns the difference between a dissimulated mode of self-instruction and one of genuine instruction by the Other.

If philosophy, theory, knowledge, can already recollect, when properly prompted, so as to produce the appropriate response "spontaneously," like an automaton, then no real teaching occurs. What occurs is a stimulus-response behavior, on the basis of mnemonic devices. The trauma of a discipline of study, of instruction in what is unknown, the inscription of the psyche with the signature of a magisterial teaching, which itself is already an open response to a prior scene of instruction, a hospitable welcoming of the Other—such a pedagogical experience of the impossible requires, enjoins, makes imperative not the powerful nonresponse of knowledge ("this, too, I must have known") but the comparatively passive response of acceptance, an ethics of yielding, but not one of total surrender (20). Between such an ethics as first philosophy and philosophy as ontology, epistemology, or maieutics, there is a gap, even an abyss, a hiatus or caesura, like an open mouth struck with the awful wonder of the scene of instruction, on the initial model of Abraham with Isaac, awaiting God's Other word. (I distinguish my allegorical use of Other from Derrida's via this difference in capitalization).

We are all in the situation of beginning by responding, because any "response comes ahead of or comes to encounter the call" (24), which itself began as and in a response. The collective or communal dimension of a teaching makes possible an ethics of hospitality and welcome, an ethics of reception: "The welcome determines the 'receiving,' the receptivity of receiving as the ethical relation" (25). The Other in discourse is to be welcomed, as in the experience of "each instant"; the Other overflows any predetermined idea on each and every student's part. As Derrida cites Levinas, "to *receive* from the other beyond the capacity of the I" (25). Reason must be thus itself *"in a position to receive"* (26), and so intermixed with, as well as differentiated from, sensibility. The aesthetic, moral, and cognitive dimensions of experience would therefore be the revisionary lineaments of a Kantian-based philosophy of critical reception.

Admittedly, the student is placed in the situation of a double bind. Derrida admits several times that such formulations as the double bind or what he calls "a sort of *oath before the letter,"* "an unconditional respect or fidelity" for and to the Other (33), are his invented formulas for the associational logic of Levinas's figures, spectral traces that Derrida fleshes out. As such, his extensions of Levinas are prosthetic elaborations that partake in "the infinite ethics of my responsibility of the other" (33). Any reading may be a sign of perjury. Thus the double bind comes in with the dilemma of either the student's nonresponse of symbolic death or the student's response that may be a perjury. The response of any student to a teaching, in the scene of instruction, may be a perjury, says Derrida, following—albeit elaborating—Levinas. But the line or border or framework definitively demarcating the difference between the pure message and its perversion cannot be, in advance, predicted, known, regulated, or prevented. And this is, for Derrida, a good thing.

Here's Derrida on the matter: "This spectral 'possibility' is not, however, the abstraction of a liminal pervertibility. It would be rather, the *impossibility* of controlling, deciding, or determining a limit, the *impossibility* of situating, by means of criteria, norms, or rules, a tenable threshold separating pervertibility from perversion" (35). Derrida's position is not, however, tantamount to a cynical postmodernization or even a revisionary neopragmatism, that the Other in discourse is what for now I can convince the ruling elites I say it is. Remember that the teaching penetrates in a manner that goes beyond the capacity of the I, in a thinking between teacher and student, in a separate space or scene delimited by, but exterior to, the already known. This scene of instruction makes for the impossibility of situating the teaching as already known for either teacher or student. This impossibility, Derrida adds, *"is necessary"*:

> It is necessary that this threshold not be at the disposal of a general knowledge or a regulated technique. It is necessary that it exceed every regulated procedure in order to open itself to what always risks being perverted (the Good, Justice, Love, Faith—and perfectibility, etc.). This is necessary, this possible hospitality to the worst is necessary so that good hospitality can have a chance, [the admittedly ambiguous] chance of letting the other come, the yes of the other no less than the yes to the other. (35)

According to Derrida's reading of the linguistic evidence, the words "hospitality," "host," "hostage," and "guest" derive from the Indo-European root word *hospes* and its variants. This allows him to follow, via Levinas's definitions of the subject as host and as hostage, the spectral play of this root word's traces, a play of traces that leaves the subject open to the Other even if that particular instance of the Other represents tyranny, exploitation, or global capital. In Derrida's reading, each subject is virtually at once host, guest, and hostage, even when at home. Of course, for his principal audience of global critics, such instruction may mean one thing, whereas for members of a "developing nation," a "host country," it may mean something very different. Derrida is aware of such differences and in fact counts on them. The formation of any structural system or totality requires the exclusion of some elements as heterogeneous. Such marginal or border elements can tell us much about the principle of composition centering the system. But every system bears the trace, the spectral imprint of what is being excluded. Whether linguistic system, nation, text, self, or culture, the system's totality gapes, like a mouth that silently articulates its present absent Other. It does not matter if that Other is hostage, past host, or future guest. All roles are interchangeable with each other in turn and in time, whose potential infinity of contingencies each moment interrupts in and as critical theory the wall-to-wall discourse of the Same. "The head of the household, the master of the house, is already a *received hôte,* already a guest in his own home" (42–43). Consequently, as Derrida goes on to add, "Hospitality thus precedes property" (45).

If Derrida is right to wager that all systems—economic, psychological, textual—function like a linguistic system, then even "the discreet gentleness of what some might nonetheless interpret as the logic of performative decrees attempting to invent a new language or a new use for old words" can serve as an ethical and a political intervention of some weight (47). What this means is that any systematic discourse "interrupts itself" (51), in order to reorder itself. At those moments, in those places, a critical revision is possible, welcome, hospitable. "One will understand nothing about hospitality if one does not understand what 'interrupting oneself' might mean, the interruption of the self by the self as other" (52). All systems end repeatedly by welcoming the Other they have excluded, if for no other reason than to replicate the act of their formation, and so to renew themselves. But in doing so, this "welcome orients, it turns the *topos* of an opening of the door and of the threshold toward the other; it offers it to the other *as* other, where the *as such* of the other slips away" from all thematic specification (54). Struck with this spectral visitation of the Other, the subject of the system renewing itself becomes the host as hostage "insofar as he is a subject put into question, obsessed (and thus besieged), persecuted, in the very place where he takes place, where, as emigrant, exile, stranger, a guest from the very beginning, he finds himself elected to or taken up by a residence before himself electing or taking up one" (55–56). Whether we are thinking of how a tradition of instruction (or of any other would-be system) is received, this structural moment of deconstructive possibility, this spectral trace of alterity, arises repeatedly and comprises, analytically speaking, a moment of openness prior to every other first moment imaginable. This a priori moment is an openness to a first critical reading of the systematic totality in question. This a priori critical reading is the specter haunting all texts, those of self or of empire. This creative moment of open response is what the resentful critic despises.

Such an a priori moment of analytic opening, which is also always already about to come, has no determinant content, is, in other words, purely formal. Which is not to say it has no spectral lineaments, outlines, or potential associations. Depending on the structure involved—text, tradition, nation-state—it has a particular orientation or point of view, a place or space or topos where the frame, the demarcations, or borderlines are burred and redoubled, in enclaves of alterity, ghettos of promise. "The trace of this visitation disjoins and *disturbs* as can happen during an unexpected, unhoped-for, or dreaded visit, expected or awaited beyond all awaiting like a messianic visit" (62). In Derrida's reading of Levinas, Sinai is the name for "the border or frontier . . . a provocation to think the passage between the ethical, the messianic eschatology, and the political at a moment in the history of humanity and of the Nation-State when the persecution of all these hostages—the foreigner, the immigrant (with or without papers), the exile, the refugee, those without a country or a state, the displaced person or populations (so many distinctions that call for careful analysis)—seems, on every continent, open to cruelty without precedent" (64). Whatever name is given for this visitation of alterity fraught with promise and terror, what "announces itself here might be called," Derrida reminds us, "a structural or *a priori* messianicity" (67). Derrida admits at this point that the "hypothesis" he is "venturing here is obviously not Levinas's, at least not in this form," but he nonetheless does so in a quest, a search and a research, that "seeks to move in his direction —perhaps to cross his path once more" (67). In such an admission, Derrida would perform here the theory of revisionary interpretation he is proposing. "Not an ahistorical messianicity, but one that belongs to a historicity without a particular and empirically determinable incarna- tion. Without revelation and without the dating of a given revelation" (67). Neither Jesus nor Marx, but a messianicity without messianism.

What Derrida doesn't mean to imply at all in saying this is that "any- thing goes" in criticism these days. To discover where the openings in a text or a tradition may be, to read the shapes of what has been excluded from the remaining figures, to become the place where text or tradition interrupts itself—all this requires scholarship, erudition, imagination, and courage. Simply pouring into the spaces of indeterminacy a pre-formed content, however laudable the political or professional aims, won't work. For long. Derrida, following Levinas, calls this hard realism "the truth of the messianic universe" (69).

If we read the text of empire, of the global economy, what do we learn?

> By means of discreet though transparent allusions, Levinas oriented our gazes toward what is happening today, not only in Israel but in Europe and in France, in Africa, America, and Asia since at least the time of the First World War and since what Hannah Arendt called *The Decline of the Nation State:* everywhere that refugees of every land, immigrants with or without citizenship, exiles or forced from their homes, whether with or without papers, from the heart of Nazi Europe to the former Yugoslavia, from the Middle East to Russia, from Zaire all the way to California, from the Church of St. Bernard to the thirteenth arrondissement in Paris, Cambodians, Armenians, Palestinians, Algerians, and so many others all for a change in the socio- and geo-political mutations, though, before this, assuming that this limit still has any pertinence in ethical conversion. (70–71)

Thanks to "the miracle of the trace" in Levinas (71), we have been prepared to receive this call of global distress, even if the figures of "Sinai" and "the Promised Land" take only spectral forms.

Precisely for this reason, however, any politics, any specific political proposal such as a state beyond all states, or in the world to come, or a United States of the Future, must be preceded by an ethical conversion, a reorientation, a turning anew toward the Other in principle and in practice, a new hospitality and welcoming via changes in international law and its enforcement. Formally speaking, this ethical reorientation, this reschooling, can only remain open and qualified:

> Now, one cannot overstate the importance of the discursive modalities that here multiply question marks, conditionals, and what might be called epochal clauses. These precautions reflect rhetorical, indeed political, caution less than they constitute ways of respecting or

greeting what remains to come—a future of which we know nothing. What comes will never belong to the order of knowledge or of fore-knowledge. (77)

Beyond the world system but *in* the world system, the spectral traces of alterity make the future openings possible.

Derrida meditates on this structural messianicity in a revealing way:

What does this [concept] imply? A difficult decision or partition: in sum, without being at peace with itself such a concept . . . returns a political *part*, it *participates* in the political even if another part of it goes beyond a certain concept of the political. The concept [of a messianic peace] exceeds itself, goes beyond its own borders, which amounts to saying that it interrupts itself or deconstructs itself so as to form a sort of enclave inside and outside of itself: "beyond/in," once again, the political interiorization of ethical or messianic transcendence. (80)

But this meditation goes further here, giving rise to the very thing it refers to, rhetorically speaking, that enclave of transcendence on either side of a border that is yet a form of interiorization, a "beyond/in" structure of the ethical with respect to the political, here performed by Derrida's "own" text:

And let us note in passing that each time this interruption of self takes place or is produced [we have been following a few examples of this for some time now] each time this delimitation of self, which might also pass for an excess or transcendence of self, is produced, each time this topological enclave affects a concept, a process of deconstruction is in progress, which is no longer a teleological process or even a simple event in the course of history. (80)

If we shift our scene of instruction from that of Derrida at work on Levinas's text to that of what is happening with the borders of many nation-states around the globe (in West Africa, the Balkans, in the South-western United States), we can witness the imperial text of the global economy suffering the phases of its own deconstruction.

For Derrida, therefore, neither empire nor anarchy comes first. The state of nature prior to empire or to empire's deconstruction is purely a formal moment in the repeated story told of a rise and fall or of a monument and its ruins. Just as text and its first reading appear together, each other's spectral double, so too all theories of an originary state of nature betray their preformed artifice. Intermixing and hybridity of elements are purely inescapable. Every nature is a prosthetic supplement too difficult to tell from any unnatural artifice. Or to put it more paradoxically, every nature is "naturally" *an-other*.

Given the formal analytic priority ("a-priority," as it were) of the ethical vis-à-vis the political, the paradoxical situation of the ethical being beyond yet in the political, what kind of subject is called to be put to work in society? Admittedly, that is, as Derrida recalls Levinas admitting, such a subjectivity would have "a phantasmatic character" (111). Here is Derrida's commentary on this confessional moment: "As host or hostage, as other, as pure alterity, a subjectivity analyzed in [Levinas's] way must be stripped of every ontological predicate. . . . And [so] the other is not reducible to its actual predicates, to what one might define or thematize about it. . . . It is naked, bared of every property, and this nudity is also its infinitely exposed vulnerability: Its skin" (111). This ontological and empirical partitioning is admittedly an abstraction, not unlike the official capitalist idea of the worker that Marx formulates, as in the passage with which we began. But this specter of pure alterity, as specter, is not nothing, nor is it so purely powerless. It is the trace of labor power under capitalism raised to the nth degree. Such "infinitely exposed vulnerability" is the skin of the worker, whatever his job or profession. And "the absence of determinable properties, of concrete predicates, of empirical visibility, is no doubt what gives to the face of the other a spectral aura" (111). The phantomization of labor in the infinite virtuality of on-line phenomenality offers, of course, intriguing parallels. Not just new subjectivities, new "bodies."

Not to ride a hobbyhorse too hard and long, I nevertheless want to quote more of Derrida's remarks on the phantom or spectral nature of the Other, where the essential work this Other does is of a dangerous ethical sort; since as Levinas says (as Derrida cites him), "it is necessary that the other be welcomed independently of his qualities."

It is necessary to welcome the other in his alterity, without waiting, and thus not to pause to recognize his real predicates. It is thus necessary, beyond all perception, to receive the other while running the risk, a risk that is always troubling, strangely troubling, like the stranger (*unheimlich*), of a hospitality offered to the guest as ghost or *Geist* or *Gast*. (111)

This dangerous risk is the risk of radical contingency. "There would be no hospitality without the chance of spectrality. But spectrality is not nothing, it exceeds, and thus deconstructs, all ontological oppositions, being and nothingness, life and death," every apparently naturalized division, textual, cultural, religious, and so on (111–12).

Spectrality is thus Derrida's name for what Levinas recognizes as the gap, abyss, or hiatus between an ungrounded and ungroundable ethics, a juridical rule between the Law and or institutional procedure to be informed by ethics. The spectral visage is the face of the Other figuratively given to this unsurpassable abyss. It is the visage of a "structural messianicity, an irrecusable and threatening promise, an eschatology without teleology, [dissociated] from every determinate messianism" (118–19). This topos without proper voice marks absolutely the time of the Other's nonresponse, one's own radical vulnerability to death in all its forms. The last word is, thereby, humanity's, the word of the global, not to say cosmic, orphan: "Let us leave the last word to Emmanuel Levinas. A last word for the orphan . . . this orphan [ever] without a father . . . : 'concern for the stranger, the widow and the orphan, a preoccupation with the other person'" (122–23). The traditional imperative of the Rabbis— renewed once again.

Each one is such an orphan, each one announces a messiah, the one before and the one to come still again, each one who has been. . . . *Adieu, A-dieu*—Indeed!

• • •

A magisterial teaching . . . the new skin of the worker . . . spectral messiahs: these figures both drawn from and elaborated beyond what Derrida says Levinas says constitute the formal a priori of an ethics before any politics, a first ethics as first philosophy. Only ethics can inform the field to be ordered by a rule of law. No world order can arise and sustain itself without the discipline of ethics. If Derrida and Foucault agree with each other (and Kant and Nietzsche) on anything, it is on this. Political, economic, and cultural economies of identity and difference presuppose the invention of self-discipline whether for an individual, a people, or a concept. The ethical moment, as Derrida articulates it here, is, however, a paradoxically unconditioned, unpredictable, contingent formality, a violent formality to be sure, and one every bit as authoritative and enigmatic as Abraham's ironic gift of prophetic speech when he tells Isaac that the Lord Himself will provide the sacrifice.[8]

To put it another way, the ethical moment is provocatively anachronic and productively anarchic. It disciplines but is itself not subject to discipline, which is one reason why, either explicitly or in disguise, the phantasmatic metafigure of a god will appear at some point in the narration of any text. Once Derrida introduces the thematics of spectrality in his text, the ghost of God, the Judeo-Christian Divine in his/her/its negative theological formless form, cannot be far behind (or ahead?): "[The chance of spectrality] can give [donner], give order(s) [ordonner] and give pardon [pardonner], and it can also not do so like God beyond essence. God without being, God uncontaminated by being—is this not the most rigorous definition of the Face of the Wholly Other? But is this not then an apprehension that is as spectral as it is spiritual?" (112). This rhetoric can be read but never (fully) erased.

The problem with Michael Hardt and Antonio Negri's *Empire* is that their titled master figure, Empire, functions like a god they do not recognize as such but nonetheless wholly believe in.[9] Consider, for one example, how they present their summary of judgment on nongovernmental organizations, those humanitarian international groups and institutions such as Amnesty International, Oxfam, and Médicians sans Frontieres that monitor and provide much-needed services around the world, especially during major crises. Moral intervention of this sort in Hardt and Negri's neo-Marxist global point of view, seen from the vantage point of their rhetorical platform in space, their god-term Empire, is nothing more than "a frontline force of imperial intervention" (36). By bringing the global communications industry into the latest crisis spot via their humanitarian activities and their critiques, such NGOs, according to Hardt and Negri, give a face not only to suffering but to the Enemy of Order that Empire must intervene to eliminate, thereby providing an ethical and imaginative basis for the imperial right of intervention. It may be true that in any particular case NGOs have functioned in this fashion, but to assimilate their critical and humanitarian role universally to the strategic operations of Empire is to allow Empire to assume, too easily, a metaphysical, even divine status. But this is precisely what the authors' more general statements appear to do. For example, here is what they say about the globalized communications industry:

> The imperial machine lives by producing a context of equilibria and/ or reducing complexities, pretending to put forward a project of universal citizenship and toward this end intensifying the effectiveness of its intervention over every element of the communicative relationship, all the while dissolving identity and history in a completely postmodernist fashion. (34)

According to Hardt and Negri, Empire is repeatedly called into existence by the widespread and intense perception of crisis, a humanitarian disaster of traumatic, virtually catastrophic proportions, occasioned primarily by political conflict. Such crisis evokes repeatedly, albeit in a piecemeal manner at first, the invention and elaboration of the military and administrative, judicial and social, mechanisms of Empire. For Hardt and Negri, Empire is simultaneously an invention of the crisis moment and the protagonist of a global allegory of domination. This is why Empire, they note early in their book, is a concept and a reality born dying, that is, a "topos" of "construction" and "decline and fall," all at the same time: "The becoming of Empire is actually realized on the bases of the same conditions that characterize its decadence and decline" (20). Although they warn at the beginning of their book against thinking of Empire as a figure for either a spontaneously generated consequence of the global free market, the unintended consequence of its worldwide invisible hand at work, or "a single power and a single center of rationality transcendent to global forces, guiding the various phases of historical development according to its conscious and all-seeing plan, something like a conspiracy theory of globalization" (13), what they say throughout their book sounds strangely like both of these things simultaneously.

Not only do they ritually practice a rhetoric of their god-term, Empire, but they also recapitulate, albeit in secular, neo-Marxist form, the myths of messianicity, but with a particular messianism in mind:

> Allow us, in conclusion, one final analogy that refers to the birth of Christianity in Europe and its expansion during the decline of

the Roman Empire. In this process an enormous potential of subjectivity was constructed and consolidated in terms of the prophecy of the world to come, a chiliastic project. This new subjectivity offers an obsolete alternative to the spirit of imperial right new ontological basis. From this perspective, Empire . . . was challenged in its totality by a completely different ethical and ontological axis. In the same way, today, given that the limits and unresolvable problem of the new imperial right are fixed, theory and practice can go beyond them, finding once again an ontological basis of antagonism—within Empire, but also against and beyond Empire, at the same level of totality. (21)

Well, whether the limits of Empire are really fixed in the aporia of an elite global class of administrators of financial and symbolic capital versus a multitude of what they call "slaves, reels, and barbarians" is something remaining, of course, to be seen (19). But the rest of this statement reads to me like the manic euphoria following a protected period of apparently inconsolable mourning, and thus as a sign of such melancholia continued by other means.

Whether or not the reality of Empire is born and dies in the repeated evocation and provocation of crisis, clearly Empire as the paradoxically doomed antagonist (or scapegoat) of Hardt and Negri's tale has been so produced and reproduced by their crisis, as "the book was begun well after the end of the Persian Gulf War and completed well before the beginning of the war in Kosovo" (xvii). As they remind us, "the reader should thus situate the argument at the midpoint between those two signal events in the construction of Empire" (xvii). Like Nietzsche's *Thus Spake Zarathustra* or Heidegger's *Contributions to Philosophy (From Enowning)*, *Empire* appears to me to be the mythopoetic theory that arises, Paul de Man once taught us all, from the "blindness-and-insight" structure of a self-deconstructing text's allegory of its own reading: or as Derrida put it in *Adieu*, "This interruption of the self by the self, if such a thing is possible, can or must be taken up by thought: this is ethical discourse—and it is also, as the limit of thematization [and regulation], hospitality. Is not hospitality an interruption of the self" (51). The problem is that Hardt and Negri, unlike Derrida, take their own story literally and so blindly.

But what could Hardt and Negri be professionally in mourning for? Besides the passing of a certain sort of Marxism, however problematically and divisively institutionalized in the world until 1989, what could it be that is so disturbing to their—and all of our—imaginary? With this question in mind, especially with respect to Michael Hardt's U.S. professional situation, I return to where I began, namely, to the deprofessionalization of American professions, as part of the routine operations of late capitalism as it incorporates the professions, with their comparatively autonomous structures of governance and their comparatively generous amount of free time disposable on an individual basis, into the communications, service, and caring industries. Such a proletarianization, however far it might go, causes a tremor if not an earthquake, especially for (but clearly not limited to) American professionals, perhaps, who are first- or at most second-generation university-educated academic intellectuals. The professional status, with all its real perks, of such intellectuals here and globally is dissolving even as I write this, and the figures, parables, fantasies, and allegories of globalization, with their diverse valences and scenes of instruction, are the compensating—and decompensating—consequences for the critical culture of the global class in its unstable and uncertain transformation, its superanimated sense of itself and of the coming future.

If I am right that the transference to the global point of view is occurring not only as the latest form of a theoretical modernization that outmodes as it fashions, deforms as it forms subjectivities, but also as a democratizing deprofessionalization, an antielitism for the new service-oriented class of intellectual proletarians wholly dependent on global capital for its technological (and emotional) investments and training, its virtual toolbox of the latest equipment, then a simultaneous abjection of traditional professionalism is happening. But rather than mount a lamentable jeremiad against this situation, I would prefer not to do so. Instead, following Derrida's lead in *The Gift of Death* as he analyzes Kierkegaard's vision of the Abraham and Isaac story (in *Fear and Trembling*) and ingeniously relates that story's irony to that in "Bartleby the Scrivener" (and as I would like to do with respect to the ironies in some of Henry James's works), I would prefer to read and so to disseminate without return or reserve Derrida on Kierkegaard on Abraham on the story of God's dramatic irony, as in the following (and concluding) passages:

Abraham says nothing, but his last words, those that respond to Isaac's question, have been recorded: "God himself will provide the lamb for the holocaust my son" . . . Abraham's total presence [is] in that word. First and foremost, he does not say anything, and in that form he says what he has to say. His response to Isaac is in the form of irony, for it is always irony when I say something and still do not say anything. . . . [But] Abraham doesn't speak in figures, fables, parables, metaphors, ellipses, or enigmas. His irony is meta-rhetorical. If he knew what was going to happen, . . . then he would have been right to have recourse to enigmatic language. But the problem is precisely that he doesn't know. Not that that makes him hesitate however. His nonknowledge doesn't in any way suspend his own decision, which remains resolute. The knight of faith must not hesitate. He accepts his responsibility by heading off towards the absolute request of the other, beyond knowledge. He decides but his absolute decision is neither guided nor controlled by knowledge. Such, in effect, is the paradoxical condition of every decision: it cannot be deduced from a form of knowledge of which it would simply be the effect, conclusion, or explication. It structurally breaches knowledge and is thus destined to nonmanifestation; a decision is, in the end, always secret. It remains secret [like the gift, like death, like the gift of death], in the very instant of its performance, and how can the concept of decision be dissociated from this figure of the instant? From the stigma of its punctuality?[10]

In Abraham's response to his crisis, we discover the absolutely imperative need of the Absolute Other, beyond the libidinally invested family or the domestic economies of the household, beyond the promised glories of peoples and nations, beyond any already known and so regulating order of strategic machination, however imperial or cosmic—Yahweh is a jealous God and acts (unlike the Christian deity) according to no human contingency scenario (who could predict a Messiah or a beloved Son of *this* God?)—and so, we discover, too, I believe, a magisterial teaching in a scene of instruction without limits, in a story about stories "monstrous yet banal" (75). Just the opposite of everything Empire and imperial, in fact most like an Empire Burlesque, perhaps, caught on film by David Lynch!

8

Ghostwork: An Uncanny

Prospect for New Americanists

● ●

"By interrupting filiation. Easier said than done."[1] This remark, extracted from Derrida's *Specters of Marx,* identifies the problematic of tradition precisely. As we know, "becoming other" than oneself, one's family, one's profession, one's culture, by interrupting but not destroying all filiation, constitutes the heir's dilemma. Derrida's comment remarks on the motivation for Marx's savage critique of Max Stirner in *The German Ideology.* It is to avoid what, according to Derrida, Marx sees as Stirner's ironic fate of being at once the docile replica and unwittingly self-mocking dummy of the Hegelian discourse he utters. To be Hegelian when one seeks to be oneself and vice versa is to be an unwitting travesty of Hegel and oneself alike: such is, for Derrida's Marx, Stirner's cautionary lot. And so Derrida's Marx must interrupt his own filiation with Hegel by scapegoating Stirner, even as Stirner inspires in Marx some of his most Hegelian moves and tropes. Or so Derrida formulates this scene of instruction. Must Oedipal ghosts always haunt any such scene, with only the names changed to momentarily identify the guilty?

There are more reasons than critical self-consciousness, of course, why "interrupting filiation," which is often a mixed blessing anyway, can in fact occur, whether desired or not. As Said demonstrates in his memoir *Out of Place,* non-Euro-American peoples often suffer displacement out of their natal cultures and become isolated in, and alienated by, a new culture, which "interrupts filiation" with a vengeance.[2] The waves of immigration, the hard life of migratory laborers, the vicissitudes of exile, the fate of being a political or an ethnic or a religious refugee—these are the catastrophic forms of "interrupting filiation." Within the sphere of more settled capitalist free-market conditions, there is another, more rationalized form as well. One may aspire to better one's circumstances, material or otherwise. And so when opportunity arises and chance proves lucky, one may suffer willingly, we say, a painful displacement in class, as well as in geographic locale and cultural status. And one's children may later bear the entire brunt of guilt that divides all such ambivalent inheritors from their old and new lives alike.

In such a situation (it is Said's, for one example), the immediate culture of the family becomes a discipline—Hegel calls it a "terrible" discipline—to be practiced and resisted. Hegel also calls the state of mind that results "the unhappy consciousness."[3] In its self-divisions and desire for recognition by, and reconciliation with, some larger, more powerful reality, he sees the limits of the human condition itself. However that may be, Marx lays specific blame for the rationalized, class-bound form of such "unhappy consciousness" and its material foundations on capitalism.[4]

Let us say, if only for argument's sake, that Hegel and Marx are both basically right. What are the consequences for contemporary intellectual culture? Said's memoir gives us one answer to such a formidable question. In his time and place, the canonical literature of his masters, the British, became the medium in which the divisions of the unhappy consciousness and its desire for authoritative recognition were openly and provisionally suspended: "Reading *Hamlet* [with my mother] as an affirmation of my status in her eyes, not as someone devalued which I had become in mine, was one of the great moments in my childhood. We were two voices to each other, two happily allied spirits in [one] language" (52). Not their own language, however, not "originally." I have quoted this passage both for its striking pathos and for its poignant sense of fragility. It is this consequence of interrupting filiation, the fragility of self and of culture that results, that increasingly haunts Said, and indeed all of us as the processes of globalization proceed apace. Such fragility, Said notes, makes for "an ersatz life" (268).

This sense of life as unreal receives one of its finest expressions and analyses in Freud's fear about the final end of his career. Freud's fear can thus provide us with a useful guide to the critic's "ghostwork."

What is this "ghostwork" to which I refer? It is what Derrida, at the opening of *Specters of Marx*, suggests that Shakespeare's *Hamlet* does best, that is, as many cultural critics have noted, give us the sense of "time being out of joint," of nature being unnatural, of reality being unreal. For Derrida, as for Said here, such unreality is a sign of the ceaseless circulation, with little or no recuperation, renewal, or repair, of radical displacements—psychological, social, cultural, whatever. By offering Freud as my guide to the unconscious imaginations of this by now general or global economy of modern displacement, I am also offering, via this revisionary portrait of a—or perhaps, for better and worse, the—representative modern intellectual, my current forecast of the potentially uncanny fate of critical culture in global America.

Not "Too Good to Be True":
A Late Freudian Fantasy of Self-Education

"A Disturbance of Memory on the Acropolis" is the title of a letter that Freud sends to Romain Rolland on the occasion of the author's seventieth birthday, on January 29, 1936.[5] Freud knows Rolland principally through their correspondence and his literary work, having met him only once, in 1924. Freud alludes to Rolland several times in his own works, most memorably by name at the opening of *Civilization and Its Discontents* (1930).

There Freud confesses to the absence of the oceanic feeling. This is the feeling of oneness with the cosmos, which, Rolland had speculated in a letter to Freud, may be at the origin of religious belief. Freud prefers his own less specialized, more commonplace theory: that infantile helplessness and subsequent longing for the father's protection against feelings of powerlessness are the realistic and emotional sources for the psychology of faith.

In "A Disturbance of Memory," the issue does not seem to be such intellectual disputes. Rather, Freud's letter itself is the issue, because it is an elaborately self-regarding, and so puzzlingly narcissistic, birthday message. To put it bluntly, to whom, or to what, is Freud's communication at this time in homage?

To be sure, Freud begins his letter with a warning to Rolland that it is "the gift of an impoverished creature" (239). The eighty-year-old Freud means that despite his best intentions, and lacking the creative power of his younger days, he can now produce little, even when pressed by circumstances, that is not evidently about himself. Nonetheless Freud intends this honesty about his excessive self-concern to mirror in a small way the love of, and devotion to, the truth, and to speaking one's mind, that Rolland, despite the European situation owing to the Nazis, still practices.

Even if we do appreciate this warning, because twelve of the letter's remaining thirteen paragraphs are still taken up with a renewal of Freud's own self-analysis, the letter gives us pause. All the details of this self-analysis make Freud's conclusion, where he finally recalls Rolland as his auditor, a surprise. It jolts the reader into wonder at the bad taste of singing not the praises of the birthday boy but the anxious obsessions of oneself. Why does Freud do this? By analyzing Freud's specific performance in the letter, I hope to answer this question and to indicate how we should read his textual performances more generally.

The substance of Freud's self-analysis in this case concerns a curious incident that occurs in 1904 when he and his younger brother, Alexander, go on holiday. Every year, Freud and his brother take a couple of weeks in late August or early September to visit Italy, or some other southern Mediterranean country, for a vacation by the sea. In 1904, because of business dealings, Freud's brother can spare only one week. So the Freud boys decide to visit Corfu via Trieste. While in Trieste, they have a meeting with one of Alexander's older business associates. He advises them against Corfu—because of the late-summer heat—and instead proposes, as cooler and more convenient, a trip to Athens.

Although they are convinced that this alternative will not work out, because of the suddenness and presumed red tape—surely they will need passports to go to Greece—the Freud boys act, nevertheless, as if they believe they can and will arrive in Athens, even as they feel irritable and depressed, restlessly wandering the streets of Trieste in preparation for their trip.

When, the next day, Freud finds himself on the Acropolis, he experiences an uncanny sensation. He feels as if he were saying to himself, "So all of this does exist just as I was told when a boy in school" (241). Freud is shocked at such a feeling because he cannot remember ever disbelieving in the reality of the Acropolis and its surrounding Athenian landscape.

To put it another way, as Freud himself says, he feels split into two selves. One self reacts to the reality of the Acropolis and the Parthenon the way a skeptic might respond should he ever see "the form of the Lock Ness Monster stranded on the lake shore" (241). The other self reacts in turn to this strange reaction, unable to equate impossible fantasy with any historical reality he has personally experienced.

Why should Freud act as if he had ever repudiated the reality of a place he always wished to see, precisely when he is finally seeing it? Why, to use technical terms he introduces here, should Freud derealize the then current scene of 1904 by displacing onto his even earlier boyhood past a skeptical projection of this sort? Of course, when he was a boy, Freud both longed to be in Athens, standing where he is standing in 1904, and, given the relative poverty of his family's circumstances then and the apparent lack of possibilities for his own later success, firmly believed he could never do so. How does this actual self-skepticism get changed into a derealizing skepticism about the world, depersonalizing the youthful Freud in the process by revising his childhood past out of existence? In short, as Freud himself underscores, in the years since this incident, he has always wanted to know how he came to have this *"psychotic"* disturbance of memory on the Acropolis (241, italics mine). Freud shares this "abnormal" episode with Alexander, of course, and it has, as a shared event, recurrently puzzled him even more than it otherwise would have, especially, he says, in recent years, precisely because it was a moment of *social* psychosis. Now, this occasion of providing a birthday message for Rolland has finally provoked a solution from him for this folie à deux.

Freud's solution to this riddle is *filial piety*. Out of guilt for having surpassed their father in appreciation of the great world and in worldly success, the Freud boys in 1904 feel depressed and discouraged at Trieste, and incredulous and confused in Athens. Whether or not such unconsciously guilt-ridden filial piety so definitively explains the incident on the Acropolis, can it somehow account for the disturbing nature of this birthday letter?

If we ask ourselves, "What role is Rolland assigned in Freud's psychodrama?" we may get the beginnings of some answers to our inquiry. In the second paragraph of the birthday letter, Freud discovers the coincidence of Rolland being just like his brother, ten years his junior. This fortuitous detail is then dropped, remaining unread by Freud. It is left there in the letter, however, apparently to be read by a perspicacious mind. Is Rolland just the kind of celebrated literary brother Freud always wished his consistently unnamed businessman brother to have been? Is Freud thus derealizing his own life and depersonalizing his brother, with a vengeance here, to more fully fantasize the "dear friend" his brother could never be?

I don't really think so. This would be too suspiciously sophisticated, and so not aesthetically appropriate, not in keeping with the traditional idea of filial piety. Where else in this letter, besides for Freud and his brother, does filial piety come in? The only explicit instance occurs when Freud refers, almost reverentially, to his own daughter, Anna, and to her forthcoming book *The Ego and the Mechanisms of Defence,* which would be published later in 1936: "An investigation is at this moment being carried on close at hand which is devoted to the study of these methods of defence: my daughter, the child analyst, is writing a book upon them" (245). We could read this remark, in light of the role unconscious guilt plays in the formation of self-inhibiting acts of filial piety, as a telling admission, a defensive confession of paternal responsibility, as well as a desired sign of reassuring childlike devotion. But who is playing the parts of father and child analyst?

There are, however, more implicit patriarchal figurations of authority in the text. Freud, for example, invokes along the way the last Moorish leader in fifteenth-century Spain and the romantic era's most titanic figure, Napoleon. The first serves as a derealizing patriarch who fails to see reality, treating the bad news of his last stronghold's fall as *non arrivée* and executing the messenger who brought it (246). The second serves as a depersonalizing emperor at, Freud mistakenly claims, his self-coronation in Notre Dame. The occasion Freud misremembers is, in fact, Napoleon's assumption of the Iron Crown of Lombardy in Milan. Napoleon supposedly comments at the time to his eldest brother, "What would *Monsieur notre Péré* have said if he could have lived to see my glory?" (247). Freud's figure of Napoleon thus demonstrates the sublime opposite of filial piety—filial enmity.

More subtly, Freud addresses Rolland in the opening and closing paragraphs in the ambivalent tonalities of both abject child and father: "All that I can find to offer you is the gift of an impoverished creature, who has 'seen better days'" (239). And later: "And now you will no longer wonder that the recollection of this incident on the Acropolis should have troubled me so often since I myself have grown old and stand in need of forbearance and can travel no more" (248). First and second childhoods hover alike over these framing remarks.

Actually, however, as the imaginative performance of this unconventional birthday message strongly suggests to me, the younger Freud of 1904 plays father to the older man in 1936 by providing him with matter to (in)form, a dark truth to illuminate for Rolland, on this birthday occasion, to bear fraternal witness to. Similarly, the older Freud of pre-Holocaust Europe makes his filial bows to all his authority figures, whatever their names, including, bizarrely, both the forty-eight-year-old psychotic figure he cuts on the Acropolis, "a generation earlier" (243), and the latter-day child analyst, safe keeper of the father's creative invention, psychoanalysis.

The commonplace phenomena to which Freud originally compares this entire experience of unconscious revisionary memory are things "too good to be true" and the overly ambitious people who are soon enough "wrecked by their own success" (242). Perhaps we could revise Freud a bit here and say that what he is now discovering is how imaginatively to become "a successful wreck," something that in the final analysis is certainly *not* "too good to be true" *for him:* "What better way of assuring oneself, on the point on which one is mistaken, than to persuade the other of the truth of what one says?"[6]

As we have just seen, Freud and his brother's experience of "unreality" when visiting, at long last, the Acropolis is but one sign of the fragility of any "new life." In Freud's case, we see how behind the facade of the revolutionary psychiatrist lies the still pious little boy to whom, for a while, the limits of his father's more conventional life can become, once again, Freud's (and Alexander's) own. Interrupting filiation in this case is a two-edged sword. Feeling out of place on the Parthenon because the Parthenon, not oneself, feels unreal is a strange but still understandable form of projection. That Freud and his brother share this experience suggests the larger social dimensions of this psychotic transference. Interrupting filiation with this "mad" aspect of cultural guilt would be, indeed, a desirable thing. And affiliating with some other aspect of that culture, or with an aspect of the larger culture (Shakespeare, say), or with aspects of some other culture (past or present) altogether, could even prove, at the last, therapeutic.

To affiliate thus, one must become open to the new influence, assume a semihelpless position, a so-called feminine passivity or receptiveness. This, anyway, is Freud's argument in his late work. As such, it anticipates Derrida's ethics of hospitality.

On Freud's Femininity

Freud's 1937 essay "Analysis Terminable and Interminable" is his definitive statement on the limits of psychoanalytic knowledge.[7] He concludes the essay when he reaches what he believes to be psychological, and perhaps even biological, "bedrock" (39). This bedrock is the strange imperative, on the part of both sexes, to repudiate femininity (39), that is, the assumption of a passive position vis-à-vis another person. All the essay's argumentative strands about the various resistances to successfully shortening or even completing an analysis are knotted together in this curious and gloomy conclusion. As such, it can serve as the perfect focal point for a discussion of Freud's femininity. By this phrase, I mean both the final conception and the particular textual manifestation of femininity in this essay.

Freud, of course, is the first major thinker in Western culture to argue, as his *Three Essays on the Theory of Sexuality* (1905) puts it, that femininity (like masculinity) is a certain set of behaviors, that is, a constitutive performance, a contingent aesthetic construction with a long history. Because I am a critical reader of such imaginative acts in texts, I am interested in Freud's femininity. Moreover, I believe that critical reading requires one to understand such aesthetic phenomena in order to discover what a theorist—indeed, what any writer—is embodying. Beyond the conscious strategies of a writer's rhetoric, the reader senses the obscure shapes of half-formed feelings and fantasies.

The original German title of Freud's essay is "Die Endliche und die Unendliche Analyse," which translates literally into English as "The Finite and the Infinite Analysis." This essay appears simultaneously in English and German psychoanalytic periodicals, with Freud's blessing on the

English title. David Zimmerman and A. L. Bento Mostardeiro, in their essay "On Teaching 'Analysis Terminable and Interminable,' " give a fair summary of the essay's main topics: "the origin of the neuroses, the duration of analysis and its termination, the constitutional strength of the drives, the possibility of patients' avoiding further psychic conflict, the alterations of ego structures and the selections of defense mechanisms, the origins of variations in ego structure, the personality of the analyst, and the repudiation [by both sexes] of . . . femininity."[8] Freud, as Zimmerman and Mostardeiro stress, returns repeatedly in the essay to the resistances to a cure.

Freud singles out, for major emphasis, the purely mechanical quantitative factor, that is, the important role that the sheer amount of energy animating the resistances plays in an analysis. He claims, in fact, that such blocking energy ultimately derives from the internalized aggression, the (self-)destructive tendency of the death drive.

Most curious, to me, in this context is the way the essay ends. The greatest of the resistances to analytic cure is the resistance to the analyst's authority, which appears as transference phenomena in the course of analysis. Freud's point is that there is a progressively stronger repudiation of femininity; in other words, this is the repudiation of all dependency on, and passivity toward, the analyst on the part of the analysand, especially, so it seems, when both are male. Such aggression is directed against the adoption of the passive or feminine position and in elementary forms arises as castration anxiety and penis envy. It also, however, inhibits the analysand's acceptance of the analyst's or anyone's influence in more complex intellectual and emotional ways.

This will to power, this "masculine protest" against passivity and dependency, derives (as Alfred Adler, Freud's erstwhile disciple, also argues) from an innate aggressiveness. The sharp difference between their views lies in the fact that Freud interprets this aggressiveness as radically destructive and self-destructive, that is, as an intimate derivative of what he terms in his late works the pure culture of the death drive. The more pragmatic Adler, for his part, sees this resistance as a potentially useful mode of a generally positive human demand for autonomy. What Freud names in his final dualism of the drives as "the repudiation of femininity" is, in other words, the negative face of masculinist individuality, one of the masks of Thanatos, that mythical opponent of Eros, who is supposed to be the builder of societies. The "great riddle of sex" in death and death in sex is, for Freud, the unending "mystery" of such conflict (39–40).

In the light—or the darkness—of this rather nihilistic conclusion, a good deal could be said about Freud's alleged misogyny, his reputed homophobia, his self-evidently "conservative" political views, his cultural pessimism, and his often extravagantly fantastic theoretical speculations. Right now, however, I want to consider why none of the professional readers of this late essay, or even high-powered theorists of reading such as Paul Ricoeur, Jacques Derrida, and Richard Rorty, mentions that most of this essay's pivotal sixth section, in which Freud for the first time treats in some detail the alterations of the ego, the distortions in the "I" that the ego's own defense mechanisms cause and that analysis would correct, centers on what appears to be a surprisingly extensive digression, as if it were a "free association" on Freud's part. This is Freud's elaborate and enthusiastic celebration of Empedocles, the pre-Socratic philosopher. So important does he consider this portrayal, by the way, that Freud publishes it separately in *Almanach der Psychoanalyse 1938*.[9]

It is here in this essay that Freud, in detail, discusses the topic of the death drive and its formative role in creating aggressive and self-destructive impulses alike. He remarks on the lack of support for this idea among his followers but then expresses pleasure when, reading a recent book on Empedocles, he found a precedent for his own dualistic theory of Eros and Thanatos, desire and destructiveness. So glad is Freud to discover an ally for his own theory that he gives up his claim to its originality in favor of Empedocles' greater genius.

Φιλία (love) and νεῖκος (strife), Freud happily explains, are what Empedocles calls Eros and Thanatos. Freud also explains, in the spirit of festive recognition, that Empedocles' theory is impersonal, mechanical, and cosmic in its dualism, whereas Freud's theory is also impersonal and mechanical, but it can be only a speculatively biological construction. Freud eagerly concedes, however, that psychologically speaking, this difference between the two theories probably doesn't finally matter that much. The antagonists of love and strife, sex and death, both solder together and defuse, in an unending series of conflicts, all the various activities of the human mind. In this ironically circuitous but imaginatively exuberant manner, Freud concludes this rather startling section of the essay by returning to his initial point: that all resistances to a cure, and especially the resistance to any efficient streamlining of analysis, reveal the death drive. The course of treatment—technically, therapeutically, and theoretically—must therefore remain uncertain and open-ended, poised unstably between being finite (or terminable) and being infinite (or interminable). Only in this way may the habit of self-destructive behavior be broken.

Now that I have rehearsed these strange and uncanny passages in Freud's essay, I want to raise two intertwined questions: What is the specific content of this speculative principle of destructiveness? And how does the celebration of Empedocles relate to this content? The principle of destructiveness and aggression, the death drive, manifests itself in the clinical setting with particular force, according to Freud, as the virtually biological imperative to resist the passive position vis-à-vis the analyst. That is, the repudiation of femininity, on the part of the analysand, with respect to accepting the analyst's authority, constitutes for Freud the fundamental reality of the death drive in the transference relationship. If we turn the tables on Freud and invoke the analyst's countertransference, or change any other variables such as the gender of one or both members of the analytic couple, it would still not alter this apparently necessary structure of contingencies one bit. The species-specific imperative appears to be that one must simply oppose being subsumed by another. Resistance to such subordination, Freud notes, can manifest itself as open hostility or passive aggression.

In the end, however, the repudiation of femininity turns out to be, Freud suddenly claims, the bad-faith alibi of motivated inertia. "The decisive thing," he concludes, "remains that the resistance [to taking the feminine position, for both sexes] prevents any change from taking place —that everything stays as it was" (39). To bring his ultimate, surprising point home, Freud provides a footnote, in which he reminds the reader that nonneurotic men and women often assume eagerly the passive position vis-à-vis another person in their sexual fantasies, in their sexual acts, and in their personal relationships to parents or other authority figures. Nonetheless Freud gives this drive to inertia a final dynamic and universalizing twist by saying, in effect, that no one wants to owe anyone else his or her redemption, which Freud realizes is what the idea of an analytic cure must feel like.

Generally speaking, by 1937, Freud has become jaundiced about human beings. And it is understandable. After suffering twenty-three operations for mouth and jaw cancer, he clearly is dying from the disease. His creation, psychoanalysis, has been taken over by Nazis in Berlin and suppressed elsewhere in the Third Reich. His books have been publicly burned, and his press has been shut down. Even his children's lives have been threatened by SS thugs. To say the least, Freud has earned the right to be jaundiced, I should think. Let us, however, also take him literally at his word and stipulate, for the sake of argument, that the specific content of the principle of destructiveness is the specialized meaning of the repudiation of femininity, that is, the neurotic's resistance to assuming a passive or dependent position vis-à-vis another, and so a defensive maneuver on the part of the desire for continued or renewed inertia—in short, the dynamic avoidance of a cure.

Given this depressing conclusion, how does Freud's paean to Empedocles function? Is it a pure digression? Or does Empedocles serve as "a big gun" on Freud's side in the debates over the death drive? Or as Freud recounts Empedocles' leap into the volcano, does this sublime vision feed his modern heir's self-destructive fantasies? Is Freud's new love for Empedocles, like his earlier confessed love for Leonardo da Vinci, a homosocial cover for renewed hero worship or for the temptation now to lapse into an apocalyptic inertia?

In a real sense, the answers to these overdetermined questions could all be given in the affirmative, but that does not really matter, because the ultimate meaning of Freud's singing the praises of Empedocles now should be clear. Freud is here bowing to the authority of another—and another male—not only by conceding Empedocles' original genius but also by confessing his self-suspicion that, even before reading the book on Empedocles, in formulating his final dualistic theory of the drives, he may have been guilty of "cryptomnesia" (32). In other words, what he took for a "new creation" of his own may have been the forgotten memory of an earlier reading from his college days (32). Far from the repudiation of femininity in any sense being exemplified here, then, Freud may in fact be teaching us what femininity particularly ought to mean: the power to give love to the figure of another. In short, Freud here practices what he preaches by renewing his own student position.

Such capacity for accepting the authority of another without resentment and with enthusiasm, this magnanimous generosity of critical appreciation, as performed nobly in Freud's passionate reading of Empedocles, makes possible the personal dimension of civilization: that openly private communication of a tradition of feeling between author and reader, master and student, past and present. Such rare acts of cultural transmission depend, in the end, on an interpretive charity, or Φιλία, which refuses the hostile νεῖκος of life. Empedocles, who was hailed by colleagues as a god for his power to heal others, leaps into a volcano when he cannot heal himself. Freud, facing the Nazis' Holocaust, holds out a dark hand here, I like to imagine, to this one of his Gentile fathers.

As we see, one must adopt the receptive, more passive position vis-à-vis the recognizing authority figure, with whom affiliation is to be consummated, and that means following Freud's lead in "Analysis Terminable and Interminable," as he relearns the lesson of affiliation, prophetically, as it were, before he can pass on to his daughter his psychoanalytic heritage. Although the established codes of the psychiatric discipline take the patriarchal surgeon as their model of practice, Freud violates their silent injunctions and unreal exemplar to practice the genius of the amateur.[10]

This is not to suggest that New Americanists will learn from the unreal scenes of global America lessons that must make them creatively receptive to all the traces of filiation emerging as possible futures out of the past and its archives, including, especially, these scenes from Freud's final years. What I hope it does suggest, however, is that they can willingly suspend the rote rejection of any of those filiations of their cultures that *seizes* them. I hope, in other words, that they remain fundamentally "un-American" in their activities in the sense that Freud in the next section gives to that term, that is, incompletely professionalized and imperfectly displaced, split and yet resourceful in their promising divisions.

Freud at Work: The Genius of the Amateur

In *Back to Freud's Texts,* Ilse Grubrich-Simitis writes: "Freud at *work*—Freud observing, listening, feeling surprised and stimulated, reading, learning, associating and fantasizing, concluding and conceiving, noting, drafting, rejecting, making fair copies, busying himself with his manuscripts, correct proofs, editing, and publishing."[11] I take this vision of Freud and his work as my guide to this chapter's next section on productive narcissism.

The first time Freud discusses the new concept of narcissism occurs in *Leonardo da Vinci and a Memory of His Childhood* (1910). The boys that Leonardo loves are, Freud says, "revivals of himself in childhood—boys whom he loves in the way in which his mother loved *him* when he was a child."[12] This is the case because Leonardo "remains unconsciously fixated to the [memory] image of his mother" (55), in the way she loved him. "He finds the objects of his love," Freud concludes, "along the path of narcissism, as we say" (55).

Whether Freud is right in identifying this new concept of narcissism as the key to understanding one type of homoerotic development is not my concern now. My point in beginning with narcissism is to underscore the idea that, in making the choice of a love object, along narcissistic lines, one is choosing not simply a mirror image of oneself. One is also choosing the memory image of the manner or style in which one was loved by the original caretaker, and it is that dynamic form of loving agency that is revived in later substitute figures. By choosing the path of narcissism, then, a person also chooses to allude repeatedly, via the virtually allegorical figures, to the unconscious love play of an earlier, almost mythical time that can only be reconstructed and performed consciously again and yet again, later.

Ironically enough, Freud explicitly makes his own narcissistic object choice at the end of this text as he confesses that his highly speculative interpretation of Leonardo, the Renaissance genius combining both artistic creator and ever-curious scientist, may suggest he has "merely written a psycho-analytic novel" (96). This may be so, Freud admits, because like "others I have succumbed to the attraction of this great and mysterious man, in whose nature one seems to detect powerful instinctual passions which can nevertheless only express themselves in so remarkably subdued a manner" (97). In other words, Leonardo has become, via this interpretive act, Freud's boy—and vice versa, of course.

But does this man that Leonardo's mother and her love play with her son also simulates become the reconstructed object and imaginative pattern of subjective agency marking Freud himself? Not exactly. Freud closes his text, his would-be psychoanalytic novel, precisely with a romantic vision of the mother figure and her way with all of us, which the story of Leonardo leads Freud to reanimate:

> May one not take objection to the findings of an enquiry which ascribes to the accidental circumstances of his parental constellation so decisive an influence on a person's fate—which, for example, makes Leonardo's fate depend on his illegitimate birth and on the barrenness of his first step-mother Donna Albiera? I think one has no right to do so. If one considers chance to be unworthy of determining our fate, it is simply a relapse into the pious view of the Universe which Leonardo himself was way on the way to overcoming when he wrote that the sun does not move. . . . We naturally feel hurt that a just God and a kindly providence do not protect us better from such influences during the most defenceless period of our lives. At the same time we are all too ready to forget that in fact everything to do with our life is chance, from our origin out of the meeting of spermatozoon and ovum onwards—chance which nevertheless has a share in the law and necessity of nature, and which merely lacks any connection with our wishes and illusions. The apportioning of the determining factors of our life between the "necessities" of our constitution and the "chances" of our childhood may still be uncertain in detail; but in general it is no longer possible to doubt the importance of the first years of our childhood. We all still show too little respect for Nature which (in the obscure words of Leonardo which recall Hamlet's lines) "is full of countless causes ["ragioni"] that never enter experience." Every one of us human beings corresponds to one of the countless experiments in which these "ragioni" of nature force their way into experience. (99–100)

God the Father and his providential order give way to Nature and her repeated chance experiments; likewise, Freud the systematic theorist of the centrality and universality of the Oedipus complex gives way to the creative muse of Nature and her "ragioni," her ever-experimental works.

In the largest sense, then, the title of this section—"Freud at Work: The Genius of the Amateur"—alludes to work of this sort, that is, to the spirit of intellectual love play and its contingency experiments. Maybe this is what R. P. Blackmur meant, in "The Critic's Job of Work" (1935), when he defined "criticism as the formal discourse of the amateur."

There is another conception of intellectual work, of course, and that is the idea that calls itself professionalism. In *Mental Ills and Bodily Cures: Psychiatric Treatment in the First Half of the Twentieth Century* (1997), Joel Braslow, a professor in the departments of psychiatry and history at the University of California and a staff psychiatrist at a California Veterans Affairs Medical Center, recounts an early childhood memory of his father, a surgeon, telling of his surgical feats over dinner one night. "One of his favorite stories," Braslow recalls, "recounted Walter Freeman teaching him how to perform the new [Nobel Prize–winning] psychiatric treatment of 'transorbital lobotomy' " on a woman patient at Camarillo State Hospital in the 1950s: "One takes a thing that looks just like an ice pick and positions it right above the eye. Using a hammer, the pick is pounded into the skull. Then ping!!! the bone breaks enough to let the ice pick slide easily into the patient's brain. You then swing the pick back and forth, cutting the nerves that connect to the front of the brain. That's it."[13]

I strike this stark contrast between the spirit of intellectual love play performed by "the Genius of the Amateur," by Freud at work, and the physical violence practiced with such gusto by the good professional Mr. Braslow, not because I like to stage a mock debate between scarecrows, or because I plan to climax my essay later by subtly conflating psychoanalytic and psychiatric practices (the talking cure is nothing like a lobotomy); rather, what I want to reveal is the ethical difference it makes when one accepts the rule of contingency and does not zealously impose on others the latest technique of professional mastery. I would say that neither Freud nor Braslow's father avoids the full range of critical judgment, even as they may designate the possible extremes of intellectual work, hypothetically at least, in theory.

Moreover, by opposing the figure of "the good professional" and "the imaginative amateur," we can envision how the former one inspires the revival of the latter, repeatedly. Now, simply because there is this allegorical exchange, however, does not necessarily mean that the difference between Freud and the senior Mr. Braslow at work matters little. Given these two kinds of "intellectual love play," naturally I prefer Freud's more chivalrous head game to Braslow's modern American "go-getterism." In fact, in *The Question of Lay Analysis* (1926), which includes his most antiprofessional remarks, Freud states this same preference and in the process envisions his life and career as a latter-day version of the circuitous journey of the romantics, with "a theoretical career" as the first and the final object of his personal intellectual quest:

> After forty-one years of medical activity, my self-knowledge tells me that I have never really been a doctor in the proper sense. I became a doctor though being compelled to deviate from my original purpose; the triumph of my life lies in my having, after a long and roundabout journey, found my way back to my earliest path. I have no knowledge of having had any craving in my early childhood to help suffering humanity. My innate sadistic disposition was not a very strong one, so that I had no need to develop this one of its derivatives. Nor did I ever play the "doctor game": my infantile curiosity evidently chose other paths. In my youth I felt an overpowering need to understand something of the riddles of the world in which we live and perhaps even to contribute something to their solution. The most hopeful means of achieving this end seemed to be to enroll myself in the medical faculty; but even after that I experimented—unsuccessfully—with zoology and chemistry, till at least, under the influence of Brucke, who carried more weight with me than anyone else in my whole life. I settled down to physiology, though in those days it was too narrowly restricted to histology. By that time I had already passed all my medical examinations; but I took no interest in anything to do with medicine till the teacher whom I so deeply respected warned me that in view of my impoverished material circumstances I could not possibly take a theoretical career. Thus I passed from the histology of the nervous system to neuropathology and then, prompted by fresh influences, I began to be concerned with the neuroses. I scarcely think, however, that my lack of a genuine medical temperament has done much damage to my patients. For it is not greatly to the advantage of patients if their doctor's therapeutic interest has too marked an emotional emphasis. They are best helped if he carries out his task coolly and keeping as close as possible to the rules.[14]

I want to pause over this long passage to make clear what I think Freud is and is not saying. It may appear at first that the antiprofessionalism of the opening section has turned by the close into a kind of hyper- or higher professionalism. The emphasis on coolness and sticking closely to the rules suggests that apparent contradiction. But what Freud is actually proposing is that one must keep one's distance, a kind of internalized distance, from too great an emotional involvement with one's profession and its latest developments. This internalized or psychic aesthetic distance allows one to follow the rules of the new science, psychoanalysis, which is to all appearances more a theoretical adventure, for analyst and patient alike, than an efficient therapeutic treatment. The basic rules of psychoanalysis are to free-associate without censorship during the analytic sessions and to agree to learn to interpret the unconscious by following the analyst's example of evenly balanced attention and tactful interpretation.

As it turns out, however, the most important rule—for Freud—is altogether different: it is the one that directs the interpreter along the path of contingencies in the spirit of "the good listener" who usually knows what time it is: "You must wait for the right moment at which you can communicate your interpretation to the patient with some prospect of success. . . . That is a question of tact, which can become more refined with experience." However, "you will be making a bad mistake if, in an effort, perhaps, at shortening the analysis, you throw your interpretations at the patient's head as soon as you have found them. . . . [Instead] wait till [the patient] has come so near to the repressed material" that there are "only a few more steps to take under the lead of the interpretation you propose" (48). The increasingly invasive bodily treatments of mental ills devised or perfected by American psychiatry in this century— hydrotherapy, malarial therapy, electroshock therapy, sterilization, lobotomy, and clitoridectomy—lead inevitably to the latest psychotropic drug therapies, according to a mass-market economic logic of the most bang for the least bucks.

Even American psychiatrists who have adopted psychoanalysis also champion the therapeutic discipline of medical "expediency" (177). Gaining material results at the hands of real professionals matters more to them than their achieving theoretical knowledge in the more uncertain context of lay analysis. In Freud's view, would-be analysts should have a broad liberal arts or humanistic education, as opposed to a purely scientific specialization. However, as manuscript variants of the partially suppressed 1927 postscript to The Question of Lay Analysis make clear, there are also several other reasons why he thinks of the Americans as the incarnation of a cynically expedient professionalism the "skeptical European" must abhor. Freud continues:

> There may be various [other] reasons for this [American professional pragmatism, doing what, at the moment, appears to work] professionally: the huge size of the country, the lack of an all-embracing organization beyond the boundaries of a city, and in addition the Americans' horror of authority, their inclination to assert personal independence in the few fields which are not yet occupied by the implacable pressure of public opinion. The same American trait [this horror of real authority], transferred from political life into scientific activity, is shown in the analytical group itself by the provision that the person of the president must change annually, so that no real leadership can be formed, essential as it would surely be in such difficult matters. . . . [Even their self-advertized] openmindedness [looks suspect]. . . . The skeptical European cannot suppress the suspicion that this [liberal] interest never penetrates very deeply, and that much reluctance and inability to make judgments lies concealed behind this [apparent] impartiality.[15]

(By the way, we are indebted for this manuscript discovery to Ilse Grubrich-Simitis and her book *Back to Freud's Texts: Making Silent Documents Speak* [1996].) Freud goes on in this vein, excoriating the lack of general education and intellectual receptiveness to be found in modern American life. Freud's America is thus the antithesis of his Leonardo. Or should I put it that his Leonardo is no all-American boy?

The most important reason Freud gives, however, for his un-American activities in mounting this diatribe against the expedient professionalism of the Americans is "that the American"—notice the adoption of the mythic singular now—"has no time" (179). This is because "time is money" (179), naturally, but more significantly, it is because for the American, it is numbers, magnitudes, sublime magnitudes—infinitely large or infinitesimally small—that matter the most. And so the American becomes blind to the contingent beauties of the winding interpretive path. In American professions, Freud says, we are instead "accustomed to the fact that every practical need creates for itself the corresponding ideology" (179). Finally, Freud concludes, there is a rationalized, professionalized, modernized sense of time that he identifies as "American time." It is incommensurate with the time of analysis. This incommensurability, Freud claims, arises because "psychic processes between the conscious and the unconscious have their own temporal conditions, which fit ill with the American demand" for immediate application of theory en masse. To Freud, then, the "American superego seems greatly to mitigate its severity toward the ego where the interests of earning money are concerned" (179–80). Putting psychotic patients on the assembly line every expedient moment to get their transorbital lobotomies—ping! ping!—is a haunting image that Freud's romantic visionary satire arouses in any chronic neurotic. Tact or transorbital lobotomy—such a choice could scare one back from the edge of psychosis, perhaps. But to be more serious now, what is the other sense of time defining what Freud identifies as "the right moment" of interpretive analysis?

"The Relation of the Poet to Day-Dreaming" (1908) suggests the beginnings of an answer. The productions of "imaginative activity"—Freud includes in this formulation dreams, daydreams, creative works, and their inspired, allusive interpretations—are not "stereotyped or unalterable."[16] "On the contrary," he says, "they fit themselves into the subject's shifting impressions of life, change with every change in [the] situation, and receive from every fresh active impression what might be called a 'date-mark'" (57). In this highly imaginative context, "the relation of phantasy to time is . . . very important" (57). Hovering between "the three moments of time which our ideation involves," "mental work is linked to some current impression, some provoking occasion in the present" able to raise up "one of the subject's major wishes into consciousness" (57). This mental work then harks back, Freud says, to "a memory of an earlier" unconscious or repressed experience, "(usually an infantile one) in which this wish was fulfilled" somehow (57). This mental work or imaginative activity now "creates a situation in relation to the future which represents the fulfillment of the wish" (57). Both the present occasion arousing the infantile wish and the memory of past fulfillment—real or imagined—imprint their temporally specific traces on the projected contingent vision of the future. "The thread of the wish" makes a text of time, but not on the model of a committee report; rather, on the literary model of an infinite romance like Freud's quest for a theoretical career discussed earlier. "Past, present and future are [thus] strung together. . . . the wish makes use of an occasion in the present to construct, on the

pattern of the past, a picture of the future" (57, 58). I say "infinite romance" because "the pattern of the past" to which Freud refers is precisely what is always at issue. It is always being contingently interpreted,
provisionally reconstructed, ironically judged as either real or imagined
or both at once, according to a self-revising Freud's intellectual genius of
the amateur at work on and in a perennially literal avant-garde love play.

The point of this essay is not, however, to recommend a critical version of what Thomas Mann in "Freud and the Future" (1936) calls the
necessary "infantilism" of the literary creator, who to create again must
learn to revel once more in the ritual imitation of a chosen mentor's
many expressions of agency, practices ranging the gamut from intimate
tracings of textual lineaments to the sublime heights of a revisionary
imagination in action, just as at the opening of this essay, when Freud
remade Leonardo into his own boy.[17] No, my point in closing is not an
echo of Mann's. Rather, it is to repeat, I suppose, after Freud to be sure, to
my colleagues in American literary studies, what Freud in *The Question of
Lay Analysis* recalls as "a common salutation when two friends meet or
part" in "our Alpine lands: Take your time" (170).

What happens, however, when "the field" in which such "passionate"
affiliation should occur is itself configured and indeed programmed in
such ways that one can only turn from it in disgust? What then? It is my
contention, following Lentricchia's lead, that this is the present and foreseeable situation of literary study. The medium of representation in the
discipline is now formed by, and made to function in, conformity with
the conventions—the lame multiculturalist codes—of what I am calling
"global America," that burlesque version of Empire. The case of Paul
de Man demonstrates this contention all too clearly.

The Aesthetics of the Real in Paul de Man

As Lindsay Waters traces the career of Paul de Man, we can see how the
revelations about his wartime journalism, made in 1987, four years after
his death, continue to haunt the mind of anyone who stills pays attention
to de Man's work.[18] I make this blunt observation because I was shocked to
find that in a recent comprehensive course book, *Literary Theory: An Anthology*, by Julia Rivkin and Michael Ryan, de Man is not even mentioned,
nor is there any argument made why this is so.[19] Given the "Left" politics of

the editors, I can only suppose the worst. De Man has been "repressed" because of the discovery that as a twenty-two-year-old journalist he wrote for the Brussels daily paper *Le Soir* what Waters calls, at the opening of his essay, "one unpardonable essay on 4 March 1941." The young de Man's newspaper column argues that if the Jews "were removed from Europe and settled elsewhere," the great tradition of modern European literature "would not be harmed" (135). Waters rightly aligns de Man's anti-Semitic judgment with the chauvinistic totalitarian politics and totalizing aesthetics of the various dictatorships of the Right and the Left rising to world power in the 1930s. A "radical" identity politics assumes an aesthetic "purity" of national character, even as it prescribes a political structure of efficient interlocking hierarchies in the state apparatus.

This aesthetic state is designed to incorporate a body politic that must rigorously exclude as abject materials all those "others" who do not prove "fit." The rationalizing and mechanized apparatus of instrumental reason inspires the romantic dream of an organic totality purged of the "unfit." In fact, these antithetical others are necessary provocations to the compensatory invention of such a dream. All aspects of this aesthetic ideology, Waters correctly argues, later drew de Man's relentless critique, which was not so much a practice of deconstruction as it was a process of "disarticulation," a literal or material uncoupling—conducted on the page, as it were—of the discourse of aesthetic ideology.[20]

In the name of what, however, does Waters argue that de Man "disarticulated" traditional aesthetics? A "true aesthetics" is his answer (134). But what can this fine phrase of de Man's mean? One way of seeing it is to say that de Man would undo the compensatory dream of organic totality so as to lay bare the underlying mindless mechanism at work producing the dream vision in the first place. Behind the Wizard of Oz's curtain was, for de Man, only the linguistic and rhetorical machinery of aesthetic illusion, including the illusion of the imperial or transcendental subject. No all-powerful master of wizardry was ever to be found.

Another way of putting this (and it is the way de Man's readings of Kant and Wordsworth, as Waters presents them, encourages us to put it) is to say that the human mind's immersion in the medium of its own invention, the figural play of language, is the spirit's abjection by and in a "nature" or "matter" whose mechanical operations the literary text truthfully produces. In the shifting figures a feeling makes in us, the trembling pathos of this true aesthetics lies.

> When de Man says that the aesthetic experience cannot be conceptualized and that what happens to humans in that experience is a matter of feeling and not cognition, some suspect him of preaching a despairing nihilism, but he is being quite flatfootedly precise. Having the aesthetic experience means travelling the passage out of the zone of cognition into the zone of power . . . which is why the aesthetic is always something politicians are trying to control and turn into an ideology of the aesthetic. For most of human history the politicians have been successful in their efforts to harness art to their purposes. There is no reason to suspect that we are exempt from this history, but de Man's call for a change—echoing as it does that of Kant and Benjamin—ought to encourage us to challenge this ideology. (156)

The spirit's abjection by nature, the father's abjection in matter, de Man's disarticulation of the aesthetic ideology into "a true aesthetics"—all are parallel processes of critique.

I want to make further sense of what for simplicity's sake I'll term this mode of critique, "the father's abjection." This phrase signals a turnabout of the phallic mother's typical abjection. The imaginary figure of the phallic mother, the mirroring object of the infant subject's desired omnipotence, dissolves in the symbolic displacements of the father's repeated "No's." This psychoanalytic "law" of early development gets reversed in Waters's reading of de Man. Such an ironic turnabout gives me "the aesthetic of the real" of my title. And I believe that it is in light of one of Lacan's rereadings of Freud that the figure of de Man Waters invokes here can best be clarified.

Lacan is fascinated by Freud's account of the father's dream of the burning child that opens "The Psychology of Dream-Processes," chapter 7 of *The Interpretation of Dreams* (1899).[21] One could say that in Seminar 11, published as *The Four Fundamental Concepts of Psychoanalysis* (1973), Lacan is haunted by this dream. It is a dream that invites an imaginary reader's curious gaze, and its being dreamed and redreamed exemplifies the unconscious at work, with all the latter's repetitions, transference phenomena, and driven impulses.

Freud recalls how a female patient, having heard an account of the dream at a lecture on dreams, proceeds "to 're-dream' it"; that is, as Freud phrases it, "to repeat some of its elements in a dream of her own, so that, by taking it over in this way, she might express her agreement with it on one particular point" (*ID*, 652). Here we have in the proverbial nutshell Lacan's four fundamental concepts of psychoanalysis: the unconscious, repetition, the transference, and the drive. The dream, which the lecturer himself had heard about before he had redreamed it, is the dream of another man, a father who has just lost his child to fever. (This lecturer is not identified by Freud.)

The father asks an old man to keep watch over the child's body, with tall candles all around it, while the father fitfully sleeps. In this troubled sleep, the father dreams that the child *"was standing by his bed"*; catching him by the arm, the child whispers *"reproachfully: 'Father, don't you see I'm burning?'"* (*ID*, 652). The father wakes up, notices "a bright glare of light" coming from the next room, and hurries into it to find that the watchman has fallen asleep and that a lighted candle has dropped onto the wrappings of one of the beloved child's arms, burning it badly (*ID*, 652).

Freud uses this dream to demonstrate the devious ways of wish fulfillment in dreams. The father, to prolong his desire to see his beloved child alive, must pay for it. He suffers the dream's bitter reproach to secure the child one more moment of imaginary life. Both symbolic guilt and real damage are the consequences (*ID*, 653).

I don't want to belabor Lacan's rereading of the dream. To do a complete analysis would require, I suspect, a reading of Lacan's entire career. Suffice it to say Lacan notices two basic things about Freud's account of the dream.[22] First, Freud's female patient, as his correspondence with Fliess makes clear, is a lesbian who disputes Freud's wish-fulfillment theory of dreams. She had adduced this dream of the dead child making this bitter reproach to prove her point, only to have it ingeniously turned against her to prove Freud's, since the dead child moves and speaks in the dream as if still alive, warning the father about the threat of fire. And secondly, Lacan notices right off that Freud is nearly finished his explanation of how this ironic dream's desired reproach nonetheless proves his theory before he notes in passing, via the reflexive personal pronoun "he himself," that the child in question is the father's beloved son: "The dead child behaved in the dream like a living one: he himself warned his father" (ID, 653).

The Oedipal pattern of revisionary interpretation becomes, in Freud's case, clear at this point. Freud must discredit not so much the tradition or "chain" of this dream's repeated significance (ID, 653) as the would-be phallic mother's claim, in the form of the lesbian patient's critique of Freud's theory, to authority over the production of meaning. Freud withholds from the reader knowledge of the child's gender, and he only discloses it in passing, because this repressed remark reveals the driven nature of Freud's desire for theoretical supremacy. Freud wants always to occupy the authoritative position of the father, which he can only do by repeatedly abjecting the mother figure. Unconscious rivalry with the father gives way here to the actual assumption of the symbolic position to abject the overreaching female, to put her silently back in her place under the patriarchy's recontinued sway. This Oedipal pattern of reading, Waters refuses.

But Lacan's rereading of the dream, even in the case of these few details I have isolated, abjects the father not *under* the name of Freud but *in* the name of Freud. That is, the subject position of authority in Western culture is itself abjected, according to the logic of a psychoanalytic interpretation put into play by Freud himself:

> If Freud, amazed, sees in this [dream] the confirmation of his theory of desire, it is certainly a sign that the dream is not a phantasy fulfilling a wish. For it is not that, in the dream, he persuades himself that the son is still alive. But the terrible vision of the dead son taking the father by the arm designates a beyond that makes itself heard in the dream. Desire manifests itself in the dream by the loss expressed in an image at the most cruel point of the object. It is only in the dream that this truly unique encounter can occur. Only a rite, an endlessly repeated act, can commemorate this not very memorable encounter—for no one can say what the death of a death is, except the father *qua* father, that is to say, no conscious being.[23]

Lacan rereads the dream of the dead son as Freud's amazed stare at the father's knowledge of the son's spectral nature, the real beyond both the specular imaginary of fantasy and the symbolic function of fatherhood. In the dream, what startles the father awake as he hears the son's warning reproach is not the son's continued life but rather his apparition as a ghost in the ritual place of such visitations, the site of dreams. Waters, to reanimate de Man, practices this other form of critical reading.

The rereading by Lacan is the secret unconscious wish animating, spectrally speaking, Freud's reading. As Lacan hears it in his revisionary fashion, Freud's abjection is to recognize, in the dream's vision, the abjection of fatherhood as an institution, as if Freud were Lacan's ideal or imaginary reader. The subjects Freud and Lacan now dissolve into the unconscious drives of language's repeated play of figural transferences.

Waters has accomplished in his reading of de Man a similar desired abjection. Like Freud, de Man already understands the knowledge of any son's ghostliness, particularly in relation to the patriarchal institutions of authority. As Waters shows, de Man's critique of aesthetic ideology, like the chain of a repeated dream, ceaselessly because mechanically would undo those institutions even more definitively than any topical political critique ever could do. The pathos of a true aesthetics, the feeling of becoming a figure, of being figural, of dissolving into mere words, is precisely the reality of the father's abjection by the nature of his own rhetoric as it dissipates and reforms, ritually, in the commemorative play of language. Beyond the empty imaginary aesthetics of reflexive identification in Lacan may indeed lie the severe symbolic displacements of figures of authority; but beyond this in de Man lies the vertiginous madness of words. What Waters, citing his authority from *Aesthetic Ideology*, rightly claims makes for "the complete loss of the symbolic" (155), a loss of all the names of the father seriatim, I now would call simply "the aesthetics of the real." And by this term I mean to invoke neither any current professional imaginary or cultural ideology, nor any symbolic order based on patriarchy, but an emergent moment of future promise ever ready to appear in the interstices of impossible boundary zones, unpredictable and unprogrammatic.

De Man's Specter

It should come as no surprise, however, that Paul de Man's criticism has been discovered to contain psychoanalytic resonances. John Guillory, in *Cultural Capital,* has even proposed that this strain in de Man's discourse, which remained unremarked or unthematized by him, may be, perversely enough, the skeleton key to de Man's work and influence.[24] As we have just seen, I believe that pursuing analogues between de Man's deconstruction and Freud's (and Lacan's) analysis can prove to be suggestive, expansive for the mind. Deep down, however, I have always suspected that de Man's attitude toward any of the critical idioms he puts into play was at once too distant and offhand to sustain a secret passion.[25] As de Man says, concerning Kant's argument from the *Critique of Judgment* about the true sublime, such "a reduction from symbolic feeling to mere words, such a loss of pathos of theatricality, and of self-reflection, is not easy to interpret and very easy to misjudge."[26] It is in just such an apathetic spirit that earlier in this same essay, "Kant's Materialism," de Man refers to Foucault's "typical" misunderstanding of Kant's transcendental explication of critical judgment as a displaced and barely disguised anthropological empiricism officially banished from Kant's discourse. "Is this . . . [alleged] return of the empirical [a return] in the sense in which we speak today of the return of the repressed?" (121).

"The return of the repressed," so casually yet pointedly deployed here, is the psychoanalytic insight par excellence, and it is now common coin. Can we determine, as Guillory thinks, what de Man's investments, professional and personal, actually were in such apparently disinterestedly phrased critical formulas? And what does it matter if we think we can?

I think we can determine that de Man's intention toward the inherited critical topoi he sets in motion was not obviously passionate, a matter of identification, nor was it, however, entirely instrumental. His investment in them was pragmatic, strategic, intelligent, and exploratory despite his great foreknowledge of all such figures. As in his foregoing use of "the return of the repressed," all his critical usages were both decorous and dutiful. Passions of a common kind, for a critic, were counterproductive, unnecessary because pathological, as Kant said. If I am right, de Man can instruct us in a key lesson about the critical vocation.

Let us return to the argument of the late essay "Kant's Materialism" just to see what we can see. This essay was originally given as a talk in 1981 at the MLA Convention in New York City at a session entitled "Kant and the Problem of the Aesthetic." At the time, as at nearly all times since its inception in the eighteenth century, the critical category of "the aesthetic" raises itself as a problem especially after Kant, because "the aesthetic" keeps getting itself interpreted by its partisans and enemies alike as an amoral, apolitical, noncognitive dimension or realm, the mind's playground, and precisely not as a forum for serious business or worldly negotiations of any sort.

De Man focuses his argument first on sections 27 to 29 of the *Critique of Judgment*, which principally concern the sublime, and then on an earlier text, Kant's *Observations on the Sentiments of the Beautiful and the Sublime* (1764). The aesthetic as a critical category represents either the serene harmony or dynamic dissonance of differentially interrelated conventional signs, whether words, colors, notes, or spaces. As such, de Man's Kant sees that "the aesthetic is the architectonic" (126), by which de Man, following Kant, means the total picture of the world, or the cosmos. It is thus the aesthetic that makes possible the cosmopolitan perspective of the Kant of his influential late essays on international order and perpetual peace. In support of this view, de Man cites a notorious passage from the *Critique of Judgment* that Kant had first used some twenty-six years earlier in the *Observations*. I cite it now in full for our convenience:

> If we call sublime the sight of a star-studded sky, we must not base this judgment on a notion of the stars as worlds inhabited by rational beings, in which the luminous points are their suns, moving purposefully and for their benefit. We must instead consider the sky as we see it [*wie man ihn sieht*], as a wide vault that contains everything. This is the only way to conceive of the sublime as the source of pure aesthetic judgment. The same is true of the sea: we must not look upon the ocean with the enriching knowledge that makes us conceive it as, for example, the vast habitat of nautical animals, or as the water supply from which, by evaporation and for the benefit of the land, clouds are being seeded, or even as an element that keeps continents apart, yet enables communication between them. All these are teleological judgments. Instead, one must see the ocean as poets do, as the eye seems to perceive it [*nach dem was der Augenshein veigt*], as a transparent mirror when it is at peace, circumscribed only by the sky, and when it is in motion, as an abyss that threatens to swallow everything. (126)

De Man's reading of this Kantian passage stresses its architectonic aspects: "Kant's architectonic vision here appears in its present form," de Man begins. "The imagery of vault, mirror, and abyss are conventional markers delimiting what is left in these scenes of starry night and tempestuous sea once all the anthropological designs and motives have been withdrawn from them. We are left with what 'the eye sees,' 'as we see it,' which is a seeing 'as the poets do' " (126). This aesthetic vision contains no human knowledge, conceives no instrumental economy. Instead, *it sees* the cosmos, "as the poets do."

This aesthetic vision can easily be mistaken for the romantic sublime, especially in a Wordsworthian mode, but de Man is careful to distinguish it from that mode and its immediate avatars in romantic poetry:

> Neither is the vision a sensation, a primary or secondary understanding in Locke's sense: the eye, left to itself, entirely ignores understanding; it only notices appearance (it is *Augenschein*) without any awareness of a dichotomy between illusions and reality—a dichotomy which belongs to teleological and not to aesthetic judgment. In other words, the transformation of nature into a building, the transformation of sky and ocean into vault and floor, is not a trope. The passage is entirely devoid of any substitutive exchange, of any negotiated economy, between nature and mind; it is free of any facing or defacing of the national world. Kant is as remote as possible from Wordsworth's mind looking "upon the speaking *face* of earth and heaven"; or of Baudelaire in "Le voyage berçant notre infini sur le fini des mers"; it is in no way possible to think of this starry gaze as an address or an apostrophe. The dynamics of the sublime mark the moment when the infinite is frozen into the materiality of stone, when no pathos, anxiety, or sympathy is conceivable; it is, indeed, the moment of a-pathos, or apathy, as the complete loss of the symbolic. (127)

This aesthetic vision, itself a vision of the aesthetic, is the true aesthetic moment, the model for its inevitable caricatures and travesties, its (self-) parodies or burlesques, in later proponents and critics. The aesthetic, in other words, is the observer's apocalyptically arrested or suspended judgment, knowledge of which can equally provide endless reflection or gratuitous, precipitous action. It is the material moment of mind, the virgin interval, a spectral latency, in which nothing appears or happens, as such, with fleeting glimpses of the necessary, purely conventional forms of our real experience of the world, seen by the fugitive cosmic eye, as the poets can best do:

> The language of the poets therefore in no way partakes of mimesis, reflection, or even perception, in the sense which would allow a link between sense experience and understanding, between perception and apperception. Realism postulates a phenomenalism of experience which is here being denied or ignored. Kant's looking at the world just as one sees it ("wie man ihn sieht") is an absolute, radical formalism that entertains no notions of reference or semiosis. Yet it is this entirely a-referential, a-phenomenal, a-pathetic formalism that will win out in the battle among affects and find access to the moral world of practical reason, practical law, and rational politics. To parody Kant's stylistic procedure of dictionary definition: the radical formalism that animates aesthetic judgment in the dynamics of the sublime is what is called materialism. Theoreticians of literature who fear they may have deserted or betrayed the world by being too formalistic are worrying about the wrong thing: in the spirit of Kant's third *Critique,* they were not nearly formalistic enough (128).

Paul de Man's specter, then, is this radical formalism as the ironic—indeed, virtually parodic—basis of all materialisms: a sort of sublime admiration, as in the guillotine.

Global America

Of course, de Man's Kantian-based "radical formalism" as the mother of all materialisms is itself a figure of speech, catachresis, the (self-)abuse of a figure to the point of (self-)parody, travesty, even burlesque. My figure for the world system of economic production and cultural representation, "global America," is a similarly catachrestic figure. Returning to late Freud, viewed in the light cast by de Man read as Lacan might read him, will enable us to see what advantage such figurative play grants us. But first I want to show that my figure of global America, that specter, nonetheless lives.

As I was sitting on a plane waiting for it to take off—I had the window seat—I noticed that the woman next to me was still busy reading her photocopies of a conference program. She had the program book with her, but she had obviously made the copies so that she could gloss them more easily on her tray table. The conference was about managerial strategies for getting one's "teams" to feel more a part of the team project, whatever it might be, and so boost morale and, hopefully, productivity. The language of the program read like that of any specialized discipline within the professional-managerial class. It was, at times, nearly impenetrably jargonistic to me, and where readable, all too easy to construe as unwitting self-parody.

I was nevertheless intrigued. One of my favorite habits of childhood and of later life, even now, is to imagine what it would be like doing someone else's work. But here was a chance to find out from the person herself, and so I did.

What "Karen" (let's call her that) did was to be an offshore project manager for the Gulf of Mexico operations of Texaco. She had recently been promoted into this leadership position, in fact, as she herself said, because of a recent scandal concerning Texaco's "glass ceiling" for women and people of color. Karen was attending the conference to hone her managerial skills and to visit the historic sites in Philadelphia, the host city for the conference. We were now flying from Pittsburgh; she had been flying originally from New Orleans.

As we talked, I realized that I didn't understand at first exactly what she did, but then after I told her I was a critical theorist and chair of Temple University's English Department (this was a few years ago), I found that her ignorance of what I did matched my own about her job. Soon, however, I did understand what she did.

When an oil company wants to locate any of its operations anywhere in the world, including the United States, it must negotiate many things with its "host" locale. (This is how she phrased it.) It was not only a matter of jobs. In Indonesia, for example, the government and the local people require that before Texaco starts a drilling or refinery operation, it must guarantee to build new, bigger roads; new housing around the facility (and not just for its own workers); and parks, playgrounds, community centers, and cultural and entertainment facilities. In sum, wherever Texaco goes, a little slice of the American dream must come too.

This is a mixed blessing, to say the least. On the one hand, it is surely better in several obvious ways, not the least of which involves a question of self-respect, that the locality hosting its own proposed exploitation by a so-called global power get some goodies out of the deal. On the other hand, however, the local culture will then have to incorporate yet another site of alien—and alienating—American imperial culture. Such "developmental" incorporation can be compared to that which a mutilated body part must suffer when a prosthetic device of some kind is surgically implanted and fitted. But this is only an analogy, which may lead us astray. Better simply to say that what Texaco brings with it will stay around long after its operations move on, and so this little slice of the American dream, for better or worse, will remain as a scar, a mark of an ersatz and ever mobile life that will produce at least one foreseeable consequence: the linkage in the popular mind, correct or not, among the processes of globalization, modernization, and Americanization, all of which, it is assumed, must produce a more homogeneous international culture of representation. Global America is the specter haunting the backs of our minds.

So what is a would-be "culture critic" to do given this prospect of global America occupying in a materially formative, even sublime fashion what Derrida refers to as the position of Khōra; that is, the place or role in the world system that administers representational inscription in all senses of the word. It is as if on all our "mystic writing pads" or "powerbooks," on each of our screens, of virtual reality and ersatz life, of simulacral spectrality, we can see somewhere emblazoned the words "Made in USA."

Naturally, such a specter, like de Man's or Kant's, may be haunting only me and a few others. But this sort of specter, that of global America, is not entirely unlike other similar specters encountered in the past by would-be critics of our culture. This is why I want to return to late Freud now to see how he dealt in the end with the biggest specter of all time, the Judeo-Christian God, precisely in the problematic context of "interrupting filiation," of receiving and not receiving a tradition. For that is, I believe, the true subject of Freud's *Moses and Monotheism*, and, indeed, of all his late work.

Because I have already discussed in chapter 5 the radically different takes one can have on this late work of Freud's, as represented by Derrida in *Archive Fever: A Freudian Impression* and Yosef Hayim Yerushalmi in *Freud's Moses: Judaism Terminable and Interminable,* I will not rehearse that discussion here, except to note, as a brief reminder, the following remarks. Derrida concludes by accusing Yerushalmi of what Marx, according to Derrida, accuses Stirner of, and this failure is also, by the way, not surprisingly, what Yerushalmi accuses Freud of: the bad faith and unhappy consciousness of the belated heir who would aspire to rival and even to overcome and yet also still fulfill the predecessor's, the imaginary father's, the tradition's—God's—"will." That such "a will" testifies to itself, bears witness of and against itself, as being fantasmatically singular but in fact is ever becoming differentially plural, like Lacan's letter insisting in the unconscious chain of signifiers performing impersonally and anonymously our subjectivities for us—such is the all-too-clearly inescapable horizon haunting our lives.

In *Moses and Monotheism,* there are plenty of ghosts to go around. They abound. As we read section II(c) of the book's long third essay, which recapitulates in a rather clumsy manner the argument of the first two essays (Freud includes two prefaces, one before each main section of the third essay to acknowledge and to explain the essay's flaws), we should note how it contains many turns on the figure of "spirit":

> At some point between [the development of speech and the end of matriarchy], there was another [moment] which shows the most affinity to what we are investigating in the history of religion. Human beings found themselves obliged in general to recognise "intellectual" [*geistige*] forces—forces, that is, which cannot be grasped by the senses (particularly by the sight) but which none the less produced undoubted and indeed extremely powerful effects. If we may rely upon the evidence of language, it was movement of the air that provided the prototype of intellectuality [*Geistigkeit*], for intellect [*Geist*] derives its name from a breath of wind—animus, "spiritus," and the Hebrew "ruach" (breath). This too led to the discovery of the mind [*Seele* (soul)] as that of the intellectual [*geistigen*] principle in individual human beings. Observations found the movement of air once again in men's breathing, which ceases when they die. To this day a dying man "breathes out his spirit" [*Seele*]. Now, however, the world of spirits [*geistenich*] lay open to men. They were prepared to attribute the soul

[*Seele*] which they had discovered in themselves to everything in Nature. The whole world was animate [*beseelt*]; and science, which came so much later, had plenty to do in divesting part of the world of its soul once more; indeed it has not completed that task even today.[27]

So many specters, so little time! (What Freud rehearses here is the development of the humanization of the cosmos that de Man shows Kant blowing away with his architectonic aesthetic vision.) There are so many ghosts in this passage that James Strachey, the volume's translator, adds a footnote (note 4) to announce to the reader just how "untranslatable" Freud can be: "It will have been seen that his last paragraph is untranslatable. '*Geist*' means not only 'intellect' but 'spirit' and 'soul.' '*Seele*' means 'soul,' 'spirit' and 'mind'" (114). I want to tease forth only one of them: *Geisterreich*. Strachey translates this word as "world of spirits," but "spirit realm" would be more literal. Laying open this realm of spirits, this kingdom, this culture of intellectual representation for and in thought, for and in transcendental (in Kant's sense) thinking, is the advance in intellectuality that, according to Freud, the special character of the Jewish people, as molded by Moses, accomplished for all humanity. Consequently, Freud concludes, envy and resentment of such an ambivalently charged development must mark the future lot of the Jews, whose God, in Genesis, designs the cosmos according to an impersonal architectonic vision.

The Global Moses

Moses and Monotheism (Der Mann Moses Und Die Monotheistische Religion: Drei Abhandlungen [The Man Moses and the Monotheistic Religion: Three Essays]) finally appears as a book in 1939, in German and English editions. Started in the early 1930s (perhaps as late as 1934), it was revised entirely twice over. Its composition was repeatedly interrupted by most of the twenty-three serious operations Freud suffered after 1923 to keep his mouth and jaw cancer at bay. Freud's efforts on the book were also harassed by the growing Nazi threats to psychoanalysis as a medical practice and publishing venture. And they were intimately intertwined with the personal crises concerning himself, his family, and his chosen intellectual heir, his daughter Anna. Freud himself was riven by doubts and anxieties about both the avowed argument of the book and what its performance at that historical moment may provoke. Freud's argument would take away from his own people the Jews their greatest hero, Moses, by making him an Egyptian, and so simultaneously remind the Catholic hierarchy of Austria of his atheism precisely when they are providing a thin protection from the Nazis for all such enlightenment intellectuals. All these radical contingencies condition, perhaps determine, the book's final misshapen construction, its broken architectonic aesthetic.

However that may be, Freud's argument, connecting back to his other ventures into social psychology, *Group Psychology and the Analysis of the Ego* (1923) and *Totem and Taboo* (1912), is that Moses was an Egyptian and a devout follower of the pharaoh Akhenaten's new world religion of monotheism; that after this ruler's fall and the swift recoil to the popular Egyptian polytheism, Moses, perhaps also a provincial administrator of some wandering Semitic tribes on the empire's periphery, chose them as his people, imposed his otherwise vanquished religion on them, and during the chaotic interregnum between Akhenaten's death and his successor's final reestablishment of order, Moses and his newly elected people escaped to discover their own promised land.

Freud's story continues. During their subsequent wanderings, the struggle between Moses' monotheism and the people's old religion of polytheism broke out once more. Moses was eventually overthrown and assassinated, thereby suffering the same fate of the first "wild legislator," the original patriarch of the primeval horde, and this people finally settled in what came to be called Israel, partially incorporating among themselves repressed identification with the man Moses and his monotheism. Among these new settlers must have been, Freud speculates, the ancestors of the Levites, the scribes and courtiers of the original Moses, who through oral traditions and written archives had kept the monotheistic heritage alive until, perhaps as much as a century or so later, a compromise was reached between the adherents of this heritage and the worshipers of the local volcano god, Yahweh. At this point, a new second Moses was fabricated from local legends to make the anthropomorphic Yahweh *the invisible* god responsible for the exodus from Egypt, so long as the former took on, bit by bit, all the principal features of spirituality belonging originally to the god of the monotheistic heritage: that sole invisible divinity of strict ethical standards who ruled all the world according to his Law, which he had graciously revealed and given in his own handwriting to his chosen people. (Here, "the return of the repressed" means the return not of the sensual but of the spiritual.)

In any event, with such a story—Freud at first subtitled this book "a historical novel"—one could explain the subsequent development of the Jewish religion, including its legalistic literalism and figurative extravagance. Its revolutionary transformation into Christianity could now be read as "the return of the repressed" in the more common sense of the term, as the return of sensuality and aggression lying beneath the mask of sweet goodness.

Freud's story of the murder of the first Moses, the Egyptian prophet of monotheism, recalls the murder of the primal father and sets into motion the Oedipus complex of unconscious guilt and obsessive-compulsive neuroses for the Jewish people. This development involves, of course, the endless work of infinite expiation, and the repeated identification with an increasingly idealized spirit of the dead father. Such a process of identification is in fact performed ritually for the people by a series of visionary prophets. This process of imaginary identification and spiritualization follows the pattern we are familiar with from individual neurotic symptomatology: from the father figure as a great hero, to a castrating rival, to an abjected mortal, to a totemlike animal at the center of a phobic defense, to the superego voice of conscience, to the invisible Big Daddy in the Sky who sent his only and most innocent Son to redeem humanity from its original sin via a beautiful, generous, albeit purely gratuitous, gift of self-sacrifice.

Freud in *Moses and Monotheism* readily and repeatedly expresses his many doubts and uncertainties concerning this narrative of Judeo-Christian religious history. But he never renounces it because it allows him to connect, via admittedly speculative analogies, the theoretical stages of individual psychological development with the cultural history of a people, the Jews, which becomes paradigmatic, in Freud's telling, for all of humanity. This visionary narrative coordinates a tragic vision of the relationship between a people and their leading figures with intellectual and moral progress, a progress in the ascetic discipline of renunciation.

What most bothers Freud about his own "spectral theory," however, is precisely how it fails to account for the consistent and persistent expression of such ascetic discipline, not principally as a harsh duty or a hypocritically espoused decorum, but as a sense of "blessing." God's having chosen the Jews as his people gives them a joy in their moral imperatives. How to account for such self-destructive joy? This paradoxical spiritual exaltation entails painful "instinctual renunciation under the pressure of the authority which replaces and prolongs the father," that is, the authority figure of individual conscience (120).

Ascetic ecstasy is not unknown to Freud, if still an uncanny phenomenon. How now to explain it? As the definitive model of what Freud terms "the narcissism of minor differences" between (and among, not to mention *within*) peoples. That is, as *moral* narcissism: "Perhaps men simply pronounce that which is more difficult is higher, and their moral pride is merely their narcissism augmented by the consciousness of difficulty overcome" (118). Given this (at first) tentatively put but ever more strongly reiterated viewpoint, Freud's theory of the Western culture of repression comes to its close.

What has Freud accomplished here? He has, I believe, given us a new, differential origin for the Judeo-Christian mythos that has defined the ways in which Western modes of representation—religious, political, aesthetic—have organized the various discursive economies of practices and disciplines, the diverse Khōra of empire. This split and spectral origin is "moral pride," "the narcissism of minor differences" being augmented by selected investments made in the several difficulties to be overcome. And it is the new capitalist world economy, it appears, as presided over by the one great specter of representation, that most exploits radical differences in identity, within the multicultural imperatives of global America, for all the futures of "spirit."

Specter of Theory: The Bad

Conscience of American Criticism

● ●

Of those relevant figures not even mentioned in Jacques Derrida's *Specters of Marx,* the omitted figure most surprising to me is that of William Blake. Derrida himself gives an ironic notice of this omission when in his *Politics of Friendship,* another volume of the early to mid-1990s, he does comment, with apparent nonchalance, not just on what one would expect, Blake's visionary conception of friendship as *true* enmity, that is, spiritual contest, but also on Blake's theory of the specter as a potentially infinite partitioning of psychic space.[1] I realize, of course, that in doing the critic's work, one both chooses and gets chosen by the figures and traditions one's formative discourses selectively, albeit repeatedly, recall. Derrida's elaborate play in *Specters of Marx* on *Hamlet* and the father's ghost, conducted in the spirit of Joyce from *Ulysses,* cannot help but evoke the influence of romantic traditions of Shakespeare on commentary and so Blake, especially as Blake stands out in this context as the eccentric romantic who is suspicious of Shakespeare's tragic genius.[2] So why doesn't Derrida when speaking of the specter in *Specters of Marx* even evoke Blake? Of course, Derrida is a trained philosopher, not a literary critic. Yet his love for, and profession of, "literature" as an institutional production of revolutionary democratic vision is well known.[3] Moreover, for many years, he taught at Yale and was a colleague of, and friend to, Paul de Man, Geoffrey Hartman, and Harold Bloom, the leading theorists of romanticism, indeed of literature, of their critical generation. Together with these prominent romanticists, Derrida published an influential essay collection helping to institutionalize theory in America, *Deconstruction and Criticism* (1979), which took Shelley's "The Triumph of Life" as the point of departure for each contribution. Admittedly, Derrida did fudge his assignment by discussing instead what arguably, along with Wallace Stevens's late visionary masterpiece *The Auroras of Autumn,* could be read as another latter-day version of Shelley's unfinished epic of entropy, Freud's *Beyond the Pleasure Principle*. (Can one ever forget, in this context, Pynchon's *Gravity's Rainbow*?) Why does Derrida forget Blake? Given that one could responsibly assume Derrida's knowledge of, if not expertise in, the canonical works of modern literary culture from Rousseau to Beckett, one must read his omission of Blake as a motivated forgetting, which Derrida's rather awkward reference to Blake in the *Politics of Friendship* would tend to confirm, somewhat belatedly.[4]

Of course, Derrida does make forgetfulness, at the opening of *Specters of Marx,* his way into his subject. It seems that he had forgotten how inaugural and central the figure of the specter is in *The Communist Manifesto*—it is that text's first noun—when he initially and rather casually suggested the title of the lecture, to be given over a two-day period (April 22 and 23, 1993), at a conference entitled "Whither Marxism?" at the University of California at Riverside, which eventually became the book we are now trying to read. Derrida realizes, years after the fact, that his selective memory allowed him to proceed in his work on the specter in Marx without becoming too frightened at the daunting prospect before him of being, apparently, totally anticipated at every turn by his chosen illustration. After all, if Marx already knows (as his text demonstrates) all that Derrida might think to know, why should Derrida even bother to begin? As we have seen throughout the other chapters in my book, what *Specters of Marx* thematizes here for Derrida, via the figure of the specter, can be manifested in a variety of ways, via this and other figures, as the aesthetic dimension of cognitive finitude, the sublime traces of willful ignorance masquerading as some sort of profession of certainty. Under the names of Foucault or Freud or even Derrida (among many other names here), I have tried to figure those aesthetic moments of potential bad faith as object lessons and cautionary tales not only of critical hubris but of imaginative instruction. "Globality," like "theory" or "politics" before it, is often just another name for the failure of (self-) education, even as such self-evidently composite, even catachrestic figures as "empire burlesque" or "global America" or "monstrous messiah" would mark the intellectual conscience of the critic, the critic's cultural superego, which late Freud theorized as America's specter, and vice versa.

To anticipate my final chapter a bit, consider, for another example, the following sentence from Cordwainer Smith's *Norstrilia*, enacting its moral climax, "the rage was followed by tears, by a guilt too deep for regret, by a self-accusation so raw and wet that it lived like one more organ inside his living body."[5] This sentence accumulates the constituents of a catachresis, turn of phrase by turn of phrase, tracing the arc of an incorporation. It proceeds from explosive externalization, through self-shattering pathos, to unconscious moralization, to a self-hatred formative for a conscience so spectrally alive that it seems more autonomous and freely destructive than any apparent organism of "life." Although we tend to forget it, the master figure that this sentence erects in the shadows of moral narcissism is a sublime self-destruction as the perfected form of its own hatred. Blake, in relation to Marx, with respect to the vision of the spectral, may be making a similar figure in Derrida here.

Blake, of course, is apropos for any discussion of the specter. His entire body of work is openly permeated with "the Spectre."[6] And the mythic terms in which Blake elaborates the Spectre implicate epistemology, psychology, social relations, revolutionary politics, historical and technological transformations on an epic, not to say apocalyptic, scale, and a messianic vision of human liberty, equality, and fraternity that is as radical today as it ever was. In short, Blake and Marx, Marx with Blake, would have been a perfect match together for the post-1989 "new world order" of global America with its triumphantly announced myths of liberal democracy, laissez-faire economies, and Internet technology—the "true" revolutionary visionaries versus the false prophets of virtuality unbound. Perhaps such "pure" oppositions chilled Derrida's ardor of pursuit?

Two of Blake's heirs may have been more appropriate to Derrida's purposes in *Specters of Marx:* Yeats and Henry James. Yeats's poetic concept of "the anti-self" (also called "the daimon") and James's fictions of "the ghost," especially "The Jolly Corner," could have helped Derrida anatomize the "spectral" literary traditions, something that after his opening remarks on *Hamlet* he barely touches in his genealogical deconstruction of Marx's specters. "The Jolly Corner," to take one brief example, tells the story of an American expatriate writer who, at the turn of the last century, returns to America to tend to his inherited properties in New York City. Spencer Brydon, our hero's visionary donkey of a name, is shocked, even appalled, by what he finds in modern America, needless to say. Everything is large, overcrowded, being torn down and rebuilt in a frenzied chaos of brute energies on display. The old things of a more refined temperament are disappearing, headed for the museum world, and are being replaced by the popular culture of immigrants, the spectacle of geopolitical interventions on a grand scale, and unimaginable commercial inventions of a mass civilization soon to be exported around the globe. But what makes "The Jolly Corner" so interesting is its Jamesian plot twist. After twenty years in Europe living the aesthetic life of a dandy litterateur, Brydon wants nothing so much as the purely impossible, that is, to meet his own specter, the ghost of all that he could have become, would necessarily have become, had he stayed in America and participated, as he must have done, in the making of this new world order of corporate culture. Brydon's specter is, then, the virtual self his decision to leave America *foreclosed*. And this spectral figure does "return" to him, in reality, one dark night when the living Brydon is almost psychotically haunting the upper levels of the property affectionately known as "the Jolly Corner," as he patrols there ever on the lookout for his ghostly, would-be alter ego. (The other property Brydon owns he has had to sell for apartments).[7]

As you can tell, I think, James's version of the specter on its face could have thrown a helpful light on Derrida's treatment of Marx, with respect to "spectrality." (Marx is Derrida's formerly unrealized alter ego, perhaps?) As Derrida takes pains to recall for us, the figure of the specter, as Marx uses it in his corpus, represents an actuality no longer in existence and a possibility, a potential, a promise (of what?), which could have, must have, existed, or may even yet again, if only. . . . As such, the specter is the bad conscience of every present moment. It is the "unhappy consciousness," in its critical thrusts as in its utopian longings. (Hegel, who Derrida does mention briefly here, is his "Blake," I assume.)

This is not just to say that Blake and Marx and Derrida are incorporated in Hegel, or that, more restrictively, Blake and Derrida think the specter in the same fashion. Derrida insists on the specter being legion or plural, the anarchic traces of all absent moments whatsoever. Blake's "Spectre" is polysemous, endlessly self-diving, but it is, in the final analysis, *one* (albeit) composite figure, the creator's shadow or dark side. Like the Darth Vader of Blake's mythic cosmos, "the specter" in the prophetic books is "the Spectre of Urthona" (the unfallen name of Los, the figure of creative imagination in the fallen world). The Spectre, by whatever name (or spelling), haunts the creative mind with fears and regrets, anxieties over creating, thereby incarnating the sublime blockage of any imaginative impulse. The ironic result is that the more the Spectre articulates itself, or is better made to minutely detail and put concretely its self-conscious doubts in a resistant work of visionary self-critique, the more the Spectre can be recognized for what it really is: not really the sole form of divinity in humankind gone bad, an autocratic reason, but primarily one power of human being equal with and to its "fellows," such as sensibility, passion, or imagination.

To put it another way, the Spectre in Blake serves to express the writer's block of the romantic visionary, the would-be prophet's Jeremiah-like frettings over legitimacy, in a time beyond belief. "What work do you do, and for whom, and why, and of what use is it to us?" The Spectre in Blake ironically incorporates in a single demonic figure the spiritual paralysis worthy of a super-Hamlet, the infinite variety of differently inadequate possible responses to such "idiot questionings." "I have searched for a joy without pain" is, in Blake, the motto of the Spectre, and *that* impossible quest is the problem in a nutshell.[8] Where taking pains is concerned, Blake's Spectre is, so to speak, a most inhospitable ghost.

The Specter of Global America

Clearly, a specter is haunting Derrida's Marx, and it is that of a global America. By the term "America" in this phrase, I don't mean what Blake meant in his prophecy of that name: the revolutionary principle that bursts forth like a glad day from the New World to enlighten peoples and nations and to inspire democratic revolutions around the globe, and especially the French Revolution. Instead, following Derrida's deconstructive lead, I mean by "America" in my paradoxical formulation "global America" several interwoven traces of historical signification, such as, for one example, Francis Fukuyama's new world order of liberal pluralist Western-styled modern democratic states, the subject of his influential and controversial book *The End of History and the Last Man*.[9]

This is the America rapidly installing itself as the centerpiece in a new hegemony of global proportions, entirely bourgeois in outlook, orientation, and aspiration, which with the blessing of a Polish pope and the support of Europe (including former Eastern Bloc states) would secure a new holy alliance against (what else?) the specters of Marxism (and now Islamic terror), via rapid and ubiquitous technological and humanitarian improvements of virtually sci-fi-like magnitude. Of course, where Fukuyama lauds these developments in principle, Derrida casts a skeptical eye at their disputed reality, as in the claim that what I am calling global America, even as the catachrestic figure it is, can represent, as Fukuyama purports, "the final solution" to the world's problems in politics, social conflicts, uneven distribution of wealth, and all the many forms of exploitation and injustice that make possible America's newly assumed symbolic role as global model and regulative ideal. This aspect of Derrida's argument in *Specters of Marx* is its least interesting one because it is so predictable.

In brief, Derrida finds Fukuyama's polemic, well, polemical. That is, it is philosophically reductive where it is not historically questionable. Lightweight *and* inaccurate! Even worse, all its major topoi—"the end of history," "the last man," America as "the Promised Land," "the Waste Land," "A Brave New World," and "A Light to the Nations" all rolled up into one—are just too familiar to Derrida and his generation of French intellectuals who in the 1950s and 1960s were weaned on the cultural pessimism and utopian politics derived from Kojève, Heidegger, Nietzsche, Hegel, and a host of others. "The end of history" and "the last man"? Please, we've heard it all before.

This surfeit of déjà vu, on Derrida's part, could have been interesting if he had explored what it could have meant in light of his own theory of spectrality as the uncanny ghostly apparition, compounded alike of unrealized promise and bitter memories of desire textually realized, which constitutes a special moment of latency, a virgin interval of blank desertion in which all the phenomena conditioning the possibility of an education, a *bildung*, converge. To speculate a bit: the Cold War liberal epoch, especially in its inaugural phase (roughly from 1947 to 1963, or from Churchill's "Iron Curtain" speech to Kennedy's assassination), was the period imaginatively preparing the way, after the traumas of World War II, for the material emergence of a new world order that was often derisively invoked by Derrida's own intellectual generation as if a bad joke. As Blake could have warned them, one may become what one beholds when one beholds it for too long.

Of even more interest, however, are the three specters of Marx—his most influential intellectual topoi—that Derrida selects from those either partially or too terribly realized. These traces of the Marxist corpus are to be discovered in the tripartite subtitle of *Specters of Marx: The State of the Debt, the Work of Mourning, and the New International.*[10] These selective specters represent Derrida's revisionary takes on the uncertain future of Marxist modes of conceiving the state, labor, and the international coordination of political struggles. The "natures," one might say, of right, of work, and of internationalism are all changing, have changed.

In saying this, I don't mean to suggest that Derrida reads deconstructively, for their philosophical pedigrees, *only* selective passages from *The Communist Manifesto, The German Ideology, The Eighteenth Brumaire of Louis Bonaparte,* and *Capital (Volume One)* that engage these three "specters" of the state, work, and international revolution. Nor do I mean to suggest that he follows literally in Marx's footsteps, as it were. Derrida's playful turn on Marx's illustrious example of commodity fetishism—the table that entreats purchase, standing on its head—renews our appreciation for Derrida's imaginative genius. Rather, Derrida transforms these themes of state, work, and internationalism into a speculative critical reflection on, a meditative essay in, the foundation of the state not solely in the legal right informing its exercise of force, or in the law of guilt and expiation, crime and punishment, but in utopian justice beyond the law, transgressing the law, which, like Kierkegaard's theory of the religious sphere as a suspension of the ethical dimension, gives the law its impossible horizon of apocalyptic futurity. Derrida's theory of "the gift" is a revision of Mauss's anthropological conception of cultural foundations in the potlatch, those festivals where we witness peoples sharing, to an extreme degree, their so-called possessions, even ritually sacrificing them in an immense bonfire to display their grand welcome for their arriving guests. For Derrida, the state is founded, ultimately, on another, if related, kind of giving: the surprising, totally expropriating excess of expenditure that welcomes with open arms every alterity, especially those in oneself, not out of pragmatic strategy, or defensive self-loathing (narcissism's other face), but, purely without reason, for its own sake alone.

In the figure of the host, hospitable to each and all around the table that may also become an altar, Derrida envisions the positive affirmation of the recognizable limits of property or of any commodity's appropriation of the position of ultimate determinative instance or "bottom-line" role. The *state* of the debt is, in other words, ever becoming radically redeemable.

Similarly, with regard to the *work* of mourning, Derrida envisions neither a manic disavowal of the ghostly other nor its melancholic piecemeal incorporation. Instead, as in the scene of instruction cited from *Norstrilia,* Derrida foresees an infinite dialogue with the dead, not as between the presently living and the no longer alive, but as among all the not yet (once again) quite fully dead or alive, the spectral living on or surviving of the "undead." This "undead" mode of spectrality does not feed off the living; it is "life." It provides food for thinking, a divine feast, perhaps.

Finally, Derrida takes "the new internationale" to mean now the errant wanderings of the latest wage slaves (from all fields, into and out of all locales), a new (de)professionalized proletariat in its nomadic diaspora over the globe ever eager to catch a glimpse of its visionary Jerusalem. What he nicknames (after Benjamin) "the messianic without messianism" (73) is Derrida's radicalized figure for this Marxist specter of "the new international." To be sure, as in James's "The Birthplace," this is no strong "messianic" passion on Derrida's part. It is "despairing" of all apocalypse (unlike Blake) and so is, like gravity compared to the ever-constant speed of light, a weak and variable, if ubiquitous, force (181). But as such, "the messianic without messianism" formally keeps, holds, the future open to wherever or whatever is coming in its endless arrival.

On Derrida's "Marx"

What is Derrida doing with/to Marx? First, he excises from the Marx corpus three spectral traces: that of the state, work, and the New International. Next, he refits them for grafting into his corpus and three of its major themes: that of debt (gift), mourning, and the messianic. Derrida can then revise Marx and his own Nietzschean (and Heideggerian), Freudian, and Benjaminian inheritances from these figures' major texts, virtually with the same stroke of the pen. Derrida retools and retrofits his corpus and traditions all at once.

More, perhaps, than any other text of his, *Specters of Marx* requires the most comprehensive sensitivity to its revisionary positioning in Derrida's career, in the career of "high theory" in France and in America, and in the course of what Hegel (or Fukuyama) might call "world historical" events and thinking. I don't propose to pursue that interpretive project here. I do want to discuss, selectively, to be sure, what in *Specters of Marx* is the "allegory of reading" that Derrida ironically performs.

Before doing so, however, I need to lay my cards on the table. I don't believe in Derrida's readings of Marx. For all his nervous dance of assertion, qualification, antic revision of assertion only suggested and not made, for all Derrida's insistent hesitation, performative contradiction, declamatory undecidability, and so on, I cannot find his readings here convincing, even for one moment. They are thoroughly tendentious and too obviously self-interested. To put it in the purely aesthetic terms of differing "tastes," I like my Marx "neat," like the best (or worst) moonshine. No soda, no rocks, no mixing. It might kill you, but when it doesn't, the world appears the better for almost doing so. Derrida, to put it more plainly, strips Marx of his pugnacious spirit, his terror, his Robespierre tendencies. Marx, after Derrida, is no threatening specter still haunting the future. He is, at best, at most, another childhood bogeyman of the Cold War starting to fade away with the coming dawn of the new millennium. Derrida dissolves away all the aspects of Marx and his heritage—violent revolution, the dictatorship of the proletariat, wholesale class warfare—that led to Lenin and Stalin and Mao, as well as to the Gulags, reeducation camps, internal exile, and the slaughter of millions. Marx knew—and Derrida blots out this knowledge—that any systemic change in the ownership of the means of material and intellectual production must mean a form of war, most likely the worst and bloodiest form. But Derrida is committed to the deconstruction of ownership, of the proper, of possession, of property, in every sense. This is after all, what Derrida thinks deconstruction is. In the figure of the *arrivant*, that coming to come of Derrida's messianic future to which one, as to one's own death, must be open, I can see Derrida arguing for his openness to whatever arrives, however monstrous. But if this means a new reign of terror, it is an extremely attenuated spook. And it just may be that only a New Terror will do the trick. (And perhaps one has been arriving since 9/11.)

In any event, a closer look at a specific act of reading will disclose, I believe, the allegory of reading that Derrida is performing, no matter what he thinks he is announcing. Derrida reads the following small passage from Marx's reading (along with Engels's, of course) in *The German Ideology*, of Max Stirner's rereading, from his *Ego and His Own*, of Hegel on "spirit" or "Geist," from *his* great work, *The Phenomenology of Spirit*. (Sounds like *communal* property to me!) Here is the Marx passage: "Now, then, the question arises: What is the spirit other than the ego? Whereas the original question was: What is the spirit, owing to its creation out of nothing, other than itself [*Was ist Geist durch seine Schöpfung aus Nichts anderes als er selbst*]? With its [slippage], Saint Max [Marx's sarcastic nickname for his revolutionary rival] jumps to the next 'transformation'" (121). Now, here are enough mirrors for everyone, I think. Max Stirner, whom Marx derisively rechristens "Saint Max," was once Marx's fellow revolutionary, Johann Caspar Schmidt, who took on the "Max Stirner" pseudonym because as a professor at the University of Berlin, he was a state employee, and had his real name been known by state officials, his revolutionary activities and writings could have gotten him fired. It goes without saying, I think, why this institutional context might appeal to Derrida's sense of irony.

Max Stirner's most famous text is his 1845 book *Der Einzige und sein Eigenthum* (literally, *The I Principle and Its Own*). As Derrida notes, it anticipates major aspects of Freud's *The Ego and the Id* (1923), which is also a text euphemistically translated, thanks to James Strachey's choice of Latin cognates for the German terms, which mean, literally, the "I" and the "It."

Derrida claims that Marx in the cited passage from *The German Ideology* wants to make and keep clear or "pure" the radical (in Marx's mind) difference between *Geist* (spirit) and *Gespent* (specter). The former is the product of a collective process of sublimation via work; the latter is like *Gase* (gas), merely the by-product of decomposition, the natural work of death. Marx wants to maintain this difference as a strong opposition because, in an apparent fit of mimetic rivalry, Marx wants to prove, Derrida claims, as in a rigorous demonstration, that "Saint Max" is an academically decadent, strangely docile son of their identical philosophical *pater*, Hegel. It is as if since only one letter, *r*, distinguishes "Marx" from "Max," which I presume may refer to "revolution," Marx wages an even stronger war of caustic, often poisonous satire against his "Saint Max." Could this be the notorious "narcissism of minor differences," which Freud often complains of?

However that may be, Derrida wants to show at work in *The German Ideology* the paradoxical *loyalty* of Marx's critique of Stirner. As he articulates such paradoxical loyalty for his "Marx," Derrida elaborates or performs an ironic commentary, a spectral scene of instruction. Such a scene instructs not only for Marx on Saint Max and, of course, Derrida on them both (together and separately). It also serves as the allegory of reading that the following passage from the spectral labyrinth of critical reflection in *Specters of Marx* states in so exemplary a fashion:

> In its first, and simple "impurity," the history of ghosts [in Marx's reading of Stirner] unfolds in several moments. Even before one watches from the comfort of one's chair what I called [Stirner's] theory of specters, the procession of the ghosts of concepts that would be these concepts of ghosts [their mere names, Marx thinks], it is important to underscore that [Stirner's theory] *betrays* its origin, namely, father Hegel. It betrays and it betrays: It allows one to see its ancestral line and it is unworthy of that ancestor. It denounces that ancestor. Stirner's Hegelian genealogy would also be a decline of the son. Stirner descends from Hegel, he is haunted by the author of *The Phenomenology of Spirit* and he cannot stand it. He spits out living ghosts like a whale suffering from indigestion. In other words, he does not comprehend Hegel as well as another one of the descendants, guess who. The latter [Marx], just as persecuted by the shadow of this great father who comes back every night, ready also to betray him or to avenge him (it is sometimes the same thing), is busy giving a lesson here in Hegelianism to brother Stirner. Stirner always slips into Hegelian language, he slides his words into "the long-familiar, orthodox-Hegelian phrases." But this unworthy heir has not understood the essentials of the will and testament, he has not read very well *The Phenomenology of Spirit*

which is his inspiration and which he wants to give us in a Christian version ("Saint Max intends to give us a phenomenology of the Christian spirit"). What has he not understood? What is the essential? On the subject of the becoming-specter of the spirit, he has not seen that, for Hegel, the world was not only spiritualized (*vergeistiget*) but despiritualized (*entgeistigt*), a thesis that the author of *The German Ideology* seems to approve: this de-spiritualization is quite correctly (*ganz richtig*) recognized by Hegel, we read. Hegel managed to relate the two movements, but our "saintly dialectician," who is ignorant of the "historical method," has not learned how to do so. What is more, if he had been a better historian, he would have ended up breaking with Hegel. For the reproach against Stirner is both that he does not understand Hegel and—this is not necessarily a contradiction—that he is too Hegelian in his genealogy of the ghost. This bad brother sees himself accused at once of being the too filial son and a bad son of Hegel. A docile son listens to his father, he mimes him but does not understand him at all, implies Marx—who would have liked to do not the opposite, that is, become another bad son, but something else by interrupting filiation. Easier said than done. In any case, the work of Stirner remains null and void. "But even if he had given us this phenomenology (which after Hegel is moreover superfluous), he would all the same have given us nothing." (121–22)

Derrida concludes this long paragraph by claiming that Marx went to such "desperate lengths" to distinguish "between spirit and specter" precisely to avoid the imagined fate of his own "Saint Max," the fate of being a docile son of father Hegel, and so really a bad son (122).

Knowingly or not (who can say for sure, and does it matter?), Derrida exhibits in this passage a Bloomian mode of critical revisionism, with all the Oedipal associations, even as the allegory of reading exposed here testifies to a virtually infinite analysis of the blindness-and-insight structure of all figurative discourse as the only possible future, a future of reading that collects, without resolving, aporias resistant to, and provocative of, theory, repeatedly. By narrating Marx's impossible situation, which he had displaced onto Stirner, Derrida *cannot* thereby break with the coils of filiation—to Marx, to Hegel—which depend not so much on human psychology as on the disseminating power of language and its spectral traces, the haunting lesson of Paul de Man's entire career, as Derrida knows.[11] Derrida's Marx is, in short, the perfection of de Man's Derrida from "The Rhetoric of Blindness."

Here is de Man's take on Derrida's initial salvo directed at Rousseau:

> Derrida did not choose to adopt this pattern [of playing off against the most talented of deluded interpreters or followers] the master's superior lucidity: instead of having Rousseau deconstruct his critics, we have Derrida deconstructing a pseudo-Rousseau by means of insights that could have been gained from the "real" Rousseau. The pattern [of misreading] is too interesting not to be deliberate.[12]

Derrida's Marx, with respect to Stirner, is the spitting image of de Man's Derrida, with respect to his Rousseau, even as de Man, Derrida, Marx, and Stirner would wish apparently to occupy the position of father Hegel. In this openly byzantine manner, *Specters of Marx* can be seen as fulfilling the logic of "The Rhetoric of Blindness" to the point that, like Marx in this essay, de Man, a specter haunting virtually every other late text by Derrida, never appears at all here, strangely enough. Could it be, given this spectral logic of the trace, that Derrida's Marx should justly be seen as de Man's own posthumous work? Hospitality and friendship, with a comic vengeance?

However all that might be, "interrupting filiation" is, according to Derrida, Marx's critical intention, an intention Stirner never recognizes or practices vis-à-vis Hegel, precisely because Stirner doesn't read his elected precursor's text "right," before he offers his revisionary interpretation. Although I don't think Derrida has gotten Marx "right," I do think he has given us a fair enough copy of what Paul de Man would have said, at his best, about Marx.[13] In our global America, the seance of spectral theory has raised the incomparable spirit of that critical comrade.[14] Ironically enough, of course.

The Figure of Figures: Transference as Abjection

Paul de Man is another name for nothing. Like Blake, he is not even mentioned in *Specters of Marx*. And yet, in Derrida's reading of Marx's reading of Stirner, we see the trace of de Man's reading of Derrida's reading of Rousseau, with this difference: de Man credits Derrida with knowing he is following the pattern of misreading he attributes to Rousseau, whereas Derrida neither gives nor takes away such credit with respect to Marx. He includes Marx in the interplay of ignorance and knowledge, like a "comrade." Derrida does not place Marx, à la de Man on Rousseau, in the position of "the father"—here occupied by "Hegel." This position, in my reading, here remains open to de Man, Derrida, Marx, or Rousseau. The position of "father," in such a romantic allegory of reading, is that of the one who is supposed to know, like the analyst in classic Freudian theory, and from whose greater knowledge we inherit *our* ignorance. As such, the source of our ignorance and authority is the limit of our abjection in this sublime transference to an explicit fiction. But while Derrida rearticulates this family romance of interpretation, as Harold Bloom would predict, he does interrupt filiation by transforming Marx "democratically," with some "justice," into a "brother (and master)-in-arms" against all critical presumption, including his own. Just as de Man had speculated that Derrida must have been doing with Rousseau. Such "interruption" of filiation resists both the sublime transference to a figure of authority and the assumption of one's hermeneutic abjection, even as transference as abjection is recognized as the problem of reading par excellence. So long as critics, especially American critics, form their identities by overlooking, dismissing, or displacing this problem of reading, then the specter of de Man (as here) will continue to haunt, with ironic genius, any empire to come.

PART FOUR

● ● ● ● ● ● ● ● ●

Reading Worlds

10

Empire Baroque: Becoming Other in Henry James

●●●●●●●●●●●●●●●●●●●●●●●●●●●●●●●●

The critic as judge is a role little reflected on anymore. This does not mean, however, that critics have abandoned making judgments. It may be, in fact, that critics now make more judgments than ever, especially judgments about the sociopolitical positions and possible implications of a writer's work and its canonical or noncanonical status. Too often, it seems to me, we fail to articulate the principles of critical judgments we aim to practice. What do critics do? What do we want? Critics, by definition, must discriminate one kind of achievement from another on the basis of some set of criteria. Consequently critics exercise judgment in making their selections, and so, in their performance, they transmit, wittingly or not, an ideal of perfection—aesthetic, political, and so on—against which they measure the writer and the work they examine. What *new* measure or standard of judgment can guide our multicultural imperatives in the emerging global frame of work?

Two recent books on Henry James pointedly raise this issue of critical judgment, but in rather different ways. Millicent Bell's *Meaning in Henry James* and Ross Posnock's *The Trial of Curiosity* deploy two different yet related strategies of recent James studies and recent criticism, generally.[1] Although relying on a now unfashionable phenomenological approach to literary signification, Bell nevertheless derives from James's self-conscious art of fiction the central critical question arising in contemporary discussions of narrative: What is the possible relationship between the human subject and the various "plots"—cultural, social, sexual, and so on—that foster and constrain the formation of significant identities, personal and institutional? For Bell, in James's fiction, from "Daisy Miller" to *The Ambassadors* (probably for reasons of space, Bell does not address *The Golden Bowl*), he stages a familiar conflict. It is between the would-be autonomous or self-defining American subject who assumes or desires the freedom to constitute, ab ovo, his or, more often in James, her own "identity story," and the social and moral conventions of class, gender, and taste. These latter construct the discursive narrative structures of genteel culture and its predetermined roles—what we would call that culture's subject positions. How in each case James elaborates this recurring conflict (comically, tragically, ironically), and so how meaning consciously arises from this agon for characters, readers, and author alike, are the questions composing the complex focus of Bell's exemplary close readings. They are written in an elegant, reader-friendly style, clearly oriented to the serious student of James at whatever level of initiation.

In our time, of course, such different figures as Richard Rorty (*Contingency, Irony, and Solidarity*), Fredric Jameson (*The Political Unconscious: Narrative as a Socially Symbolic Act*), Paul Ricoeur (*Time and Narrative*), and Jean-François Lyotard (*The Postmodern Condition*), among many others, all argue that in the absence of the grand narratives of traditional myth and religion or their Enlightenment replacements—the myths of liberal progress and scientific rationality—human beings can become subjects only through the comparatively "local" (versus previously "universal") production of an interpretative community's specific "story" of identity and difference. In this context, Bell's close analysis of the manner in which meaning gets performed in James's fiction is clearly pertinent and timely, even though she does not bother to refer to a single one of these theorists of narrative meaning or to their practices of overt cultural critique. Instead Bell practices critical judgment as immanent critique. She works entirely from within James, to put into question such contemporary perspectives, by means of her brilliantly adept ventriloquizing through James's representative fictions. Provided we read him closely enough, as she has done, in the implicit light of contemporary narrative concerns, however formally untheorized by Bell, James can still speak to us. Thanks to Bell's careful articulation of his work, its intricate forms of signification still have exemplary lessons to impart to us today.

Ross Posnock, in his cultural study, adopts a different, more openly critical stance, but one that also retains, explicitly so, the focus on the contemporary scene. He presents James's late achievements, particularly *The American Scene,* "the Autobiography," and *The Ambassadors,* as one work of cultural critique that can measure up to his and, especially, our own masters in this intellectual mode of critical judgment. These masters include, among others, William James (first of all), Veblen, Santayana, Bourne, Dewey, Weber, Simmel, Benjamin, Adorno, Foucault, Rorty, and Jameson. The multitudinous murmur with which James opens *The American Scene* (1907) comes to mind: "Here was the expensive [in the form of seaside villas for the nouveau riche] as a power unguided, un-directed, practically unapplied, really exerting itself in a void that could make it no response, that had nothing—poor, gentle, patient, rueful, but altogether helpless void!—to offer in return."[2]

This model of "response" makes, ironically enough, a perfect emblem for Posnock's own exhaustive procedure of staging an elaborate dialogue between James's work and all these other cultural critics of modernity. One feels, too often, that in this style of dialogue, James's work becomes a resounding void resonant with the echoes of these other voices. Posnock's aim, however, is laudable. He wants to demonstrate, at length, that Henry James is as serious an intellectual critic of modern culture as any of these other figures, and especially his brother, William James. In fact, Posnock claims that Henry James practices a form of pragmatist curiosity that, despite canonical interpretations to the contrary, embraces, rather than merely opposes or evades, the emerging new world of American moder-nity, which is something far better than what William James achieves by means of his more influential harangues and preachments. Henry, not William, James is the one who, like Whitman, can better embrace multitudes—or so Posnock aims to show. Yet in pursuing this laudable critical goal, Posnock renovates James's late "houses" of fiction, personal reminiscence, and travel writing into what resembles a suburban mall flea market of currently received ideas, ideas that, like his sound bites of James's prose, are torn from their original contexts and thrown together despite their different modes, levels, and genres of discourse. Here is one early, comparatively uncluttered example of what I mean:

If bourgeois respectability in the late nineteenth-century capitalist world, says Sartre, embodies "antinature" (critique 771–72), or the suppression of desire, in both of his major phases James in effect stages nature's revolt. Yet antinature—the condition of culture— "bears without cracking the strongest pressure" James throws on it (*Art*, p. 304). (4)

This "dialogue" between James and Sartre (from his *Critique of Dialectical Reason*) actually echoes more clearly Adorno's position, from his *Aesthetic Theory*, that modernist art stages nature's revolt against a repressively rationalizing modern culture. In any event, this passage really is talking at cross-purposes. Someone unfamiliar with James, however, would never know it from Posnock's manner of "snippet" citation. To take the most pertinent instance: Posnock quotes the phrase from James, "bears without cracking the strongest pressure," from the preface to *The Wings of the Dove* as collected in R. P. Blackmur's *The Art of the Novel*, which brings together all the prefaces. In context, the phrase, which originally reads "bear without cracking," refers not to "antinature—the condition of culture" at all but to James's "ideal" of enjoyment in complicating, as much as possible, the aesthetic surface of his fiction with multiple points of view and ambiguities of meaning that put the greatest possible demand on a reader's attention. Here is James without distorting excision: "The enjoyment of a work of art, the acceptance of irresistible illusion, constituting, to my sense, our highest experience of 'luxury,' the luxury is not greatest, by my consequent measure, when the work asks for as little attention as possible. It is greatest, it is delightfully, divinely great, when we feel the surface, like the thick ice of the skater's pond, bear without cracking the strongest pressure we throw on it."[3] I don't doubt that there are allusions galore in this passage—to Coleridge's willing suspension of disbelief, Wordsworth's hierarchy of pleasure, Schiller's idea of aesthetic illusion, Gibbon's analysis of Roman "luxury," Goethe's divine immediacy, just to name a few—but any connection, however prophetic, to Sartre's (and Adorno's) neo-Marxist critique of bourgeois modernity and culture's antinature escapes me, as far as concerns this particular passage in its original context. But adducing a neo-Marxist repertoire, rather than, say, a romantic one—however more actually appropriate the latter—is a smarter protocol of (mis-)reading nowadays, given poststructuralist and multiculturalist agendas, even when it translates James (and probably everyone else in the foregoing passage) with considerable garbling and so exhibits a poor quality of judgment.

Both Bell and Posnock, then, allow the demands of relevance to the professional audience's latest concerns to constrain the exercise of historical imagination as they perform their acts of criticism. Bell does so sotto voce, Posnock with bravura arias addressed to the "pit." Of the two contemporarily oriented (or "presentist") approaches, I prefer Bell's perfected ventriloquism because it gets the citations right and foregrounds James, whereas Posnock's improvised rock opera backgrounds James and everyone else to the role of the critic's chorus. I wonder if another, more truly historical approach is possible, even if only as a regulative ideal for critical judgment. However that may be, the standard of judgment in Bell and Posnock alike, to judge from their practices, is one of revisionary relevance. Their "subjects" are to be revised, made commodifiable, metaphorically from within by close reading in Bell, or metonymically via a cheek-by-jowl adjacency in Posnock, and all for contemporary consumption.

This situation is a general one, and not the fault of any individual. We can mark its beginning in Roland Barthes's 1964 essay "The Structuralist Activity." Barthes influentially argues that the critical act is fundamentally productive. The critic can only deploy present-day discourses of analysis —linguistic, psychoanalytic, philosophical—in order to dissolve, so as to re-create, the object under examination and so give to this new object produced by the critic, this simulacrum, the only kind of rule of formation and function the object can ever have, a law of signification forever in the present tense.[4] The historical imagination, perhaps especially in the New Historicism, has increasingly disappeared as critics read back into past texts and cultures our latter-day fascination with the problematics of power, imperialism, and repression. In remarking this changed situation, I do not propose in response simply to ride the dead horse of the historical imagination. If we are condemned to an inescapable contemporaneity, we can at least develop an ethics of judgment to evaluate the differences between the kinds of such critical practice. What follows is my version, briefly sketched, of an ethics, which I will then use to more closely judge Bell's and Posnock's representative acts of judgment.

Unlike purely logical or determinant judgment in philosophy and theoretical science, in which a particular is subsumed by a universal law, critical judgment is a species of reflective judgment, in which the particular has no immediately known and certain universal law, and so the critical act consists in discovering, via research and analysis, the most plausible judgment representing the law of the particular, its governing rule of combination and activity. "All human beings are mortal; Sappho is a human being; Sappho is mortal." This is the fundamental form of logical judgment. "Sappho is a lesbian poet and died, apparently, for love." This is the kind of particular statement for which the critic goes in self-conscious quest of a possible general rule, via research and analysis, a quest that is always one of approximation and so revisable in light of new research and more persuasive analysis. This approximate nature makes criticism an instance of reflective judgment.

The particular, when it is a complex literary text such as one of James's late fictions, verges on being a contingent singularity, which makes the discovery of an adequate form of reflective judgment giving a general rule for such texts virtually an impossible critical act. The more impossible or problematic the final form of reflective judgment becomes, however, the "better" the criticism must become to be adequate to the object of attention. By "better," I mean the more ethically concerned to respect the text's strange autonomy vis-à-vis not "the world" but our designs to use the resisting text instrumentally for our purposes. The critical imperative is, I propose, to recognize a text, however else it can be used, as its own end in itself, much as we would hope our texts would be received. Beyond the purely instrumental value of any text, there must also be a playful, gratuitous excess, a rational pleasure, however small or great, freely given and intelligently to be received; otherwise the text could not be the product of a human being, since it is precisely this aesthetic measure of rational agency that defines the very idea of humanity as distinctively different from other beings and open to the "games" of argument, debate, dialogue, and persuasion. We human beings have no other claim to distinction.

Each text for the critic, in this light, is a problematic substance in the development of reflective judgment along these ethical lines. And this critical imperative to respect and recognize, to avow, publicly, the achievement of another as other—that is, as also its own end in itself, beyond professional opportunism or personal resentment—provides the rationale, the ethical position of transformation for the critical subject.

The practice of reading for the form of this excess, this aesthetic gift of rational pleasure, is something the critic willingly imposes, as an ascetic self-discipline, on the elaborated act of judgment. The critic's goal in this process of ethical self-stylization is to create memorable images of the relation to oneself as a final state of self-overcoming. This goal is a coproduction, by primary and secondary texts together, of influential examples of free human judgment offered to public discussion and general appropriation, to reciprocal adjudication, without any reservations, except those implicated, of course, by the ideals of respect and recognition. This regulative ideal is, admittedly, the fiction of the quality of judgment. It nonetheless appears especially appropriate to the study of James.

James himself in *The Ambassadors* provides a "novel" anatomy of the education of critical judgment. Lambert Strether occupies the critic's position throughout the novel, progressing in his assessment of the uncontrolled perceptions of Paris society that he allows, experimentally, to wash over him. Part of his learning experience involves Strether's realizing that whereas he may experience these perceptions impressionistically as uncontrolled, every perception that matters arises from a systematic attempt to manage appearances, since it is in the interest of Chad Newsome, Madame de Vionnet, and their circle to keep Strether believing, for as long as possible, in the pair's performance of their virtuous attachment. What finally matters to James in this case is that Strether first frees himself from his New England preconception about Madame de Vionnet as the scarlet *femme du monde,* and then he can recognize and respect each of the changing impressions of her infinitely various yet harmonious beauty of performance. From a respectable woman in a plain black dress surprisingly like the women of Woolett, to a noble aristocrat surrounded by the relics of her private order and with a private honor, to her pale, transfixed, meditative apparition in Notre Dame, to her final appearances as if a condemned martyr, ready for the Terror's scaffold, or, as if Shakespeare's Cleopatra at the last, a mere maid woman lamenting the impending loss of her lover, Madame de Vionnet educates Strether's critical judgment not only in the ways of worldly passion but in the truth of human subjectivity. She is, like each of us, a creature of the contingent scene, an agent of the conditions being represented via the performance necessarily given. In short, Strether learns that even those who arrange appearances cannot really produce their full meanings or control their consequences. His judgment, in response to this realization of human agency's limits, is a growing sympathy for others, no matter how they may desperately deceive, even as he comes to hold himself to a strict ideal of not taking personal advantage of them on the basis of his new worldly knowledge. This is why Strether must return, as Mrs. Newsome's failed ambassador, from Paris to Woolett, without anything material to compensate him for his losses—of financial support and social status—except the memory of all his weighed impressions. To have materially profited from anyone else's vulnerability would be cheaply opportunistic and so personally dishonorable.

Like Strether, James implies, critics must try to free themselves, as much as humanly possible, from their merely local preconceptions, so as to submit themselves to the discipline of learning to judge uncontrolled— for them—"alien" perceptions. Critics can then improvise, in respectful response to the changing scene of judgment, the recognitions of the reciprocal limitations and mutual responsibilities of authors and readers. Adequacy to this ethical ideal of critical judgment, James seems to say through Strether's career, counts the most for the critic of life, regardless of the relative capacity for historical imagination. James does also dramatize, however, Strether's renewal of this capacity when he first visits Madame de Vionnet, in her reclusive old house, in the ancient part of Paris, seated among her select hereditary things, relics of a private order, in a modern age of aggressive novelty, publicity, and self-promotion. But even more important than this restored historical sense, I believe that doing justice to the creatures of the changing scene, which includes, of course, oneself, constitutes the emerging ethical principle that James, as the novel progresses, has Strether more and more perfectly exemplify. Such justice requires the dialectical ability both to appreciate the powers and limitations of others, their radical human finitude, and to hold oneself to the highest standard of critical integrity. Mere material or professional gain must be scorned in light of any enlargement of the imagination that the complex process of critical judgment provokes.

Bell's reading of Kate Croy in her chapter on *The Wings of the Dove* gives a good example of the contemporary possibilities of critical judgment. Bell sees Kate as "a representative of that modern pragmatic consciousness" and "philosophic materialism" for whom "the distinction between the dictated and the freely chosen course has begun to disappear" (305). Bell sees Kate in this fashion, she claims, because Kate, who wants Densher, her lover, to marry Milly Theale, a dying American heiress, for the money they will eventually share, can even dismiss, to achieve her design, sexual jealousy because, to Bell, Kate's "will [is] fused with a conscious recognition of conditions that impose themselves and dictate the kinds of accommodation that make for survival" (305). Kate Croy designs her plot *against* the plots of others such as her Aunt Maud, who plans to marry her off to coldly egotistical Lord Mark. Kate's plot also works within the larger plot of the novel, which requires her gradual reduction to a conventional melodramatic villainess. In both cases, her aim, for Bell, is to marry "circumstances to her desires," which, to me, means to provide real support for her increasingly destitute family, her dependent lover, and her passion-starved, sick rich friend. Kate remains faithful to this complex counterdesign even as Densher, belatedly gaining a bad conscience, vainly rejects Milly's generous posthumous bequest and so scrupulously wrecks the beauty of Kate's original vision.

This portrait of Kate Croy foregrounds the main strengths and weaknesses of Bell's study. It stresses the important relationship between the paradoxical sense of character in James as both psychologically isolated from, and socially enmeshed in, "plots," narratives of all kinds—material, sexual, personal, literary, and authorial. As seen in his famous remarks about Isabel Archer and the making of *The Portrait of a Lady,* James usually conceives of a certain kind of character first and then devises the circumstances or "scene" of an appropriate developing fate for the character to affront, thereby making for a tragic or comic drama of misrecognitions. Bell rightly remarks on the peculiarly romantic and American— that is, Emersonian—assumption about self and world underlying this Jamesian practice of a generative conflict of clashing semantic possibilities. This purely aesthetic adequacy of character and conditions is, for the reader, an intended contingency. It is like that of Strether, on his romp in the French countryside, accidentally discovering Chad and Madame de Vionnet clearly in their habit of intimacy. The fitting sense of felt life in this aesthetic illusion, and the fine ethical discrimination such a fateful scene of contingent discovery provokes, justify James's general practice.

In suggesting that Kate Croy in *Wings* is a pragmatist and a materialist, for whom the distinction between dictated and chosen courses of action has begun to disappear, Bell thereby makes this character into a prototype of Rorty's or Fish's "neopragmatism" and of Eagleton's or Jameson's "neo-Marxism." Of course, pragmatism and materialism existed in James's time, having their first heyday then. But they did so not precisely in the terms formulated by Bell to transform Kate into their mouthpiece. These terms, familiar to us from the current critical scene, are essentially the pragmatism and materialism of our time. Bell does not document and discriminate Kate's affinities with, and differences from, these late-nineteenth-century views, even as she does demonstrate, from within the novel's text, by selective close reading, the plausibility of her take on Kate Croy. The problem with this demonstration is that even from within the text, Kate appears as a character in a naturalistic narrative. She affronts characters—Milly and Densher—in narratives of tragic romance and experimental impressionism, respectively. The novel's melodramatic plot structure and conventions strain to hold together these different narrative modes, with, to James's prefatory ear, many cracking sounds. Kate Croy is, then, not simply an ur-practitioner of contemporary cynical reason. In fact, for James, Kate is, as his preface suggests, as much a victim of circumstances, despite her ruthless strength of will and her over-developed sense of duty to her lover and family, as the melodramatic, pragmatic purveyor of a sinister, materialistic design.

To make Kate, as Bell does, the muse of contemporary critical real-politik is a brilliant stroke, scoring a direct hit on the profession of literary study today, but Kate is something both more and less than this. She is more in that she really does seem to believe that giving her secret lover to her publicly avowed best friend for a while will grant Milly the passion she deserves to experience before she has to die. Kate, in other words, is also a pathetically rationalizing romantic idealist, as well as everything else she is, who is forced by overwhelming circumstances and a determined nature to play, for a woman in her position, the game of the times as best she can. And Kate is also less, by the novel's famous conclusion, as James (to his open regret) reduces her in the final scene, to a latter-day, female, money-hungry Mephistopheles, who yet is given the best Eve-like exit line in all of James: "We shall never be again as we were!"[5] In short, to judge Kate Croy a pragmatist and a materialist muse, as Bell does, may work wonderfully well to intervene, sotto voce, in current debates about the formative role of narrative in the contingent construction of identities—personal, social, and cultural—and so to highlight, subtly, the dangers of certain contemporary critical postures associated with the names of Fish and Eagleton; but to make such a judgment also means that the full dimension of Kate's character and fate, as well as that of the novel's achievement, and especially of its complexity's provocative ethical challenge to critical judgment, ends up getting woefully shortchanged. I'm not calling, however, for extensive comparisons of Kate Croy's beliefs and practices to those of contemporaneous pragmatists and materialists. Nor am I saying Bell should avoid ventriloquizing via James and Kate to intervene discreetly in current debates. To do the former is to ask for another kind of book. To do the latter would have lost James a potential venue of contemporary appreciation. I am in fact saying that the quality of judgment demands as fully adequate a critical response as possible to the complexities of the text being examined, within the terms of the criticism practiced, which in this case is close reading informed by a phenomenological understanding of intentional signification in language that, ironically enough, stresses the open-ended, narrative structure of literary works that a later designing reader is repeatedly to complete. In light of Bell's own assumptions, then, Kate Croy, despite her superior intelligence, is more a poor creature of conditions, as her many occasions of smothered irony attest, than she is a would-be pragmatic master of the marriage game. She is more kin to Dreiser's Sister Carrie than she is to James's closet materialist, Gilbert Osmond, that cold mastermind of a diabolic design, although she also clearly is, in part, derived from him and Madame Merle in *The Portrait of a Lady*. This complexity should call forth, in turn, a critical form of judgment that would make more of her, and of James's ambivalent and self-betraying relationship to his character, for whom in the preface he professes, remorsefully, to care, but to whom, nevertheless, he admits, he has failed to do full justice. But Bell's strikingly allusive, closely ventriloquized intervention into the contemporary narrative theory wars cannot fully afford to do so. There is simply no place for such complexity of response now. Critical respect, for oneself and for the "other," in this instance, James's fictional achievement, ought to determine in the end, however, such critical care for the quality of judgment.

Posnock, to his credit, openly joins contemporary critical debates. His argument, made at some length and in a conspicuously allusive style, is comparatively simple.

In sum, Henry James may be mired in the nativist prejudices of his class, yet he is unique in submitting them to the "tonic shock" of total immersion [in the new industrialism of urban immigrants and the nouveau riche world]. When he literally confronts and interacts with the object of his disgust in 1904 [as recounted in *The American Scene,* lamented in the Autobiography, and anticipated in the conclusion to *The Ambassadors*], he revises his congealed responses and dependency on reified assumptions. In exploring New York City his powers of discrimination are put to their severest test, and they grow more inclusive [like Whitman's]. His wayward, avid curiosity, which brings him to "the very heart of the New York whirlpool" [of modernity], embodies a dynamic of mobile involvements that puts him in contact with a variety of people, classes, institutions, and locales in his year of traveling from New Hampshire to California and from Florida to Chicago. (13)

For Posnock, James in all his late work is the embodiment of the figure of "the restless analyst" that this same returning prodigal son puts into play throughout *The American Scene*—along with a variety of rather different figures, such as the pilgrim and the martyr, none of which Posnock, given his agenda, can elaborate on. James, in this fashion, puts on trial his own pragmatically opportune curiosity by carefully weighing its resiliency, scope, fairness, and strength of receptivity for "alien" impressions, for which, once gathered, James would go to the stake. Like Lambert Strether in *The Ambassadors* when facing Paris and France again after a lifetime elsewhere, so James in facing New York City and America again after a comparative lapse of time (a quarter century) discovers uncontrolled perceptions washing over him. And as with Strether, so, too, with James, what saves him for us is the greater openness of his embrace of the "alien" than we could have expected given his genteel origins. Nevertheless we must still remark on the relative continuity of his constraining prejudices, all-too-"proper" suspicions, and rather patronizing aperçus, especially about Jewish immigrants on New York City's lower East Side. James, for Posnock, nevertheless exhibits, on the whole, a mobility of identity at odds with both the contemporaneous genteel type of the hypersensitive expatriate aesthete and the later canonical representation of him as the all-controlling "Master" of the human scene. Thanks to his perpetually self-revising pragmatism, his curiosity would go virtually against any preconception, however ingrained, for the sake of a genuine impression, no matter how threateningly modern—hence the main and subtitles of this book. James thus puts into practice, according to Posnock, a continually moving subject position, that of "the restless analyst," for the later literary intellectual, as a cultural critic, repeatedly to occupy. James (and Posnock after him) would embrace in this manner multitudes. Posnock's crowded canvas of different critical figures—their names are legion—attempts to demonstrate just how capaciously Whitmannian a hug his James can give.

In reading *The Ambassadors,* for example, Posnock summons Adorno (from *Aesthetic Theory*) on "traumophilia—the capacity to shudder, to suffer bewilderment or tremor" (240); William James (from *The Varieties of Religious Experience*) on "ontological wonder-sickness" or "diseased curiosity" (242); Georg Simmel (from *The Philosophy of Money*) on "the dialectic of the self's hoarding and expansion" (244); and finally Henry James himself (from *The American Scene*) on the new social type of desexualized individual subject appropriate to the "Hotel World" of American imperial modernity (248). This new social type, Posnock finds James saying, as if James were Weber, represents instrumental reason's bureaucratization of life in technically precise forms of organization that mirror the new forms of class stratification then emerging. Posnock's argument is that by finally imposing on *The Ambassadors* a formal perfection that entails scenes of Strether's repeated renunciation of all material gain from his recent experiences, in the name of his ideal collection of aesthetic impressions of exquisite bewilderment, James unwittingly performs in his novel the new subject position of modernity. This latter is best represented here by Chad Newsome's ultimate devotion to the art of pure fakery, modern advertising. Ironically, James's cultural criticism in *The American Scene* condemns this subject position a few years later as the demonic spirit of the Hotel World, engineering collective scenes of isolated aesthetic delights for no one in particular. Thus Strether, already a feminized male in an American business culture that assigns art and morality to the mistresses of the domestic sphere, repeats Chad's ironically "sacrificial" development, in a finer tone. He needlessly rejects Maria Gostrey, according to Posnock, as Chad in principle had already rejected Madame de Vionnet, in a final scene between the two middle-aged "critics" of social life that James in his preface recognizes is themati-cally unnecessary but technically required for purely formal symmetry. Consequently, Posnock concludes, James in *The Ambassadors* is guilty of performing the attitude he condemns in *The American Scene*. In short, the mind of the "Master" and the mastermind of the Disney empire are more alike than not.

As we know, however, Strether does have his reasons for not accepting Maria's offer to make a lighter, more carefree world for Strether amid her various collectibles.[6] First there is her lust for collecting all kinds of things, including people, as if they, too, were things to be typed and pigeonholed. Next there is the fact that she is not Madame de Vionnet, but a paler version of the femme du monde, and once one has looked perfection in the face, pale imitations simply will not do. Then there is the fact that she abandons Strether when he most needs her, when he first meets Madame de Vionnet. Although she later claims she does so because she wants him to be able "to toddle alone" in society, she also wants, more importantly, to wash her hands, Pilate-like, of the whole affair. She stays in the south of France, supposedly tending a sick friend, to avoid either telling Strether the truth about Chad and Madame de Vionnet or telling him a lie, as Little Bilham does, and so joining the conspiracy to keep him happily in his self-destructively ideal illusion about their supposed virtuous attachment. In either case, Maria Gostrey, whatever her other merits as his friend, hardly remains above suspicion. Given all these reasons, Strether does have some cause to reject her offer. But then why does James in the preface stress the purely formal aspect of this scene? It is not so much to parallel, in a finer tone, Chad's already assumed but unspoken decision to reject Madame de Vionnet for the art of advertis-ing. Rather, it is to complete the formal symmetry of Strether's leave-takings (first Madame de Vionnet, then Chad, and now Maria), so as to underscore his resurgent Puritan heritage. For it is he, and not Chad, who on his return to Woolett, can truly combine in a single figure the features of the pagan and the gentleman, the newly emergent partisan of aesthetic culture and the recently recovered martyr to the ideal of self-sacrifice. The novel early on establishes this prospect as one of the projected sub-lime conclusions to occur outside its narrative frame, which is primarily focused on the tragic fate of noble beauty (Madame de Vionnet's) in the modern world. Does James, in these concerns for formal symmetry and technical execution, attempt to master this novel of mobile, bewildering impressions, to close them down, as it were, within the confines of his textual perfection and so practice the spirit of the Hotel World he preaches against in *The American Scene*? As my preceding remarks all suggest in different ways, I don't think so.

I find Posnock's act of critical judgment in this instance, which is typical of the whole book, to be highly problematic. Not only are there the reasons given in the foregoing paragraphs that suggest a more plausible way of reading James's formal experimentation in *The Ambassadors*, one inspiring rather than precluding open-ended speculation, but there is the whole question of Posnock's procedure, his critical method of summoning the often inappropriate specular chorus of theoretical ghosts, which drowns out what James is trying to say. For example, what James in the preface to *The Princess Casamassima* terms "the quality of bewilderment," which he claims is the end the novel genre serves, is an aesthetic idea that owes far more to Keats's notion of "negative capability" than it does to what Posnock says it does, in Strether's case in *The Ambassadors*, Adorno's "traumophilia" or any other later conception Posnock evokes.[7] To remain in doubts, uncertainties, mysteries without any irritable reaching after fact or reason—the way Keats claims Shakespeare does in his creation of memorable characters—is the ideal that defines the aesthetic passion Strether, like all of James's finest characters, who share in his own creativity of response, must also suffer. Moreover, by ignoring the literary genealogy—from Keats through Thackeray to James himself—to which James clearly alludes in this famous preface, Posnock necessarily reads ahistorically and narrowly, in an extraliterary, overly theoretical fashion. He thereby refuses to grant James all the most important aspects of his donnée for the novel. Such a refusal is ungenerous and indeed coercive, setting up James's performance in *The Ambassadors* to be knocked down by his later cultural critique in *The American Scene*, which may reflect a change of mind, or a deepening of insight, or, perhaps, just the difference between the genres of the novel and travel writing, as James understood and practiced them. Finally, Posnock's drawing of the analogy between what R. P. Blackmur in his introduction to *The Art of the Novel* calls the "executive form" of a James novel and the executive mode of corporate individualism is a style of critical judgment that I think is simply unsup-portable.[8] This analogy makes a relationship of near identity between two radically different kinds of intentional acts: literary and managerial. The individual intentional act productive of the complex literary work of art, in this case, may result in a problematic formalization of the fictional experience; but that it is fictional experience, formalized by an individual intentional act, given to the critical reader warts and all, makes the case of *The Ambassadors,* whatever its faults, something far different than a for-profit-only mindless corporate product in the Hotel World. Posnock, in other words, commits a category mistake. To make his point more plausi-ble, even if one really wanted to do so, would require carefully de-tailed comparisons between like entities, that is, between this novel and others—and not such wildly divergent things as a novel and a corporate institution. After the necessarily qualified historical analyses and media-tions were made at some abstract level, perhaps, a judgment could re-sponsibly and fairly be made about discursive practices within a culture at a particular historical moment, but this is not what Posnock has per-formed in *The Trial of Curiosity.* Instead he deploys his myriad of critical voices like a Wagnerian chorus to drown out not only James's sensible voice but also the still clear tone of special pleading haunting the quality of his own judgments. Despite his presumably admirable end, to make James possible—or is it safe?—for cultural critique, as possible for us today as Andrew Ross, Posnock's elected means of judgment too often fails, as here, to do full justice to James's actual achievement in the latter's own chosen terms, which, to me, is where any critical work has at least to begin.

Bell and Posnock, in their different yet related ways, are clearly react-ing to what the age now demands from every canonical author, James included: a multicultural image, however spectral or partially formed, reflecting back from the pages of the canonical text at the politically correct reader, which can then be filled in or completed, according to the profession's current disciplinary practices. I don't know what is worse: the James who is the genteel antimodern aesthete of the canon, or the James who contains multitudes of all class, sexual, ethnic, and racial positions, as a trial of his curiosity and the experimental goal of his revolt, in the name of his characters, against traditional narrative convention. Bell, on the one hand, chooses to make James speak critically of the central problem confronting our theories of human subjectivity—the formative role played by narrative in constructing and constraining identity (personal and social), and the consequent need to demonstrate—within limits—the possibilities of revision, especially, in Bell's view, for James's protofeminist heroines. Posnock, on the other hand, has James become one member of a symphony of a thousand—a virtual Bedlam of Bakhtinian heteroglossia—all testifying to the radical mobility of the subject position, and so pragmatically declaring the material existence of self-revision for all, even for, perhaps, a "wanted" white Euro-American male, dead or alive?

I admire the performances of both Bell and Posnock in terms of the obvious labor and passionate investment in their critical projects. They display, against great odds, given their aim to "save" James for us and the current state of criticism, a sheer stylistic felicity that merits close attention. But I must also wonder and worry about what is happening in the profession to the quality of judgment when two such fine critics finally sacrifice their particular subject— James—to the disciplinary imperative to give the multicultural age an acceptable image of the latest proper subject. Another recent book is an even clearer case in point.

John Carlos Rowe, for instance, concludes his recent book *The Other Henry James* with a chapter on "the art of teaching" his subject.[9] In the process of explaining his new pedagogy for teaching Henry James, with new critical approaches and methods, Rowe gives his readers a compact history of the practices of literary study, and their theoretical rationales, during the twentieth century, for virtually all levels of the teaching of literature: high school, undergraduate, and graduate. By comparing Rowe's profiles of the beginning and end points of this critical history, we can see at work the familiar complex politics of literary study in American higher education and what such politics bode for our future. Here are Rowe's concluding remarks:

> If we are to connect [Henry James's] modernity with our postmodern condition, then his influence, reception, and limitations must be considered in our understanding of globally diverse literatures. Viewed in this way, the scholarly revival of Henry James should be part of the curricular reforms under way throughout higher education that have as their long-term goal a more inclusive representation of nationality,

ethnicity, gender, and sexual preference in the literatures and cultures we teach our students. (198)

Let's examine what Rowe is calling for, and why. The first thing to notice, I think, is that Rowe assumes that there is an interregnum, an abysmal division, between Henry James's "modernity" and "our post-modern condition" (198). What can this mean? As he makes clear in the rest of this chapter, and indeed in the rest of the book, by James's modernity Rowe means "the elitist" and "the aestheticist" aspects of Henry James (186), which Rowe notes work together as representative of "a historical struggle that is long past, won decisively by a powerful middle class" (186), with one result being, for current teachers of James, that our students must find his work fraught with "difference, narrowness, and irrelevance" (182). Rowe assumes that we all know, from our postmodern position on the lip of the abyss, that formal experimentation, focus on upper-class Anglo-American life at the turn of the last century, and the failure to include clear and positive representations of people of color, gays, and "new women" (feminists) must mean that James and his liberal culture are at best irrelevant and at worst instruments of repression. Now, to his credit, Rowe is going to argue that his own portrait of James is really one-sided and incomplete, but he does tie its powerful influence not so much to the work itself as to its narrow and now irrelevant reception by formalist critics, beginning in the 1920s with Percy Lubbock's *The Craft of Fiction* (1921).

Interestingly enough, what Rowe points out as the offensive modernity of formalist approaches to James's work sounds less genteel and exclusive, and even more democratically romantic and transcendentalist than we would have supposed. Here are the representative passages from Lubbock that Rowe adduces to make his case:

> If you ask Henry James whether he "likes" some book under discussion, the roll and twinkle of his eye at the simplicity of the question is a lesson in itself, and one that a young critic will never forget. Where, he seems to say, on the loose fabric of a mere preference or distaste will be found the marks of the long wear and tear of discrimination that are the true critic's honourable and recognizable warrant? [After all, it was] a large unhurried mind, solitarily working and never ceasing to work, entirely indifferent to the changes and chances of the popular

cry, it was this that gave its sonorous gravity to Henry James's opinion of the theory he rated when all was said, to be the vessel of the essence of life—a book. [Consequently] the reader of a novel—by which I mean the critical reader—is himself a novelist; he is the maker of a book which may or may not please his taste when it is finished, but of a book for which he must take his own share of responsibility. (184)

Rowe's animus is directed at this idea of the author and the critical reader working together to produce, on the model of the former, a figure of the novelist that the latter should impersonate via the critical reader's careful and responsible realization of the author's scripts and directions. Although a strict New Critic would find Lubbock's critical imperative too impressionistic, Rowe makes clear, in an extensive footnote at this point, that "this apparently liberating appeal [to the reader to become an active participant in the reading process] is central not only to formalist aesthetics but also to phenomenological, structuralist, and poststructuralist approaches to literature, to mention only the most obvious" (230). Rowe goes on to cite and indict in this footnote (note 8) Poulet, Barthes, and Derrida as strangely infected with this only apparently liberating imperative, which Lubbock formulates, and which, to me, sounds like Emerson or Blake, among other romantic figures. What Rowe most objects to, I believe, is what Harold Bloom, basing himself on the psychoanalytic concepts of transference, influence anxiety, and authoritative identification, describes as the scene of instruction, which all language and text-based approaches to literature construct out of the encounter of author and reader, so as to create what Lubbock calls "the novelist" or the critical reader's conscience. In other works, what Rowe objects to, finds hopelessly modernist and not part of our postmodern condition, is the personal ethical struggle for meaning between author and reader, the agon or contest that gives birth to a composite if spectral figure, what Lubbock christens "the novelist" that each critical reader can become:

The formalist Henry James had his own special part to play, of course, in the development of the institutionalized study of literature in terms of aesthetic techniques. Percy Lubbock's *The Craft of Fiction* . . . established the image of the "great writer" as the model for the discriminating critic and reader, both of whom ought to avoid scrupulously the hasty judgments of evaluative critics writing for the popular press and intent on telling careless readers which books they should like. . . . In Lubbock's terms, then, Jamesian difficulty is equated with the singular genius of the major author, possessed of a subjectivity that refuses "entirely" the "changes and chances of the popular cry," and thus somehow exemplary of what the reader should become. . . . On the face of things, Lubbock's elevation of the reader from passive recipient to active participant in the fictional act is liberating. (184–85)

Rowe sees the figure of the novelist that James and his critical reader wrestle with each other to create merely as a "compensation" for the latter as he or she, by and in such work, performs "*the* [essential] task of critical reading and repeatedly *legitimates* the novel as a properly artistic genre" for the profession of literary study in America (185). For Rowe, such compensation and legitimation are the modernist carrot and stick respectively for the critical reader as mule, which fate, thanks to our postmodern condition, we can gleefully bypass on our way to the airport to take off for a grand conference in Sun City, South Africa, on Henry James and globalization. By taking refuge in our postmodern condition of politically correct multiculturalism, making the world safe for global capitalism, Rowe forecloses the reality of the critical transference, the experience of reading as it projects the prosopopoeia, the spectral figures of what Lubbock calls "the novelist," each one of us can become, and so no critical judgment of one's own needs to be made, only the empty iteration of the latest global fashion in professional groupthink and opportunistic critical exploitation:

If we consciously acknowledge the need to change not just the texts but also the orders in which they are taught, then we should look for new configurations in which Henry James may profitably be taught with W. E. B. DuBois, Kate Chopin, Charlotte Perkins Gilman, Zora Neale Hurston, *Black Elk Speaks,* John Dos Passos, John Steinbeck, Tillie Olsen, Jean Rhys, Chinua Achebe, Margaret Atwood, Maxine Hong Kingston, Louise Erdrich, Jose Donoso, Jorge Luis Borges, Kazuo Ishiguro, Salman Rushdie, and a host of other Euro-American, Asian American, African American, Native American, African, postcolonial, gay and lesbian, and women writers who have contributed to the several other "modernisms" available to us in our postmodern condition. (198)

Whatever we do to fulfill this new critical agenda, and so legitimate the teaching of Henry James and, more generally, the study of literature to a postmodern global clientele apparently ever seeking self-affirming representations of themselves, Rowe warns us against ever doing what we used to do, which is "simply to reread Henry James as an American and English writer" (198). As we shall see shortly, however, the ultimate irony of this situation is that from James's point of view, the act of critical judgment that writer and reader share is already open to all who care enough to read closely enough.

Before turning to James's version of judgment, however, I want to lay out the ethical basis for my criticism of Rowe, and the move he makes, first to abject James's modernity in its early-twentieth-century American or Anglo-American context, so as to transfer the identification of critical reader and author not to a composite figure that Lubbock calls "the novelist" but to the Whitmannian catalog disseminating the latest names already circulating as tokens of the cultural capital in the field among "knowing" professionals. For me, the composite figure that author and critical reader make together, what T. S. Eliot in another context calls "the familiar compound ghost," is what Jacques Derrida identified in his recent work as the figure of "spectrality." Spectrality is itself, of course, a figure. It is the figure of the limit on future possibility that is always already ever about to come. That is to say, the specter that haunts both author and critical reader alike is precisely this sublime figure for the unending contest between master and slave that informs and shapes them equally in somewhat different ways, as the critical reader constitutes the author's imaginative designs and the author defines the critical reader's acts of constitution. This spectral couple produces one version of the literary intellectual's conscience. To understand better how this aesthetic process of ethical self-formation occurs, I want to examine, in a comparative context, James's theory of judgment before closely reading his most successful late novelistic performances of judgment.

Henry James's Version of Judgment

A sentence from Nietzsche's *Beyond Good and Evil* guides my thinking: "The 'work,' whether of the artist or the philosopher, invents the man who has created it, who is supposed to have created it."[10] As the entire passage makes clear, this ironic work of (self-)invention also arises in the cases of "the great statesman, the conqueror, the discoverer" (218). All of these figures are invented and "disguised" by their "creations, often beyond recognition" (218). Consequently, for "the crowd," after the work in question succeeds, the creator is re-created according to the venerable myth of genius or the great man as the crowd's own piece of "wretched minor fiction" (218). So powerful is this aesthetic illusion of the successful work, so contagious is it, that it serves as the rule of the "counterfeit" constituting "the world of historical values" (218). It serves, for a central example, as the model of misunderstanding inspiring the social production of a culture's ultimate values as "gods": "And who knows whether what happened in all great cases so far was not always the same: that the crowd adored a god—and that the 'god' was merely a poor sacrificial animal" expiating the guilt of the tribe with respect to its ancestors (218).

I take Nietzsche's complex speculation to be the following: insofar as a "work" of statesmanship forming a people into a nation, a "work" of conquest gaining the materials for the formation of a people, a "work" of discovery opening a new field of reality to explore, and a "work" of art or philosophy producing a new aesthetic or rational order achieves "success" with "the crowd," this success retroactively creates, via a process of contagion, the standard image of its creator and so disguises the creator's own invented image for his condition, which is one of radical contingency, risk, and suffering. Just as the growing numbers of disciples of a new religion progressively see in their scapegoat-founder and in his words more and more of the lineaments of divinity, so, too, in these other cases "the crowd" misreads them.

Nietzsche's point is even more radical, however, than this statement may make it sound. He is saying that the ontological condition for the production of any identity involves a foundational contingency of cultural work. At least two different, perhaps conflicting, images of identity arise as productions or inventions: the creator's and the crowd's. Both are "works" disclosing and disguising the wholly conditional nature of any identity, but according to different sets of values—one singular, the other common. The truth of a work, individual or collective, is, in case after case, a contest of images, a contagion of masks, a work itself of fiction.

All forms of morality, whether of aristocratic or democratic kinds, would rationalize this radical contingency or contagious fictionality of identity, individual and cultural, according to different metafictional "tables of the law," different hierarchies of value. As we know, in his later work, Nietzsche attempts to distinguish from a "supra-moral" perspective the virtues and vices of aristocratic (or "master") and democratic (or "slave") moralities (201). As Nietzsche argues in *Ecce Homo*, all modern individuals and cultures are complex mixtures of both kinds of moralities or metafictional measures for regulating the pandemic contagion of fictionality or aesthetic illusion. For Nietzsche, the most interesting and promising cases, like himself, are beings composed by a sharply staged contest, a repeatedly improvised drama, of antithetical virtues and vices, the dangerous game or play of the divided soul, what we now call the split self or, more formally, the multiple subject positions of human agency. I am not concerned here either to follow or to dispute Nietzsche's critique of moralities, which is a critique of the metafictional measures of human cultures. Instead I just want to note that for him, regardless of kind, morality per se seeks to rationalize and disguise the radical contingency and fictionality of any form of identity. Concealing the work of any identity formation with a unifying image or name makes possible all politics of identity. What I call, in connection with Henry James's theory and practice, the critique of fiction refers to this recognition of the fictional limits of identity and the pragmatic ethical consequences of such recognition for the modern novelist.

As an implicit commentary on Nietzsche's nominalistic analysis of identity formations, Heidegger's remarks from "The Origin of the Work of Art" (1934–1936) on the agonistic "play of beings" make for an interesting and important elaboration.[11] They make the work of producing aesthetic illusion no longer simply a matter of subjective imaginative agency and cultural influences; they make this work of contagious appearances a matter of formal relations in the larger process of concealment and disclosure that defines, for Heidegger, Being's ambiguous coming (in) to the appearance of truth in the case of each being or entity, including, especially, that of "Dasein" or human being (there). I cite the passage in full because of its provocatively effective difficulty:

> One being places itself in front of another being, the one helps to hide the other, the former obscures the latter, few obstruct many, one denies all. Here concealment is not simple refusal. Rather, a being

appears, but it presents itself as other than it is. This concealment is dissembling. If one being did not simulate another, we could not make mistakes or act mistakenly in regard to beings; we could not go astray and transgress, and especially could never over-reach ourselves. That a being should be able to deceive as semblance is the condition for our being able to be deceived, not conversely. Concealment can be a refusal or merely a dissembling. We are never fully certain whether it is the one or the other. Concealment conceals and dissembles itself. This means: the open place in the midst of Being, the clearing [of Being], is never a rigid stage with a permanently raised curtain on which the play of beings runs its course. Rather, the clearing happens as this double concealment [of refusal and dissembling].[12]

There is a constitutional inaccessibility of entities (what Heidegger sees as a protective dissembling on the ontological level that produces aesthetic semblance) that makes for epistemological errancy and moral transgression, for what feels like an entity's refusal to fully appear and to still conceal itself from our view.

Each entity, that is, appears masked as it is. This openly masked appearance makes each entity ambiguous—both itself and other than itself. It is like the way an itinerant actor improvises a role on a provisional country stage, appearing both as the person the actor is and as the other, the momentary persona, that the improvised speech exhibits. (Perhaps a better analogy might be the way Robin Williams appears during a television interview.) The improvised personae are indeed contagious appearances that conceal as much as they reveal. I like to think of each being, as Heidegger here presents them, in this light—as such an unpredictable repertoire of improvised figures making their appearances against the background of Being's openly concealing masked revelation of any identity formation's radically contingent fictionality. Custom, convention, culture—as exemplified and elaborated in morality—attempt to perform a single coherent politics of identity in systematic efforts to stabilize, regularize, and normalize, to make comprehensively predictable, a nonetheless selective range of permitted roles that beings assume in accordance with some centralized ideal. In this moralizing context, beings bring Being to questionable light without question. Nevertheless, as Heidegger's remarks show, each entity is a working of fiction not only in Nietzsche's senses of "individual" and "social" production (or revisionary invention) but in an ontological sense, as well. In short, any phenomenon defined by a name is, however disguised by custom, a conflicted fictional construction produced in each moment according to one or another improvised design made available (but not necessary) by the diverse contests of cultural existence. Agency, then, can never in principle be restricted and localized only as a pragmatic matter of perspective and discourse. It must remain an ontological matter we should not forget.

Foucault, in the end, has the clearest sense of what this radically contingent fictionality conditions for the modern writer. In a September 1983 interview, nine months before his death, he comments on "the obscure desire of a person who writes" in a way that concretizes the Nietzschean-Heideggerian problematic of fiction:

> One writes to become someone other than who one is. . . . There is an attempt at modifying one's way of being through the act of writing. . . . Therefore, I believe that it is better to try to understand that someone who is a writer is not simply doing his work in his books, in what he publishes, but that his major work is, in the end, himself in the process of writing his books. The private life of an individual, his sexual preferences, and his work are interrelated not because his work translates his sexual life, but because the work includes the whole life as well as the text. The work is more than the work: the subject who is writing is part of the work.[13]

The work the writer writes is not only the publicly visible and conventionally accepted work, but the entire existence of the writer is itself also a work, a project, that incorporates the "life" and the "work" in the ordinary senses of those terms. As Nietzsche puts it, the work in the extended sense creates the person, and as Heidegger elaborates this point, any being is like that of the writer or the creator in that it openly works to produce a protective semblance of itself as it discloses this truth of Being. Foucault's critical understanding of his own "project" (in a Sartrean sense) grounds this Nietzschean-Heideggerian critical ontology of fiction in modern cultural contests of subjectivity and sexuality, a grounding that provides me with a general horizon for my subsequent remarks on Henry James.

But first the central question of this chapter. Given Nietzsche's Dionysian and Heidegger's hermeneutic sublimes, it could be argued that "contagious appearances" arise from the "works" of "fiction" of all beings as such and that finding some way to oversee and regulate, to supervise and discipline, this pandemic fictionality would indeed be the order of the day, an order of things Foucault spent his life detailing and exposing as fictional in his avowedly "critical fictions."[14] In the light of the spread of "contagious appearances" as the ontological, epistemological, political, and moral conditions of radical contingency, which a state culture tries to control and conventionalize, how does a supposed master of reflexive fiction conceive of his work?

My text for answering this question is the preface to *The Golden Bowl*. I choose this final preface because James uses it as the occasion to speak generally about aesthetic representation in several of its different modes. He speaks first about his narrative "system" of restricted point of view,[15] next about the critical distinction between traditional fictional and modern photographic art, then about the surprising agon of self-revision—its dramatic acts, scenes, and different agents of "re-representation" (*AN*, 335) and "re-appropriation" (336)—and finally, he speaks, in a visionary vein, about the responsible pleasures of being a writer.

James concludes the preface with what I would call an American version of "the writer's faith," a postromantic credo in the Wordsworthian mold. Our acts of writing, James affirms, are not merely private and contingent, like our ordinary everyday acts, whose reality and consequences may become unremembered or may remain nameless. Instead, like our unique acts of kindness and love, but more certainly and securely so because they are inscribed accounts, our acts of writing are necessary links in what James envisions as "the whole chain of relation and responsibility" constituting society (*AN*, 348). And because each act of writing is also necessarily a matter of selection, it is an act of judgment, as well. Writing, in James's ethical imagination, is thereby "conduct with a vengeance, since it is conduct minutely and publicly attested" (348). Both Emerson and Habermas could live with that. Perversely enough, perhaps, James finds this morally constraining condition, as Nietzsche or Foucault also suggest, vigorously and dialectically empowering. Holding oneself "accountable" to oneself as a model for becoming responsible to others, in the repeated act of writing, makes up, for James, his writing's "exquisite law" and paradoxically dutiful "joy," what he terms his writing's "one sovereign truth" (348).

This one sovereign truth of his writing both informs and arises from the writer's radical dispersion among what we now so cumbersomely call multiple subject positions, including some of a vaguely religious, liberally mythical, and even socially mystical inflection. It is as if the writer, in the writing, makes up in miniature a society of different discursive subjects, or, as James might better phrase it, a society of imaginative souls. The writer's one sovereign truth, in other words, is to become, in the writing, a community of diverse constituent parts, in several strong senses of the word, whether we choose to Bakhtinianize this Jamesian vision or not. However well we may believe James puts this vision into practice, in any particular case, it is nonetheless a novel idea, I believe, in principle.

In the preface's first part, James reminds us that his system of fictional narration is that of restricted point of view (*AN*, 331); this is a third-person account of things generally limited to one center of consciousness or, in some cases, to one of several at a time. James opens this discussion of point of view by generally distinguishing between "the muffled majesty" of a sovereign but "irresponsible authorship" (328), which assumes that omniscience should "reign" in the novel with respect to character, and his own innovative method of characterization: "I get down into the arena and do my best to live and breathe and rub shoulders and converse with the persons engaged in the struggle that provides for the others in the circling tiers the entertainment of the great game [of life]" (328). And yet, as James admits, he practices, as best he can, "invisibility" (328). "There is," as he says, "no other participant, of course, than each of the real, the deeply involved and immersed and more or less bleeding participants" (328). This means, I take it, that the James narrator effaces himself and plays the role of the imaginative, compassionate, and ideally discreet reporter, the mimic register of his central characters' own accounts of, and perspectives on, their conflicts in the great game of the arena. James is not, however, a real participant, no broadly self-dramatizing narrator. When such a figure does appear, especially in the tales, we know immediately that it is not really our man James, but "just" another character. Nor is James a purely distanced spectator—ever—despite his fascination for the spectatorial type and the acquisitive or lustful eye of the collector.

But he is no Olympian connoisseur. Neither is he, clearly, gladiator or martyr, decadent Epicurean or omnipotent emperor. Rather, as he says later, James is "the historian" of what I call his genteel combatants' savage civilities (341). Although it is a traditional figure for the novelist, "the historian," as James conceives of and practices this spectral role, is more like what we would now call a "ghostwriter" for some celebrity's reflections on life, except that James is the ghostwriter for his own imagined creations' embodied perspectives. Perhaps James is a refined spectral reporter.

We can see more precisely what this means when James turns to explain the apparent breaks in his systemically restricted point of view in *The Golden Bowl* (*AN,* 331). He notes, rightly, that the Assinghams, especially Fanny, assume throughout the novel the position of important, albeit less-than-major, centers of consciousness, even though James also still maintains that as intended, the Prince and the Princess do indeed preside as the informing consciousness of their respectively titled volumes. James accounts for this Assingham contingency—he had not originally planned on such a full role for his *ficelle,* Fanny, for example—by saying that what she or her husband, or, for that matter, any of the other characters, perceive and respond to is primarily exhibited in light of, and is colored by, the consciousness of the Prince or the Princess. How everyone else—other characters, readers, the author himself—perceives when reading themselves in(to) the novel depends on how this royal pair's exhibitions inspire all of these others to see and to feel. It is as if the Prince and the Princess participate in the author's imaginative power, as if they share narrative sovereignty with him, once he creates them and releases them to their textual fates. They clearly stimulate in the other characters what an author stimulates in a reader: a contagious hallucination, a visionary phantasmagoria, an aesthetic "semblance" (332). As James spells it out, a fortuitous creative "contagion" shapes the imaginative responses of author, narrator, central character, other characters, and readers more or less alike.

This is a curiously democratic aesthetic, an American or Emersonian conception of the sublime, that is yet not a case of mass hysteria à la Whitman, since author, reader, and the more intelligent of James's reflective characters recognize and judge the fictional quality of what they perceive. This is one reason why his characters comment so often on how beautiful this or that appears to be. Ideally, James concludes, readers complete their productive experience of reading only when they put into some medium of their own, in their own words, their sense of what they have read. This contagious emanation of creativity, for which the image of the golden chain is most apt, explains why James believes that his narrative system of restricted point of view remains significantly intact in *The Golden Bowl*. The Assinghams cannot help but become, in turn, creative as they respond to the genius of the Prince and the Princess. Similarly, we cannot help but become, in our turn, creative vis-à-vis them. And James cannot help himself but become, again, in his turn, creative vis-à-vis his own imaginative productions as he originally envisions and performs them, or even now as he rereads them. This curious poetics of sovereignty—a democratically aesthetic sovereignty—also explains, I believe, why James thinks he can become an invisibly moving and dispersed spectral presence in the arena of life's great game and do something different in the novel genre from anything Thackeray and George Eliot have already done. That is, James, in the writing, is the stage for the performance by characters, narrator, author, and reader of a democratically saving immanence, whether Neoplatonic or Christian or Hegelian in origins. If the creative power of imaginative innovation contagiously disseminates itself among characters and readers, so that they too become authorial, then by the logic of the contagion figure that, whether madness or disease is thought of, swings potentially in all ways at once, James must also become creaturely.

Two figures—"the poet" and "the god"—dominate the preface's fourth and final, most religious-sounding, myth-laden, and also ethically responsible part. These figures follow a whole series of others—"the historian," "the docile reader," "the revisionist," "Scott," "Balzac," and so on—which represent one after another aspect of imaginative agency. For James, the poet is like the rhapsode in Plato's *Ion*. The poet is the archetypal title for the creative responsiveness that works, via whatever genre, to inspire by sublime contagion in readers their own species of imaginative production (*AN*, 332, 341). So great can be the poet's work of responsive performance to the impersonal creative power flowing through him or her that it can even lure or seduce the ultimate figure, the god, to descend so as to inhabit the created form, whatever it may be: lyric poem, drama, novel. The particular age's version of the poet thus plays, whatever the poet's gender or sexual orientation, the muse to the god—whether in the mode of visionary madman or madwoman, popular playwright, or prose master. The poet in this generic perspective projects and produces the age's own unique shrine to house the god. The god is the figure, then, for the mysterious, impersonal, indeed anonymous and so pre-Oedipal and pregendered but not asexual, purely contingent power of imaginative agency. No one individual can possess this power, but any one self or part of self may participate in it to one degree or other, depending, as Longinus might say, on the quality of the response. James sees this quality arise from the often bewildering fiction of (self-)judgment, which is inspired by this power's contagious emanations of aesthetic semblance. Lambert Strether's nobly Pyrrhic career of judgment in *The Ambassadors* is just one ironic case in point. Even material objects, via their shining appearances, can become creative entities, as with the golden bowl that entitles its novel (*AN,* 342).

I could speculate on the sources for James's vision of judgment in this preface. Romantic, occult, and transcendental resonances resound. More precisely, I hear echoes of Wordsworthian pantheism, the Emersonian and Swedenborgian notions of James's father, James's own sublime reflections on Shakespeare's, Balzac's, and Milton's practices of beauty. For one example, the pervasive light imagery in the preface reflects this last inflection, especially in the familiar Miltonic epithet "the fields of light" (*AN,* 341). Appropriately enough, James uses this epithet to conclude his identification of the best poetry with the best prose, precisely in their vital rhythmical rightness for articulation by a living voice. There are also, of course, the biblical and Blakean allusions of the novel's title.[16] But for this occasion, I will simply note how all these possible resonances contribute to the broadly religious, liberally mythical, and democratically mystical rhetoric of imaginative ethical agency in the final preface. James, in reviewing the whole of the New York Edition of the *Collected Works,* finds that it is good.

It is, as I have called it, the writer's faith that accounts for James's radical differences from other writers of his time and so makes him possible, indeed necessary, for us today. I still find it extraordinary and exhilarating, for example, that James can speak of all these personae, masks, figures, subject positions—all these disseminated selves or contagious emanations—both pleasurably and as forming "the whole chain of relation and responsibility" of society, what he characterizes, after Emerson and Arnold, as if it were society's defining and indeed constitutive trait: "conduct with a vengeance," that is, "conduct minutely and publicly attested" in and through writing (*AN*, 348). James, in other words, is not only radically different from others of his time, neither reductive ideologue nor genteel aesthete; he is, I dare suggest, still very different, perhaps more different than we can know, even as we recognize our concerns in him, precisely from us, with our often unthinking multicultural imperatives and global critical horizon.

James's Baroque Images

In the preface to *The Awkward Age* (1899), James complains that this novel is one of his "comparative monsters" (375), by which he means that what began as a simple germ of a story idea became in the execution more and more elaborate, as if the author had lost control over what he was doing, or at least did not possess "mastery" over its unfolding and refolding. This is a frequent lament in James and has often been understood as mere feigning.[17] But I always wondered: What if it were true? In any event, not only did the imaginative relation of James to his story begin with the accident of receiving a certain story idea from the London of his day, but its execution also proceeded on its course contingently. And precisely because of this double contingency—of "origin" and "career"— it is not surprising that in *The Awkward Age* the central theme selfconsciously becomes the awkwardness of modernity's material and moral contingency. Story idea, compositional practice, and novelistic theme: an overdetermined sense of contingency pervades all. And technically this contingent "vision" appears in the text, of course, as the ironic play of point of view, or the dramatic exhibition of radical perspectivism, as the narrating discourse mimics and produces the changing "centers of consciousness" of the primary characters in the novel. In the preface to *The Awkward Age*, James even mentions his exercise in cubalistic geometry, as he tried in his notebooks, to plot the mooring "scenes," that is, the configurations of "conscious centers" in the circulation of "the vicious circle" of his little society (his term) surrounding and illuminating his central situation—the fate of an adolescent girl.

The difficulty with all this in James lies in the images that his late works particularly exhibit. They are infinitely suggestive and totally unorganic. Whether referring reflexively to character, action, structure, or motif, these contingent Jamesian images are "monstrous" (his term), mechanical, and patently allegorical—only there are no agreed-on principles, codes, or stock of ideas available to make sense of them. Like the unwinding of a tightly wound nightmare spring, they unfold in ways that refold significance in an open appearance of secrecy, a Möbius strip of self-presentation: "We are shut up," James concludes, regarding his novels, "wholly to cross relations," "relations [are] all within the action itself" (389). (As the bizarrely surreal image of the porcelain pagoda opening Book II of *The Golden Bowl* demonstrates.) There is no master semantic hierarchy, only crisscrossing codes and images.

Here are a few simpler examples: One character, Mr. Michett, says to another, Nanda, in *The Awkward Age* that "what may happen is after all incalculable. There's just a little chuck of the dice, and for three minutes we win" a new impression (238). Consequently, he ironically concludes, "I do forget . . . with a facility that makes me, for bits, for little patches . . . cease to be; so that my life is spotted all over with momentary states in which I'm as the dead of whom nothing is said but good" (238). As if in some unfathomable concurrence with this strange view, Nanda responds shortly: "Doesn't one become a sort of a little drainpipe with everything flowing through?" (243). When Mr. Michett tries to make the image more romantic and graceful, or more traditionally acceptable, by saying that Nanda is more like "a little aeolian harp set in the drawing-room window and vibrating in the breeze of conversation," Nanda quickly retorts that "the harp gives out a sound, and we . . . give out none" (244). In other words, Mr. Michett now lightly concludes that what they—as modernity's finest—take in, they keep. "Well, it sticks to us" is how Nanda glosses what Mr. Michett says on the subject of modern subjectivity. Just imagine: it is the epistemology of the toilet that defines us! For me, all of James's significant images perform like these characters and their ironic self-images. They try not to give out a sound, and everything sticks to them. They are their own imaginary readers and ours.

This is where, for me, Gilles Deleuze comes in. One of the reasons we turn to theory is to get help with conceptualizing an analytic problem in a new way. With some remarks in *The Fold,* Deleuze gives me such help.[18]

For Deleuze, the short definition of the baroque as an aesthetic category is the imaginative principle of "the fold to infinity" in mathematics, philosophy, architecture, art, and literature (38). An infinite becoming shaped in an ever-returning organized figure of itself with no history, with only this folding form of ever becoming itself. In topology, the Möbius strip is a familiar example. In cosmology, Stephen Hawking has proposed that the entire universe is a bounded infinity, a great cosmic sphere. If we pursue this new concept of the Baroque further, we find that Deleuze analyzes the change in the nature of the human subject that follows from this idea. The human subject, and the content of its subjectivity, become point of view, perspective. But this reduction of subjectivity to perspectiveness "does not mean a dependence in respect to a pregiven or defined subject; to the contrary," Deleuze suggests, "a subject will be what comes to the point of view, or rather what remains in the point of view. . . . The point of view is not what varies with the subject . . . it is, to the contrary, the condition in which an eventual subject apprehends a variation (metamorphosis)." Deleuze concludes this discussion: "For Leibnitz, for Nietzsche, for William and Henry James, and for Whitehead as well," perspectivism amounts to a relativism, "but not the relativism we take for granted. It is not a variation of truth according to the subject, but the condition in which the truth of a variation appears to [and as] the subject. This is the very idea of Baroque perspective" (19, 20).

Deleuze provides me with a new way to think of my problem with James's Ovidian or metamorphic images. The images are not "a variation of truth according to the subject," not a common reality, historical and actual, seen from the character's imaginative point of view. Rather, these images constitute "the condition in which the truth of a variation appears to the subject." They constitute the aesthetic medium in which a nonnarrativized truth, the truth of a new differential variation—a drainpipe derived from an aeolian harp—appears to, in, and as, an eventual subject: the imaginary reader James envisions in his preface to *The Golden Bowl*. Rather than inventing images as symptoms of their subjects' pathology, James invents—uncontrollably?—images of eventual subjectivities that no one subject can contain and understand. This concept of the eventual subject as the belated reader of itself defines the baroque image. In James's aesthetic practice, especially in the late work, the ever-changing circulation of society's subjects perpetually becomes the fold to infinity, in Deleuze's sense.

Becoming Other: The Conscience of the Reader in Late James

I begin once again with that haunting passage in Heidegger's "Origin of the Work of Art."

> One being places itself in front of another being, the one helps to hide the other, the former obscures the latter, few obstruct many, one denies all. Here concealment is not simple refusal. Rather, a being appears, but it presents itself as other than it is. This concealment is dissembling. If one being did not simulate another, we could not make mistakes or act mistakenly in regard to beings; we could not go astray and transgress, and especially could never overreach ourselves. That a being should be able to deceive as semblance is the condition for our being able to be deceived, not conversely. Concealment can be a refusal or merely a dissembling. We are never fully certain whether it is the one or the other. Concealment conceals and dissembles itself. This means: the open place in the midst of beings, the clearing [of being], is never a rigid stage with a permanently raised curtain on which the play of beings runs its course. Rather, the clearing happens as this double concealment [of refusal and dissembling].[19]

Heidegger reflects here (much as Derrida or de Man would) on the distinction between "natural" appearance as immediate presentation and mediated appearance as artful or aesthetic representation. All the significant reflections in the history of Western aesthetic theory have been founded on this distinction. Heidegger shows there is no clear certainty concerning this distinction. Instead there is a process and production of becoming other implicit in being itself and inherent in the presentation and representation of any being. Appearing, presenting, representing, staging or performing, simulating, deceiving, refusing to appear except as other, dissembling, self-concealing—all these essential contingencies constitute what I call "the allusion of being." By this ontological formula, I refer to the aspiration on the part of any being to persist, as if in secure possession of the supposed full presence of being itself. Such self-delusion would emulate the illusion of being as presence. It holds out the false promise of a permanent appearance far beyond what Heidegger, in "The Anaximander Fragment," sees as the just term of finite existence.[20] Being, especially now, as we will see, takes the form of this ironically exemplary illusiveness or chronic dissemblance. Making mistakes, acting mistakenly, going astray, transgressing, overreaching, being deceived, being hidden or obscured by another, being obstructed or denied by another, never securing certainty, erring and being errant—all these existential contingencies constitute what I call "the bewilderment of existence." By this existential formula, I refer to the human condition's appearance in what Heidegger's "Age of the World Picture" calls "the moral-aesthetic anthropology" of modern humanism. This modern humanism's moral-aesthetic worldview culminates in "Americanism" and the idolization of "the gigantic." I see the latter as the worship of the mathematical sublime of sheer mass in every sense.[21] As Heidegger notes in one of his appendixes to this essay, "Americanism," like "modernity," is essentially "ancient" and "something European." Moreover, the "American interpretation of Americanism by means of pragmatism" is "an as-yet-uncomprehended species" of "the metaphysical essence of the modern age" or "the gigantic" (153). Being as illusion and existence as bewilderment define for Heidegger the American phase of modernity. The long-forgotten oblivion of the ontological difference between being itself and beings comes here and now to fruition, as it were.

Heidegger's reflections in "The Origin of the Work of Art" constitute a significant revision of his fundamental ontology of existence as exhibited in *Being and Time*. This revision implies an anarchic determination of historical contingencies. The state characteristic of existence now is not simply anxiety or dread; it is also cognitive error or bewilderment. Similarly, being now discloses itself not simply as destructive negation but also as uncanny contingency of dissemblance or aesthetic illusion. Within the technological and media framework of the modern age, existence as bewilderment especially discloses the appearance of being as dissemblance. Care now concerns the occasions of bewilderment in facing illusion. Given this fundamental relationship between bewilderment and illusion, therefore, resentful usurpation of position and pandemic aestheticization of the earth reign supreme. What happened in the former Yugoslavia, among other places even closer to home, as carried by CNN into our living rooms, should not surprise anyone. The material elimination of entire peoples in the name of a single ideal national identity captures one terrible dimension of this fundamental relationship between being as illusion and existence as bewilderment. If bewilderment and illusion define, respectively, existence and being in modernity, what place can art, specifically imaginative literature or fiction in the most fundamental sense, have; what role can it fruitfully play? I think Paul Ricoeur in *Oneself as Another* offers the beginning of a suggestion. He argues that

> the affection of the self by the other than self finds in fiction a privileged milieu for thought experiment that cannot be eclipsed by the "real" relations of interlocution and interaction. Quite the opposite, the reception of works of fiction contributes to the imaginary and symbolic constitution of the actual exchanges of words and action. Being-affected in the fictive mode is therefore incorporated into the self's being-affected in the "real" mode.[22]

Ricoeur means by this that fiction reflexively partakes of illusion and bewilderment, fiction can help to constitute the conscience of the reader in a primary way. What follows is in part my development of Ricoeur's basic position. Ricoeur's argument relies on the analyses of conscience in Heidegger's *Being and Time,* in Nietzsche's *On the Genealogy of Morals,* and to a lesser extent in Freud's *The Ego and the Id.* Being affected by fiction means that fiction constitutes the imaginary and symbolic yet historically contingent core of conscience. This contingent core contains both the conventional injunction of public mores, what Heidegger calls the "they," and the authentic conscience's summons to "my own" existence, or Dasein. This summons is mediated by the monumental figure of the transcultural hero in the heart and the voice of the friend. These two fugitive figures in *Being and Time* Derrida has usefully foregrounded. The summons is from the self to the self. Because the self is always already becoming other than the self, this call is a call to face resolutely the self's finitude. This means the self is to take up the burden of creatively repeating or retrieving a now chosen tradition, liberating it from the dead weight of conventionality. In this Heideggerian context, Nietzsche's analysis of ressentiment, slave morality, and noble magnanimity fits perhaps rather too neatly. Nonetheless, as Ricoeur suggests, the appropriateness seems largely compelling. The slave of conventional morality, a figure imbued with ressentiment through and through, contrasts strikingly with the master of noble magnanimity, that final dialectical product of the ethical stylization and refinement of aristocratic barbarism. For

Ricoeur, following a Hegelian-inspired reading of Nietzsche, the noble soul sublates these oppositions of barbaric master and resentful salve. The noble mind commingles two souls within one breast via a productive (versus reactive) aesthetics of existence, to borrow Foucault's phrase from his late work for the internalized dialectic of erotic mentorship. This aesthetics of existence primarily plays itself out hermeneutically. It consists of a mutual reading of the figures of master and pupil making up the composite soul, the oneself, of friendship's mediative works. Finally, Ricoeur argues, the sublimation of the Oedipal crisis in the figure of the mortal patriarch institutes the final phase of what Freud in *The Ego and the Id* calls the imaginary father. This is the figure embodying each self's polymorphously perverse and ambiguously gendered pre-Oedipal history. This sublimation of later gender-specific and earlier ambiguously gendered figures from the different phases of the self's libidinal economy results, ideally, in the formation of conscience. This conscience would live the dialectic of customary morality and personally innovative ethics, of law and practice, beyond the various, crudely reductive oppositions of gender, power, and social relations. Becoming other, then, is at once an aesthetic, ethical, and ontological condition. For Ricoeur, fiction is the reflexive production of bewildering illusion for ironically instructive purposes. Fiction, in other words, is the field of what he terms "thought-experiment," which makes possible the complex summons, sublation, and sublimation known as conscience.

Ricoeur sees conscience as the contingent essence of the self. Conscience is necessarily character, for it shows the self's reflexive promise of becoming the same again and yet differently so. By repeatedly listening to the internalized composite other of conscience, the self continues an identification and dialogue with a fuller range of its imaginative contingencies than otherwise available, repeatedly betraying them in every sense. This is especially so because the self continually lapses into what appears less than this ideally internalized, composite other. The self via conscience would openly and continually mediate the received and revised fictions making up the self's essentially narrative identity.

The self receives initially from the society around it, especially its family, an already figured identity. This given identity is imbued with the sedimented associations of a preestablished system of role and meaning from various cultural media. The self then uses the discourses available to it in its society—religious, ethical, imaginary, and so on—to configure this initially figured self, to produce and stage another context or scene of dramatic transformation. The aim is to perform a new role for a re-figured self according to the original dictates of a projected design based on a continually developing sense of judgment. How the self's projected design relates to those of others (is it, in essence, a coercively dissembling, would-be definitive illusion, or not?) determines whether the refigured self basically appears as it was originally envisioned or whether it has been definitively perverted into something far worse. This ironic perver-sion usually results from the self's critical blindness, or what I would call a self-insistent bewilderment. The social recognition of this revisionary interpretive dialectic of figuration, configuration, and refiguration is fun-damental, and it entails a critique of judgment inspired by fiction. I be-lieve that one place for the social recognition of the self-formation of the readers' conscience can still be the academy. The academy is—selectively, to be sure—the place where what Kant in *Critique of Judgment* defines as "reflective judgment" can still happen. This kind of judgment repeatedly proceeds from the particular case in quest of the universal that the par-ticular may plausibly be said to exemplify. In principle, however, this quest is without conclusion. Reflective judgment is unlike determinant judgment, Kant's favored form, which subsumes the particular imme-diately under the known rule of the hierarchical universal, as a particular species is subsumed under a common genus.[23] The academy constitutes the conflict of the faculties around his difference between reflective and determinant judgment, as in the familiar division between the human-ities and the natural sciences.

Henry James's late works, especially including *The Wings of the Dove*, form for me a composite test case for my briefly sketched critique of fiction. By "critique of fiction," I mean to suggest a project more basic and comprehensive than a theoretical criticism of a literary genre, since the history of fiction as illusion spans various discourses and periods, as well as implicating various figures and disciplines. In any event, this recourse to James is not as arbitrary as it may at first appear. For his contempo-raries, James is the most philosophical and analytical of novelists, even to a fault. In his notorious late-Edwardian parody, *Boon,* H. G. Wells claims, only partly tongue in cheek, that one "can't now talk of literature without going through James. James is unavoidable. He is to literature what Kant is to philosophy—a partially comprehensible essential, an inevitable introduction.[24] Similarly, in her 1916 monograph, Rebecca West wittily remarks that James's late characters and narrators expend more "intellectual force" on what she sees as analytically snooping into life's dirty secrets than Kant spent on constructing *The Critique of Pure Reason*.[25] We have to pass beyond the figure of the hypersensitive master enshrined by Pound, Eliot, and two generations of formalist critics. The author who possesses a mind so fine no idea ever penetrates it is not the historical James, nor, for that matter, does this formulation mean in Eliot what it comes to mean in his epigones. James is for his contemporaries, and should be again for us, a cosmopolitan American intellectual who at the turn of the so-called American century reflects provocatively in his late fiction on the finite cultural practices of intellectual agency.

Near the end of *The Ambassadors,* for example, Maria Gostrey and Lambert Strether at last discuss the "basis" for his mistaken belief in the virtuous attachment of Chad Newsome and Madame de Vionnet. It was Maria herself who had discouraged his various moments of doubt, some of which are as grandly cynical as his more habitual moments of belief are grandly romantic. Strether, she also realizes, remains ambiguously open-ended in his judgments, even when he now knows the truth.

In response to her remark that "things must have a basis,"[26] Strether tells her simply—it is perhaps his sole utterance for which this adverb can be used—that "a basis seemed to me just what her beauty supplied." "Her beauty of person?" Maria asks. Strether answers: "Well, her beauty of everything. The impression she makes. She has such variety and yet such harmony." To Strether's suggestive claim, Maria concludes, with indulgent irony: "You're complete" (493).

We thus learn that the basis on which Strether builds his changing views, acts against his own practical self-interest, and conducts his social relations for most of the novel is this elementary judgment of beauty. We see it first in action concerning Chad's beautiful transformation from a provincial New England youth into a refined man of the world; and then we see it in relation to the author of Chad's new urbane self, his secret lover, Madame de Vionnet.

Although baldly phrased, we recognize in Strether's invocation of variety in harmony a common idea of imaginative beauty found in Coleridge and some German romantic poets and thinkers and for them best exemplified by Shakespeare—in this instance of Strether's judgment, it would be Shakespeare's Cleopatra. They claim that beauty, especially the formal perfection of the reflective work of art, is an organic unity in multiplicity similar to what is sometimes found accidentally in nature. (Both Wordsworth and Schiller, among others, make this kind of claim in their own ways.) Because Madame de Vionnet has a beauty of person more like a reflective work of art than like spontaneous nature, this quality is seductively bewildering to Strether. In fact, it is sufficient for Strether to justify, in his most sublime flights, Chad's or any man's ideal devotion to her without prospective recompense and indeed with considerable material loss in view. The foundation for Strether's judgment is that Madame de Vionnet is worth trying to save from the condemnation and exclusion of Chad's family precisely and solely for her beauty and for the beauty of any possible imaginative relationship to her. Strether's basis, in short, is fundamentally an aesthetic one. It is an aesthetic idea—the idea of the aesthetic itself. Her beauty, even now that he knows the truth and knows how Chad and she have tricked him, is still strong enough for Strether to insist that Chad should stick to her, despite everything, and that for Chad to do anything less would make him in Strether's intentionally melodramatic epithet "a cursed beast" (491).

I'm interested in this otherwise anticlimactic late scene because it makes clear how judgments of value, for Strether, that minor figure of imagination and editor of a small review, are based on a romantic conception of the aesthetic, and how the aesthetic, so conceived, founds not only changing views but changing actions. I count Strether's decision to go over to Madame de Vionnet's side, into what he figuratively terms her "boat," and then "to pull the oars for all they're worth" (338), a significant form of action. Of course, it is an ironic reversal of his original intention. This reversal also definitively changes his social relations and financial prospects. This becomes painfully clear as Strether argues his "lady fair's" case with Chad's unfortunately married sister, the severely hypocritical Sarah Pocock. For Strether, then, there is an aesthetic foundation for interpersonal exchanges and actions, and this aesthetic foundation is informed by the judgment of beauty made.

Judging something or someone beautiful is an aesthetic matter having social consequences. What the conditions are for making the judgment of beauty, for claiming that a person or a thing is beautiful, and what the consequences are of acting on this judgment—these conditions and consequences constitute the prime subject matter for James, especially in the late work. Let me be clear about this: ascribing the predicate "beautiful" to a person or a thing in a sentence of the type "This is beautiful" is a critical act of judgment that certain conditions make possible and from which certain consequences flow. Judgments of beauty disclose what James, as we'll see, calls irresistible illusion, even as they arise out of what, as we'll also see, he calls bewilderment. They are both symptomatic and proleptic, revelatory and predictive, signs of the unhappy consciousness and the beautiful soul, as Hegelian perspective suggests. Acts of judgment constitute the true soul of the Jamesian drama, however melodramatic the external scenes of action, reversal, and revelation may become. Such fictive acts of judgment make up the Jamesian conscience and constitute what, following Schiller and Arnold, James means by "aesthetic education."

As early as "The Parisian Stage," an 1872 review for *The Nation,* James speaks of the necessity for Americans who want to gain an "aesthetic education" in the world of national types and characters to compare their theater firsthand with those of other countries, especially with France's.[27] His point is that the theaters of different countries function as the cultural factories for manufacturing and refining the traits we recognize as composing the national qualities and characters of a country. Even when the theater in question performs a foreign work, the way the actors perform it, the traditions of acting and presentation, contribute to the constitution of the national character of the country where the play is being put on. James in this review first holds out what becomes his longstanding hope that the novel may take over this function as this genre surpasses drama in popularity. James envisions the novel as producing those cognitive classifications making for the perceived differences among national characters. It would also produce the recognition of socioeconomic status necessary for defining class and class consciousness. Finally, in its ability to capture the nuances of gesture and form in the style of scene and the structure of narration, the novel would provide that aesthetic education in worldly matters of modern culture that James, after Schiller and Arnold, wants for his readers—in this case, his American readers in particular. Class in its several senses of cognitive classification, socioeconomic hierarchy, and style constitutes for James worldly knowledge. And James wants his readers to possess literacy in such urbanity as part of their intellectual consciences, much as we may want our students to possess visual literacy, since in his time urbanity counts as much as lightning recognition of the image and ubiquitous publicity do in our own. The novel for James is, as we'll see, the place where bewilderment and illusion together produce the measure of judgment of the modern age from within the emerging limits of modernity itself. Seeing the nexus of bewilderment and illusion, James would construct the measure of judgment by forming the conscience of the reader, with the reader conceived as what we would abstractly call a subject position occupied in turn by character, narrator, author, and critically enlightened public.

Another scene where the critical judgment of fictional beauty matters highlights its significant conditions and consequences. In *The Wings of the Dove*, Kate Croy needs to ensure Merton Densher's commitment to her original design of marrying him off to a dying but rich Milly Theale so as to give Milly a taste of life and to get for herself and Densher, her secret fiancé, cold hard cash. So Kate solemnly exclaims the ironically prophetic judgment: "I verily believe I shall hate you if you spoil for me the beauty of what I see!"[28] To fully appreciate this scene of judgment, we need to recall the story of the novel in some detail. (*The Golden Bowl*, really an epic prose-poem in the symbolist mode, virtually requires a book of critical commentary itself.)

The Wings of the Dove (1901) consists of three major discourses, one for each of its major characters or "points of view." There is a romantic discourse of religious and mythical symbolism associated with Milly Theale. She is the dying young American heiress of all ages, the angel with a thumping bank account, the biblical-resounding dove of the title and latter-day fairy-tale princess. This romantic discourse is largely mediated by Susan Stringham, Milly's chosen mentor, popular romancer, and James's ficelle. It represents an aristocratic or noble consciousness of high glory, self-sacrifice, and heroic resolution when confronting the prospect of early death. This is the kind of consciousness that Arnold's "barbarians" in *Culture and Anarchy* should but do not possess. Lord Mark is here James's "barbarian" who out of pure spite will disclose all the destructive secrets. There is also a naturalistic discourse of commercial exchange value associated with Kate Croy, that perfection of the English "girl," whose wastrel gentleman father and dependent family have fallen on hard times. Kate will do anything, including sacrifice Densher to Milly and vice versa, to achieve her design. It is Kate, after all, who early on explains to Milly how, in endless pursuit of personal gain, each member of English society works, and in turn is worked by, every other member, thereby ensuring the smooth operation of society's wheels within wheels. Kate often feels smothered by this demonic vision, even as she must practice it. This naturalistic discourse, somewhat atypically here in James, represents a middle-class, positivistic, "utilitarian" business consciousness, the Philistine mind-set that Arnold excoriates. Maud Lowder, Kate's wealthy aunt and the Britannia of the marketplace, plays this role by refusing to sanction Kate's and Densher's prospects and by planning to marry off Kate to Lord Mark. Finally, there is the psychosexual discourse of aesthetic impressionism associated with Merton Densher. He is the still radically unformed, belated young English gentleman of ideas. He follows Arnold's Hellenic principle with a vengeance and revels in the free play of the mind. Back in the private theater of his Venetian rooms, after he possesses Kate fully, he also revels far less disinterestedly by repeatedly rerunning the scene of his long-delayed sexual conquest. Like his famous school-inspector mentor, however, this "critic," too, is reduced to making a living the hard way—in Densher's case, by doing journalism, especially profiles of the American national character. This psychosexual discourse represents the chronic adolescence and confused identifications of the newly emergent consciousness found in middle-class professions and modern media, or in what we could call the ur-culture industry. The lower-class consciousness, by the way, is represented in the novel primarily by the servant, especially Milly Theale's Venetian servant, Eugenio. Ironically, she has inherited him from Christina Light, the Jamesian femme fatale of both *Roderick Hudson* and *The Princess Casamassima*. Only Eugenio fully recognizes Densher as a "mountebank" who is after Milly's money (469). And only Eugenio fully mirrors back at Densher this image so forcefully that a blush of shame arises on Densher's face. The basis of this recognition scene is the principle that it takes an experienced and reformed one, Eugenio, to know an embarrassed one, Densher, that perpetual novice in all things.

Densher is the most fluid of the three major characters. Significantly, he appears as the still-white-hot metal soon to be struck finally into permanent form as if a newly minted coinage. Equally significant, Milly and Kate appear as two sides of the same coin or medallion, as well as embodying two different kinds of portraiture, Italian high Renaissance (the famous Bronziono painting scene), and English academic modernism, respectively. Kate and Milly also apparently represent the material realm of stage melodrama and the spiritual realm of close drama. I say apparently because as the novel proceeds, it complicates all these polar oppositions by deploying the same figures of resentment, jealousy, and exchange value for every one. Between these two increasingly bewildering muses, Milly and Kate, Densher in the novel's last third tears apart and reconstructs himself. Densher largely forms his conscience via the beautiful fictions of his and Milly's time-passing conversations about such distracting yet "stretchable" topics as the American national character and the American girl. They talk of such things in Milly's Venetian palace to avoid speaking either of her impending demise or of her embarrassing and compromising love for him, the man whose love Kate Croy only appears not to requite. In this compromised sense, Densher can keep close to Milly, and so he remains apparently true to Kate's originally projected design; and yet he never need openly lie to Milly either by proclaiming his love for her or by denying the reciprocated love between Kate and himself they have so often privately avowed. The novel ends, ironically, with Milly's will bequeathing Densher a small fortune even after she has learned of this dissimulation from a resentful Lord Mark, whose coldly calculating bargain of marriage Milly had earlier refused. As Kate bluntly puts it, Densher has gained a new, authentic conscience via a belated love for, and identification with, the nobly idealized image of a dead girl. This loving identification is something that Densher's admiration for Sir Luke Strett, Milly's surgeon-physician and "master of a thousand knives," facilitates (242). It is as if Sir Luke and Milly together compose Densher's imaginary father figure, that ambiguously gendered composite model for his newly emergent conscience. Clearly, Densher cannot now take the money and also marry Kate. He therefore decides that Kate must choose between the money and their marriage. As such, James appears to intend that Densher represent the conscience of the reader in the novel. Kate finally decides that since they can never be again as they were, she has no real choice left after all. We leave the novel on her exit line to this effect, as if we could almost see and hear the theater curtains coming down, closing in, and beginning to veil the final tableau.

Thus Densher, in gaining a conscience and an ideal love to identify with, retrospectively, does indeed in the end spoil the original vision of Kate's beautiful design for all concerned, even as the project appears to be finally realizing itself in Milly's posthumous and seemingly noble bequest. So when Kate concludes the novel by judging that "we shall never be again as we were" (509), we in our turn must conclude, I think, that she does not hate him as she foresaw she would do once he spoiled the beauty of the design as she first envisioned it.

Here we see that the judgment of beauty entails in James a judgment on intention, design, vision. What is being judged beautiful and ultimately spoiled is a project. A vision is being carried out, enacted to its conclusion. An idea is being realized in the novel's world, apparently coming to a permanent presence. A plot, in the sense of narrative composition and of ethical complication, is working itself out as a dialectical configuration of roles. Strether in *The Ambassadors,* for one example, ends up in the position of the critic devoted to beauty who in making his judgment remakes himself in relation to others, refiguring himself in his and Maria Gostrey's eyes as "better," as able, in her words, to "toddle" in society now on his own. Kate Croy throughout *The Wings of the Dove,* for another example, would position herself as the author of a self-declared beautiful vision or design (however demonic for some of us), which she attempts to realize in her world, only to have it spoiled by her primary instrument of the demonic design's execution, Densher, her ever reluctant coconspirator. Kate's vision hasn't failed her, but her chosen "hero" surely has.

The judgment of beauty in James not only invokes conditions, such as Kate's and Densher's lack of material resources, and consequences, such as their total moral transformation; the judgment of beauty also has an anticipatory, self-fulfilling prophetic aspect to it. Yet what is said to be and not to be beautiful is, despite Kant, an open-ended matter of taste, in principle. So ambiguity and uncertainty inform in a radical way the judgment of beauty and also, then, the aesthetic and cultural basis for the future of any kind of social agency portrayed in James. At the climax of *What Maisie Knew,* for instance, young Maisie Farang makes a conditional offer of permanent relationship to Sir Claude. He is her preferred and putative guardian. This offer, in its classical symmetry of reciprocal sacrifices, suggests a basic idea of beauty, a finely developed judgment of taste, and even an emerging tragic sense of life. What it does not suggest is a commonly recognized moral sense among the members of her class including Sir Claude, who all become disoriented by the uncanny innocence of her formulation: "I'll let [Mrs. Wix, the objectionable governess] go, if, if, if . . . you'll give up Mrs. Beale" [Sir Claude's equally objectionable spouse].[29] In *The Golden Bowl*, Princess Maggie uses such seemingly innocent judgments to create the beautiful American "humbuggery" of apparent normality that saves her marriage with what the novel designates as the imaginative maxims of "fictive reasons."[30] James thus raises the defensive hypocrisy of a pretended innocence and a pretended normality to the level of an art form, or at least to that of a rational craft.

James risks his provocation because he must, for the Jamesian character has no core identity other than these judgments of taste. The Jamesian character moves from one judgment to another. The opposing pulls of novelty and consistency compose the story of a life always attempting to design itself and often attempting to impose this ever-emerging design definitively on others, out of either resentment or fear: resentment at the perceived success of other lives, fear of becoming assimilated to other people's designs. The larger social and international conditions and analogues for this aesthetic psychology of modern humanistic culture should be clear. And James exhibits this revisionary aesthetic psychology, with all its ramifications, for us to judge in our turn—and at the peril of our own self-betrayal of motive and design.

Consider some related late examples. Early in *The Spoils of Poynton*, Fleda Vetch judges herself at first to be far from beautiful when she sees herself as others see her, as "parasitical" to her wealthier relations and friends, as, in short, "a leech."[31] But using the discourse of moral heroism from the fiction she reads, Fleda attempts to configure this initial figuration of herself in a more attractive light. She judges that a woman can be as morally heroic as a man. Accordingly, she conceives her beautiful design for bringing Mrs. Gereth and her son back together and so for saving the aesthetically exquisite Poynton estate from Mona Brigstock, the son's prospective bride and arch-Philistine. The successful working out of this design, Fleda believes, will demonstrate a new heroically refigured self to the satisfying recognition of all in a dramatic scene of final judgment. Instead, thanks to her meddling, Fleda in the end returns to find Poynton a burning ruin, an apt representation of the novel's world of fateful contingency. Similarly, Nanda Brookenham in *The Awkward Age* recognizes how tainted she must appear to be by the loose talk of her mother's modern salon when she figures herself as "a sort of drainpipe with everything flowing through it to which something must stick."[32] But because of her selective assimilation to a more appreciative and older configuration, Mr. Longdon's discourse of romantic gallantry, Nanda ends up, as she once envisioned, refigured as a beautifully ironic yet lofty symbol of modernity: "Nanda was once more—and completely now—enthroned in high justice" (311). Finally, Princess Maggie in *The Golden Bowl* initially judges herself to be "a small creeping thing" (168), like the favorite figure of the "snail" in her father's vast collection (143), only to configure herself, thanks to society's pervasive classical and Christian discourses, as a knowing and willing "scapegoat" (487). Hers is a refigured self of beautiful abjection worthy of Nietzsche's theory of *ressentiment*. In a climactic scene enacted before all the others, Maggie receives the Judas kiss from Charlotte Stant Verver, her new stepmother, her best friend, and her husband's lover, as if Maggie were another betrayed Christ. As we would expect, however, this is an ironically triumphant act on Charlotte's part. It seals her fate. For thanks to Maggie's subtle influence, Adam Verver, James's fictional version of Andrew Carnegie and Maggie's indulgent god-like father, pulls the imaginary silken cord around Charlotte's neck so that he can lead his younger, wayward, and now inwardly wailing wife into American exile, where together they will educate the sublime wilderness in the beauty of high culture (544) while Maggie resurrects herself and her marriage to the Prince. Finally, the plays on and with the biblically resounding figure of "the dove" in *The Wings of the Dove* obviously foreground and eventually make central similar symbolic transformations.

James's characters and narrators are thus virtually perfect examples of what Paul Ricoeur calls in *Oneself as Another* "narrative identity." This means that the narrative self is a self-revising narrative ensemble of various mediating discourses and vocabularies, a composite mobile identity of self-designation, which "can only correspond to the [open-ended and] discordant concordance of the [developing] story itself" (142), as the story enacts itself in and as the novel's world. This story in late James, as I have suggested, largely concerns the progress of the judgment of taste in all its different aesthetic, social, and, ultimately, ontological implications. Taste, that is, stands between the conditions of class and the moral consequences of acting on the judgment of taste, at the threshold of larger, even ontological, meanings. Let me just note here that I follow Ricoeur in distinguishing between morality and ethics in that morality refers to conventional codes or mores and ethics refers to socially conditioned yet nonetheless individual situation-based innovations in such codes.

Because "class" is a term that will increasingly appear in my argument, I should say more specifically here what I take it to mean. "Class" is a term that has to be thought of in several ways. We see it operate cognitively, with little of its socioeconomic resonance, in the sense of how the world appears to be organized into sets, groupings, orders of beings, types of objects and persons, species. Maria Gostrey in *The Ambassadors* is called a master of typologies, having a pigeonhole for each object or person. Class in the sense of philosophical, epistemological, or cognitive classification is as important in Henry as in William James. The socioeconomic sense of class is even more evident, of course, as my example of Kate Croy and Merton Densher suggests and as my discussions in preceding chapters demonstrate. Class in this sense makes possible different kinds of access to the materials of culture necessary in making judgments of taste and of the beautiful. But how a character responds to the beautiful once one kind of access or another opens up is not strictly determined by the class origins or aspirations of the character. Although neither of Mrs. Newsome's commercial class (but still of her "set") nor of Madame de Vionnet's aristocratic class (but now in the same "boat" with her), Lambert Strether, for example, reacts to the beautiful in a way clearly his own, even if with more substantial affinities, perhaps, to Madame de Vionnet's sense of beauty.

Class in the strictly socioeconomic sense is, of course, a notoriously slippery concept for an often shifting reality. In *Making Sense of Marx,* Jon Elster demonstrates how complicated and inexact analyses of class often are, even when Marx himself is doing the analysis.[33] Is, for example, the clergy a class or a caste or a proto-profession? Should it be lumped in, as Marx does, with the landed aristocracy, even in the late Middle Ages? What about newer professions, such as academia and the modern mass media, which together form for Adorno and Horkheimer the basis of the so-called "culture industry"? Given the conflict-riven mobility of class consciousness and class aspirations, why should we define membership in a class as simply based on the amount and kind of material wealth or on the degree of actual ownership of the means of material production? Cultural production and cultural capital—are these metaphorical conceptions and analogies more than rhetorically adequate and appropriate? If so, how so?

For thinking about these general questions of socioeconomic class as I analyze James, I largely follow Richard Bushman's lead in *The Refinement of America*. Bushman studies how genteel culture and capitalism combine to produce modern mass consumer society. By 1900, more people than ever before can aspire to an upper-class lifestyle simply because they can now afford to buy the objects affiliated with that class, or later, merely their mass-produced simulacra. As Bushman sees it, this development is a double-edged sword. It reinforces certain aspects of the status quo, but it also promotes the designs of middle- and lower-class people who would usurp the lifestyle of the upper classes by acquiring the portable property of upper-class objects, stylish fashions, and fine interior house decorations. Such things are originally the possessions of the upper classes, especially the aristocracy in England and America in the eighteenth century. In the nineteenth century, these items identify the middle class of genteel culture: "Genteel culture was not an inheritance; it could be acquired by purchase. . . . In this context, the purchase of a Wedgwood vase became an act of cultural usurpation. . . . In a certain way the Wedgwood vase was a revolutionary presumption, an invasion of aristocratic circles by an excluded class. Genteel consumerism was a form of cultural revolution."[34] My remarks about socioeconomic class, with respect to characters such as Kate Croy and Fleda Vetch and their desire for beautiful things, should be understood in light of what Bushman has to say in his conclusion. He looks forward here from the story of eighteenth- and mid-nineteenth-century America he has recounted toward the emergence of modern international culture at the turn of the century, which is to be dominated by America and all things American. Bushman thus practically confirms Heidegger's theoretical sense of our modernity and its radical play of appearances.

Besides these two senses of class as cognitively and socioeconomically defined, there is also implied the sense of class as style, as in the expression "so-and-so has real class." This sense of class pervades late James, even to the point of self-parody, for Strether at least, when we recall that it is the manner by which Chad Newsome knows how to enter a theater box late that first defines the younger man's beautiful transformation for his older ironic champion. Finally, as one of my students in a seminar on James put it, there is also the sense of class as a site for, or a scene of, education and judgment.

The cognitive, socioeconomic, and aesthetic senses of class often exhibit themselves in the classroom all at once, since students are grouped, judged, and classified according to their cognitive ability; nowadays they often disclose their class affiliations and origins; and they often attempt in their manner of talking and writing to demonstrate how they understand class as they make critical judgments. Judgments of beauty, in James or in a course on James, I have found, are overdetermined, reflexive, social acts, as a reading of Pierre Bourdieu's magisterial analysis *Distinction* suggests. The fiction of late James is the fiction of judgment, and it is as much a classroom as the classroom is a "set" place of reading fictions.

I want at this point to try to put together my framework for analyzing James by giving a typical profile of a Jamesian scene of judgment and by suggesting how class in its several different but related senses functions in such a scene. A character (or, in the tales, a narrator) categorizes or classifies himself or herself (or is categorized or classified) as an outsider because of different socioeconomic and/or national origins. This character or narrator has gained, almost miraculously, access to the collective archive, the amassed cultural wealth of a society. This is the "romance" dimension of Jamesian "realism." The character or narrator now performs on the new state a surprisingly dramatic role we can evaluate. In this context, making the judgment of beauty usually takes one of two forms. On the one hand, the character or narrator realizes that the culture is irresistibly beautiful and that despite some uncertainty and much bewilderment, the sense of beauty is finally enough to justify society's evils. Lambert Strether, despite his Yankee antipathy to Old World aristocracies, after all, sides with one of their finest productions, Madame de Vionnet. In this first case, the character of narrator acts accordingly by trying to save the beautiful from some kind of ruin. At best, character or narrator gets in compensation for his or her pains imaginary possessions, just as Strether returns to America with a treasure of European, particularly Parisian, impressions. On the other hand, the character or narrator decides that his or her design to appropriate the material resources necessary to acquire a portion of the culture's aesthetic wealth is more beautiful than anything or anyone else. In this second case especially, aesthetic judgments on what the characters or narrators behold make their beautiful designs fraught with a visionary intensity. This sublime visionary intensity indicates a destructively romantic project, an irresistible illusion, which they often consider worth the sacrifice of honor, love, and friendship, so blinded and bewildered have they become. This is a Jamesian opposition between an appreciative socializing reception (or hard-won "disinterestedness") and radical acquisitiveness (or too easy "self-interestedness"). It recalls and revises the distinction in Kant between taste and genius. Characters such as Fleda Vetch and Kate Croy can be seen in light of this distinction. In fact, however, Fleda combines both kinds of response to beauty in her ironically destructive design of aesthetic salvation. One could also make a similar judgment about the Jamesian narrator of *The Sacred Fount*.

You will notice that I have used forms of the word "bewilderment" and "illusion" for both kinds of judgments of beauty—those self-bewildering projects of irresistible illusion. I'll call these different but related projects, respectively, the Strether kind of imaginative appreciation and the Kate Croy kind of material acquisition. The former project remains an ideal revisionism, whereas the latter project entails a literal usurpation. As I've already suggested, the most interesting situations occur when these opposing poles collapse into each other. Yet clearly marking these polar oppositions is analytically, heuristically helpful. I have used this nexus of bewilderment and illusion to lay out the Heideggerian basis of my argument, but I derive the terms equally from James himself. I will now elaborate on what James means by bewilderment, and shortly, I'll develop what he means by illusion in connection with later comments on *The Wings of the Dove*. James remarks in the preface to *The Princess Casamassima* that

> the whole thing comes to depend thus on the quality of bewilderment characteristic of one's creature, the quality involved in the given case or supplied by one's data. There are doubtless many such qualities [of bewilderment], ranging from vague and crepuscular to the sharpest and most critical; and we have but to imagine one of these later to see how easily—from the moment it gets its head at all—it may insist on playing a part. There we have then at once a case of feeling, of ever so

many possible feelings, stretched across the scene, like an attached thread on which the pearls of interest are strung.[35]

Analytically considered, the Jamesian character faces the competing beauties of the culture he or she judges and the nature of his or her own designs on it and its beautiful members. The Jamesian scene of judgment is a scene dependent for its condition of possibility on class in its various senses and entails moral and material consequences of some considerable import. It is primarily a scene of sustained bewilderment, fully recognized as such by the character or not, in which we, the readers, can appreciate and evaluate the quality of the bewilderment that the character undergoes as he or she makes his or her judgment of beauty and acts accordingly in light of one or another kind of irresistible illusion. For one example, there is the moment at Milly Theale's party in her Venetian palace when Kate Croy resentfully envisions herself as one day wearing Milly's long, winding string of lavish pearls, which Milly is now suggestively fingering before Kate's wide eyes. In this fashion, Kate imagines herself as finally becoming a beautiful "bejewelled dove," too. (Whether there is a lesbian dimension to this exhibition I'll leave to others to decide.) This is a projected visionary scene of material transformation that Densher now realizes he will never be able to help to make possible (490). Or for another example, there is the moment when Amerigo in *The Golden Bowl* finally succumbs to Charlotte's design for their adulterous affair. He does so, you'll recall, when he judges their prospective affair as being what Charlotte has always suggested it to be, the "too beautiful" solution to their impossible marriages (259). The quality of bewilderment thus often results in a self-betraying judgment made on the beauty of one's own kind of irresistible illusion.

James in this preface to *The Princess Casamassima* cites Thackeray as his sources for what he means by "the quality of bewilderment" and glosses the phrase by calling it "the condition . . . on which Thackeray so much insists in the interests of his exhibited careers, the condition of a humbled heart, a bowed head, a patient wonder, a suspended judgment, before the 'awful will' and the mysterious decrees of Providence" (238). My own sense of what James really means sends me back again to the romantics. Here I want to stress Keats on Shakespeare and his power of "negative capability." Later I will cite a Wordsworthian connection. There is a difference, however, between what James, Keats, and Thackeray mean. Even if James is closer in spirit to Keats, he is interested in the act of judgment performed amid bewilderment that reveals, in its quality, in its nature, the differences of motive and design, morality and feeling, that its characters undergo, without final recourse to divine providence or demonic skepticism. Ultimately, for most of his characters, the realm of the Jamesian scene of judgment remains worldly, contingent, human, avoiding the extremes of transcendental foundations. It is a realm founded on persistent doubts, uncertainties, perplexities, whether this bewilderment is initially recognized or not, and no matter how it is finally recognized, comically or tragically. This bewilderment in the face of irresistible illusion provides the characteristic drama in late James.

In *The Sacred Fount*, however, as read more than fifty years ago by R. P. Blackmur, there does appear to be a spectrally religious, albeit demonic, allegory barely buried. Blackmur uncovers this religious allegory via this strange novel's affinities with James's many late tales of haunted characters and narrators. The narrator of *The Sacred Fount* cries out at the end that he is caught between "bewilderment and joy" as his bizarre vampiric theory of the exchange of life-forces within a circle of two supposedly adulterous couples breaks down after being verbally assaulted by one of the women, Mrs. Brissenden (303). Her "right" and "beautiful" argumentative "tone" (311), something the narrator does not possess but admires, dispels the "sublime theory" (311), and the self-parodic Jamesian narrator, admitting defeat, leaves the weekend at the country estate early and alone.

Blackmur sees in this climax both James's recognition of the truth that social life requires lies and illusions to be lived at all and James's revelation, by invidious comparison, of the truly successful author's masterful role as the providential "conscience of his characters."[36] Blackmur sees James as virtually the divine mirror of their secret souls. This is a role that the novel's narrator can only demonically aspire to perform and unwittingly ends up parodying in his obsessive overreadings of those souls he would narrate as if he were their author. Blackmur's reading thus has James play the role of the gnostic alien god, in jealous relation to his narrator, who is thus consigned in this reading to the role of the botching, self-conscious, poor man's devil, the Demiurge. Whatever the case may be with this aesthetic metaphysics of the implied author, the dramatic crux of *The Sacred Fount,* as in the rest of late James, lies in the fact that the narrator's sublime theory breaks down precisely because he judges the beauty of Mrs. Brissenden's tone of argument to be just right. The formal, reflective determination of worldly beauty, as Kant in *The Critique of Judgment* would have it, takes precedence over the sublime. This is so no matter how methodologically useful and suggestively fraught or haunted by intimation of infinitude the sublime's indeterminate transcendentalism and vague religiosity appear to be.

One cannot help but recognize in the plight of James's characters, however, the way James displaces Thackeray's religious sublime, that condition of the latter's bewildered creatures before the "awful will" of an otherworldly power, to the "this-worldly" aesthetic realm of the late fiction. One could allegorize what James means by "the quality of bewilderment." We could read his characters' struggles with their suspended judgments, when their beautiful designs finally break down, as partial recognitions of their author's superior bewildering power of irresistible illusion. This aesthetic allegory would be open to a religious lesson, I suppose, but need not be limited to it. How the characters react to the collapse of their beautiful designs when confronted by the grand design (or grand illusion) of the larger plot in which they play their parts does make for interesting drama. As such, we can understand why James endorses the "quality of bewilderment" as an intense and complex measure of character vitality, reader interest, and authorial creation of narrative line and formal structure. I would suggest, to complete this line of thinking, that the author's grand design does not so much act as divine providence with either narrowly conventional or heterodox moral intentions as it acts like contingent fate with significant consequences, some of which are reflexively aesthetic and surprisingly ethical. This is especially so, as we'll see, when the author's own grand design also appears to suffer a breakdown. I would also suggest that in this difficult fashion, James's fiction stages the ontological difference between being and beings as radical formal contradiction.

In *The Wings of the Dove,* for example, there is a scene at the National Gallery in which Milly Theale observes her American "compatriots" swarming over the great museum on a Sunday in early August. For Milly, who is confronting fatal illness, they can do nothing to help her deal with living the last of her life in Europe. They seem to her to be "cut out as by scissors, coloured, labelled, mounted" (240). Milly recognizes in one of their faces especially "resentment humanised," but just barely so; this is resentment at all things European and different, as she overhears these "generic" Americans making their own negative judgments on the few singular British and other European types they observe (241). Because it is August, all these characters are rather oddly in London.

This is a characteristically Jamesian scene, one definitive for what comes to be known as the modernist and the literary. First, the protagonist stands in opposition to the world by virtue of circumstances that make for alienation. Milly's illness, her being the last survivor of the general wreck of her family, her nascent cosmopolitanism, her upper-class monied status, her somewhat more informed aesthetic sensibility, her being hopelessly in love with a man she knows is in love with another woman—all these plausible fictional contingencies make up the embodied alienation, her perspective of irony, her unhappy consciousness, if not her beautiful because so clearly suffering soul. She is thus momentarily in a position like that of her expatriated author, able to see her American compatriots as generic stereotypes, as thin and flat as the cultural world from which they come. But if the scene only dramatized this alienation, it would be conventionally romantic and not originally modernist. That the Americans judged by Milly to be no more than cutout and mounted stereotypes in the museum of national characters are in turn shown judging others, by their own lights, in a similarly harsh way—this irony makes one reflect on the status of Milly's own American form of judgment and its possible relationship to the point of view of the novel or to that of its author. How much of Milly's judgment is just the bewildered projection of her irresistible illusion becomes a real question as her American compatriots, who are now other for her, make their similar judgments, which make others of everyone around them. Is othering people the American mode of becoming other, par excellence? We even begin to wonder if Milly is other now for us, or by extension is the Jamesian narrator, or the author. Is the point of all this fuss with point of view, James's radical perspectivism and specular scenes, that each of us is really other to ourselves as well as for others, even if we rarely if ever dramatically know it? Do we really seek answers to these questions? Well, we don't, of course, at least if we read this scene in the best modernist way. Instead, we read it as irony at play, perhaps absolute irony at absolute play, contained, if at all, only by the reflexive chimera of so-called "organic form."

The reader's bewilderment is naturally mirrored by, and contingent on, the bewilderment of the characters. Milly reflects a bit earlier in the novel on the perceived differences between "the American mind" and "the monster" of English society (232). Her reflections remind one of those hypothetical cases found in analytic philosophy. Milly realizes, the closely mimicking narrator interpolates, that "in certain connections the American mind broke down. It seemed at least—the American mind as sitting there thrilled and dazzled in Milly—not to understand English society without a separate confrontation with all the cases" (232). That is, when confronting a complex society such as English society, the American mind cannot synthesize and generalize from one or two representative cases.

> It couldn't proceed by—there was some technical term she lacked until Milly suggested [to herself] both analogy and induction, and then, differently, instinct, none of which were right: It had to be led up and introduced to each aspect of the monster, enabled to walk all around it, whether for the consequent exaggerated ecstacy or the still more . . . disproportionate shock. (232)

In other words, when facing the sublime monster of English society, the American mind apparently does not possess the capacity for determinant judgment, which generalizes on the basis of representative cases in light of a universal premise.

As we have already noted, however, ten pages later in the novel, the American mind embodied in Milly and her compatriots does not proceed only by reflective judgment, which formulates the rule of each individual case in its inductive, ever-approximating quest for a general rule for all such cases; instead, the American mind, whether judging itself or others, proceeds by determinant judgment. It universalizes from the thinnest and most typical of features and is informed by a comparatively poor sense of taste in its selection of universal premises. This is an abuse of judgment, but this very abuse nevertheless attests to the existence of the capacity for such judgment. One could argue that since Milly is generally a finer representative of the American mind than her compatriots, there is no contradiction between what is said about her, earlier or later, and the museum Americans, only that there is a significant degree of difference. But as I have suggested, James's novel goes out of its way to highlight Milly's potential self-implication in the mode of judgment she would condemn in her compatriots. As Milly is bewildered by English society, therefore, so the reader is now bewildered by Milly Theale in this way (among others), and indeed by the entire contradictory novel her character is intended to center.

When we turn to the author's 1907 preface to the novel for help, we get none, apparently. To underscore my point, I need to mention an essay by George McFadden. He cites (among many other things) James's admission to Ford Madox Heuffer (soon to become Ford Madox Ford) that "I let my system [of experimentation] betray me [and my original intentions]."[37] One of these is to be fairer to Kate by developing a fuller portrait of her cynically calculating father, Lionel Croy, something the finished novel fails to do, at least to James's own satisfaction. Bewilderment and illusion, it would appear, thus take, beautifully, the measure of the supposed master's judgment, as James fails to be fairer to Kate, among the other betrayals of his original intentions, and so he feels guilty here in not living up to the high standards of his intellectual conscience, a guilt that returns to haunt the novel's last scene. Not only does James in his preface confess to having lost control of his novel, of not having finely executed his original design, and of botching the central chapter and of having foreshortened too much here and elaborated too much there (among other failures he self-consciously notes); he also announces as his aesthetic principle the very creation of difficulty leading to bewilderment that we have already seen in contradictory action:

> The enjoyment of a work of art, the acceptance of an irresistible illusion, constituting, to my sense, our highest experience of "luxury," the luxury is not the greatest, by my consequent measure, when the work asks for as little attention as possible. It is greatest, it is delightfully, divinely great, when we feel the surface, like the thick ice of the skater's pond, bear without cracking the strongest pressure we throw on it. (The sound of the crack one may recognise, but never surely to call it a luxury.) (49)

James at the end here alludes to the practice of testing to see if the ice of a frozen pond will still hold a skater by placing objects of increasing weight on it until the right weight is reached, or the ice cracks. In this context, bewilderment, for readers as for characters, is the result of the aesthetic principle of difficulty perfected by James. James courts his own (and our) bewilderment and breakdown of control by building up and laying on thick the weighty self-conscious complications of, and attention to, the myriad of details of his "irresistible illusion." The risk of self-contradiction is run precisely to test how far illusion may go before it becomes resistible, ironically enough, and so gives way and gives itself away; that is, in James's conceit, before we too hear the sound of the crack, and suspend our willing suspension of disbelief. At various points in rereading and revising this novel for the New York Edition, James apparently hears the sound of the crack, which is, as he implies, no luxury for him, even if it proves ironically instructive to us.

Despite my prominent echoing of Coleridge, I believe that James in this passage primarily revises two scenes from Wordsworth. (Americanists may also recall here Emerson's visionary snow puddle from *Nature*.) In his preface to *The Lyrical Ballads*, Wordsworth remarks on the hierarchy of pleasure distinguishing one mind from another. There is, on the one hand, the savage torpor of sensationalism. This is how Wordsworth characterizes the pleasure of the uneducated democratic populace in a modern urban and commercial culture that caters to the least common denominator of fashionable and fickle taste. There is, on the other hand, the more refined pleasure taken in poetry and in the different kinds of poetry. The highest poetic pleasure is that which results from the recollection, preservation, and reflection of the original emotion. Such poetry produces a tranquil state of yet more than usual excitement. This unusual state arises originally out of a sublimity more naturally refined than newspapers and romances afford us. Although Wordsworth does not say so, poetry clearly dissimulates this refined illusion and benign bewilderment. Or so James's revision allows us to see.

Between these opposing poles of high and low pleasure, and so of high- and low-mindedness, of high and low culture, one can imagine a spectrum or hierarchy of pleasures, minds, cultures, each phase or level of which defines a different kind of taste.[38] In addition to this Wordsworthian sense of aesthetic pleasure informing the foregoing passage in James's preface on the enjoyment of the work of art as the highest experience of luxury, there is also another Wordsworthian scene, I think, informing James's spectral figure of the skater in his expression "the skater's pond." I'm thinking of the skating scene of instructive dizziness in *The Prelude*.[39] These Wordsworthian traces, however, are transformed by James into his conceptions of irresistible illusion and the quality of bewilderment. And it is with such revisionary transformation that I am here concerned.

Wordsworth's experience of permanent natural forms becomes James's highest experience of luxury, and luxury is the Jamesian name for the enjoyment, the pleasure, taken in the work of art as an irresistible aesthetic illusion leading to different qualities of bewilderment. Irresistible natural reality has become irresistible poetic illusion. The skater's instructive dizziness has become the reader's quality of bewilderment. The pleasure of poetry has become the luxury of enjoyment taken in fiction. James's idea of bewilderment derives in part from the overloading of attention—the imagination's being engrossed in and by intellectual contingencies—in a way surprisingly related to Wordsworth's imagination of sublime nature in his poetry. The test of aesthetic illusion in James—how much complication can we stand before we say enough, and so say no to the illusion of art—has a Wordsworthian origin. Bewilderment, in fact, is ever present in a scene of instructive dizziness such as one from *The Prelude* that recalls an experience of ice-skating as a scene of the young mind's education by, and judgment on, nature. In James, bewilderment is the condition induced by the ironic play of perspective as the primary means of our aesthetic education in the highest experience of luxury, the irresistible illusion of great, divinely great art. The measure of judgment in James, for characters, readers, and author, is therefore this complex relationship between bewilderment and illusion.

What has helped to transform the original romantic topoi from the realm of nature in Wordsworth to that of worldly art in James is, I believe, the supervention of the discourse of class as a basis for the terms of the revision. Class in late James is a revisionary transformer, as it were. Wordsworth, despite his horror at modern democracy's savage torpor of sensationalistic culture, stands opposed to visions of luxury. But James uses the term "luxury"—which derives from the Latin *voluptuous* and, as such, rings throughout Gibbon's *Decline and Fall of the Roman Empire,* a favorite work of James's at this time—because he wants to indicate the primary condition of possibility for experiencing art in the way he desires his reader to do so, namely, the capacity to appreciate all sorts of "luxury," especially art; and yet he also wants to detach, via the scare quotes, the term "luxury" from its original class contest and use it to transform the romantic aesthetic he inherits into one more appropriate to his later, so-called liberal democratic phase in the class history of modern nation-states. James wants to be able to claim, following Arnold, Emerson, Wordsworth, and Schiller, that the "luxury" of art is imaginatively affordable, regardless of its class origins, to all those who can and do choose to read for the pleasure of difficulty, a choice and a capacity that modern education in the forms of fiction can develop with comparatively less restriction than the class system in the narrow socioeconomic sense would seem to allow. Class as a cognitive and ethical style is an affordable luxury for those willing to work for it, even as class as socioeconomic status may be less available, however pervasive the myth of the American dream may become.

Author, narrator, character, reader: all these figures of interpretation put into circulation by James's ironic play of point of view engage in explicit and implicit judgments. These judgments are most often judgments of beauty that disclose the state of their respective aesthetic educations. Even more tellingly, such judgments disclose the state of bewilderment these figures experience as they face the irresistible illusion of what they deem to be beautiful. For some, the beautiful is their own materially acquisitive designs and self-betraying resentful projects. Less often, for others, it is the inherited cultural wealth, the refined luxury, of the collective archive, on which they do their more imaginatively appreciative revisions, much as James does here on Wordsworth, or Strether does apropos the romantic beauty of Madame de Vionnet, a beauty that, as I've already suggested, is a latter-day version of Shakespeare's Cleopatra and her "infinite variety." A spectrum of possible responses results from this revisionary situation, which can become a hierarchy of judgment in any particular scene or work. The world of nature and its more permanent objects have been replaced by the world of modern society and its shifting strata and personnel. As we have seen from James's preface to *The Wings of the Dove*, however, the presumed authority figure among all these other figures, the author, may just have to confess to knowing and accomplishing far less than he would have liked in this brave new modern world. In James, then, there is no certain and fixed "master" of the novel form. The measure of judgment for all concerned occurs each time as a radically uncertain, contingent act.

Bewilderment, known, repressed, projected onto others, recognized and taken upon oneself—this is the condition of human existence in James. Its positive mode is sympathetic identification with other bewildered existences. Illusion, disclosed by bewilderment, is the mode of being, the manner in and by which being appears or manifests itself and traces its withdrawal in and as what I, after Heidegger, call dissimulation or dissemblance. Its positive mode is art, the reflexive aesthetic illusion exposing as it uses the appearances of beauty and class for its own purposes. In James, human existence, what Heidegger terms Dasein, is bewilderment, a repeatedly becoming other; and in James, being, Heidegger's Sein, is illusion or untruth. There is a reciprocal, dialogic relationship, of Dasein and Sein, of bewilderment and illusion, in Heidegger, in James. This relationship I call the measure of judgment. This measure of judgment is not simply the subjective disillusionment of the bewildered human existence ironically reflecting on the illusion of being; nor it is the de facto judgment implicitly passed by this mode of being as illusion on the beautiful projects of human existence. Rather, the measure of judgment is an open process of critical recognition and reflection that knows no end, has no origin, and becomes irresistibly bewildering in and as the conscience of the reader.

As if in uncanny anticipation of this last point of the 1907 preface, Milly Theale in *The Wings of the Dove* (1901) repeatedly receives a weird impression of Kate Croy. Milly sees Kate as a part of an identity she knows the total of which stands directly only before Merton Densher (174, 229, 299). Milly curiously delights in this strange experience, finds it stimulating to her appetite for motive, and terms it "seeing abysses" in people rather than in mountain prospects (174). It is as if Kate, often portrayed as the consummate actress, in beautifully dissimulating an appearance of disconnection from Densher for the purposes of her secret plot, nonetheless discloses thereby the sublimely spectral presence of what the absent "total of her being" must be for her other's intentionally unwitting yet nonetheless conspiratorially intimate gaze, before which she presents and exhibits herself apparently in full immediacy (229). A knowing bewilderment of considerable ethical weight results for Milly from such clear play of illusion, such "beautiful" untruth of sublime truth, as Milly Theale and Martin Heidegger might together declare. Milly, like James, hears the sound of the crack in the very artifice that would captivate. The acceptance of irresistible illusion is our highest pleasure precisely so long as we can recognize such luxury as both afforded by class status and generally productive of a difficult art of reading always potentially subversive of any kind of artifice.

In this ironic light, Kate Croy's famous exit line previously cited, "We shall never again be as we were" (509), could function, among other more obvious ways, as an existential recognition of revisionary repetition's failure and so of her consequent entrapment within the configurations of a larger design than her own. Milly Theale's posthumous bequest to Merton Densher would not constitute this larger design, because Milly's intention to go ahead with the bequest, despite knowing all, only helps to complete the fiction of the grand design. Admittedly, Milly's intention is contingently formative of Densher's conscience, but it has its essential origin elsewhere. It lies in the entire plot. Despite her best efforts to refigure her self otherwise, as another "bejewelled dove" like Milly, Kate Croy is doomed finally to figure as a melodramatically evil, if still rather perversely fascinating, villainess. The ultimate effort of James's grand design, despite his best intentions and for which he should perhaps feel some remorse, is to vulgarize Kate Croy. He reduces her to the melodramatic role of the failed author of a sordid plot, that of arranging for her clandestine lover to marry a dying young American heiress, so that Merton Densher and she can abscond with the gold. Kate Croy is the only character to rival her author in power and subtlety of design and so is virtually James's major female emanation in the novel. Kate, after all, first titles Milly "the dove," as if to author Milly as the trained or captive centerpiece of her ambiguous plot. Her melodramatic transformation testifies, I suggest, to James's act of reducing his latter-day version of the Gnostic Sophia, with her passion for error, to the mundane level of a pure vulgarity. The veiling "wings of the dove" covering in the end Kate Croy and Merton Densher would then refer equally to the class differences—in all my senses—between them and Milly Theale and to the cloth "wings" of her author's two-volume novel now theatrically closing, as she would exit its final tableau, around her terrible cry. James would thus be the author as jealous god of last judgments, deeply implicated in and indicated by the irresistible illusion of the novel's most vital character's function as his incarnate bad conscience. The quality of bewilderment, even as Kate now recognizes and responds to, as she reads, the demonic fate befalling her, would thus continue to reverberate, formally and reflexively, in the clearing of James's self-betraying art, as if forever otherwise. Such would be indeed a "luxurious" class act—on James's part at least. James both cares that he has reduced Kate and cares enough for her to release her to her self-elected fate. This duality in the creator's mind produces the novel as a double-edged sword of judgment from the reader's perspective of (self-)critical conscience. For me, therefore, Kate Croy best embodies the conscience of the reader in this novel and in the rest of late James. If you, too, find this provocative revision so, this would surely be a becoming other, in every sense, and with a vengeance.

I conclude with the complete passage, alluded to previously from *The Wings of the Dove*, my "intertext," if you will, to which the preceding analysis serves as a critical prolegomena for a future study that I hope can do full justice to this novel, to James, and to what I envision as the anatomy of judgment and the critique of fiction we still need:

> "But she's too nice," Kate returned with appreciation. "Everything suits her so—especially her pearls. . . ." Densher, though aware he had seen them before, had perhaps not "really" looked at them, and had thus not done justice to the embodied poetry . . . which owed them part of its style. Kate's face, as she considered them, struck him: the long, priceless chain, wound twice round the neck, hung, heavy and pure, down the front of the wearer's breast—so far down that Milly's trick, evidently unconscious, of holding and vaguely fingering and entwining a part of it, conduced presumably to convenience. "She's a dove," Kate went on, "and one somehow doesn't think of doves as bejewelled. Yet they suit her down to the ground." "Yes—down to the ground is the word." . . . Milly was indeed a dove; this was the figure, though it most applied to her spirit. Yet he knew in a moment that Kate was just now, for reasons hidden from him, exceptionally under the impression of that element of wealth in her which was a power, which was a great power, and which was dove-like only so far as one remembered that doves have wings and wondrous flights, have them as well as tender tints and soft sounds. . . . "Pearls have such a magic that they suit every one." "They would uncommonly suit you," he

frankly returned. As she saw herself, suddenly, he saw her—she would have been splendid; and with it he felt more what she was thinking of. Milly's royal ornament had—under pressure now not wholly occult—taken on the character of a symbol of differences, differences of which the vision was actually in Kate's face. It might have been in her face too that, well as she certainly would look in pearls, pearls were exactly what Merton Densher would never be able to give her. Wasn't that the great difference that Milly tonight symbolised? She unconsciously represented to Kate, and Kate took it in at every pore, that there was nobody with whom she had less in common than a remarkably handsome girl married to a man unable to make her on any such lines as that the least little present. (389–90)

Perhaps Derrida's "absolute" arrivant or ever-spectral newcomer may give us the global perspective on James's "Baroque" fiction of judgment that we still need, especially with respect to *The Golden Bowl* and its exquisite prophecy of our global America.

11

Planet Buyer and the Catmaster:

A Critical Future for Transference

● ●

Nietzsche retells the legend of Buddha's "tremendous, gruesome shadow," which his disciples exhibited long after their master's death, crouching in a cave. Since the Judeo-Christian God is now dead, and given this "way of men" in religious matters, Nietzsche reasons, "there may be caves for thousands of years in which his shadow will be shown—and we—we still have to vanquish his shadow, too."[1] My retelling in chapter 8 of Freud's revisionary analysis of the self-destructive split at the origin of the spiritual realm—its basis in moral narcissism—concluded with the specter of global America virtually haunting the cultural critic's every imaginative horizon, no matter what the geopolitical realities are. And chapters 9 and 10 invoked the specter of theory, Paul de Man, and the practice of reading in Henry James, to reforge for critical culture in global America a "bad" conscience about its social status and political "bad faith."

I am not, however, a latecomer to the subject of the specter. My first book, *Tragic Knowledge: Yeats's Autobiography and Hermeneutics* (1981), reads Yeats's account of his life in terms of his theory of the "anti-self" or "daimon," that spirit of the dead grafted, via the mask, to the core of the living self and opposing it with a passionate ferocity and loving persistence that turn a life into a heroic contest with one's fate. My second book, *The Romance of Interpretation: Visionary Criticism from Pater to de Man* (1985), reads the work and careers of Pater, Frye, Hartman, Bloom, and de Man in light of the desire to turn themselves, via their different theories (aesthetic, mythic, phenomenological, psychoanalytic, and deconstructive), into the "spectral messiah" for the profession of literary study, at the tragic cost of creating for literary study various "scapegoat muses" out of the texts, figures, techniques, and people that helped to take them to the top. Similarly, my next book, *Lionel Trilling: The Work of Liberation* (1988), tracced what I called the diverse "spectral politics" at play in the making of Trilling's representative career as a social critic in Cold War America. And finally, in *Radical Parody: American Culture and Critical Agency after Foucault* (1992), I argued via many different cases in contemporary criticism for the emergence of a new critical genre, "radical parody," which was "the spectral double," the ironic pastiche of radical social criticism, a mode of discourse too often unconsciously subversive of the politically correct intentions of its self-deceived users, including, perhaps especially, myself.

In this book, I have been attempting to show the different ways in which American critics in the last decade have negotiated a curious double movement, whereby they cite what I call "the abjection of America," enacted by American-oriented global elites (economic and cultural), as the motive for performing their own "global transference," their leap into "globality" or "globalization" studies, whether expressed as cynical realpolitik or utopian idealism (however muted). In this self-betraying fashion, they can renew their professional identities now that the theory and the culture wars have passed, by assuming, intellectually and institutionally, their self-appointed roles as the administrators and managers of the international order and culture of that latest specter of divinity, global America. Thus empire and identity are ever intertwined.

A good shorthand way of conceiving of "the spectral," whether one is considering Blake or Freud or Derrida, is to think of it as an anachronistic experience of temporality, as the ghost of future guilt to come. As such, the spectral displays the narrative structure of romantic fantasy, even as it exists virtually as a purely infinite limit. The pattern of transference and abjection may indeed arise in the past, but it is experienced as coming out of the future, albeit according to an uncanny course of action, in which moral narcissism may become abject narcissism.

The Abjection of America

Abjection is a psychoanalytic concept that refers to the child's mental process by which the figure of the mother suffers a horrific reduction in status and value. This reduction is usually symbolized as a miserable fall from an ideal state of purity and power to a physical state of total defilement. As such, abjection prepares the way for both the endowment of the father figure with the power and authority to prohibit incest, real or fantasized, and the reorientation of the child to the reality of other people's desires. These other desires must often conflict with the child's desire for the exclusive possession of the mother's narcissistic reflexive attention, as that attention manifests itself in speech, in discourse solely about the child's desire. Thus the institution of the father's "No," the law prohibiting incest or the folie à deux par excellence, revises self-reference into social reference.

The neatness of this developmental-psychoanalytic conception of abjection belies certain apparent contradictions in this conception, as well as hiding abjection's other dimensions. In order for the mother's abjection to make way for the father's ascension, an ego, however fragile, must exist and serve as a means of activating and transferring, in a directed linear fashion, such emotional investments and disinvestments. But if such a synthesizing ego exists beyond the mother's authority over the child's body, why the developmental necessity of abjection and reidentification? In addition, the linear developmental pattern depends on an experience of temporality that is nonlinear but not synchronous, a kind of original belatedness. Only after the fact of abjection can the narcissistically invested ego emerge to identify with the imaginary father, but to identify with the imaginary father makes possible the achievement of the mother's abjection. This radical reversal of times, in which what was first becomes last and last first, haunts the developmental schema with the irony of bad faith.

The moment of abjection does not propel a developmental history so much as it compromises, like perversion, all such progressive schemata. Because the mother is generally the primary caregiver in human society, the mother exercises authority, however conscious or unconscious, over the process by which erotogenic zones are demarcated over the surface of the child's body. The child's first sense of self is thus a semiotic and prelinguistic one. That is, cognitively, the child experiences itself and its world via a semiotic inscription of its body. Touches, caresses, gestures, and looks create oral, anal, and genital zones and define fragmentally both the self the child dimly perceives and the world the child feels possessed of. Any narcissistic investment of the child's ego requires the additional action of subsuming the semiotic under the symbolic (and verbal), of abjecting the mother's imaginary authority and elevating the father's moral law.

As have done many critics and theorists, especially Julia Kristeva in *Powers of Horror,* I also want to expand the concept of abjection from its particular psychoanalytic focus to a broader cultural context. But rather than follow Kristeva's lead and discuss the function of abjection in the formation of an anti-Semitic and chauvinistic imagination of a writer, or see abjection's socialized appearance in the corruption of victimization by bad faith, I want to analyze the literary strategy of *abjecting the father* as a critical democratic imagination now available to us, thanks to the sustained and systematic critiques of multicultural, feminist, gay and lesbian, African American, neopragmatist, and New Historicist critics, all of whom, for convenience's sake, we can term "New Americanists." To abject the father is to return to the semiotic, the aesthetic, and the "feminine" definition of the incipient self and world encoded in and by the figurative play of texts structured by the symbolic conventions of rationalized fictions of all sorts. The net effect of the work of New Americanists is to effect such a return. I will assume the general presence of such work, even as I will also choose here not to single out any one critic or group as quintessentially "New Americanist," since such spotlighting is not useful, given both my previous discussions and my chosen text's radically contemporary nature. Instead, in reading later "Minor Heroism," by Allan Gurganus, I want to demonstrate that one future of American literature, thanks to American studies and its recent focus on narratives of identity and national fantasy, exists right now. But before doing so I need to address in more detail my psychosocial use of the psychoanalytic concept of abjection as an ironic literary strategy of a revisionary critical imagination of America.

We understand the main problem with using psychoanalytic concepts for social analyses. The biological and physical dimensions of psychoanalytic discourse, no matter how metaphorical we take them to be, create false expectations that the clinical and cultural phenomena psychoanalysis examines can be treated, even cured, as if psychoanalysis were an empirically based medical science of the body (not the mind), and as if these phenomena were unalterable or recurrent, typical features of some kind of human nature. The concept of abjection in psychoanalysis assumes a developmental pattern in which the child must abject the phallic mother on the way to recognizing the father's ultimate authority over all expressions of desire, if the child is to become a so-called normal adult.

Given this tendency of psychoanalytic concepts to entail a naturalizing attitude toward, and a universalizing myth of, cultural phenomena, why use any of them at all, and especially why use "abjection," which invokes a drive to naturalize with a vengeance? After all, isn't abjection basically akin to pulling the pedestal down so that the mother eats dirt? And isn't this iconoclastic drive finally in the service of recognizing the father's exclusive possession of the phallus, the traditional symbol of patriarchal power?

In fact, I don't believe that abjection as a psychological mechanism necessarily concerns gender at all. Rather, abjection concerns *number,* an elementary mathematical equation, and not a natural dynamic of the family romance. Lacan's impossible matheme and Borromean knots are more appropriate here. As one might well ask, what is this equation? *Whatever is first must become last, and whatever is second must become first, and so on, ad infinitum.* That is, the dynamic of abjection is not a natural, biologically determined process at all. It is instead a cognitive and rhetorical process, contingently conditioned, of the revisionary imagination, of the will to revise the past.

Let's take (once again) the example of Freud at the opening of chapter 7, "The Psychology of the Dream-Processes," from *The Interpretation of Dreams.*[2] To rehearse his theory of dreams as disguised wish fulfillment, you recall that Freud recounts the dream of a female patient who hears about this dream originally from a male lecturer on dreams—it's not Freud—and she proceeds to repeat the dream, apparently without significant variation.

The dream is that of a father who has lost his son to fever. Exhausted, he asks an old manservant to stand watch in an adjoining room over the son's body surrounded by burning tapers. In his dream, the father witnesses his son reproach him, pulling his arm and inquiring, *"Father, can't you see that I am burning?"* (652). As the father awakens, he catches sight of a glare coming from where the son's body lies. He rushes into the room to discover that the old manservant has fallen asleep at his post and a lit taper has dropped onto the son's arm, severely burning it.

Freud's female patient, a lesbian, had recounted this dream polemically, to argue against Freud's theory of wish fulfillment, since presumably no father would wish to be reproached by his dead son. What the lecturer on dreams, from whom she first heard this dream, has said about it she omits to tell Freud. She thereby becomes the first teller of the dream's meaning, even as she remains in this sequence or set the second teller of the dream itself, just as the lecturer was its first teller—excluding its presumed original teller, of course, the father himself, about whom no one knows anything, not even his name. As she deprives the lecturer of his interpretation, thereby reducing the lecturer to a mere source of her own critical significance, she would also deprive Freud of his theory. But Freud goes on to show that the same dream content—*"Father, can't you see that I am burning?"*—can accommodate a potentially infinite series of meanings: the father's, the lecturer's, the patient's, Freud's, and so on. Freud's meaning for the dream is twofold: the father wishes to see his son alive so much, even if just for one more moment, that he suffers the guilt of the son's reproach, which becomes truthful belatedly. The father's dream delays him from preventing significant damage to the dead son's arm from the fallen taper. Just as the second known teller of the dream, the female patient, had supplanted the first known teller, the lecturer on dreams, so now Freud replaces his patient as the first teller—not of the dream itself, or of one of its meanings, but of the theory of how the mechanisms of the dream processes makes any and all of its overdetermined meanings possible.

Lacan, of course, in *The Four Fundamental Concepts of Psychoanalysis* (Seminar Eleven), goes on to reconceptualize this theory, using and reusing this dream and its interpretations throughout the volume, which is one reason I won't plumb the complexities of Lacan's reading of Freud's reading of his female patient's reading of the lecturer's account of the living father's dream interpretation of the dead son's ghostly reproachfulness. To use Lacan's language for a moment, however, we can conclude that whoever possesses the key to new meaning or the phallus suffers in turn the repeated abjection of that meaning by yet newer meanings, ad infinitum, as imaginary priority, gets symbolically displaced and re-established in the never-ending equations of the real.[3] In sum, an ironically "infinite calculus," as opposed to any infinitesimal calculus, reigns here, much as Lacan suggests in "The Seminar on 'The Purloined Letter.' "

As an interpretive economy of the revisionary imagination, this technique of abjection appears starkly in a story by Allan Gurganus from his 1991 collection *White People*.[4] The very fact that Gurganus, most famous as the author of *The Oldest Living Confederate Widow Tells All*, which was also a network miniseries, can entitle this short-story volume as he does suggests the strength and range of the multicultural critique mounted by the New Americanists. After all, to specify "white people" as such implies that you are not assuming that they constitute automatically the social and cultural norm. In fact, as the volume's best story "Minor Heroism: Something about My Father" demonstrates, the idea of a representative norm has been replaced by the reality of an aesthetic practice of life that recognizes no one norm but makes pragmatic use of the formative values of all sorts of identities, including female, African American, gay, and Cold War liberal. The story's aim is to conduct the abjection of the Cold War father figure, an abjection that not only reverses the psychoanalytic abjection of the phallic mother but also constitutes in principle the definitive abjection of "America," as that term has been known in and by American studies here and around the globe.

"Minor Heroism" consists of two parts and an addendum. The first part, "At War, at Home," is as long as the second part, "My Elder Son," and the addendum put together. I'll return to this deliberate structural lack of classical balance and decorous proportion shortly. "At War, at Home" is apparently built on a series of dramatic contrasts between the heroic and horrific exploits of the narrator's father, a bombardier who participated in the firebombing of Dresden, and the domestic and professional routine of the humdrum postwar era. Such contrasts are best represented by a photograph of this tall, blond, strikingly handsome flyboy war hero being kissed by Betty Grable as it circulates on the home front both during and immediately after World War II. At first, the photograph literally stands larger than life, in stark relief, on the stage where Eleanor Roosevelt and the hero's shy mother exchange admiring words for this hero as they rally the rural Virginia townsfolk to buy war bonds. Then the photograph marks the spot in the narrator's house where the load-bearing walls are conjoined, as if it were holding the house up and together. Finally, the photograph becomes in its faded yellow newspaper copies both a reminder of how the narrator's father got a job selling insurance by cashing in on his brief moment of fame and a later inspiration above the beds of young men all over town as they fantasize their own more explicit "minor heroics" with Betty Grable. The war hero of "national fantasy," the narrator remarks, has turned into a model of "identity" for pimply loners (214).

This severe opposition between the heroic and the domestic worlds, however, has been elided metaphorically from the story's opening, when the narrator uses the conceit of smoke-cured hams to connect his father's fraternity experience "hanging out" at the University of Virginia with his "hanging over" the differently curative burning of German cities. In a long passage, the narrator recounts his childhood vision of the firebombing of Dresden. He imagines it as an Alice-in-Wonderland explosion of dinner china and kitchen utensils, an uncanny punning holocaust that manages to suggest how the domestic and the heroic worlds are madly one in "the black deluge" of hot oil now covering and cooking the globe. Above this ironically abject spectacle, the exalted specter of his father's prodigious bomber returns home (214).

"At War, at Home," the title of this first part of the story, could better be read, therefore, without the delicately positioned comma. This part ends with the narrator's father commanding his young sons to help him incinerate and crush tent caterpillars, as if he planned a fully equipped military operation, a war game that Bradley, the younger son, revels in, but that sickens Bryan, the older son and narrator: "Shut up down there, you two. You'll do your job and keep your mouths closed. These things are going to get to other trees. . . . This is an emergency, so quit squealing like sissies and stomp them. That clear?" (216–17).

At war at home? Clearly. But the images we take away with us from this first part of "Minor Heroism" are images of abjection, such as the "clusters of black caterpillars, pounds of them, toppling from their webs, falling to the ground and steaming," causing this minor war hero's young sons to make "girlish noises" as they start hopping on "the smoldering worms" (216). Perverse images of blackness, of physical dissolution, of femininity, of Cold War paranoia and male panic, trace the arc of the father's fall into Cold War abjection. This is a portrait made possible by

Gurganus's imaginative receptivity to his mentor's strong critique of America. John Cheever's later works, such as *Bullitt Park* and *Falconer*, herald a revisionary imagination of America that continues in the multicultural discourses of the New Americanists.

The second part of "Minor Heroism," entitled "My Elder Son," represents a complete shift in point of view. Gurganus suspends his narrator to allow the latter's father to speak his own piece. Largely a confession of helplessness before the transformation of his elder son into an openly gay writer, this second part, the father's self-portrait in his own words and style, is a tour de force of progressively climactic revelations of the father's physical violence against his elder son, even when the latter is twenty-seven years old. These revelations are, of course, horribly rationalized as the son's fault, but more importantly than this, they serve as dramatic representations to further humiliate and abject the father ironically through his own words. Bryan, the elder son and narrator of this story's first part and of the "Addendum," does respond to his father's latest assault. He wraps his head in white cotton gauze like a mummy and goes off to church with his surprised parents. He is really unhurt and a practicing atheist. In this way, he may tell the people at church "exactly who's responsible for this" New Year's morning nightmare of signifying whiteness (223).

This clever revenge of the resentful weak against the normally strong, the father predicts, will come to dominate his elder son's fictional career in the future: "Someday he'll probably publish a story or a whole book about what a tyrant I've been. I can imagine a chapter listing all the times I ever raised my voice or hit him" (224). In fact, not only does the elder-son narrator allow his father to displace him in this story, but Bryan uses his father's own words not just to indict homophobia but also to divine a motive for forgiveness, thereby liberating his literary work from the predicted all-consuming resentment. "I wanted too much for him," the father claims, concluding his part, "and considering all the ways you can go wrong with a son," he adds, "it seems the one he would be quickest to forgive" (224).

If the story had ended at this point, it would have been like an ironic Jamesian conditional sentence, one of whose clauses would be perpetually overturning the other. But the story does not end here. It continues into a third part, the short "Addendum," which gives the entire story a classical three-part shape of beginning, middle, and end, but in a deliberately unequal fashion of virtually grotesque proportions. To continue my sentence analogy, it is as if that ironically self-overturning conditional sentence preceded a gnomic sentence fragment.

This is not to say that the "Addendum" is obviously unclear. On the surface, it is Bryan's narrative of an earlier incident from his childhood. After being slapped by his father "two times in one week" (226), he begins anxiously to anticipate another slap. This is because he at first and for the longest time refuses to show his father the drawing he is completing at the breakfast table. The drawing is a portrait of his father in uniform, posed in the kitchen before the threshold of the dining room, framed by his mother's potted houseplants. Here's how the narrator puts it: "In this drawing I am doing, a tall red man holds the hand of a small white boy. The man wears a decorative uniform: policeman, soldier, milkman. He is much taller than the child, but his right arm has been conveniently elongated, elasticized like a sling or bandage so it easily supports the boy's white hand" (224).

This "conveniently elongated, elasticized" red-uniformed right arm, looking like "a sling or bandage so it easily supports the boyish figure of the narrator's white hand," represents at once the visionary conflation of heroic, disciplinary, and domestic worlds via the associated figures of "policeman, soldier, milkman" (224), and their imaginary abjection in the surreally fluent symbolization of the father's right arm, as if it were simultaneously deformed, wounded, and unreal. The right arm of the father appears as an aesthetic convenience. It is already suggestive of the limp-wristed stereotype for the son that this father should recognize and despise, as well as the long arm of authority.

When the narrator finally shows his father the drawing, however, the father doesn't recognize this trait. This is because the more the father demands, with rising anger, that the boy show him the drawing, the faster the boy scribbles his black crayon over one of the figures in the picture. As the suspense grows, we expect that the boy has blackened the bemedaled father out. In fact, however, he has blackened himself out. In totally writing his own childish self-image out, the narrator, in this later account of the final scene, underscores the pathetic appeal of the father's own abject narcissism, which has imprisoned him in an imaginary electrified cage, as if a bestial war criminal permanently cut off from all love by his own blindly mad choices:

> "So, there I am. Those are sure some ears you gave me. What are these round things here on front? Are those medals? Medals for what?" He hesitates to risk a guess. I look back from the venetian blinds and stare at him. He sits studying the drawing, his face rosy, jovial now. More than anything, I want suddenly to hug him, to move forward and throw my arms around his neck. I want to cry and have him hold me. Lift me off the floor and up into the air and hold me. Instead, there seems to be a layer of electricity around him. I know I will be shocked for touching him with no reason. Somewhere in the house an alarm will sound, the grandfather clock will gong all out of sequence, the door chimes will go wild, sirens will howl out of the heating ducts, and four balls will crash through every window in the place. I look at him and, in answer to his question, shrug.
>
> He holds the drawing out for me to take. He's done with it. Slipping past his chair, I saunter to the back door and, on my way outside, turn around. I see him seated in stripes of light at the vacant family table. Sad, he holds my own drawing out to me as if offering a gift or an apology or some artwork of his own. Something changes in me, seeing him like this, but as I pass into the sunlight I fight to keep my voice quite cool and formal and call back, "I'm finished, Daddy. You may keep it now. It's yours." (228)

The narrator's remembered final remark, his strategically placed last word here—"I'm finished, Daddy. You may keep it now. It's yours"—reminds us of the father's earlier complaint that one day when he is six or so, his elder son "drops calling you Dad and changes you to Father" (221). And so, in this touching, not to say stinging, manner, the father is forgiven by the story, even as his crimes against his elder son are not forgotten by it. These crimes against humanity form "the stripes of light" that mark the father's glorious standard of normality and actual abject place, as the American subject of this ironic portrait, which is pointedly focused on "the vacant family table" (228).

As we can then see, by "the abjection of America," I mean the revisionary aesthetic representation of white male American individuality as a specifically marked, distinctively and contingently determined identity, whose most salient historical determination is not pseudo-universality but a particular form of Cold War liberal psychology: *abject narcissism*. This ironic imagination of abjection entails a critical dynamic of interpretation that depends on the cultural work of New Americanists and discloses the contingent formula or law of contemporary revisionism: *Whatever is first must become last, and what is second must become first, and so on, ad infinitum.*

As the boy narrator thinks after fooling his father this time and liberating himself, with a palpable breath of wonder, from the family romance's various double binds, "Good for something . . . my own imagination, it has just spared me a whipping" (228). Either as almost received here, of course, or as given virtually later. This story is, to my mind, "major" heroism by this "minor." By reading himself out of the obvious snares of the Oedipal plot, this boy begins a journey that both recalls that of the author and yet remains formally open to contingency, suspended, as it is, in a future of all such possible "mindful" transferences in the reader's position, ever to come.

What follows now is the analysis of another story of abjection by a different writer that seeks to realize literally, apocalyptically, this pure futurity of transference. But first, since the story is not well known or easily available, here is some pertinent background.

The Future of Transference

Paul M. A. Linebarger (1913–1966) published science fiction stories under the name Cordwainer Smith from 1950 until his death in 1966. Most of the stories appeared in *Galaxy,* a science fiction magazine edited then by Frederik Pohl, Smith's greatest champion. Linebarger also wrote articles and books under his own name, as well as other pseudonyms, on a variety of subjects, including his primary areas of experience and expertise, China and the history of psychological warfare. Born in America but raised in China, Japan, Germany, and France, Linebarger during the 1950s and 1960s held a professorship in the Asiatic Politics Program at Johns Hopkins University. Given his family's close personal ties to the Taiwan government—his father had funded the original 1910 democratic uprising—and his own interest in the literary and philosophical culture of China, Smith's job consisted primarily in sharing his knowledge with budding diplomats. He spied periodically for the United States in the Far East from World War II and the Korean War, through a number of small wars in the 1950s, to the early days of the Vietnam War. (Officially, his position was listed as a civilian consultant to Army Intelligence.) In and out of psychoanalysis for severe depression during this entire period, Smith late in life gave up the strict Methodist religion of his childhood for the more tolerant Episcopalian Christianity of the time. Although he published a mainstream literary novel and a couple of experimental spy novels, he completed only one science fiction novel as Cordwainer Smith, *Norstrilia* (1966), but a goodly number of tales, which were collected in 1993 by James A. Mann in a large omnibus volume entitled *The Rediscovery of Man*.[5] Smith is survived by his second wife, Genevieve, who continues to occasionally publish Smith's drafts of stories and his daughter Rosana Hart who runs an on-line "fanzine" about her father.

Although never wildly popular, several of his stories are considered classics in the field, including (among others) "Scanners Live in Vain" (1950), "The Ballad of Lost C'Mell" (1963), "The Lady Who Sailed the *Soul*" (1960), and, among my personal favorites, "A Planet Named Shayol" (1961), which makes Kafka's "In the Penal Colony" look like a Disney World simulation. "A Planet Named Shayol" describes a prison colony world in which the prisoners are forced to grow spare body parts by aliens ("light beings") who invade their bodies in the most painful ways imaginable. All of Smith's stories trace the saga of future history in terms of the Lords and Ladies of the Instrumentality. Covering a period of fifteen thousand years, the stories chart the descent of humanity into a new dark age, the development of a super race (the Lords and Ladies of the Instrumentality) to administer terrestrial affairs (with the episodic aid of mysterious aliens), the breeding of an under-race from animal stocks— the Underpeople, as they are called, turn out to be the real super-race— and the rediscovery of humanity. This last development consists largely in the Lords and Ladies of the Instrumentality's reintroducing flawed human beings and their wholly contingent practices into the cosmic moral and political system to ensure that an inspired finitude, a veritable genius for helplessness, a fortunate pathos does not cease to exist again. A "brave new world" order having led to sterility and stasis, an agenda of improvisation proves necessary. Telepathic mastery, faster-than-light travel, and latent sadomasochistic elements mark Smith's universe.

Does this mean that the vision of Smith's stories is humanistic, despite their often antihumanistic details and plotlines? Actually, given the central role of the Underpeople in his work, it has more affinities with the animal rights and Green movements. For Smith, the human, like the animal, is identified with the unpredictable both in weakness and strength. A mechanical regularity appalls; a painful wonder is preferred.

Within the genre of science fiction, Smith's work shares major features with what is called "new-wave" science fiction. In the late 1960s and early 1970s, a new generation of science fiction writers, emulating masters such as Ray Bradbury, Theodore Sturgeon, and the Robert Heinlein of *Stranger in a Strange Land* (1961), began to write works that displaced the hard-science core characteristic of traditional science fiction and replaced it with surrealistic fantasy. In addition, these younger writers often wrote in highly allusive, indeed lushly lyrical ways, clearly indicating their mainstream literary ambitions. Of these writers, Harlan Ellison, with his series of edited anthologies, all of which were entitled *Dangerous Visions,* as well as with his own controversial yet award-winning stories such as "I Have No Mouth and I Must Scream" (1968), has always looked back to Smith's stories as prototypical of the new wave in science fiction. New-wave writers such as Roger Zelazny, Samuel R. Delany, and Robert Silverberg, whose *Downward to Earth* (1969) models itself in theme, plot, structure, point of view, and style on Joseph Conrad's *Heart of Darkness,* rarely mention Smith's work, preferring to cite the more immediately cinematic work of Philip K. Dick as a prophetic ancestor. Smith's conceptual visions are rarely visual and when so are purely surreal. One reason for the curious neglect of Smith's work is its general unavailability. Lacking a major publisher, his work has been out of print for long periods of time. Even more to the point, I think, Smith's work has a strain of visionary cruelty in it, which reduces the protagonists in the stories to a truly pitiable state of abjection. The prisoners in "A Planet Named Shayol," for example, who are there the longest, are no more than mindless, pulpy worms turning and turning in the pink desert sands to escape the latest alien assaults. It is not too extreme to say that in many of his stories, Smith displays a sado-masochistic flair worthy of the moments of sheer physical terror in Blake's illuminated prophetic poems. Such unrelieved heroic pathos, reminiscent of most of Shelley's *Prometheus Unbound,* contrasts strikingly with science fiction's conventional protagonists and their new-wave counterparts, all of whom, like typical action heroes, however more reflective the new-wave type may be, always choose to strike out or strike back in big ways. Is this pathetic abjection of his heroes the real reason for Smith's relative oblivion? I think it is, in part. For it even goes beyond the genre's adolescent analogies with romantic daydreams and the mixture of shame and passivity such analogies often engender. But the fate of the characters serves to critique the psychoanalytic subtexts (about adaptation and adjustment) often underlying the phantasmagoric surfaces of Smith's tales.

To recognize these subtexts, however, one must understand, for any particular story, the aspect of the psychoanalytic process in its theoretical, technical, and therapeutic dimensions that Smith is often ironically commenting on by means of his story. For one example, as we will see later in detail, an early story, "The Burning of the Brain" (1958), gives a savage twist to the idea of transference. Now, transference is the keystone of the psychoanalytic process. During analysis, resistance to treatment inevitably arises and takes the form of a repetition of unresolved erotic and aggressive feelings from childhood and their projection on the person of the analyst. Such resistance to getting well, in conflict with the demand to be made well, is the typical mark of neurosis. And falling in love with one's analyst, substituting a sexual relationship for an intellectual identification, submitting to the compulsion of love but not to the authority of knowledge, is the most natural and effective way to sabotage treatment. Managing the transference in its positive and negative modes of love and hatred, and looking for its incipient signs and for those of the analyst's countertransference, become the primary tasks of treatment, the technical mastery of which a wealth of psychoanalytic theory would support.

The theory of transference is, of course, a subject with a huge bibliography. For my purposes here, Jacques Lacan's concept is apropos. Lacan develops his basic idea of transference during the 1950s and early 1960s, that is, at the same time that Smith is going through his most intensive analysis and creating his most important stories. Of course, this could be a historical accident. But the connection I am making between Smith and Lacan also derives from the anthropological and linguistic framework in which both of them conceive their work. Smith's experiences in China and the Far East more generally got thought through in the framework of his professional formation. Although a professor in the Asiatic Politics Program at Johns Hopkins, his studies of the Confucian tradition and the elite and folk literary traditions, and his versatility with the Chinese language and other languages, enabled him to perceive the ritual functions of the symbolic dimension in the shaping of human subjectivity in a way that parallels Lacan's work with structural linguistics and structural anthropology. For Smith and Lacan at this time, the processes of symbolic investiture—being made a figure of authority—are central to their visions. Moreover, as an expert during the height of the Cold War in the history and strategic uses of psychological warfare and its relationship with game theory and symbolic logic, Smith sounds as if he would have been the ideal partner in a Lacanian dialogue.[6] In any event, this symbolic discourse possesses both of them alike.

Lacan's theory of transference stresses the cognitive and power aspects of the relationship between the analyst, the subject who is supposed to know and so whose authoritative influence is supposed to be corrective, and the patient, the subject who is demanding to be cured and resisting the fulfillment of that demand at every turn. For Lacan, the analyst really doesn't know but pretends to a knowledge that only the particular contingencies of the analytic situation may reveal to both patient and analyst in time. Like the difficult games of love in courtly romance, analysis sets into motion, via transference and countertransference in all their positive and negative forms, a creative process of mutual mythmaking between analyst and patient. The aim of this process is to transfer both parties from the position of unwilling actors in the potentially endless repetition of a script written for them both by others (parents, siblings, teachers, etc.) and by what Lacan wittily terms the Big Other. The Big Other, for Lacan, comprises the ritual practices and symbolic structures that organize society, especially the transmission of society's culture from one generation to the next. Here is Lacan: "What better way of assuring oneself, on the point on which one is mistaken, than to persuade the other of the truth of what one says" (489). The transference thus discloses the fundamental structure of romantic love as a reciprocal self-deception that each is the other's perfect complement, as if each personality were the ideal reading, the appreciative interpretation, of the other: "In persuading the other that he has that which may complement us, we assure ourselves of being able to continue to misunderstand what we lack" (489). Thus, in analysis, the analyst persuades the patient to complete "the circle of deception" akin to that which constitutes romantic love (489), but with the following difference: the analytic process trains the analyst to be just as imaginatively open to the patient's resistances, as cues to the critical reading of the analytic situation and the analyst's assumption of authoritative knowing that the patient is producing, as it trains the patient to be aware of the analyst's resistances. That is, in analysis there is ecstasy only in fiction. The analytic process is an education in reading the cues that both analyst and patient produce as their respective critical readings of each other's resistances. Authority resides in the process, not in any one person. Transference and countertransference in this ironic, doubled way can inspire the interplay of co-creation between analyst and patient, an interplay in which each is the other's equally appreciative and critical first reader, as both receive from one another their own unconscious messages in symbolic form. Ideally speaking, in the analytic situation, each would become in turn the other's student and mentor, repeatedly.

The most useful way of showing Lacan's theory of transference at work when analyzing a literary text (and, I would argue, especially one of Smith's stories) is to see this dynamic between analyst and patient as a dramatization of the split in the psyche that results in experiences suffering a double inscription in the mind. Experiences of whatever kind, real, imagined, recalled, are registered in both the primary and secondary psychic systems, that is, in both the unconscious and the conscious mind. Analyst and patient are the allegorical characters in this drama of psychic splitting. Working together, each may assume for a moment at a time the position of revisionary author of this drama, what I am calling the first reader of each other's unconscious script, which when made conscious can form one coherent work for freely chosen future performances. Just as when one writer dies leaving a manuscript incomplete or unrevised and another writer revises and completes this work, so too analyst and patient may serve for each other such a creative function. Similarly, I would claim, in literary texts, and particularly in Smith's tales, as we will see, characters interchangeably play the revisionary commentator on each other's life scenarios. Moreover, we see in Smith's tales the effects of his allegorical dramatization of this critical transference on him, the author of the tale, as it is registered in the formal aesthetic qualities of the narrator's prose. Smith, in short, becomes the first reader of his own Cold War American cosmic fantasies.

Consider, for example, "The Burning of the Brain" (1958). The story traces the fates of three characters: Captain Magno Taliano, who pilots a planoform ship skipping through subspace around the universe; his wife, Dolores Oh, once fabulously and fatally beautiful and now by her own choice an embittered, withered crone; and his young niece, Dita of the Great South House. Like Smith's other heroes, Taliano is physically passive while his mind, via telepathy, powers the ship through subspace. His wife, Dolores Oh, wanting to be sure that he loves her for "a *me* more than the beauty" of her face (178), refuses "the ordinary rejuvenescence" of the drugs and operations that could keep her young for a thousand years (177). And Dita, after a visit, is returning with them from their home on Sherman's Planet to her unnamed home aboard her uncle's ship, the *Wu-Feinstein,* "the finest ship of mankind to sail out amid the roughnesses and uncertainties of two-dimensional space" (178).

In this story, Smith intertwines the technically difficult contingencies of subspace flight with the emotional conflicts of these characters. Moving faster than light through two-dimensional space causes human beings immense pain and is a place haunted by other-dimensional alien creatures, such as the invisible dragons that stalk and feast off mental energies, leaving their prey empty husks. They are called dragons because they burn out the brains of their victims, leaving in their minds as traces of their work spectral images of dragons. The Go-Captains, which is what the pilots of the subspace planoform ships are called, must skip strategically into and out of two-dimensional subspace just long enough to keep the pain to a minimum and to better evade the dragons. (The Stop-Captains, equivalent to tugboat captains, drive small ships that help bring the large planoform ships into their spaceports.) With their highly developed telepathic power, the Go-Captains can keep most of the pain at bay. And with the addition to their crews of pinlighters, specialized telepaths whose powers are amplified by innovative computer programs and the brains of their Partners, a race of selectively bred cats whose additional brain power helps to focus the pinlighters' surgically precise counterattacks on the dragons, the Go-Captains can pilot ships, like the *Wu-Feinstein,* whose interior is constructed as a replica of Mount Vernon, in which the passengers travel in comfort and according to the model of the latest retro lifestyle favored by future ship-design fashions. I like to remind you that this tale comes from 1958, not from today.

To orient themselves in making these jumps between dimensions of space, the Go-Captains require what are called "locksheets." These are star maps with the coordinates of all the stars in the immediate vicinity and all the permutations of possible errors in subspace jumping. These many additional maps, taken altogether, make up what looks like the intricate brickwork of a wall that, when they are piloting their ships, the Go-Captains stare at in their self-hypnotic telepathic trances. To have a successful career as a Go-Captain is rare; to practice one's piloting like an art is rarer still. And Go-Captain Magno Taliano is a genius of the craft.

Unfortunately, his wife, Dolores Oh, is the queen of resentment. Although she justifies her decision to allow herself to age naturally by saying it is based on her desire to be loved for her true self alone and not the beauty of her face, this justification is merely a bad-faith rationalization. As Dolores Oh reveals in her casual shipboard conversation with Dita— this is Dita's main analytic function in the story, to get Dolores and her husband, Go-Captain Taliano, to reveal themselves—Dolores sorely misses how men used to fight over her, once to the death, and how then she would spurn the victor for his superficial infatuation with her fabulous beauty, asking incredulously, "What do you think I am, anyhow?" (182). When Dita meets Dolores earlier on Sherman's Planet, she is unprepared for what she finds. Beneath the ritual civil greeting there is "a sucking pump of hideous anxiety" (178). And behind the formal friendliness of Dolores Oh's greeting, there is "the driest of mockeries, the greeting itself an attack" (178).

Dita discovers in the case of her uncle that he is all—and only—what he appears to be: the faithful husband of Dolores Oh, whose very presence supports his wife in the very sense of her existence. "[Dita] looked at the ruined face of Dolores Oh, at the dreaming terror in Dolores's eyes, and she realized that Dolores had passed all limits of nightmare and had become a veritable demon of regret, a possessive ghost who sucked the vitality from her husband, who dreaded companionship, hated friendship, rejected even the most casual of acquaintances, because she feared forever and without limit that there was really nothing to herself, and feared that without Magno Taliano she would be more lost than the blackest of whirlpools in the nothing between the stars" (179). Smith may be influenced by Sartre's *No Exit* here—Smith followed intellectual currents closely and was quite familiar with French existentialism, in its original language. To understand the language of this sentence and the portrait it paints of Dolores Oh, one must put it in a larger cultural frame. Smith's studies of Chinese literature focused on quest forms, and as his story "Drunkboat" (based on Rimbaud's poem, "Le bateau ivre") suggests, his knowledge of modern Western literature had similar roots. Therefore one perspective that incorporates the entire romance tradition, going back to medieval quest-romance, then onto its rediscovery and revision in Renaissance epics, and its return in its visionary psychological forms with romanticism and its continuing aftermath, would seem to be specifically apropos. Dolores Oh is, quite simply, less an existentially sketched character than she is an allegorical type. She is more an allegorical personification of what Blake calls "the Female Will," by which he means what Nietzsche means by the psychology of resentment, than she is a realistic representation. For people who experience their own passivity and reactiveness as forms of suffering and abjection, the psychology of resentment seeks to discover someone else—anyone else—to blame and punish for these feelings. We should thus view the characters in Smith's stories as if they were names generated by the visionary play of his language for various psychic states through which any person, given the right circumstances, can pass. Where the problem arises for these characters, of course, is when they get fixated in any one state. This is precisely Dolores Oh's painful dilemma, a kind of double-bind situation she put herself into, a state that borders on paranoid schizophrenia. The technical problem that brings these emotional issues to a head is that, for some unexplained reason, the locksheets our Go-Captain faces on the wall before him as he jumps into subspace are all duplicates of the one used to begin the flight. And so the *Wu-Feinstein* is now to be lost apparently in one of Dolores Oh's black whirlpools between the stars.

We never learn whether Dolores Oh has had anything to do with the lost locksheets. But a sort of unconscious brand of telekinesis would not be a surprise, given Smith's own analytic imagination. In any event, what we do learn is that Dita witnesses her uncle continue to respond in love and with courage as he pilots the ship in his state of telepathic trance. He agrees to the rescue plan his pinlighters propose. They will probe his midbrain telepathically, augmented by their Partners, to find in his cortex, which is a human being's emotional core of personality, the spectral lineaments of star coordinates imprinted there by years of experience. The pinlighters' probe will burn out his brain, cell by cell, just as if he were finally falling victim to his subspace rivals, the phantom dragons. As Go-Captain Taliano agrees to the plan, he turns to his niece, offering his self-sacrifice to her in his hollow entranced voice: *"If I do this I shall be a fool or a child or a dead man, but I will do it for you"* (183). Because his telepathic powers are great enough to drive the ship, Taliano must turn them on his own brain as the pinlighters do to ensure the successful outcome of their search. The final state he is left in is reminiscent of the aftereffects of frontal lobotomy or repeated electroshock therapy. But I believe that the real therapeutic model for the tragic process of communication leading up to this pathetic outcome is a literal transference of personality.

Dolores Oh, as you would expect, is publicly grief stricken but privately thrilled by the prospect of her celebrated husband's envisioned fate. Dita's fledgling telepathic ability senses Dolores's duplicity, loud and clear: "Dolores's hand leapt to her mouth. Her gesture of grief was as automatic as the striking of a snake. Dita sensed that her aunt had been waiting a hundred years and more for disaster, that her aunt had craved ruin for her husband the way that some people crave love and others crave death" (182). Go-Captain Taliano, meanwhile, makes the best of his looming second infancy, when he intones now to his wife: *"As I die you shall at last be sure I love you"* (184). Of course, he does not die. Instead he becomes at the tale's end a complete baby: "Magno Taliano had risen from the chair and was being led from the room by his wife and consort, Dolores Oh. He had the amiable smile of an idiot, and his face for the first time in more than a hundred years trembled with shy and silly love" (185). In this ironic fashion, our now former Go-Captain represents the fate of the ironic "future" traditional hero of quest-romance and its literary and critical descendants. Dolores Oh, as we have seen, represents the vast future history of seemingly unconquerable resentment. What about Dita?

Dita uses her telepathy to support her uncle's mind as the pinlighters probe the core of his brain for the knowledge they need. In the process, her empathetic imagination perfects her telepathic powers. As a result, from now on, Dita can speak "mind-to-mind with pure telepathy" (184). In addition, as the pinlighters evaporate each cell in their search, Taliano's talents get unconsciously transferred to Dita: "As your uncle burned out his brain," one of the pinlighters informs her, "you picked up his skills. Can't you sense it? You are a Go-Captain yourself and one of the greatest of us" (185). Dita has received into her sympathetic psyche her uncle's heroic personality. She has recognized and rejected her aunt's path of resentment. And Dita has thereby been able to assume his professional genius, as well.

What "The Burning of the Brain" allegorizes in its visionary parable is psychoanalytic transference, but with a critical difference. Dita functions through the story as the catalyst who gets others to talk, and as they do so, she reads their language closely for what and how it says what it says. She also literally reads their unspoken, their unconscious minds. From this de facto position of apprentice-analyst in training, Dita progresses via her sympathetic imagination and critical intelligence to the position of the heroic genius whose genius is but willingly to suffer, as if such genius were the archetypal state of mind of the patient in its pure form. Not only does Smith reverse, as does Lacan in his theory, the expected power positions between neophyte analyst and professional master, but he also turns Dita's amateur ability to read people into authentic critical author-ity. Just as Taliano is Smith's critical interpretation of the hero in romance narratives and the unsympathetic Dolores Oh is his critique of all that would block the creative imagination, so Dita is Smith's representation of what I call the figure of "the first reader." This is the trope, you recall, I am using to refer to the position of imaginative priority that the critical transference produces. This position arises spontaneously from the un-expected knowledge that Dita has unconsciously internalized from her Go-Captain uncle's burned-out brain. And what is such knowledge? Smith's narrator gives its feel earlier in the story, as follows: "Only in the planoforming room did the Go-Captain know what happened. The Go-Captain, his pinlighters sitting beside him, took the ship from one com-pression to another, leaping hotly and frantically through space, some-times a hundred light-years, jump, jump, jump, jump until the ship, the light touches of the captain's mind guiding it, passed the perils of millions upon millions of worlds, came out at its appointed destination, and settled as lightly as one feather resting upon others, settled into an embroidered and decorated countryside where the passengers could move as easily away from their journey as if they had done nothing more than to pass an afternoon in a pleasant old house by the side of a river" (179–80). This intricate passage's reflexive incantatory diction and elevated rhetoric, its elaborated imagery and rhythms, are like the poetic high style of the epic simile Smith has Dita use earlier to capture her aunt's true state of mind underlying her display of grief (179). Such "poetic" features mark the passage as an instance of the romantic sublime, I think, as it occurs in the so-called minor genre of science fiction. Such sublime passages, wherever they occur, perform the momentary identification of the character's and the narrator's points of view, even as these scenes of imaginative instruction thereby symbolize and project the momentary coalescence of the reader's and the author's identities, a coalescence that is always still about to come. It is in this temporally ironic manner—an aesthetic with all its own pathos of gain and loss—that the future appears in Smith's fiction as the critical transference. To put this another way, "the rediscovery of man" is ever an apocalyptic hope.

Is, then, the moment of the critical transference also but an illusion, just one of a more refined nature? Does Smith's literalization of transference via telepathy and future technology function as an implicit critique of the idea of one personality being transmitted into another psyche? This critical question recalls Lacan's recognition of the classic psychoanalytic transference as depicting "the circle of deception" characteristic of romantic love. Given such mutual self-deception of loves, in which each persuades the other that only the other can complete oneself, both lovers, narcissistically reinforced, may continue in their systems of self-deception nicely insulated from the destructive truth of the real. But if we think of "The Burning of the Brain" as representing the model of a single mind, then the unconscious transmission of personality via the critical transference performed literally in the story and expressed symptomatically in its sublime passages could be seen as a scene of instruction staged between character and narrator and prophetic of that between reader and author, so as to reveal the reversible superimposition of one point of view onto another, an imaginative analysis that would break down, momentarily at least, the barriers between psychic systems, and so would enlarge formally the creative power of human vision.

Consider, in conclusion, an analogy with a very different story, Joyce's

"The Dead." When the vision of the snow falling generally all over Ireland appears in Gabriel Conroy's mind at the story's end, the language of that vision is far beyond his imaginative power, even while its content, as it were, is within his scope; character and author—and sympathetic reader—become one in that moment of cosmic apocalypse. Such a prospect of identity projects the vision of a mind capable of encompassing, appreciatively, the universe. Smith is more modest in his dreams: he would envision one mind appreciating another, even in that other's, however radically alien, abjection: the narcissism of major likenesses, perhaps?

Although "The Burning of the Brain" was published in 1958, the fate of its quintessentially American-like Captain Taliano resembles that which has overtaken that more recent popular icon Dutch Reagan. However that may be, I have wanted to show via Smith's tale how the Cold War liberal discourses of literary romance, science fiction, and psychoanalyses sketch out in advance the "locksheet," the spectral topology, so to speak, of our emerging geopolitical and cultural futures, a future of the abjection of America, as in the fate of our Go-Captain, and a future of global—not to say, virtually cosmic—transference, as in the freedom of our newly empowered "Dita of the Great South House."

With an even greater prescience, Smith, in his one science fiction novel, *Norstrilia*, foreshadows our endless future of multicultural transferences in a cosmic scene of instruction.

Planet Buyer and the Catmaster

My section heading refers to the protagonist and his clinical psychologist in the science fiction novel *Norstrilia* (1966).[7] I confess that I chose this heading, in part, because what it says no longer sounds so surreally far-fetched. In the nearly forty years since it was just conceived and composed, *Norstrilia*'s two intersecting plotlines tell stories whose sci-fi premises now are virtually matters of course. Let me also say, at the outset, that neither Rod McBan, the planet buyer, nor C'william the Catmaster, who are, respectively, the novel's hero and its pivotal figure, command in themselves, ultimately, our interest. Like the pseudonym "Cordwainer Smith" that the novel's author Paul Linebarger makes use of, these characters begin in wonder—both of them are genetically engineered telepaths to some degree, one bred from human, the other from feline, stock—but end in anticlimax. Given this would-be utopian text, containing a dystopian vision, what else should one expect?

Why do I say that Rod McBan and C'william stand at the centers of story lines whose sci-fi premises no longer sound far-fetched? When we read that McBan and his supercomputer play the future financial markets so well that he ends up having bought the entire Earth, or that C'william is a humanoid bred from cat stock to serve as the one and only clinical psychologist to The Underpeople, the race of humanoid slaves bred from a variety of animal origins, we not only recall earlier science fiction classics, perhaps speculative texts by H. G. Wells (*The Island of Dr. Moreau*) or Aldous Huxley (*Brave New World*), we also recognize the pragmatic ambitions held currently by a Bill Gates or any number of genetic biologists working on other than sheep clones under the banner of "the posthuman imagination." When we also understand that these two plotlines of personal ambition and social revolution come together in a way that appears at once to be totally deterministic and radically contingent, and yet is also remarkably prefigurative of "the messianic without messianism" in Jacques Derrida's *Specters of Marx*, then we can begin to see, I think, the real interest of this novel.

Of course, the awesome becoming the ordinary is the typical bane of the science fiction genre. What makes this standard fate so different in this case is the visionary irony of the narrator in *Norstrilia*. Although the novel is set fifteen thousand years in the future, the narrator assumes the perspective of the even farther distant historian or chronicler of the events recounted, a rather bemused and at times cynically knowing point of view and posture. If becoming outmoded is the fate of every form of modernity, the cosmic modernity in this text already presumes this knowledge and so by its tone of cynical knowingness would forestall, if not preclude outright, ironically enough, the need for a wholesale obsolescence. To complicate things further, the omniscient narrative point of view does vary, appropriately, according to whether the Rod McBan or The Underpeople plotline is dominant, with third-person-limited point of view being adopted for them both at times. This variation in narrative point of view is not, however, a chronic and irregular oscillation, since most of the planet-buyer story gets told in the novel's first half, which allows its second half to focus on the Underpeople's plight. The Underpeople story comes to incorporate McBan once: to save his life, he is transformed and now passes for a handsome if somewhat dumb humanoid feline, with thirty-centimeter-long whiskers, who has as his mate, C'mell, the most beautiful and exciting "girly-girl" on earth, who is the crucial link between the present ruling order and the revolutionary future. (More about C'mell and her profession later.)

The ruling order calls itself "the Instrumentality of Mankind," and it is composed of "Lords and Ladies" who, possessing great and unique telepathic powers of different sorts, have been selected to rule all others in the known universe. They oversee and administer the affairs of humanity. They are figures of tremendous power, whose authority is unquestioned among ordinary folks, and whose access to force and resources is apparently unlimited. The Instrumentality was established after human beings, for the most part, blew themselves up with atomic weapons at the beginning of the twenty-first century, with their immediate descendants falling into a prehistoric, postapocalyptic barbarism, where "Wild Ones" and "Man-Hunters" struggle for each other's nonexistence.

Once order was restored, some few thousand years from our time, the Instrumentality, with the occasional unpredictable interventions of the Daimoni, a mysterious alien race from either another dimension or a far distant future, begin to administer human affairs, supervising the colonization of the cosmos. The invention of faster-than-light drive and the discovery of the "santaclara" drug, "stroon," which gives virtual immortality to humans, makes possible this centuries-long project of colonization. The Underpeople were bred to serve humanity not so much in its colonial mission as to do the cosmic scut work, especially the dirty work on Manhome, the Earth. That is, to take care of the various needs of the human body.

Norstrilia opens a few hundred years after "the rediscovery of Man," some fifteen thousand years from the twentieth century. "The Rediscovery of Man" is the latest project of the Instrumentality, the cosmic administration. After the planets that could be colonized in the galaxy were settled and developed, the perfection of life began, ironically enough, to take its toll. The imperfect is our paradise. To remediate this fatal perfection, the Instrumentality decides to reintroduce into the universe, on a carefully selected basis, the creative moment of pure randomness, surprise, contingency, luck, fortune. Lord Jestacost—how appropriately named—is the Chief of the Instrumentality in charge of chance, the administrator of unintended consequences, which includes unexpected deaths and births.

Norstrilia tells the complex tale of the revolutionary moment when the old order of dystopic determinism is giving way to a new order of utopian contingency. Only the secret cosmic alliance between the Instrumentality and the Underpeople, as it is forced to accommodate the surprising developments of the Rod McBan plot, grants the possibility of the future history that the reader is now reading, nearly a millennium and a half before the fact. The diverse dislocations of this reading experience are mirrored to infinity when we remember that *Norstrilia* is a novel of early to mid-1960s, the height of the Cold War, which yet straddles in its piecemeal publication history (1964, 1968, 1975) the beginning and the final end of active countercultural politics on a grand scale. If we also keep in mind the uncanny parallels between the novel's themes and our own "new millennium" of the Internet, global positioning satellites, the Human Genome Project, and all the other specters of global progress (and repression) that haunt us with sublime visions of abjection, we might start to believe again in the romantic genre of visionary prophecy. (For just one example of what I mean: The Instrumentality reintroduces, as virtual realities, that is, as formal and revisable institutional structures of identity, "nations and nationalities," because such multicosmic, not to say, multicultural, identity politics help humanity to resist the universal homogenization of life. Multiculturalism, even multispeciesism, is a cosmic moral imperative in Smith's prophetic vision.)

In fact, it is the generic code of visionary romance that Smith's novel and Derrida's later work share with the major narrative poetry of the romantics. If we return to the section heading, "Planet Buyer and the Catmaster," and note that it alludes to the scene of critical transference that climaxes Rod McBan's self-transformation so that he may finally participate to the full in the revolution of the Underpeople still to come, and if we understand that such a cathartic work of self-mourning, of confronting the other in oneself, precedes, as Derrida (or James) also stresses, all revolutionary change, then we may begin to see the literary conventions informing the major texts of such otherwise different figures as Blake, Marx, Freud, and Derrida.

Although we can also see this pattern of transference and abjection in Milton, in the movement, for example, from *Lycidas* to *Paradise Lost,* Blake's short epic *Milton* portrays it most completely and clearly. Before the Blakean bard figure can sing his epic vision in Jerusalem, he must confront in the other—here Milton himself—the spectral form of his own desire for fame and worldly power. Once he has suffered transference upon the Miltonic other and experienced via that figure his own abject narcissism, the Blakean bard can "concretize his error" imaginatively and move on, a chastened poet, to his greater vision of human liberty. We have seen this pattern at work as a scene of instruction in recent literature and criticism, and have seen it again in James's fiction and Derrida's *Specters of Marx* in previous chapters. But now we must turn to *Norstrilia* to see what Smith does with this romantic pattern of visionary identity.

Rod McBan comes from a farmer culture, the planet called Old North Australia, "Norstrilia" for short. As old as the Instrumentality, this culture preserves the spartan lifestyle of frontier (or Outback?) sheep herders. On this planet, the sheep grow gigantic in suffering from a viral-like parasite whose by-product, stroon, grants virtual immortality and so produces near infinite wealth. Because stroon cannot be successfully duplicated or artificially synthesized, the Old North Australians have a monopoly on the future of life in the cosmos. To keep their planet in precarious balance, however, requires that all their children at age sixteen must pass a test to see if they are fit to survive. Those that do not possess the genetic mutation of telepathy and whose subsequent returns to infancy—up to four rebirths are permitted—fail to develop their recessive powers must be executed via another drug that makes them giggle themselves to death.

Rod McBan's telepathy appears intermittently. When he does "heir" or "spier" (hear other minds or speak to them), he can penetrate their innermost defensive shields—a rare gift—and can deliver a "brain bomb" of such potent rage and absolute hatred that he suggests to his tribunal of judges at the time of his test, after his fourth childhood, that he would make yet another great secret weapon in the Norstrilian planetary defense arsenal.[8] This ingenious suggestion, along with what appears to be the chance intervention of Lord Redlady, a demoted chief of the Instrumentality exiled from Manhome (Earth) to the provinces for similar volatile telepathic powers, allows Rod to escape the giggle death, an unprecedented development in Norstrilian history. He wonders, then: "Had he made it [happen] . . . or was it chance which had done it for him?" (28).

But our hero has even more pressing practical problems to deal with. It seems that an old childhood enemy—a *first* childhood enemy—Houghton Syme, whose pathetic allergy to stroon causes him perpetual resentment in place of perpetual life, and so for others endless pain, has become by default (only the "impaired" enter administration) Norstrilia's "Onseck," or Honorary Secretary, the highest governmental post. Syme is now plotting McBan's assassination, since he has escaped the giggle death. To overcome Syme's murderous intentions, McBan turns to "the Old Broken Treasures in the Gap," the ancient "drama-cubes" and other futuristic archival materials, for guidance. After reviewing his favorite cube, Shakespeare's *Hamlet,* McBan decides to leave home, at least for a while, and so he now turns to the family's secret supercomputer, which directs him to maximize for his trip, via elaborate but rigorous speculation in the interplanetary financial markets, especially in stroon futures, his personal fortune. One major consequence is that his government goes into a crisis, and so the Instrumentality, to preserve its own considerable stroon investments, sells Rod McBan the Earth so that it may charge him an exorbitant tax rate on his off-Earth earnings and an even more exorbitant flat-tax fee on his earthly profits. In the chapter entitled "FOE money, SAD money," Smith, who did covert work for Army Intelligence, gives a convincingly detailed account of such cosmic speculations (69–88). A kind of Cold War liberal internationalism of a country club Republican kind provides the template for a thirty-sixth-century economy.

The Rod McBan "planet buyer" story connects with that of the Underpeople via the character of C'mell. C'mell is the leading "girly-girl," perhaps, in the universe. This institution of being a "girly-girl" is not prostitution in the pure sense of the world. The Instrumentality breeds the most seductive humanoid females from the most promising feline stock. These "girly-girls" are trained to serve on Earth "outworlders" when they come to Manhome for recreation and reinvestment. Hospitality management is the girly-girl's business, and the endless postponement of climactic satisfaction, in every possible fashion, is the girly-girl's professional discipline. And C'mell, Lord Jestacost's double agent among The Underpeople (or is he their double agent among the Lords and Ladies of the Instrumentality?), is the greatest sublime tease of them all.

Through C'mell, Rod McBan has come to Earth in one huge subspace jump after first being disassembled. He is then reassembled on Mars and transformed into a cat person for a safe trip to Manhome. McBan, via C'mell, unites the Instrumentality and its myriad of contingency plans with the revolutionary fate of what The Underpeople call their movement of hope: "the Holy Insurgency." Ultimately, McBan will be persuaded by E'telekeli, The Underpeople's prophetic leader, a superhybrid mutated out of alien Daimoni and bald eagle genes, to give his unimaginable wealth for a foundation named in McBan's father's honor, which, with the Instrumentality's tacit blessing, will support the future work of The Underpeople as these former slaves are progressively recognized as the equals—at the least—of their titular masters.

Although a few of The Underpeople, including E'lamelanie, E'telekeli's own daughter, believe that McBan may be "the Promised One," the Messiah who will lead all people into a new epoch of liberty, equality, and fraternity, McBan turns out not to be this "Promised One." The Messiah, according to his nonchalant prophet, E'telekeli, is always already ever about to come yet once more still again: "Rod? A promised speaker of the truth? Oh, no" (215). According to the Smith narrator, the Messiah is not so much a person as a figure of the creative moment itself, and not simply the subject position of enduring "the timeless torment of undated hope . . . the strain of waiting for something that might happen now or a million years from now" (215). This moment of time out of time is never outmoded because it is never finally, definitively arrived at, even as it supersedes all other moments; this is the spectral moment of pure anarchic and anachronistic possibility, and so a moment both indeterminate and overdetermined at once, the virginal interval of the creative response ever to come, or the future itself.

After McBan's wild-card financial speculation and gift giving radically transforms the Underpeople's prospects, but before he is granted this formal utopian vision of the messianic redemption ever to come, our hero, as we would expect given the romance genre, must suffer a stark confrontation with his own ghosts. Discovering the Catmaster, C'william, in his "Department Store of Hearts' Desire," a monumental collective archive of documents, objects, and holographic records of humanity's entire cultural past, Rod McBan learns that he must enter "the Hate Hall" to find out who he really is, what he really wants, confront the secret sharer, the spectral demonic other in himself, so that he might really choose at last all of his inheritance from universal human history. What McBan does indeed encounter, in the remembered shapes of Syme's surreal revenge plots, is his own disavowed guilt over his parents' death, who were obliterated one day as they were shipping out to Earth when Rod, in his fourth infancy, let loose an uncontrollable blast of abandonment rage in his first brain bomb. McBan now sees initially "the waste and spoilage of the human race," "the wrecks and residues of abandoned settlements and forgotten colonies" (159). And then he sees his parents' spaceship. It had gone "milky in mid-trip, dissolving into traceless nothing. . . . He was an almighty baby, so enormous he could scoop them up with his right hand" (160). McBan realizes that he experienced their leaving as a wish for him to die, and so he had struck out at his own unconscious fantasy and had destroyed them, not it. "His mind roared back at itself. . . . The rage was followed by tears, by a guilt too deep for regret, by a self-accusation so raw and wet that it lived like one more organ inside his living body" (160).

McBan's self, as psychoanalysis would predict, has here been revealed to be prosthetically augmented at its core by a savage superego whose severe conscience functions solely to induce a strict and chronic self-mourning, "a guilt too deep for regret," "a self-accusation so raw and wet that it lived like one more organ inside his living body" (160). This self-destructive reduplication of life within life is a literalized version of psychoanalytic truth, but such life *en abîme* is essentially our fate. Ironically enough, the technical supplement of consciousness in such critical self-consciousness and self-hatred takes on in its unconscious symbolic representations the role of an organic simulation of normative agency, individual or corporate. Given this terrible vision of the paradoxical sources of identity in the radical dispossession of self in absolute self-alienation, McBan can now sense who he really may become:

It wasn't his telepathic deformity. . . . It was himself, the "Me-subtle" inside him, which was wrong, all wrong. He was the baby worth killing who had killed instead. . . . His own naked life lay before him like a freshly dissected cadaver. . . . Rod rose to his feet. His hands were wet. He touched his face and he realized that the had been weeping with his face cupped in his hands. . . . There was one thing he wanted.

He wanted Houghton Syme not to hate him. . . . He had forgiven his last enemy. He had forgiven himself. (160–61)

McBan wants nothing that the Department Store of Hearts' Desire can give except this moment in which, expecting nothing, he sees who he must gratuitously forgive. In a cosmos ruled by a general economy of exchange, such unexpected *gifting* could not be conceived. McBan wants to return to Norstrilia to ensure that the imprisoned Syme receives all of his allotted time in freedom. Only thus in turn may Syme, with his already shortened life, possibly become receptive to the incalculable.

This representative pattern of self-discovery, with all its Christian and messianic overtones, is in the final analysis secular, romantic, and humanistic. It is what Blake in Milton elaborates as the concretion of error, the consolidation of self-hatred and resentment into a spectral image fully revealed as the ghost of future potential otherwise not even to be imagined, not to say, to be realized if forgiveness is not always forthcoming. *Norstrilia* is in this great tradition of visionary poetry.

And so, of course, is psychoanalysis, at least in its theory of transference. Transference involves a figure or situation in the present that reminds us of one from the past, either consciously or unconsciously, and thereby shapes how we will perceive and react to the present figure or situation. Erotic and aggressive investments from our pasts influence us repeatedly. Identifications acting behind our backs, as it were, betray our secrets. Within analysis, supposedly, transference can occur in a more focused and impersonalizing way, via the analysand relationship, positive and negative, with the analyst, whose relationship to the analysand informs the countertransference. The artificial and constructed nature of the analytic transference allows for a harmless revelation of one's passions in the form of various resistances, including the most notorious resistance to any analysis, falling in love. The intrapsychic, as well as the interpsychic, dimension of the analytic transference, how the person you currently love unconsciously recalls your Uncle Willy, who always stood for your otherwise missing conscience, can more readily be examined in therapy or romantic poetry.

Naturally, the analytic situation as it constructs transference places one party in the position of the subject who is supposed to know, and the other party in that of the subject who is supposed to get known. But this imbalance can be addressed by recalling the details of any countertransference, which shows that the subject who is supposed to know needs the subject who is supposed to get known in order to know him- or herself at all. The aestheticizing and objectivizing dimensions of the analytic process are usually all too apparent. Similarly, as we see throughout this book, the positions of author and reader, in terms of imaginative authority, are really not fixed but are fluid.

One can see how mastering the transference, as the process is called in analysis, could have important consequences. No one wants only to be taken for an avatar of someone's Uncle Willy. This is especially true if being Uncle Willy in a lover's psychodrama means putting up with way too much shit, not to mention the horrors of physical abuse. But what's so important about transference in literary and cultural studies? With a couple of examples from Freud's 1910 study *Leonardo and a Memory of His Childhood*, I hope to show why understanding what I call "the critical transference" can be important, too.[9]

Early in the study, Freud quotes two different statements attributed to Leonardo in which he expresses the view that not until one knows something thoroughly can one love it. "For in truth," Leonardo says in the second quoted statement, "great love springs from great knowledge of the beloved object, and if you know it but little you will be able to love it only a little or not at all . . ." (21). Freud immediately claims that this statement is obviously false as an important psychological fact, since most of us love impulsively without knowledge and learn the lesson of our congenital ignorance thereafter, repeatedly. But the value of Leonardo's observation for Freud lies in its categorically imperative nature for Leonardo himself. Clearly Leonardo believes that he should only love where he has known. However, rather than accuse Leonardo, as his contemporaries did, of coldness, Freud reads into Leonardo's words the best-case, and not the worst-case, interpretation:

> His affects were controlled and subjected to the instinct for research; he did not love and hate, but asked himself about the origin and significance of what he was to love or hate. Thus he was bound at first to appear indifferent to good and evil, beauty and ugliness. During this work of investigation love and hate threw off their positive or negative signs and were both alike transformed into intellectual inter-

est. In reality Leonardo was not devoid of passion; he did not lack the divine spark which is directly or indirectly the driving force—*il primo motore*—behind all human activity. He had merely converted his passion into a thirst for knowledge; he then applied himself to investigation with the persistence, constancy and penetration which is derived from passion, and at the climax of intellectual labour, when knowledge had been won, he allowed the long restrained affect to break loose and to flow away freely, as a steam of water drawn from a river is allowed to flow away when its work is done. (22)

Just in case we don't get it, Freud repeats the sexual language: "When, at the climax of a discovery, he could survey a large portion of the whole nexus, he was overcome by emotion, and in ecstatic language praised the splendour of the part of creation that he had studied, or—in religious phraseology—the greatness of his Creator" (22). Freud identifies with what he perceives as Leonardo's sublimation of his erotic drive in his intellectual passion for knowledge. And so he magnanimously attributes the best-case interpretation to Leonardo's characteristic practices and judgments.

This transference of the critical reader on the author of a text, whether expressed positively as here or negatively, cannot be avoided. It can only be displaced onto the subjects and themes in a text, or on the representative status of the text, or on the techniques or formal dimensions, or on the cultural resonances, and so on. Thus how one manages the critical transference matters, since it is the way tradition in the specific sense of texts to be read or in the more general sense of cultural representations to be known gets formed and passed on. Freud's charity in Leonardo's case, his magnanimity, is not in the final analysis disinterested, but it is contingently gratuitous. Freud didn't have to give Leonardo this much benefit of the doubt to identify with him enough to catch the reader's attention. Why did Freud perform what he later in this study admits is his deep affection for Leonardo? Is he caught in the throes of an overwhelmingly homosocial, even latently gay, identification?

Actually, I think Freud performs his identification with Leonardo, as well as states it, because in becoming Leonardo's reader, Freud comes to know the lineaments of what he still does not know, and he is grateful for this intimate knowledge of his own finitude. Late in this study, Freud comments on the final paintings of Leonardo, those of Leda and the Swan, Bacchus, and Saint John the Baptist, in this manner:

> These pictures breathe a mystical air into whose secret one dares not penetrate; at the very most one can attempt to establish their connection with Leonardo's earlier creations. The figures are still androgynous [as in the Mona Lisa and smiling heads of young women] but no longer in the sense of the vulture phantasy [and its celebration of the phallic mother]. They are beautiful youths of feminine delicacy and with effeminate forms; they do not cast their eyes down, but gaze in mysterious triumph, as if they knew of a great achievement of happiness, about which silence must be kept. The familiar smile of fascination leads one to guess that it is a secret of love. It is possible that in these figures [of knowledge] Leonardo has denied the unhappiness of his erotic life and has triumphed over it in his art, by representing the wishes of the boy, infatuated with his mother, as fulfilled in this blissful union of the male and female natures. (77)

These figures, like Syme for McBan or Smith for us, are (as Derrida might put it) the figures of the impossible, romantic figures of infinite finitude, like James's greatest heroines.

Of course, the analogy between the analytic transference and the critical transference is an imperfect one; it limps, so to speak, all the way. But one thing it does allow us to see is that for a cultural heritage to continue, whatever its contents, the critical transference must occur. Hopefully, perhaps, it will occur more in the style of Freud and Leonardo than in any other. Using Smith as our guide, our personal visions are necessary prefaces to any communal renewal.

Norstrilia ends, however, on a disturbing note. Rod McBan, twenty years later, married his long-suffering distant cousin Lavinia, and together they have two twin boys, Ted and Rick, who have just faced the test in the Garden of Death, as it is called, the one their father nearly failed when he turned sixteen for the fourth time. This time, on the first try, Ted passes, but Rick fails: "It was the Lord Redlady, unconventional to the end, who broke the sign to them. He held up one finger. Only one. . . . Rick, the darker twin, stood all alone. All alone, and laughing. Laughing. . . ."

Just as stroon cannot be synthesized and Norstrilian character appears immutable, so inexorable custom would seem to command that this catastrophe must be so, without hope of appeal or revision. Except that Ted and his father Rod *exchange words* about this uncanny fate, that on this first try one of the twins, Rick, must laugh himself to death:

> After a long time they had done their formal courtesies. Rod pulled Ted to his feet. "Hullo, boy. You made it. You know *what* you are?" Mechanically, the boy recited, "Roderick Frederick Ronald William MacArthur McBan to the hundred-and-fifty-second, Sir and Father!"
>
> Then the boy broke for just a moment. He pointed at Rick, who was still laughing, off by himself, and then plunged for his father's hug: "Oh, dad! Why me? Why *me?*" (222)

I take this ending to mean, among several possible things, that Norstrilia had in fact incorporated into its rites of passage and commanding custom, into its social conscience or cultural superego, the example of Rod McBan, that contingent singularity, that vestige of the monstrous messiah ever to come that splits all origins and twins them, endlessly reversing priorities. Rick suffers the giggle death because he is a *pure* telepath and so must die the first time. Ted survives because like Rod, his father, he is a more human, impure mutation. This, in any event, is how I read the open ending of Smith's *Norstrilia.*

Specters, alien monsters, runaway technology, faster-than-light financial markets, apocalyptic turning points in world history, a formal promise of messianic vision, an infinite work of (self-)mourning, the inaugural role of Shakespeare's *Hamlet,* the renewed imperative to select from one's inheritance after interrupting unconscious filiation, cosmopolitanism on a grand scale, transformation of human and all nature, with a vengeance —I could continue in this vein, but won't. I am not describing *Norstrilia.* I am describing *Specters of Marx.* What should one make of such an extraordinary sharing of representational features? Before I offer my answer to this question, I want to suggest that *Norstrilia* and *Specters of Marx* also share formal features. Both texts are organized around *two* leading plotlines, the revolutionary and the psychoanalytic, the communal dimension of the critical transference being performed, via romantic irony, as the suspension of all final resolution. In noting this, it is not my intention to suggest that both texts are postmodern and written by the same composite authorial figure: a Paul Blake de Man.

Obviously, what is working in and through both texts is a discourse of modernity, or a family of modern discourses, which allows us to recognize such resemblances and identities, as well as to note their vital differences. I want to suggest further, and on this suggestion I will conclude the chapter and the book, that the putting into play of the discourse of modernity, in a Cold War liberal but popular literary variant and in its high-theory spectral echo of apocalypse, testifies uncannily to the cosmic aspirations of global America, a prospect that this book would look on with a colder (but not hostile) critical eye.

NOTES

Introduction: We Welcoming Others, or What's Wrong with the Global Point of View?

1   William Harmon and C. Hugh Holman, eds., *A Handbook to Literature,* 7th ed. (Upper Saddle River, N.J.: Prentice Hall, 1996), 72.

2   Henry James, *The Wings of the Dove,* ed. John Bayley (New York: Penguin, 1986), 400.

3   Michael Hardt and Antonio Negri, *Empire* (Cambridge: Harvard University Press, 2000).

4   Jacques Derrida, *Aporias,* trans. Thomas Dutoit (Stanford: Stanford University Press, 1993), 79.

5   For a comprehensive discussion of "the principle of ruin" as "spectrality," see Jacques Derrida, *Politics of Friendship,* trans. George Collins (New York: Verso, 1997), chap. 5: "On Absolute Hostility: The Course of Philosophy and the Spectre of the Political," 112–37. Although Derrida, surprisingly enough, does not remark on Blake's use of the figure of "the Spectre" in *Specters of Marx,* he does mention it in *Politics in Friendship.* See 72–73, 73–74 n. 20, and chap. 2, "Loving in Friendship: Perhaps—the Noun and the Adverb," 26–48.

6   On this topic see Jacques Derrida, *Specters of Marx: The State of the Debt, the Work of Mourning, and the New International,* trans. Peggy Kamuf (New York: Routledge, 1944).

7   On this topic, see the special issue "The University" of the international journal of literature and culture, *boundary 2* 27, no. 1 (spring 2000).

8   See, for example, my *Radical Parody: American Culture and Critical Agency after Foucault* (New York: Columbia University Press, 1991).

9   Derrida derives his term *arrivant*, which can mean "arrival," "newcomer," or "arriving" and therefore blurs any hard-and-fast distinctions among object, subject, and process, from Hélène Cixous, *La* (Paris: Gallimard, 1976), 132. See Derrida's *Aporias*, 86 nn. 13 and 14. For more on this topic, see *Of Hospitality: Anne Dufourmantelle Invites Jacques Derrida to Respond*, trans. Rachel Bowlby (Stanford: Stanford University Press, 2000).

10   On this Benjaminian theme, see Derrida, *Specters of Marx*, 55, 154, 180–81 n. 2. See also Derrida's response to his Marxist critics, "Marx and Sons," in *Ghostly Demarcations: A Symposium on Jacques Derrida's "Specters of Marx,"* ed. Michael Sprinker (New York: Verso, 2000), 213–69. For one of the better critiques, from this perspective, see Werner Hanacher, "Lingua Amissa: The Messianism of Commodity-Language and Derrida's *Specters of Marx*," 168–212. For another response by Derrida on the subject of the future as having the form of "a messianic promise," see his "History of the Lie: Prolegomena," in *Futures of Jacques Derrida*, ed. Richard Rand (Stanford: Stanford University Press, 2001), 65–94.

11   Daniel T. O'Hara and Alan Singer, eds., "Thinking through Art: Aesthetic Agency and Global Modernity," a special issue of *boundary 2* 25, no. 1 (spring 1998).

12   I began with Robert D. Kaplan, *The Coming Anarchy: Shattering the Dreams of the Post Cold War* (New York: Random House, 2000). For more of this, see hereafter.

13   *PMLA* 116, no. 1 (January 2001): "Special Topic: Globalizing Literary Studies," 16–188. In this context, two recent collections, one in anthropology, the other in theology and religion studies, provide interesting contracts: Arjun Appadurai, ed., *Globalization* (Durham, N.C.: Duke University Press, 2001); and Dwight N. Hopkins et al., eds., *Religions/Globalizations: Theories and Cases* (Durham, N.C.: Duke University Press, 2001).

14   Bruce Robbins, *Feeling Global: Internationalism in Distress* (New York: New York University Press, 1999), 3.

15   It is to be understood that when I say "America" here I mean the United States, unless I specify otherwise. For more on this usage, see William V. Spanos, *America's Shadow: An Anatomy of Empire* (Minneapolis: University of Minnesota Press, 2000).

16   Although not concerned specifically with this spy satellite network, John le Carré's novel *Single and Single* (New York: Pocket Books, 1999) is generally very illuminating on the cloak-and-dagger aspects of the new world order.

17   The one common, albeit complex, feature of globalization appears to be the rise to dominance of the celebrity system and the service tourism industries, and the consequent deprofessionalization of traditionally middle-class professions, especially university teaching.

18   Robbins, *Feeling Global*, 3–4.

19   Samuel P. Huntington, *The Clash of Civilizations and the Remaking of World Order* (New York: Simon and Schuster, 1996).

20   For more examples, see *boundary 2* 26, no. 3 (fall 1999), esp. "Left Conservatism: A Workshop," 1–61. See also, in this issue, three very different analyses of global-

ism: Terry Cochran, "Thinking at the Edge of the Galaxy: Pierre Lévy's World Projection," 63–85; Donald E. Pease, "After the Tocqueville Revival; or The Return of the Political," 87–114; and Pheny Cheah, "Spectral Nationality: The Living On [sur-vie] of the Postcolonial Nation in Neocolonial Globalization," 225–52. Derrida's concept of "spectrality," of the survival or living on of "textual," "archival," and "inscriptional" identities and differences (disseminated traces), is here given exemplary life.

21 If one wanted to do a reading of the emerging "global studies" in Paul de Man, one could recall his redefinition of romantic figural language as the scene (of instruction in) "anacoluthon" or "parabasis." This is "any grammatical or syntactical discontinuity in which a construction interrupts another before it is completed." This figure occasions "a sudden revelation of the discontinuity between two rhetorical codes." See Paul de Man, *Allegories of Reading: Figural Language in Rousseau, Nietzsche, Rilke, and Proust* (New Haven: Yale University Press, 1979), 289 and 300 respectively. Derrida's spectrality, like other figures of globalization, is the anacoluthon or parabasis of theory.

22 Paul A. Bové, "Editor's Note," special issue, "The University," *boundary 2* 27, no. 1 (YEAR): 1.

23 Robert D. Kaplan, *The Coming Anarchy: Shattering the Dreams of the Post Cold War* (New York: Random House, 2000), 24. Kaplan is here citing Tad Harrer-Dixon, who is quoting Daniel Deudney. And I, of course, and now, you. . . .

24 Mick Foley, *Mankind: Have a Nice Day! A Tale of Blood and Sweatsocks* (New York: Regan Books, 1999), 488. Foley has published another number one nonfiction best-seller entitled *Foley Is Good: And the Real Word Is Faker than Wrestling* (New York: Regan Books, 2001).

25 John le Carré, *Single and Single* (New York: Pocket Books, 2000). The original Scribner hardcover edition appeared in 1999.

Chapter One: Edward W. Said and the Fate of Critical Culture

1 Seamus Deane, "Under Eastern and Western Eyes," *boundary 2* 28, no. 1 (spring 2001): 1–18.

2 Edward W. Said, "Globalizing Literary Study," *PMLA* 116, no. 1 (January 2001): 64–68.

3 Edward W. Said, *Out of Place: A Memoir* (New York: Alfred A. Knopf, 1999).

4 Edward W. Said, *Reflections on Exile and Other Essays* (Cambridge: Harvard University Press, 2000).

Chapter Two: Why Foucault No Longer Matters

1 Michel Foucault, *Madness and Civilization: A History of Insanity in the Age of Reason,* trans. Richard Howard (New York: Random House, 1973); *The Birth of*

the Clinic, trans. A. M. Sheridan Smith (London: Tavistock, 1976); *Death and the Labyrinth: The World of Raymond Roussel,* trans. Charles Ruas (London: Athlone, 1987).

2   I have discussed this matter at greater length in my *Radical Parody: American Culture and Critical Agency after Foucault* (New York: Columbia University Press, 1992), chaps. 3 and 4, pp. 60–95.

3   The entire phrase, "the ironic heroization of the present," comes from "What Is Enlightenment?" (42), about which see my note 10 below. It refers to the modern intellectual practice, especially found in modern art and literature, which Baudelaire first identified and perfected for poetry, that entails "an exercise in which extreme attention to what is real is confronted with the practice of a liberty that simultaneously respects this reality and violates it" ("What Is Enlightenment?" 41). That is, the formal resources of art known as pastiche and parody both present the real and represent, via its formal mode, its immanent critique. For more on this topic, see "What Was Foucault?" in my *Radical Parody,* 37–59.

4   Briefly put, "radical parody" is "the exaggerated imitation of a recognizably characteristic position or style the parodist in question shares with others by virtue of a network of ideological and professional identifications and association. . . . the intended target of such parody [is] some common aspect or other of the intellectual parodist's own mode of scholarly production" (*Radical Parody,* 49). Here I also discuss the relation of "radical parody" to Fredric Jameson's conception of postmodern pastiche in his *Postmodernism, or The Cultural Logic of Late Capitalism* (Durham, N.C.: Duke University Press, 1990). For a more detailed discussion of what Foucault means by "oneself," see *Radical Parody,* chaps. 4 and 9. Chapter 9 discusses Deleuze's reading of this figure in his book *Foucault,* trans. Seán Hand (Minneapolis: University of Minnesota Press, 1988).

5   For a thorough discussion of this matter, see Christopher Norris, " 'What Is Enlightenment?' Kant according to Foucault," in *Reconstructing Foucault,* ed. Ricardo Miguel-Alonzo (Amsterdam: Rodolphi, 1995), 51–134.

6   For a statement of Rorty's influential position, see his "Moral Identity and Private Autonomy" and the discussion following it in *Michel Foucault, Philosopher: Essays Translated from the French and German,* trans. Timothy J. Armstrong (New York: Routledge, 1992), 328–35. Unlike Taylor or Said, who criticize Foucault for what they see as his deterministic vision of power and the nonrelationship of his later and earlier work, Rorty argues that there are two Foucaults: the Foucault involved in private self-creation (and this is the Foucault who recognized himself in the late work), and the Foucault who would impose a totalizing vision on existence in the interest of promoting a transformation of the public sphere (and this second Foucault is the problem). Thus even Rorty finds the late work inconsistent with the earlier work, but whereas others lament this late work, even while they may criticize aspects of the earlier work, he praises it precisely for its recognition of the true aim of all intellectual work, self-creation or private autonomy. I argue for a coherent and valuable continuity in Foucault's career and that the

later work, as the earlier in its own way, transcends the reductive binary opposition of public and private.

7 For more on this point, see my *Radical Parody,* 74–83.

8 See Rorty, "Moral Identity and Private Autonomy"; also Norris's discussion of this and similar positions in " 'What Is Enlightenment?' Kant according to Foucault."

9 See Raymond Bellour, "Towards Fiction," in *Michel Foucault, Philosopher,* 148–56.

10 "What Is Enlightenment?" in *The Foucault Reader,* ed. Paul Rabinow (New York: Pantheon, 1984), 42. Quotations from *The Foucault Reader* hereafter cited in the text as *FR*.

11 Foucault conceives of self-fashioning as a spiritual exercise originally invented by the Greeks and perfected by the Roman Stoics. He was led, in part, to do so by the work of Pierre Hadot, who responds very critically to Foucault in "Reflections on the Notion of 'The Cultivation of the Self,' " in *Michel Foucault, Philosopher,* 225–32. Because I am not a classicist, I cannot really judge who has the better case. My own view is that what Foucault has to say about "the cultivation of the self" in ancient or modern culture matters more as a present revision, an experiment in learning to think differently in the future, for himself and for us, than as a conventional scholarly representation of the distant or more recent past.

12 See Norris, " 'What Is Enlightenment?' Kant according to Foucault," for a complete and critical airing of such charges.

13 See Paul A. Bové, *Intellectuals in Power: A Genealogy of Critical Humanism* (New York: Columbia University Press, 1986), 209–37, and Bové's foreword to Gilles Deleuze, *Foucault.*

14 See Norris, " 'What Is Enlightenment?' Kant according to Foucault," who summarizes the issue as follows: "In short: there is a near-schizophrenic splitting of roles between (1) Foucault the 'public' intellectual, [somehow] thinking and writing on behalf of those subjects oppressed by the discourses of instituted power/knowledge, and (2) Foucault the avowed aesthete, avatar of Nietzsche and Baudelaire, who espouses an ethos [impossible by his own reasoning] or private self-fashioning and an attitude of sovereign disdain toward the principles and values of enlightened critique" (101). Or also see p. 74: "This raises the question as to how it is possible to envisage an *ethics*—in any meaningful sense of that term—which would treat the subject as indeed nothing more than an imaginary locus, a side-effect of language, or a product of those transient discursive formations that constitute the history of Western thought. It seems to emphasize that this question haunts Foucault's writings up to the end, and he never managed to address or resolve it to his own satisfaction." As we see, I strongly disagree with this critical consensus because I follow Foucault in the second and third volumes of *The History of Sexuality* and in his late interviews in noting the important distinction between cultures and the kinds of moral codes they have—a single coercively centralizing form or a plurality of elective ethical possibilities—and

noting, as well, the resemblance Foucault sees between the ancient epoch of the Stoic's "cultivation of the self" and our own "postmodern" epoch. The subject, unlike the way Norris characterizes it, is not the same in every epoch. It is only one "modern" (Renaissance to mid-twentieth-century) form of subjectivity, albeit with its origins in earlier epochs and its vestiges in our own time, but this modern subject is never presumed to be by Foucault *the* sole definition of human subjectivity. Making possible alternative forms of "reason" by comparing the modern instrumental sort to other kinds in Western history is, after all, Foucault's career-long project. He may have been mistaken about the possibilities of our postmodern epoch, but that is a separate matter, which I also address here.

15 See, for example, Charles W. Anderson, *Prescribing the Life of the Mind: An Essay on the Purpose of the University, the Aims of Liberal Education, the Competence of Citizens, and the Cultivation of Practical Reason* (Madison: University of Wisconsin Press, 1993). By "practical reason," Anderson means the calculative understanding developed in modern technological society and applied instrumentally to cultural education as the model of human judgment.

16 Of course, there are distinctions to be made among these critics. Allan Megill's chapter in his *Prophets of Extremity: Nietzsche, Heidegger, Foucault, Derrida* (Berkeley: University of California Press, 1985), while critical, is interesting for its suggestion that Foucault's *Archaeology of Knowledge* is deliberately a parody of Descartes's *Meditations*. Meanwhile, most of the essays in *Foucault: A Critical Reader*, ed. David Couzens Hoy (Oxford: Blackwell, 1986), especially those by Ian Hacking, Richard Rorty, Michael Walzer, Charles Taylor, Habermas, and Arnold I. Davidson, are often reductively critical and polemically distorted to the point of "straw man" caricature. Similarly, the chapters in Geoffrey Galt Harphan, *The Ascetic Imperative in Culture and Criticism* (Chicago: University of Chicago Press, 1987), and in Nancy Fraser, *Unruly Practices: Power, Discourse, and Gender in Contemporary Social Theory* (Minneapolis: University of Minnesota Press, 1989), are polemical misreadings of Foucault that ignore important distinctions and reformulations of the kind I discuss here. Two of the strongest and fairest critiques remain Edward W. Said, "Traveling Theory," in *The World, the Text, and the Critic* (Cambridge: Harvard University Press, 1983), and Frank Lentricchia, "Michel Foucault's Fantasy for Humanists," in *Ariel and the Police* (Madison: University of Wisconsin Press, 1988).

17 For an excellent analysis of this critical desire, see Paul A. Bové, "Intellectuals at War: Michel Foucault and the Analytics of Power," in *Intellectuals in Power*, and his foreword to Deleuze, *Foucault*. See also his "Power and Freedom: Opposition and the Humanities," *October* 53, no. 3 (summer 1990): 78–92.

18 On this feature of Foucault's work, see the aperçus in Jonathan Arac, *Critical Genealogies: Historical Situations for Postmodern Literary Studies* (New York: Columbia University Press, 1987), and his editor's introduction to *After Foucault: Humanistic Knowledge, Postmodern Challenges* (New Brunswick: Rutgers University Press, 1988).

19 On this topic, see "Aesthetic Relations: Michel Foucault and the Fate of Friend-ship," in my *Radical Parody*, 74–95. The problematic of friendship truly haunts Foucault's understanding of ancient culture as he traces how the nonreciprocal relationship of boy and man, student and mentor, gets transformed into a more open and yet self-disciplined game of love, thanks to Platonic and later Stoic elaborations. The reciprocity needed for genuine friendship does arise but, iron-ically enough, as he tells the story, can only be perfected in the final Stoic conception of the heterosexual couple and the responsible practice of the mar-ried state. Nonetheless, I argue in this chapter and assume here that friendship is possible between "author" and "reader," at the site of the text, as ever reversible roles or revisionary positions, much as Foucault himself practices "reading" vis-à-vis his source texts.

20 For a serious discussion of the aesthetic in the context of these equally inadequate critical responses, see "An Interview with Edward W. Said," conducted by Paul A. Bové and Joseph A. Bittigieg on the occasion of the publication of *Culture and Imperialism*, a critique that takes the aesthetic seriously in both its political connections and its formal imaginative dimensions. This interview appears in *boundary 2* 20, no. 1 (spring 1993): 1–35.

21 In *Romanticism, Nationalism, and the Revolt against Theory* (Chicago: University of Chicago Press, 1993), David Simpson makes a compelling case for the system-atic misconstrual of the aesthetics, especially as it informs the development of critical theory, first via the German romantics and then via French elaborations, owing to an Anglo-American nationalist ethos that values common sense, prac-ticality, and plain speaking and misreads the aesthetic and theory in terms of Jacobin politics, abstract methodology, and otherworldly or irresponsible spec-ulation.

22 On this topic, see Thomas Hurks, *Perfectionism* (New York: Oxford University Press, 1993). The exact relationship of Foucault's ethics to Kant's position in *Foundations of the Metaphysics of Morals* remains to be explored, as does its relation to Aristotle's view.

23 See W. B. Yeats, "The Circus Animals' Desertion," in *The Collected Works of W. B. Yeats*, vol. 1, *The Poems*, rev. ed., ed. Richard J. Finneran (New York: Macmillan, 1983, 1989), 346–48.

24 Foucault, *The History of Sexuality*, vol. 2, *The Use of Pleasure*, trans. Robert Hurley (New York: Pantheon, 1985), 9.

25 The literature of the culture wars, which began with Allan Bloom's 1987 best-seller *The Closing of the American Mind* (New York: Simon and Schuster, 1987), has grown enormously. A good overview of the debate can be found in Christo-pher Newfield "What Was Political Correctness?" *Critical Inquiry* 19 (winter 1993): 308–36. Similarly, see Marianna Torgovnick, "Hartman's Dilemma: *Minor Prophecies: The Literary Essay in the Culture Wars*," *ADE Bulletin* 104 (spring 1993): 52–55. David Bromwich, in *Politics by Other Means: Higher Education and Group Thinking* (New Haven: Yale University Press, 1992), makes a case against

both "Left" and "Right" identity politics, although he is hardest on those among whose members he would count himself—those on the "Left." But perhaps the strongest critique of this kind is in Edward W. Said's "The Politics of Knowledge," *Raritan* 11, no. 1 (summer 1991): 17–31. An interesting reflection by a participant in the public debates about "political correctness" and the NEH and the NEA can be found in Catharine R. Stimpson, "Dirty Minds, Dirty Bodies, Clean Speech," *Michigan Quarterly Review* 32 (summer 1993): 317–37. For Foucault-inspired positions on this debate, see the essays in *Foucault and Education: Disciplines and Knowledge,* ed. Stephen J. Ball (New York: Routledge, 1990), and the introduction to my *Radical Parody,* 1–12. The most suggestive reading of these debates, which argues that they are part of a concerted effort to overcome the memory of the various subversive challenges to the disciplinary and administrative structures of critical humanism and the "liberal" university, can be found in two recent books by William V. Spanos: *The End of Education* (Minneapolis: University of Minnesota Press, 1992), and *Heidegger and Criticism: Retrieving the Cultural Politics of Destruction* (Minneapolis: University of Minnesota Press, 1993). The sensational revelations about Foucault's life in two recent biographies, Didier Eribon's *Michel Foucault,* trans. Betsy Wing (Cambridge: Harvard University Press, 1991), and especially James Miller's *The Passion of Michel Foucault* (New York: Simon and Schuster, 1993), have only distracted from what intellectual contribution his late work could make in any serious discussion of *Bildung* and pedagogy.

26 W. B. Yeats, "Byzantium," in *The Poems,* 249.

27 Although most critics believe Nietzsche's *On the Genealogy of Morals* (trans. Walter Kaufmann [New York: Vintage, 1967]) is only a critique of the ascetic ideal, it is actually a complex dialectical reflection on the positive self-empowering aspects of the long scourge of humankind, asceticism. I follow Nietzsche and Foucault in believing that what does separate us out as a species is that human beings are the sole ascetic animals delighting in forming our minds, bodies, and souls according to either a centrally imposed, single normative ideal or a more diverse array of revisable and self-chosen examples. The second situation is, for Foucault, preferable, and it may yet be emerging in our time, although I have my doubts.

28 On this topic, see "What Was Foucault?" in my *Radical Parody,* 37–59.

29 For more on this dialectical interchange—"oneself as another, another as oneself"—see Paul Ricoeur, *Oneself as Another,* trans. Kathleen Blamey (Chicago: University of Chicago Press, 1992), especially the section "Conscience," 341–56, which discusses Heidegger's, Nietzsche's, and Freud's theories on the subject.

30 My own view is closest to Said's in "The Politics of Knowledge": "A great deal of recent theoretical speculation has proposed that works of literature are completely determined in their responses by their respective cultural situations, to a point where no value, no reading, no interpretation can be anything other than the merest reflection of some immediate interest. All readings and all writings are reduced to an assumed ideological emanation. . . . Although I risk oversimplifica-

tion, it is probably correct to say that it does not finally matter *who* wrote what, but rather *how* a work is written and *how* it is read. The idea that because Plato and Aristotle are male and the products of a slave society they should be disqualified from receiving contemporary attention is as limited an idea as suggesting that *only* their work, because it is addressed to and about elites, should be read today. Marginality and homelessness are not in my opinion to be gloried in; they are to be brought to an end, so that more, and not fewer, people can enjoy the benefits of what has for centuries been denied the victims of race, class, or gender" (29–30, 31). Via the figure of "oneself," which is simultaneously "oneself as another," an agon of conflict subjects to be ethically stylized for each person and for a society as a whole, Foucault's late work could contribute to the realization of Said's vision here, if only it could be generally appreciated.

31 Michel Foucault, *The History of Sexuality,* vol. 3, *The Care of the Self,* trans. Robert Hurley (New York: Pantheon, 1986), 65.

32 I base my gloomy view of the possibilities of our cultural moment on many things, not least of which is the spectacle of America's leading philosopher, Richard Rorty, making such simplistic and distorted statements about Foucault in "Moral Identity and Private Autonomy" as the following: "Foucault was for much of the time, a 'knight of autonomy' " (229). To say such a thing—or to be allowed to say such a thing—when all the documented evidence of the work and career says otherwise testifies to the sad state of affairs in American intellectual culture, which can only grow worse, more Rorty-esque, as his epigones proliferate, with the consequence being our constitutional incapacity for the Foucauldian work of thought as an ascetic self-stylization or "aesthetics of existence," dependent on reading/writing/listening/responding with imaginative and critical appreciation.

33 Margaret Toye, "Care of the Self or Care of the Other? Towards a Poststructuralist Ethics of Pedagogy," in *Critical Ethics: Text, Theory, and Responsibility,* ed. Dominic Rainsford and Tim Woods (New York: St. Martin's Press, 1999), 203–19.

34 Jacques Derrida, *Politics of Friendship,* trans. George Collins (London: Verso, 1997). Derrida, while critical of Foucault in this context, can nonetheless use other figures—Levinas, Blanchot—to construct a sustained, intricate, and comprehensive (but still infinite) reading.

35 Jacques Derrida, *Given Time: 1. Counterfeit Money,* trans. Peggy Kamuf (Chicago: University of Chicago Press, 1992), 27. For Derrida's complete discussion, see his *The Gift of Death,* trans. David Wills (Chicago: University of Chicago Press, 1995).

36 See Derrida, *Politics of Friendship,* 5. Here he both recognizes and disavows all such gifts, ironically enough: "Who never dreams of such a scene? But who does not abhor this theatre? Who would not see therein the repetition of a disdainful and ridiculous staging, the putting to death of friendship itself?" But as Derrida's elaborate analysis goes on to show, such death is de rigueur to any politics at all.

Chapter Three: Lentricchia's Frankness and the Place of Literature

1   Frank Lentricchia, *The Edge of Night: A Confession* (New York: Knopf, 1992), 121.
2   Stanley Fish, "Why Literary Criticism Is like Virtue," *London Review of Books* 15, no. 11 (10 June 1993): 11–16. On the cover, the title is given as "Why I Am a Literary Critic."
3   "An interview with Edward Said," *boundary 2* 20, no. 1 (spring 1993): 1–25.
4   The best overview of the project of *The Use of Pleasure* and *The Care of the Self*, volumes 2 and 3 in *The History of Sexuality,* is Foucault's own, which is to be found in three late interviews: "On the Genealogy of Ethics: An Overview of Work in Progress," "Politics and Ethics: An Interview," and "Polemics, Politics, and Problemizations: An Interview with Michel Foucault," all of which are in Paul Rabinow, ed., *The Foucault Reader* (New York: Pantheon, 1984), 340–90.
5   For more on this subject, see my *Radical Parody: American Culture and Critical Agency after Foucault* (New York: Columbia University Press, 1992), 60–95.
6   Frank Lentricchia, "Philosophers of Modernism at Harvard, circa 1900," *SAQ* 89, no. 4 (fall 1996): 787–834.
7   For further discussion of *Modernist Quartet* and of Lentricchia's relationship to aestheticism, see my *Radical Parody,* 245–70.
8   For further discussion, see the chapter on T. S. Eliot in Lentricchia's *Modernist Quartet* (New York: Cambridge University Press, 1994).
9   Frank Lentricchia, "My Kinsman, T. S. Eliot," *Raritan* 11, no. 4 (spring 1992): 1–23. See also Mark Edmundson, ed., *The Academy Writes Back* (New York: Viking, 1993).
10 T. S. Eliot, "Tradition and the Individual Talent," in *Selected Prose of T. S. Eliot,* ed. Frank Kermode (New York: Harcourt Brace Jovanovich, 1975), 40.
11 From the original manuscript of *Edge 'a Night,* 173.
12 Frank Lentricchia, *The Music of the Inferno: A Novel* (Albany: SUNY Press, 1999), 84.
13 Jacques Derrida, *"Khōra,"* in *On the Name,* trans. Thomas Dutort, David Wovel, John P. Leavey Jr., and Ian McLeod (Stanford: Stanford University Press, 1995), 99.

Chapter Four: Redesigning the Lessons of Literature

1   Henry James, *The Reverberator,* in *The Novels and Tales of Henry James*, New York Edition, vol. 13 (New York: Charles Scribner's Sons, 1908), 13–14.
2   Wlad Godzich, *The Culture of Literacy* (Cambridge: Harvard University Press, 1994), 1–35.
3   John Guillory, *Cultural Capital: The Problem of Literary Canon Formation* (Chicago: University of Chicago Press, 1993), esp. 36–56.
4   Mette Hjort, *The Strategy of Letters* (Cambridge: Harvard University Press, 1993), 17–43.

Chapter Five: The Return to Ethics and the Specter of Reading

1   Cornel West, "The New Cultural Politics of Difference," in *Beyond a Dream Deferred: Multicultural Education and the Politics of Excellence,* ed. Becky W. Thompson and Sangeeta Tyage (Minneapolis: University of Minnesota Press, 1963), 18–40.

2   Jane Tompkins, "The I's Have It," interview by Alan Begley, *Lingua Franca: The Review of Academic Life* 4, no. 3 (March–April 1994): 54–59.

3   Wlad Godzich, *The Culture of Literacy* (Cambridge: Harvard University Press, 1994).

4   Arnold Davidson, "Ethics as Ascetics: Foucault, the History of Ethics, and Ancient Thought," in *The Cambridge Companion to Foucault,* ed. Gary Gutting (Cambridge: Cambridge University Press, 1994), 115.

5   Friedrich Nietzsche, *On the Genealogy of Morals and Ecce Homo,* ed. Walter Kaufmann (New York: Vintage, 1967), 120.

6   Jahan Ramazani, *Poetry of Mourning: The Modern Elegy from Hardy to Heaney* (Chicago: University of Chicago Press, 1994).

7   Jack Gilbert, *The Great Fires: Poems, 1982–1992* (New York: Knopf, 1994), 12.

8   Nietzsche, *On the Genealogy of Morals,* 15.

9   Jacques Derrida, *Archive Fever: A Freudian Impression,* trans. Eric Prenowitz (Chicago: University of Chicago Press, 1996).

10 Dominic Rainsford and Tim Woods, eds., *Critical Ethics: Text, Theory, and Responsibility* (London: Macmillan, 1999).

11 Edward W. Said, *Out of Place* (New York: Alfred A. Knopf, 1999), 137.

Chapter Six: Class in a Global Light

1   The history of the term "class" before Marx links it with the emergence of those natural, life, and social sciences such as chemistry, biology, and political economy (among others) for which thinking by means of tables, graphs, schemata—what Foucault sees as the theoretical grids of modern scientific rationality—is a habitual representational practice. That is, the mapping of nature's body in the periodic table of chemical elements, of the human body in medical anatomy, and of the social body in class analysis are interlinked activities in the emerging discourse of instrumental reason. Before the nineteenth century, the sense of class distinctions appeared embodied in literature via the principle of decorum; how one spoke marked one's social and even moral status.

2   Václav Havel, "Our Troubled Quest for Meaning in a Postmodern World," *Philadelphia Inquirer,* 6 July 1994, A7.

3   Patricia Meyer Spacks, "The Academic Marketplace: Who Pays the Costs?" *MLA Newsletter* 26, no. 2 (summer 1994): 3.

4   Jon Elster, *Making Sense of Marx: Studies in Marxism and Social Theory* (New York: Cambridge University Press, 1985), 331.

5   Wlad Godzich, *The Culture of Literacy* (Cambridge: Harvard University Press, 1994), 22.

6   Henry James, "The Birthplace," in *The Jolly Corner and Other Tales,* ed. Roger Gard (New York: Penguin, 1990), 111.

Chapter Seven: Transference and Abjection

1   For a different take on these developments, see Jacques Derrida, *Adieu: To Emmanuel Levinas*, trans. Pascade-Anne Brault and Michael Naas (Stanford: Stanford University Press, 1999), 101.

2   See Bruce Robins, *Feeling Global: Internationalism in Distress* (New York: New York University Press, 1999).

3   Jon Elster, ed., *Karl Marx: A Reader* (Cambridge: Cambridge University Press, 1986), 139.

4   See the preceding chapter for further discussion of these institutional developments.

5   See, for further discussion, Paul A. Bové, "Editor's Note," Special Issue, "The University," *boundary 2* 27, no. 1 (2000).

6   See, for example, Donald E. Pease, "After the Tocqueville Revival; or, The Return of the Political," *boundary 2* 26, no. 3 (1999): 87–114.

7   *Adieu* also discusses the tortured affiliation of Levinas with Kant and the problematic relationship of Levinas's Talmudic sources to contemporary feminism.

8   See, for further discussion, Jacques Derrida, *The Gift of Death,* trans. David Wells (Chicago: University of Chicago Press, 1995), and Derrida, *Given Time: 1. Counterfeit Money,* trans. Peggy Kamuf (Chicago: University of Chicago Press, 1992).

9   Michael Hardt and Antonio Negri, *Empire* (Cambridge: Harvard University Press, 2000).

10 Derrida, *The Gift of Death,* 74, 76–77. For his discussion of the paradoxical relationships between the worldwide resurgence of religion, which opposes the values of modernity, and the new global reality of capitalist, techno-scientific rationality and telecommunications, see Jacques Derrida, "Faith and Knowledge: the Two Sources of 'Religion' at the Limits of Reason Alone," in *Religion,* ed. Jacques Derrida and Gianni Vattimo (Stanford: Stanford University Press, 1998), 1–78. In this monograph-length essay, Derrida coins the name *mondialatinisation* (globalatinization) to refer to "this strange phenomenon of the present historical other and death and radical evil—can come as a surprise at any moment" (17–18). "Chora," the latter term (from the Greek *khōra* in Plato's *Timaeus*), refers to "the open interior of a corpus, of a system, of a language or a culture," a configuration of spacing, a topology of elements that cannot be reappropriated into "a consistent self-interpretation" (19). In this book, "global America" is my messianic moment to come. These "formal structures" inform every text, of course, even that of an entire historical moment.

Chapter Eight: Ghostwork

1 Jacques Derrida, *Specters of Marx: The State of the Debt, the Work of Mourning, and the New International,* trans. Peggy Kamuf (New York: Routledge, 1994), 122.

2 Edward W. Said, *Out of Place: A Memoir* (New York: Knopf, 1999).

3 I have presumed that this topos of modern philosophy is familiar enough to need no special glossing or commentary.

4 See Derrida, *Specters of Marx,* 75–95, for an interesting elaboration.

5 In James Strachey, ed., *The Standard Edition of the Complete Psychological Works of Sigmund Freud,* vol. 22 (London: Hogarth Press, 1960), 239–48. Hereafter all references to Freud's letter to Rolland Romain are cited in the text by page number only.

6 Jacques Lacan, "Presence of the Analyst," in *Essential Papers on Transference,* ed. Aaron H. Esman, M.D. (New York: New York University Press, 1990), 489. For a Lacanian reading of this incident, see Susan Sugarman, *Freud on the Acropolis: Reflections on a Paradoxical Response to the Real* (New York: Basic, 1998).

7 Freud's essay "Analysis Terminable and Interminable" is reprinted in its entirety, as published in *The Standard Edition of the Complete Psychological Works of Sigmund Freud,* in Joseph Sandler, *On Freud's "Analysis Terminable and Interminable"* (New Haven: Yale University Press, 1991), 3–40. Subsequent quotations from Freud's essay come from Sandler's work and are cited in the text by page number only.

8 David Zimmerman and A. L. Bento Mostardeiro, "On Teaching 'Analysis Terminable and Interminable,'" in Sandler, *Freud's "Analysis Terminable and Interminable,"* 78.

9 Regarding the publication of Freud's essay in *Almanach der Psychoanalyse 1938,* see the editor's note to "Analysis Terminable and Interminable," in *The Standard Edition of the Complete Psychological Works of Sigmund Freud,* trans. and ed. James Strachey, vol. 23 (London: Hogarth Press, 1964), 211–15, esp. 211.

10 See, for one example, Paul E. Stepansky, *Freud, Surgery, and the Surgeons* (Hillsdale, N.J.: Analytic Press, 1999).

11 Ilse Grubrich-Simitis, *Back to Freud's Texts: Making Silent Documents Speak* (New Haven: Yale University Press, 1996).

12 Sigmund Freud, *Leonardo da Vinci and a Memory of His Childhood* (New York: Norton, 1989), 55.

13 Joel Braslow, *Mental Ills and Bodily Cures: Psychiatric Treatment in the First Half of the Twentieth Century* (Berkeley: University of California Press, 1997).

14 Sigmund Freud, *The Question of Lay Analysis* (New York: Norton, 1989).

15 Ilse Grubrich-Simitis, *Back to Freud's Texts,* 177–78.

16 Sigmund Freud, "The Poet's Relation to Day-Dreaming," in *Authorship from Plato to the Postmodern: A Reader,* ed. Seán Burke (Edinburgh: Edinburgh University Press, 1995), 54–62.

17 Thomas Mann, "Freud and the Future," in *Selected Essays* (New York: Vintage, 1957), 303–24.

18 Lindsay Waters's essay "On Paul de Man's Effort to Re-anchor a True in Our Feelings" appears in *boundary 2* 26, no. 2 (summer 1999): 133–56.

19 Julia Rivkin and Michael Ryan, *Literary Theory: An Anthology* (London: Blackwell, 1998).

20 See Paul de Man, *Aesthetic Ideology* (Minneapolis: University of Minnesota Press, 1996), for a complete discussion of this topic.

21 Sigmund Freud, *The Interpretation of Dreams,* trans. James Strachey, Pelican Freud Library, vol. 4 (Harmondsworth, Middlesex, England: Penguin, 1975). Hereafter cited in the text as *ID*.

22 Jacques Lacan, *The Four Fundamental Concepts of Psychoanalysis,* trans. Alan Sheridan (New York: W. W. Norton, 1978), 59.

23 Ibid., 59.

24 John Guillory, *Cultural Capital: The Problem of Literary Canon Formation* (Chicago: University of Chicago Press, 1993).

25 See my chapter on de Man in *The Romance of Interpretation: Visionary Criticism from Pater to de Man* (New York: Columbia University Press, 1985).

26 Paul de Man, "Kant's Materialism," in *Aesthetic Ideology* (Minneapolis: University of Minnesota Press, 1996), 123.

27 Sigmund Freud, *Moses and Monotheism,* in *The Standard Edition of the Complete Psychological Works of Sigmund Freud,* vol. 23, ed. James Strachey (London: Hogarth Press, 1964), 114.

Chapter Nine: Specter of Theory

1 Jacques Derrida, *Politics of Friendship,* trans. George Collins (New York: Verso, 1997), 73–74 n. 20.

2 Blake, a true visionary, resists the tragic sublime, which requires the death of the other to excite our sense of terror and pity.

3 See Jacques Derrida, *On the Name,* trans. Peggy Kamuf (Stanford: Stanford University Press, 1995).

4 Derrida, *Politics of Friendship,* 73–74 n. 20, and chap. 2, pp. 26–48.

5 Cordwainer Smith, *Norstrilia* (Framingham, Mass.: NESFA Press, 1998), 161.

6 When referring to Blake's use of the term, I will capitalize it, "the Spectre," following his usage.

7 Henry James, "The Jolly Corner," In *Complete Stories,* vol. 5 (New York: Library of America, 1996), 697–731.

8 William Blake, "The Book of Urizen," in *Complete Poetry and Prose,* 2d ed., ed. David V. Erdman, with commentary by Harold Bloom (New York: Oxford, 1997), 141.

9 Francis Fukuyama, *The End of History and the Last Man* (New York: Freso Press, 1992).

10 Jacques Derrida, *Specters of Marx: The State of the Debt, the Work of Mourning, and the New International,* trans. Peggy Kamuf (New York: Routledge, 1994). See also Michael Sprinker, ed., *Ghostly Demarcations: A Symposium on Jacques Derrida's "Specters of Marx"* (New York: Verso, 2000). This is a collection of useful essays on Derrida's later work generally.

11 Derrida has written so many different things on de Man, including an entire volume, *Memoirs,* trans. Peggy Kamuf (New York: Columbia University Press, 1989), that it is fair to say, I think, that de Man, for Derrida, represents *not* solely a person now deceased, not solely a professional project of American deconstruction, not solely an idea of intellectual life, but also the function of language that performs the dispossession of subjectivity in the impersonal, anonymous mechanical processes of *différance.*

12 Paul de Man, *Blindness and Insight: Essays in the Rhetoric of Contemporary Criticism* (New York: Oxford University Press, 1971), 139–40.

13 One of the projected but unfinished chapters of *Aesthetic Ideology* was to be devoted to Kierkegaard and Marx.

14 Although the terms "transference" and "abjection" are of psychoanalytic origins, they actually refer to rhetorical movements, that of anacoluthon (at the level of sentence syntax) and parabasis (at the narrative level)—which are both illustrated here—movements of trope, figurative turnings that break grammatical and aesthetic surfaces, punctuating the illusion of reality in any mode of fictionality.

Chapter Ten: Empire Baroque

1 Millicent Bell, *Meaning in Henry James* (Cambridge: Harvard University Press, 1991); and Ross Posnock, *The Trial of Curiosity: Henry James, William James, and the Challenge of Modernity* (New York: Oxford University Press, 1991).

2 Henry James, *The American Scene in Collected Travel Writings: Great Britain and America,* ed. Richard Howard (New York: Library of America, 1993), 363–64.

3 Henry James, "Preface to *The Wings of the Dove,*" in *Henry James: The Art of the Novel,* ed. R. P. Blackmur (New York: Scribner's, 1934, 1984), 304–5.

4 Roland Barthes, "The Structuralist Activity," in *Critical Theory since Plato,* rev. ed., ed. Hazard Adams (New York: Harcourt, Brace, Jovanovich, 1992), 1128–30.

5 Henry James, *The Wings of the Dove,* ed. John Bayley (New York: Penguin, 1986), 509.

6 Henry James, *The Ambassadors,* ed. Harry Levin (New York: Penguin, 1986).

7 Henry James, "The Preface to *The Princess Casamassima,*" in *The Art of the Novel,* ed. R. P. Blackmur (New York: Scribners, 1984), 66.

8 Ibid., xviii.

9 John Carlos Rowe, *The Other Henry James* (Durham, N.C.: Duke University Press, 1998).

10 Friedrich Nietzsche, *Beyond Good and Evil,* trans. Walter Kaufmann (New York: Vintage, 1966), 218.

11 Martin Heidegger, "The Origin of the Work of Art," in *Poetry, Language, Thought,* trans. Albert Hofstadter (New York: Harper and Row, 1971), 54.

12 Ibid.

13 "Postscript: An Interview with Michel Foucault," in *Death and the Labyrinth: The World of Raymond Roussel,* by Michel Foucault, trans. Charles Ruas, with an introduction by John Ashbery (Berkeley and Los Angeles: University of California Press, 1986), 182, 184.

14 As quoted in James Miller, *The Passion of Michel Foucault* (New York: Simon and Schuster, 1993), 130, 211.

15 Henry James, *The Art of the Novel,* introduction by R. P. Blackmur, foreword by R. W. B. Lewis, fiftieth anniversary edition (Boston: Northeastern University Press, 1984), 331. Hereafter cited in the text as *AN.*

16 See Eccles. 12.6 and 12.7: "Or ever the silver cord be loosed / Or the golden bowl be broken, / Or the pitcher be broken at the fountain, / Or the wheel broken at the cistern. / Then shall the dust return to the earth as it was." See also William Blake, "The Book of Thel": "Can wisdom be kept in a silver rod, / Or love in a golden bowl." For these references, consult Robert L. Gale, *A Henry James Encyclopedia* (New York: Greenwood Press, 1989), 264. And for the best discussion of James's revisionary acts in his late career, see Philip Horne, *Henry James and Revision* (Clarendon: Oxford University Press, 1990).

17 Henry James, *The Awkward Age* (New York: Alfred A. Knopf, 1993).

18 Gilles Deleuze, *The Fold,* trans. Tom Conley (Minneapolis: University of Minnesota Press, 1992).

19 Heidegger, "The Origin of the Work of Art," 54.

20 Martin Heidegger, "The Anaximander Fragment," in *Early Greek Thinking,* trans. David Farrell Krell and Frank A. Capuzzi (New York: Harper and Row, 1975), 46.

21 Martin Heidegger, "The Age of the World Picture," in *The Question Concerning Technology and Other Essays,* trans. William Lovitt (New York: Harper and Row, 1977), 135, 153.

22 Paul Ricoeur, *Oneself as Another,* trans. Kathleen Blamey (Chicago: University of Chicago Press, 1992), 330.

23 Immanuel Kant, *Critique of Judgment,* trans. Werner S. Pluhar (Indianapolis: Hackett, 1987), 18–20.

24 H. G. Wells, "Selections from *Boon,*" in *Henry James and H. G. Wells: A Record of Their Friendship, Their Debate on the Art of Fiction, and Their Quarrel,* ed. Leon Edel and Gordon N. Ray (Urbana: University of Illinois Press, 1958), 242.

25 Rebecca West, *Henry James* (London, 1816), in *Henry James: Critical Assessments,* vol. 1, *Memories, Views, and Writers,* ed. Graham Clarke (New York: Routledge, 1991), 126. It is to this critical biography that I owe my interest in "bewilderment" in Henry James, however fine Paul Armstrong's work on this topic is.

26 Henry James, *The Ambassadors* (New York: Penguin, 1986), 493.

27 Henry James, "The Parisian Stage," in *The Scenic Art,* ed. Allan Wade (New Brunswick, N.J.: Rutgers University Press, 1948), 11.

28   James, *The Wings of the Dove*, 269.

29   Henry James, *What Maisie Knew* (New York: Penguin, 1986), 254–55.

30   Henry James, *The Golden Bowl* (New York: Penguin, 1987), 517.

31   Henry James, *The Spoils of Poynton* (New York: Penguin, 1987), 60, 73.

32   Henry James, *The Awkward Age* (New York: Penguin, 1987), 210.

33   Jon Elster, *Making Sense of Marx* (New York: Cambridge University Press, 1985), esp. chap. 6, "Classes," 318–98.

34   Richard L. Bushman, *The Refinement of America: Persons, Houses, Cities* (New York: Alfred A. Knopf, 1991), 410.

35   Henry James, "From the Preface to *The Princess Casamassima,*" in *Theory of Fiction,* ed. James A. Miller (Lincoln: University of Nebraska Press, 1972), 238.

36   R. P. Blackmur, *"The Sacred Fount,"* in *Studies in Henry James,* ed. Veronica A. Makowsky (New York: New Directions, 1983), 67–68.

37   George McFadden, "Henry James's Remorse for *The Wings of the Dove,*" *Henry James Review* 9, no. 2 (spring 1988): 120.

38   William Wordsworth, "Selections" (from the preface to *The Lyrical Ballads*), in *English Romantic Writers,* ed. David Perkins (New York: Harcourt, Brace and World, 1967), 322.

39   Ibid., 24.

Chapter Eleven: Planet Buyer and The Catmaster

1   Friedrich Nietzsche, *The Gay Science,* trans. Walter Kaufmann (New York: Vintage Books, 1974), 167.

2   Sigmund Freud, *The Interpretation of Dreams,* trans. James Strachey (Harmondsworth, Middlesex, England: Penguin Books, 1976).

3   Jacques Lacan, *The Four Fundamental Concepts of Psychoanalysis,* trans. Alan Sheridan (New York: W. W. Norton, 1977), 59.

4   Allan Gurganus, "Minor Heroism: Something about My Father," in *The Vintage Book of Contemporary American Short Stories,* ed. Tobias Wolff (New York: Vintage, 1994). Although this story is originally from the early 1970s (composed and published in 1972–1973), it appears finally in a 1991 collection from Knopf, *White People,* as the leadoff story. A strong continuity from the countercultural revolutions of the earlier era thus clearly informs the academic multiculturalism of the New Americanists, whose greatest impact can perhaps be measured by the generation it took before a collection like *White People* could be fully conceived and then produced by a commercial press.

5   James A. Mann, ed., *The Rediscovery of Man: The Complete Short Science Fiction* (Framingham, Mass.: NESFA Press, 1993). All biographical information comes from the introduction by John J. Pierce, vii–xiii.

6   Jacques Lacan, "The Presence of the Analyst," in *Essential Papers on Transference,* ed. Aaron H. Esman, M.D. (New York: New York University Press, 1990), 489.

7   Cordwainer Smith, *Norstrilia* (Framingham, Mass.: NESFA Press, 1998).

8   Smith, in "Mother Hilton's Little Kittens," in Mann, *The Rediscovery of Man*, discusses some of the other weapons.

9   Sigmund Freud, *Leonardo da Vinci and a Memory of His Childhood*, trans. James Strachey (New York: Norton, 1989).

BIBLIOGRAPHY

Arac, Jonathan. *Critical Genealogies: Historical Situations for Postmodern Literary Studies*. New York: Columbia University Press, 1987.

——. Introduction to *After Foucault: Humanistic Knowledge, Postmodern Challenges*, ed. Jonathan Arac. New Brunswick: Rutgers University Press, 1988.

Anderson, Charles W. *Prescribing the Life of the Mind: An Essay on the Purpose of the University, the Aims of Liberal Education, the Competence of Citizens, and the Cultivation of Practical Reason*. Madison: University of Wisconsin Press, 1993.

Appadurai, Arjun, ed. *Globalization*. Durham, N.C.: Duke University Press, 2001.

Ball, Stephen J., ed. *Foucault and Education: Disciplines and Knowledge*. New York: Routledge, 1990.

Barthes, Roland. "The Structuralist Activity." In *Critical Theory since Plato*, rev. ed., ed. Hazard Adams. New York: Harcourt, Brace, Jovanovich, 1992.

Begley, Alan. "The I's Have It." *Lingua Franca: The Review of Academic Life* 4, no. 3 (March–April 1994): 54–59.

Bell, Millicent. *Meaning in Henry James*. Cambridge: Harvard University Press, 1991.

Bellour, Raymond. "Towards Fiction." In *Michel Foucault, Philosopher*. New York: Free Press, 1990.

Blackmur, R. P. *"The Sacred Fount."* In *Studies in Henry James*, ed. Veronica A. Makowsky. New York: New Directions, 1983.

Blake, William. "The Book of Urizen." In *Complete Poetry and Prose*, 2d ed., ed. David V. Erdman. New York: Oxford, 1997.

Bloom, Allan. *The Closing of the American Mind*. New York: Simon and Schuster, 1987.

Bové, Paul A. *Intellectuals in Power: A Genealogy of Critical Humanism*. New York: Columbia University Press, 1986.

———. Editor's Note. *boundary 2* 27, no. 1 (spring 2000). Special Issue: "The University."

Braslow, Joel. *Mental Ills and Bodily Cures: Psychiatric Treatment in the First Half of the Twentieth Century.* Berkeley: University of California Press, 1997.

Bromwich, David. *Politics by Other Means: Higher Education and Group Thinking.* New Haven: Yale University Press, 1992.

Bushman, Richard L. *The Refinement of America: Persons, Houses, Cities.* New York: Alfred A. Knopf, 1991.

Cheah, Pheng. "Spectral Nationality: The Living On [sur-vie] of the Postcolonial Nation in Neocolonial Globalization." *boundary 2* 26, no. 3 (fall 1999): 225–52.

Cochran, Terry. "Thinking at the Edge of the Galaxy: Pierre Lévy's World Projection." *boundary 2* 26, no. 3 (fall 1999): 63–85.

Connery, Christopher L. "Left Conservatism: A Workshop." *boundary 2* 26, no. 3 (fall 1999): 1–53.

Davidson, Arnold. "Ethics as Ascetics: Foucault, the History of Ethics, and Ancient Thought." In *The Cambridge Companion to Foucault,* ed. Gary Gutting. Cambridge: Cambridge University Press, 1994.

Deane, Seamus. "Under Eastern and Western Eyes." *boundary 2* 28, no. 1 (spring 2001): 1–18.

D'haen, Theo, and Haris Bertens, eds. *Narrative Turns and Minor Genres in Postmodernism.* Amsterdam: Rodopi, 1995.

Deleuze, Gilles. *The Fold.* Trans. Tom Conley. Minneapolis: University of Minnesota Press, 1992.

de Man, Paul. *Blindness and Insight: Essays in the Rhetoric of Contemporary Criticism.* New York: Oxford University Press, 1971.

———. *Allegories of Reading: Figural Language in Rousseau, Nietzsche, Rilke, and Proust.* New Haven: Yale University Press, 1979.

———. *Aesthetic Ideology.* Minneapolis: University of Minnesota Press, 1996.

Derrida, Jacques. *Memoirs.* Trans. Peggy Kamuf. New York: Columbia University Press, 1989.

———. *Given Time: 1. Counterfeit Money.* Trans. Peggy Kamuf. Chicago: University of Chicago Press, 1992.

———. *Aporias.* Trans. Thomas Dutoit. Stanford: Stanford University Press, 1993.

———. *Specters of Marx: The State of the Debt, the Work of Mourning, and the New International.* Trans. Peggy Kamuf. New York: Routledge, 1994.

———. *The Gift of Death.* Trans. David Wills. Chicago: University of Chicago Press, 1995.

———. "*Khōra.*" Trans. Thomas Dutort, David Wovel, John P. Leavey Jr., and Ian McLeod. In *On the Name,* ed. Peggy Kamuf. Stanford: Stanford University Press, 1995.

———. *Archive Fever: A Freudian Impression.* Trans. Eric Prenowitz. Chicago: University of Chicago Press, 1996.

———. *Politics of Friendship.* Trans. George Collins. London: Verso, 1997.

——. "Faith and Knowledge: The Two Sources of 'Religion' at the Limits of Reason Alone." In *Religion,* ed. Jacques Derrida and Gianni Vattimo. Stanford: Stanford University Press, 1998.

——. *Adieu: To Emmanuel Levinas.* Trans. Pascade-Anne Brault and Michael Naas. Stanford: Stanford University Press, 1999.

——. "Marx and Sons." In *Ghostly Demarcations: A Symposium on Jacques Derrida's "Specters of Marx,"* ed. Michael Sprinker. New York: Verso, 1999.

——. *Of Hospitality: Anne Dufourmantelle Invites Jacques Derrida to Respond.* Trans. Rachel Bowlby. Stanford: Stanford University Press, 2000.

——. "History of the Lie: Prolegomena." In *Futures of Jacques Derrida,* ed. Richard Rand. Stanford: Stanford University Press, 2001.

Edmundson, Mark, ed. *The Academy Writes Back.* New York: Viking, 1993.

Eliot, T. S. "Tradition and the Individual Talent." In *Selected Prose of T. S. Eliot,* ed. Frank Kermode. New York: Harcourt Brace Jovanovich, 1975.

Elster, Jon. *Making Sense of Marx: Studies in Marxism and Social Theory.* New York: Cambridge University Press, 1985.

——, ed. *Karl Marx: A Reader.* Cambridge: Cambridge University Press, 1986.

Eribon, Didier. *Michel Foucault.* Trans. Betsy Wing. Cambridge: Harvard University Press, 1991.

Fish, Stanley. "Why Literary Criticism Is like Virtue." *London Review of Books* 15, no. 11 (10 June 1993): 11–16.

Foley, Mick. *Mankind: Have a Nice Day! A Tale of Blood and Sweatsocks.* New York: Regan Books, 1999.

——. *Foley Is Good: And the Real Word Is Faker than Wrestling.* New York: Regan Books, 2001.

Foucault, Michel. *Madness and Civilization: A History of Insanity in the Age of Reason.* Trans. Richard Howard. New York: Random House, 1973.

——. *The Birth of the Clinic.* Trans. A. M. S. Smith. London: Tavistock, 1976.

——. "What Is Enlightenment?" In *The Foucault Reader,* ed. Paul Rabinow. New York: Pantheon, 1984.

——. *The Care of the Self.* Trans. Robert Hurley. Vol. 3 of *The History of Sexuality.* New York: Pantheon, 1986.

——. "Interview." In *Death and the Labyrinth: The World of Raymond Roussel.* Trans. Charles Ruas. Berkeley and Los Angeles: University of California Press, 1986.

——. *Death and the Labyrinth: The World of Raymond Roussel.* Trans. Charles Ruas. London: Athlone, 1987.

Fraser, Nancy. *Unruly Practices: Power, Discourse, and Gender in Contemporary Social Theory.* Minneapolis: University of Minnesota Press, 1989.

Freud, Sigmund. *Moses and Monotheism.* In *The Standard Edition of the Complete Psychological Works of Sigmund Freud,* vol. 2, ed. and trans. James Strachey. London: Hogarth Press, 1964.

——. *The Interpretation of Dreams.* Trans. James Strachey. Vol. 4 of the Pelican Freud Library. Harmondsworth, Middlesex, England: Penguin, 1975.

——. *Leonardo da Vinci and a Memory of His Childhood*. New York: Norton, 1989.

——. *The Question of Lay Analysis*. New York: Norton, 1989.

——. "The Poet's Relation to Day-Dreaming." In *Authorship from Plato to the Postmodern: A Reader,* ed. Seán Burke. Edinburgh: Edinburgh University Press, 1995.

Gale, Robert L. *A Henry James Encyclopedia*. New York: Greenwood Press, 1989.

Gilbert, Jack. *The Great Fires: Poems, 1982–1992*. New York: Knopf, 1994.

Godzich, Wlad. *The Culture of Literacy*. Cambridge: Harvard University Press, 1994.

Grubrich-Simitis, Ilse. *Back to Freud's Texts: Making Silent Documents Speak*. New Haven: Yale University Press, 1996.

Guillory, John. *Cultural Capital: The Problem of Literary Canon Formation*. Chicago: University of Chicago Press, 1993.

Gunn, Gilles, et al. Special Topic: "Globalizing Literary Studies." *PMLA* 116, no. 1 (January 2001): 16–188.

Gurganus, Allan. "Minor Heroism: Something about My Father." In *The Vintage Book of Contemporary American Short Stories,* ed. Tobias Wolff. New York: Vintage, 1994.

Hamacher, Werner. "Lingua Amissa: The Messianism of Commodity-Language and Derrida's *Specters of Marx.*" In *Ghostlier Demarcations: A Symposium on Jacques Derrida's "Specters of Marx,"* ed. Michael Sprinker. New York: Verso, 1999.

Hardt, Michael, and Antonio Negri. *Empire*. Cambridge: Harvard University Press, 2000.

Harmon, William, and C. Hugh Holman, eds. *A Handbook to Literature*. 7th ed. Upper Saddle River, N.J.: Prentice-Hall, 1996.

Harpham, Geoffrey G. *The Ascetic Imperative in Culture and Criticism*. Chicago: University of Chicago Press, 1987.

Havel, Václav. "Our Troubled Quest for Meaning in a Postmodern World." *Philadelphia Inquirer,* 6 July 1994, A7.

Heidegger, Martin. "The Origin of the Work of Art." In *Poetry, Language, Thought,* trans. Albert Hofstadter. New York: Harper and Row, 1971.

——. "The Anaximander Fragment." In *Early Greek Thinking,* trans. David Farrell Krell and Frank A. Capuzzi. New York: Harper and Row, 1975.

——. "The Age of the World Picture." In *The Question concerning Technology and Other Essays,* trans. William Lovitt. New York: Harper and Row, 1977.

Hjort, Mette. *The Strategy of Letters*. Cambridge: Harvard University Press, 1993.

Hopkins, Dwight N., Lois Ann Lorentzen, Eduardo Mendieta, and David Batstone, eds. *Religions/Globalizations: Theories and Cases*. Durham, N.C.: Duke University Press, 2001.

Horne, Philip. *Henry James and Revision*. Clarendon: Oxford University Press, 1990.

Hoy, David C., ed. *Foucault: A Critical Reader*. Oxford: Blackwell, 1986.

Huntington, Samuel P. *The Clash of Civilizations and the Remaking of World Order*. New York: Simon and Schuster, 1996.

Hurka, Thomas. *Perfectionism*. New York: Oxford University Press, 1993.

James, Henry. *The Reverberator.* In *The Novels and Tales of Henry James,* vol. 13 of the New York Edition. New York: Charles Scribner's Sons, 1908.

——. "The Parisian Stage." In *The Scenic Art,* ed. Allan Wade. New Brunswick, N.J.: Rutgers University Press, 1948.

——. *The Art of the Novel.* Fiftieth anniversary edition. Boston: Northeastern University Press, 1984.

——. *The Ambassadors.* Ed. Harry Levin. New York: Penguin, 1986.

——. *What Maisie Knew.* New York: Penguin, 1986.

——. *The Wings of the Dove.* Ed. John Bayley. New York: Penguin, 1986.

——. *The Golden Bowl.* New York: Penguin, 1987.

——. *The Spoils of Poynton.* New York: Penguin, 1987.

——. *The American Scene in Collected Travel Writings: Great Britain and America.* Ed. Richard Howard. New York: Library of America, 1993.

——. *The Awkward Age.* New York: Alfred A. Knopf, 1993.

——. "The Jolly Corner." In *Complete Stories,* vol. 5. New York: Library of America, 1996.

Kant, Immanuel. *Critique of Judgment.* Trans. Werner S. Pluhar. Indianapolis: Hackett, 1987.

Kaplan, Robert D. *The Coming Anarchy: Shattering the Dreams of the Post Cold War.* New York: Random House, 2000.

Lacan, Jacques. *The Four Fundamental Concepts of Psychoanalysis.* Trans. Alan Sheridan. New York: W. W. Norton, 1978.

——. "Presence of the Analyst." In *Essential Papers on Transference,* ed. Aaron H. Esman, M.D. New York: New York University Press, 1999.

le Carré, John. *Single and Single.* New York: Pocket Books, 1999.

Lentricchia, Frank. "Michel Foucault's Fantasy for Humanists." In *Ariel and the Police.* Madison: University of Wisconsin Press, 1988.

——. "My Kinsman, T. S. Eliot." *Raritan* 11, no. 4 (spring 1992): 1–23.

——. *The Edge of Night.* New York: Knopf, 1992.

——. *Modernist Quartet.* New York: Cambridge University Press, 1994.

——. "Philosophers of Modernism at Harvard, circa 1900." *SAQ* 89, no. 4 (fall 1996): 787–834.

——. *The Music of the Inferno: A Novel.* Albany: SUNY Press, 1999.

Mann, James A., ed. *The Rediscovery of Man: The Complete Short Science Fiction.* Framingham, Mass.: NESFA Press, 1993.

Mann, Thomas. "Freud and the Future." In *Selected Essays.* New York: Vintage, 1957.

McFadden, George. "Henry James's Remorse for *The Wings of the Dove.*" *Henry James Review* 9, no. 2 (spring 1988): 118–35.

Megill, Allan. *Prophets of Extremity: Nietzsche, Heidegger, Foucault, Derrida.* Berkeley: University of California Press, 1985.

Miguel-Alonzo, Ricardo. *Reconstructing Foucault: Essays in the Wake of the EOS.* Amsterdam: Rodopi, 1994.

Miller, James. *The Passion of Michel Foucault*. New York: Simon and Schuster, 1993.

Newfield, Christopher. "What Was Political Correctness?" *Critical Inquiry* 19 (winter 1993): 308–36.

Nietzsche, Friedrich. *Beyond Good and Evil*. Trans. Walter Kaufmann. New York: Vintage, 1966.

——. *On the Genealogy of Morals and Ecce Homo*. Ed. Walter Kaufmann. New York: Vintage, 1967.

——. *The Gay Science*. Trans. Walter Kaufmann. New York: Vintage, 1974.

Norris, Christopher. " 'What Is Enlightenment?' Kant according to Foucault." In *Reconstructing Foucault: Essays in the Wake of the 80s*, Postmodern Studies Series 10, ed. Ricardo Miguel-Alfonso and Silvia Caporale-Bizzini. Atlanta: Rodopi, 1994.

O'Hara, Daniel T. *The Romance of Interpretation: Visionary Criticism from Pater to de Man*. New York: Columbia University Press, 1985.

——. *Radical Parody: American Culture and Critical Agency after Foucault*. New York: Columbia University Press, 1992.

O'Hara, Daniel T., and Alan Singer, eds. "Thinking through Art: Aesthetic Agency and Global Modernity." Special Issue, *boundary 2* 25, no. 1 (spring 1998): 1–5.

Pease, Donald E. "After the Tocqueville Revival; or, The Return of the Political." *boundary 2* 26, no. 3 (fall 1999): 87–114.

Posnock, Ross. *The Trial of Curiosity: Henry James, William James, and the Challenge of Modernity*. New York: Oxford University Press, 1991.

Rabinow, Paul, ed. *The Foucault Reader*. New York: Pantheon, 1984.

Rainsford, Dominic, and Tim Woods, eds. *Critical Ethics: Text, Theory, and Responsibility*. London: Macmillan, 1999.

Ramazani, Jahan. *Poetry of Mourning: The Modern Elegy from Hardy to Heaney*. Chicago: University of Chicago Press, 1994.

Ricoeur, Paul. *Oneself as Another*. Trans. Kathleen Blamey. Chicago: University of Chicago Press, 1992.

Rivkin, Julia, and Michael Ryan. *Literary Theory: An Anthology*. London: Blackwell, 1998.

Robbins, Bruce. *Feeling Global: Internationalism in Distress*. New York: New York University Press, 1999.

Rorty, Richard. "Moral Identity and Private Autonomy." In *Michel Foucault, Philosopher: Essays Translated from the French and German*, trans. Timothy J. Armstrong. New York: Routledge, 1992.

Rowe, John Carlos. *The Other Henry James*. Durham: Duke University Press, 1998.

Said, Edward W. "Traveling Theory." In *The World, the Text, and the Critic*. Cambridge: Harvard University Press, 1983.

——. "The Politics of Knowledge." *Raritan* 11, no. 1 (summer 1991): 17–31.

——. Interview. *boundary 2* 20, no. 1 (spring 1993): 1–25.

——. *Out of Place: A Memoir*. New York: Alfred A. Knopf, 1999.

——. *Reflections on Exile and Other Essays*. Cambridge: Harvard University Press, 2000.

——. "Globalizing Literary Study." *PMLA* 116, no. 1 (January 2001): 64–68.

Sandler, Joseph, ed. *On Freud's "Analysis Terminable and Interminable."* New Haven: Yale University Press, 1991.

Simpson, David. *Romanticism, Nationalism, and the Revolt against Theory*. Chicago: University of Chicago Press, 1993.

Smith, Cordwainer. "Mother Hilton's Little Kittens." In *The Rediscovery of Man*. Framingham, Mass.: NESFA Press, 1993.

——. *Norstrilia*. Framingham, Mass.: NESFA Press, 1998.

Spacks, Patricia Meyer. "The Academic Marketplace: Who Pays the Costs?" *MLA Newsletter* 26, no. 2 (summer 1994): 1–5.

Spanos, William V. *The End of Education*. Minneapolis: University of Minnesota Press, 1992.

——. *Heidegger and Criticism: Retrieving the Cultural Politics of Destruction*. Minneapolis: University of Minnesota Press, 1993.

——. *America's Shadow: An Anatomy of Empire*. Minneapolis: University of Minnesota Press, 2000.

Sprinker, Michael, ed. *Ghostly Demarcations: A Symposium on Jacques Derrida's "Specters of Marx."* New York: Verso, 2000.

Stepansky, Paul E. *Freud, Surgery, and the Surgeons*. Hillsdale, N.J.: Analytic Press, 1999.

Stimpson, Catharine R. "Dirty Minds, Dirty Bodies, Clean Speech." *Michigan Quarterly Review* 32 (summer 1993): 317–37.

Strachey, James, ed. *The Standard Edition of the Complete Psychological Works of Sigmund Freud*. 22 vols. London: Hogarth Press, 1960.

Sugarman, Susan. *Freud on the Acropolis: Reflections on a Paradoxical Response to the Real*. New York: Basic, 1998.

Torgovnick, Marianna. "Hartman's Dilemma: *Minor Prophecies: The Literary Essay in the Culture Wars*." *ADE Bulletin* 104 (spring 1993): 52–55.

Toye, Margaret. "Care of the Self or Care of the Other? Towards a Poststructuralist Ethics of Pedagogy." In *Critical Ethics: Text, Theory, and Responsibility*, ed. Dominic Rainsford and Tim Woods. New York: St. Martin's Press, 1999.

Waters, Lindsay. "On Paul de Man's Effort to Re-anchor a True in Our Feelings." *boundary 2* 26, no. 2 (summer 1999): 133–56.

Wells, H. G. "Selections from *Boon*." In *Henry James and H. G. Wells: A Record of Their Friendship, Their Debate on the Art of Fiction, and Their Quarrel*, ed. Leon Edel and Gordon N. Ray. Urbana: University of Illinois Press, 1958.

West, Cornel. "The New Cultural Politics of Difference." In *Beyond a Dream Deferred: Multicultural Education and the Politics of Excellence*, ed. Becky W. Thompson and Sangeeta Tyage. Minneapolis: University of Minnesota Press, 1993.

West, Rebecca. *Henry James*. Vol. 1 of *Henry James: Critical Assessments: Memories, Views, and Writers*, ed. Graham Clarke. New York: Routledge, 1991.

Yeats, W. B. "The Circus Animals' Desertion" and "Byzantium." In *The Poems*, rev.

ed., vol. 2 of *The Collected Works of W. B. Yeats,* ed. Richard J. Finneran. New York: Macmillan, 1983.

Zimmerman, David, and A. L. Bento Mostardeiro. "On Teaching 'Analysis Terminable and Interminable.'" In *On Freud's "Analysis Terminable and Interminable,"* ed. Joseph Sandler. New Haven: Yale University Press, 1991.

INDEX

Daniel T. O'Hara is a professor of English and the editor
of *The Faculty Herald* at Temple University. He is the
author of *Radical Parody: American Culture and Critical
Agency after Foucault* (Columbia, 1992); *Lionel Trilling:
The Work of Liberation* (Wisconsin, 1988); *The Romance
of Interpretation: Visionary Criticism from Pater to de
Man* (Columbia, 1985); *Tragic Knowledge: Yeats's
Autobiography and Hermeneutics* (Columbia, 1981). He
has also edited *Why Nietzsche Now?* (Indiana, 1985); and
with Paul A. Bové and William V. Spanos, *The Question
of Textuality: Strategies of Reading in Contemporary
American Criticism* (Indiana, 1982). He serves on the
editorial boards of *Annals of Scholarship*, *Journal of
Modern Literature*, and *boundary 2*. He is also the review
editor for these last two journals. Currently, he is
completing a new book, *The Poetics of Liberal Culture*.

Library of Congress Cataloging-in-Publication Data
O'Hara, Daniel T.
    Empire burlesque : the fate of critical culture in global
America / Daniel T. O'Hara.
        p. cm. — (New Americanists)
Includes bibliographical references and index.
    ISBN 0-8223-3032-6 (cloth : alk. paper)
    ISBN 0-8223-3019-9 (pbk. : alk. paper)
    1. Criticism—United States—History—20th century.
2. American literature—History and criticism—Theory,
etc. 3. United States—Civilization—Foreign influences.
4. Literature—History and criticism—Theory, etc.
5. Mass media and culture—United States. 6. United
States—Civilization—1970–   7. Journalism—United States.
I. Title. II. Series.
PS78 .O38 2003 801'.95'097309045—dc21 2002014076